...st page. AUG 14

...l Japanese comic format, this book reads from right to left—so action, sound effects, and word balloons are completely reversed. This preserves the orientation of the original artwork—plus, it's fun! Check out the diagram shown here to get the hang of things, and then turn to the other side of the book to get started!

House of

from groundbreaking manga creator
Natsume Ono!

The ronin Akitsu Masanosuke was working as a bodyguard in Edo, but due to his shy personality, he kept being let go from his bodyguard jobs despite his magnificent sword skills. Unable to find new work, he wanders around town and meets a man, the playboy who calls himself Yaichi. Even though Yaichi and Masanosuke had just met for the first time, Yaichi treats Masanosuke to a meal and offers to hire him as a bodyguard. Despite the mysteries that surround Yaichi, Masanosuke takes the job. He soon finds out that Yaichi is the leader of a group of kidnappers who call themselves the "Five Leaves." Now Masanosuke is faced with the dilemma of whether to join the Five Leaves and share in the profits of kidnapping, or to resist becoming a criminal.

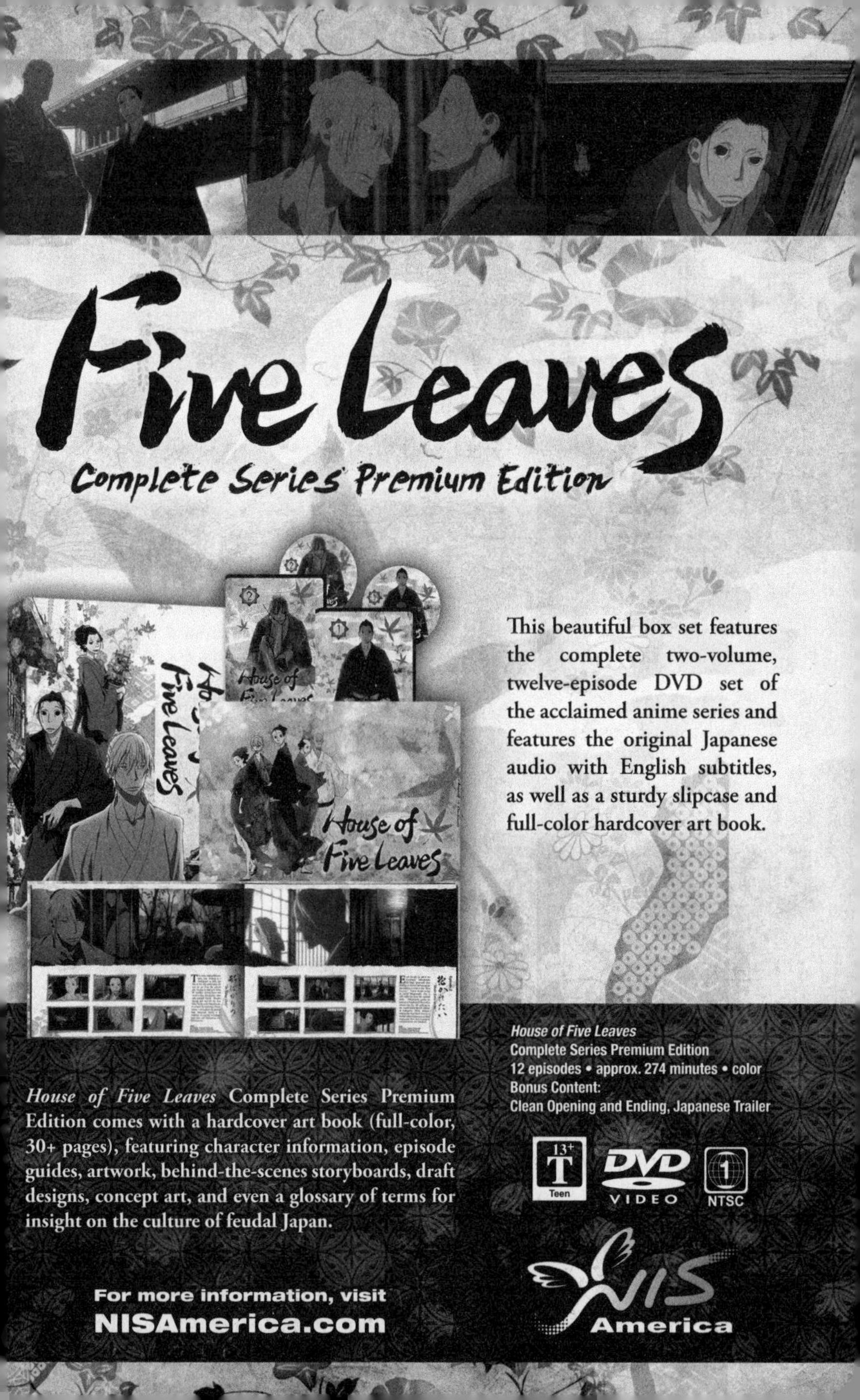
Five Leaves
Complete Series Premium Edition
House of Five Leaves
This beautiful box set features the complete two-volume, twelve-episode DVD set of the acclaimed anime series and features the original Japanese audio with English subtitles, as well as a sturdy slipcase and full-color hardcover art book.
House of Five Leaves Complete Series Premium Edition comes with a hardcover art book (full-color, 30+ pages), featuring character information, episode guides, artwork, behind-the-scenes storyboards, draft designs, concept art, and even a glossary of terms for insight on the culture of feudal Japan.
House of Five Leaves
Complete Series Premium Edition
12 episodes • approx. 274 minutes • color
Bonus Content:
Clean Opening and Ending, Japanese Trailer
13+ T Teen
DVD VIDEO
1 NTSC
For more information, visit
NISAmerica.com
NIS America

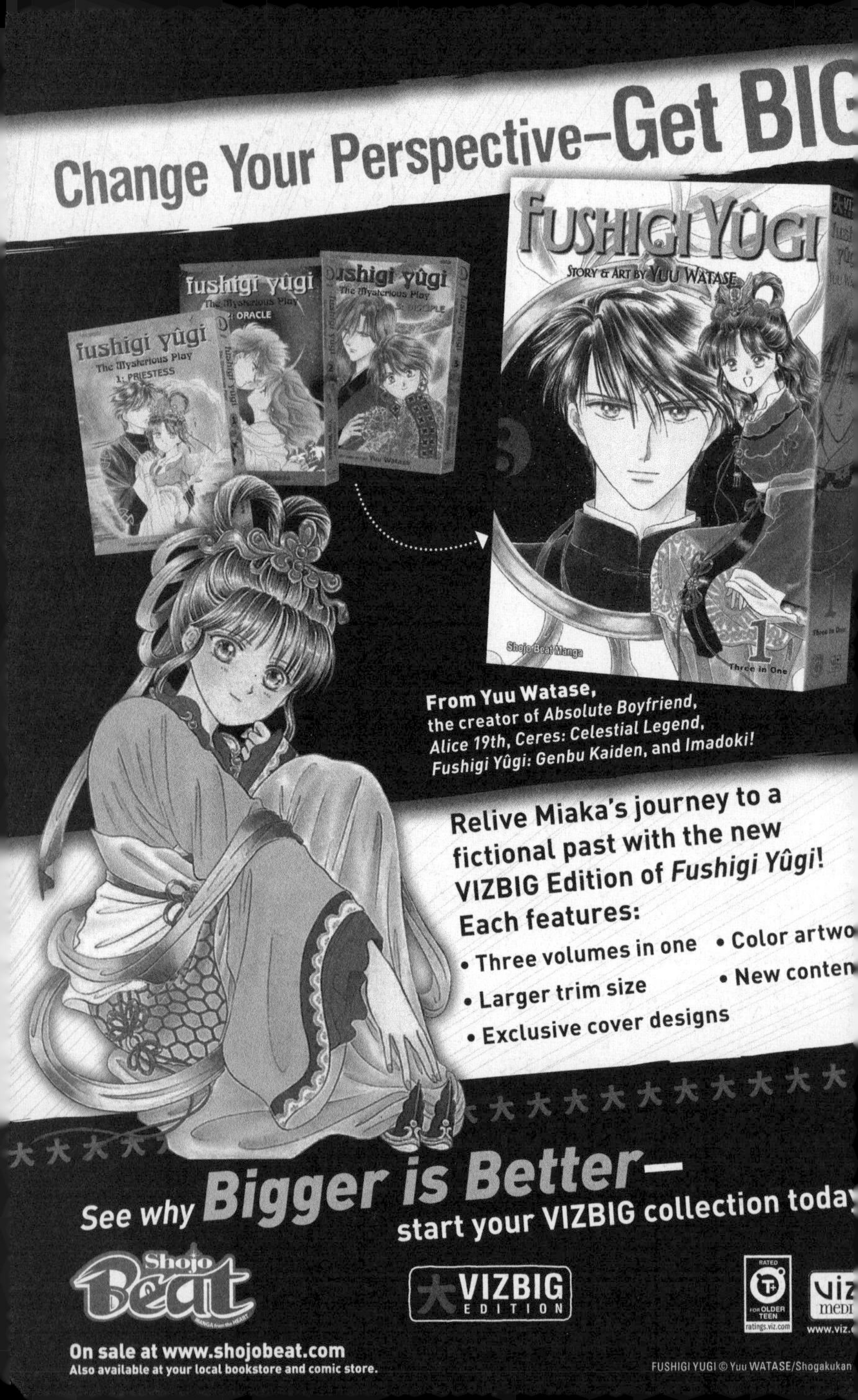

Change Your Perspective–Get BIG
fushigi yûgi
The Mysterious Play
1: PRIESTESS
fushigi yûgi
The Mysterious Play
2: ORACLE
ushigi yûgi
The Mysterious Play
FUSHIGI YÛGI
STORY & ART BY YUU WATASE
Shojo Beat Manga
1
Three in One
From Yuu Watase,
the creator of Absolute Boyfriend,
Alice 19th, Ceres: Celestial Legend,
Fushigi Yûgi: Genbu Kaiden, and Imadoki!
Relive Miaka's journey to a fictional past with the new VIZBIG Edition of Fushigi Yûgi!
Each features:
• Three volumes in one
• Larger trim size
• Exclusive cover designs
• Color artwo
• New conten
See why Bigger is Better—
start your VIZBIG collection toda
Shojo Beat
MANGA from the HEART
VIZBIG EDITION
RATED T+ FOR OLDER TEEN
ratings.viz.com
VIZ media
www.viz.
On sale at www.shojobeat.com
Also available at your local bookstore and comic store.
FUSHIGI YUGI © Yuu WATASE/Shogakukan

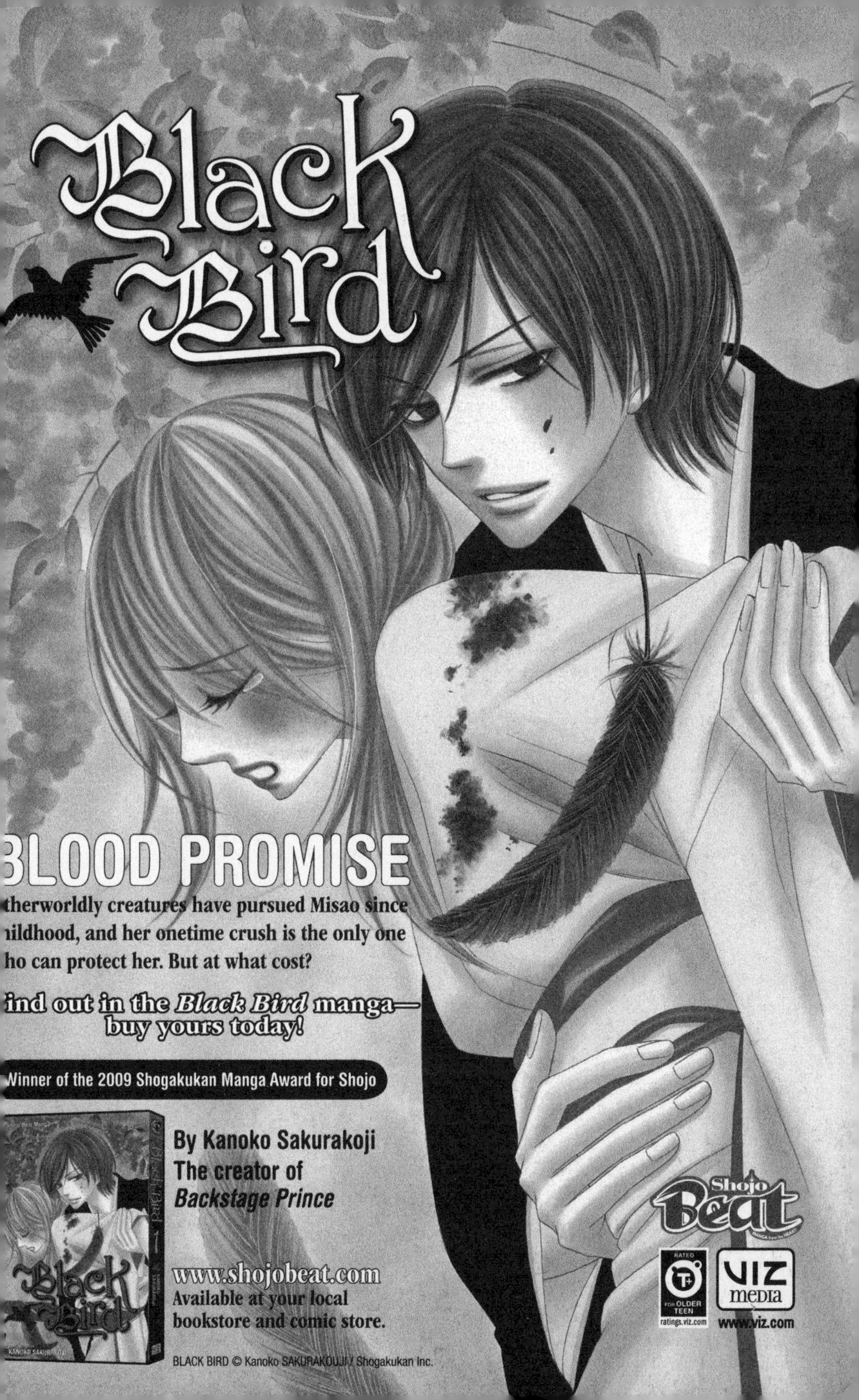

Black Bird
BLOOD PROMISE
therworldly creatures have pursued Misao since
ildhood, and her onetime crush is the only one
ho can protect her. But at what cost?
ind out in the Black Bird manga—
buy yours today!
Winner of the 2009 Shogakukan Manga Award for Shojo
By Kanoko Sakurakoji
The creator of
Backstage Prince
www.shojobeat.com
Available at your local
bookstore and comic store.
Shojo Beat
RATED T+ FOR OLDER TEEN
ratings.viz.com
VIZ media
www.viz.com
BLACK BIRD © Kanoko SAKURAKOUJI / Shogakukan Inc.

DAWN OF THE ARCANA
VOLUME 1
Shojo Beat Edition

STORY AND ART BY
REI TOMA

© 2009 Rei TOMA/Shogakukan
All rights reserved.
Original Japanese edition "REIMEI NO ARCANA"
published by SHOGAKUKAN Inc.

Translation & Adaptation/Alexander O. Smith
Touch-up Art & Lettering/Freeman Wong
Design/Yukiko Whitley
Editor/Amy Yu

Printed in the U.S.A.

Published by VIZ Media, LLC
P.O. Box 77010
San Francisco, CA 94107

10 9 8 7 6 5 4 3
First printing, December 2011
Third printing, June 2013

www.viz.com   www.shojobeat.com

Dawn of the Arcana

XII
I
II
XI
X
III
IX
IIII
VIII
V
VII
VI

1

Story & Art by
Rei Toma

Dawn of the Arcana

Volume 1

CONTENTS

XII

XI

X

IX

VIII

VII

VI

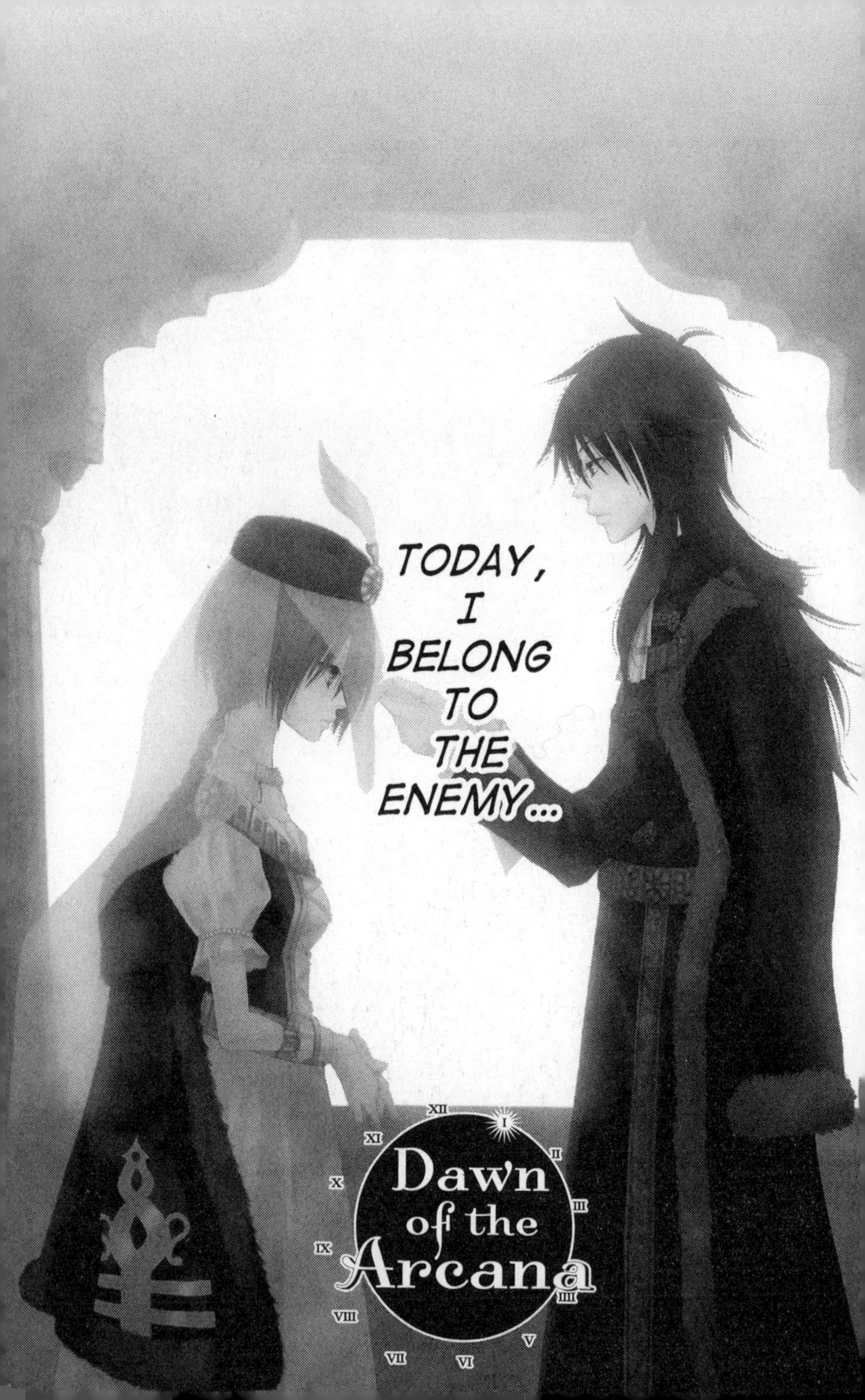
TODAY, I BELONG TO THE ENEMY...
Dawn of the Arcana

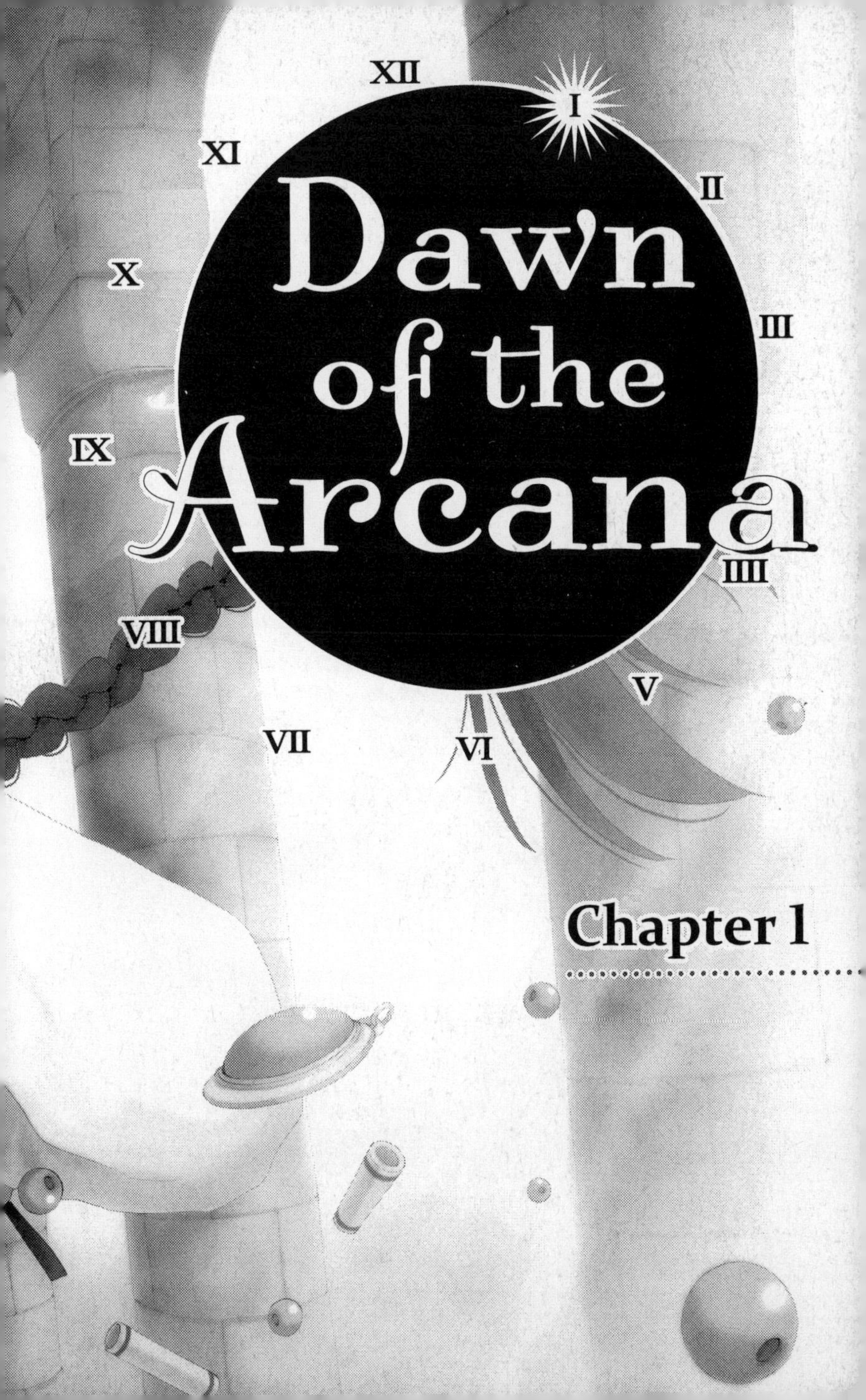
Dawn of the Arcana
Chapter 1

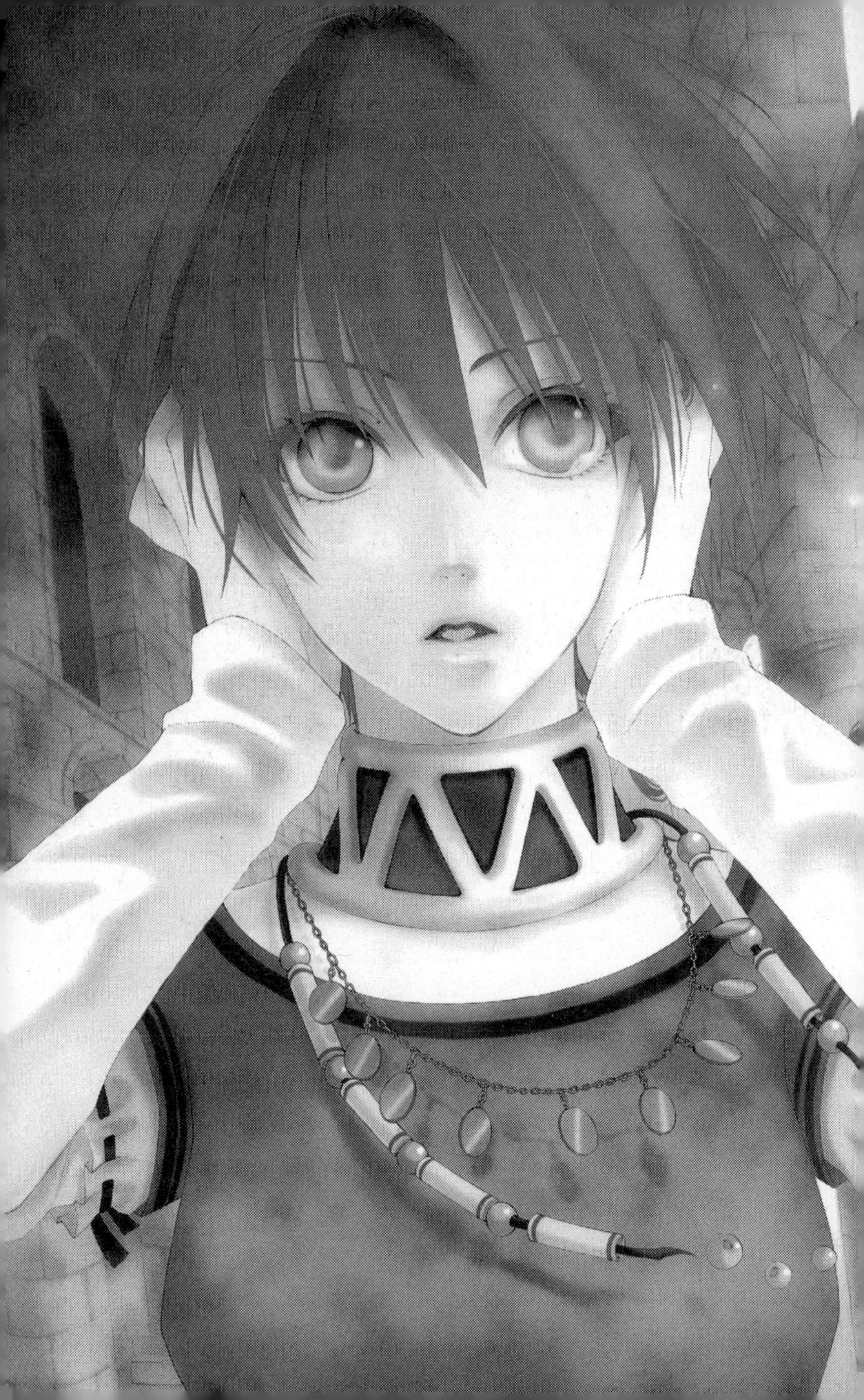

Author's Rambling Space (Sort of. No, really.)

Hello! I'm Rei Toma. This is volume 1 of my first work of fantasy, an event worth commemorating.
I'm not particularly good at talking about my works, so I'm casually going to write stuff. I don't know what good it will do, but I have two pages to fill. So if you've got some time to kill, stick around. (*Laugh*)
Aah… What to write...

How about some behind-the-scenes chitchat…
The appearance of the half-man, half-beast character "Loki" in *Dawn of the Arcana* is very different now than when I had imagined him. Originally he was much more beast-like. His face, for example. It was almost entirely canine. Shaggy hair and all. (*Laugh*) I had the image of a somber little puppy, quietly watching over Nakaba…
But after much consideration, I settled on his current appearance.
I figured I had to work in a bit of that "feminine moe element."
As for Nakaba, there weren't many changes to her appearance.
Caesar's hairstyle and eyes changed a little though. (*Laugh*)
For now, between Caesar and Loki, Loki seems more popular, judging from the letters I've received. Probably because Caesar is a little stupid and often mean…
But what would the readers have thought if Loki had been a hairy dog? I wonder…
And that's my ramble. (*Laugh*)

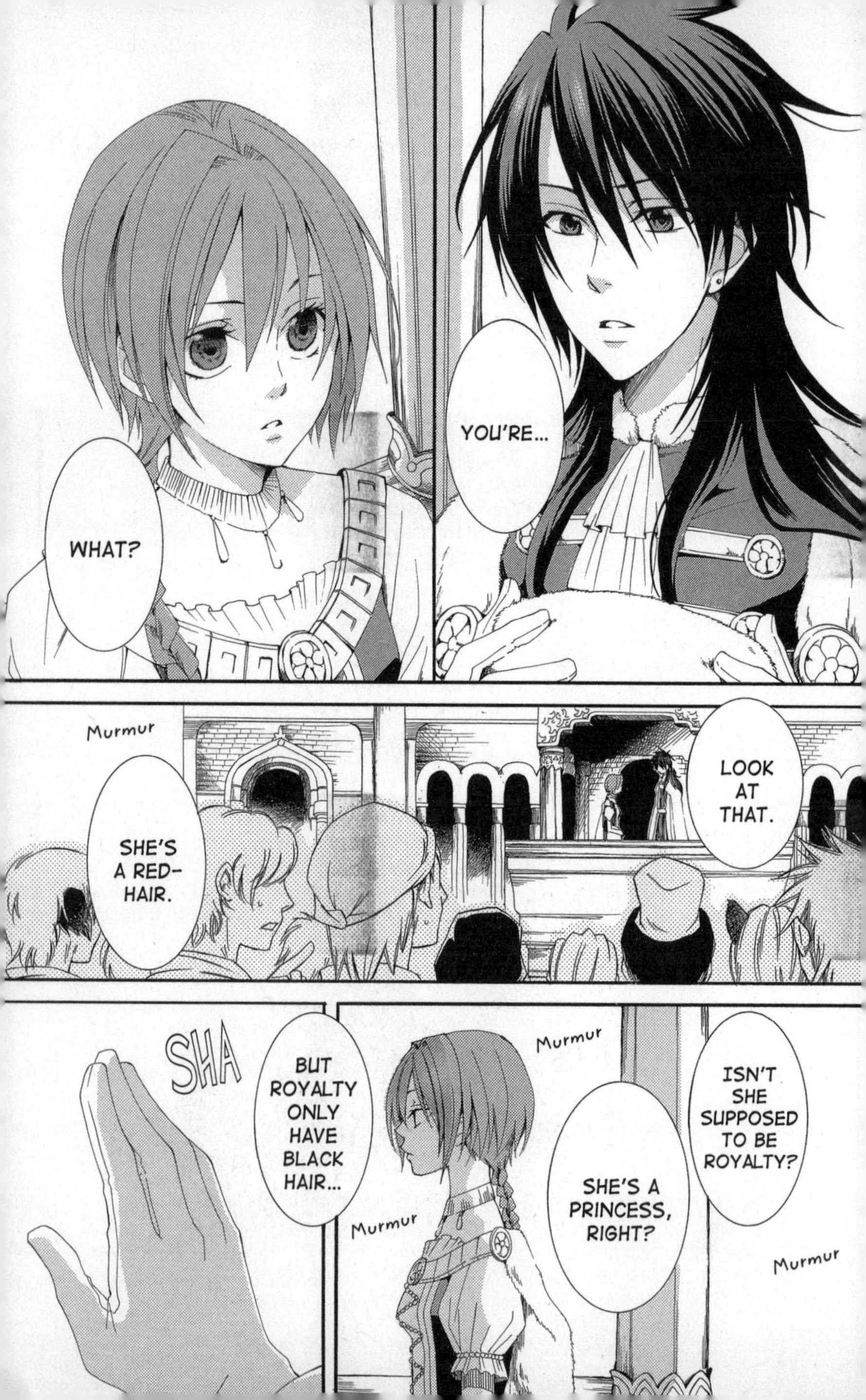

YOU'RE...
WHAT?
LOOK AT THAT.
Murmur
SHE'S A RED-HAIR.
ISN'T SHE SUPPOSED TO BE ROYALTY?
Murmur
SHE'S A PRINCESS, RIGHT?
Murmur
BUT ROYALTY ONLY HAVE BLACK HAIR...
Murmur
SHA

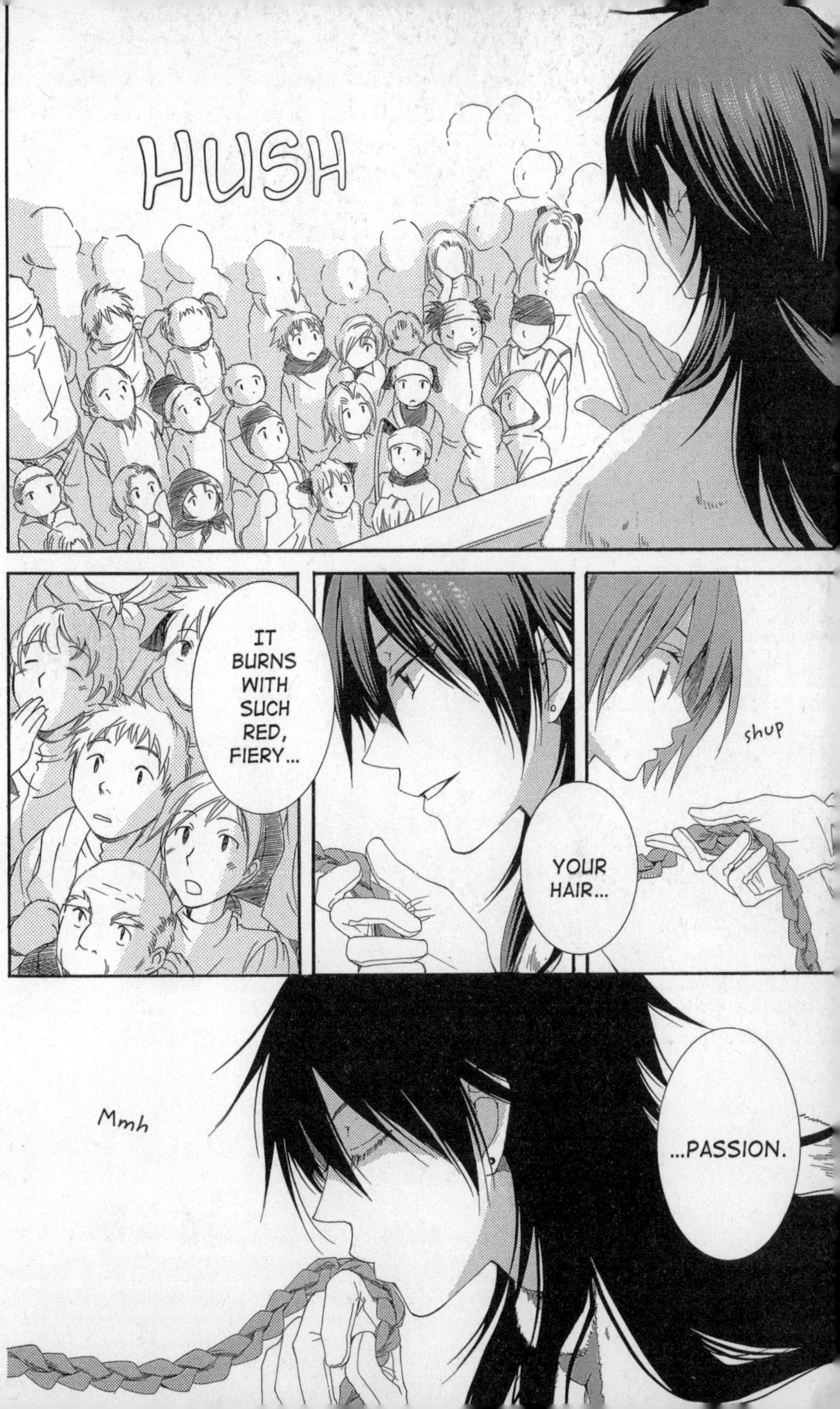
HUSH
shup
YOUR HAIR...
IT BURNS WITH SUCH RED, FIERY...
...PASSION.
Mmh

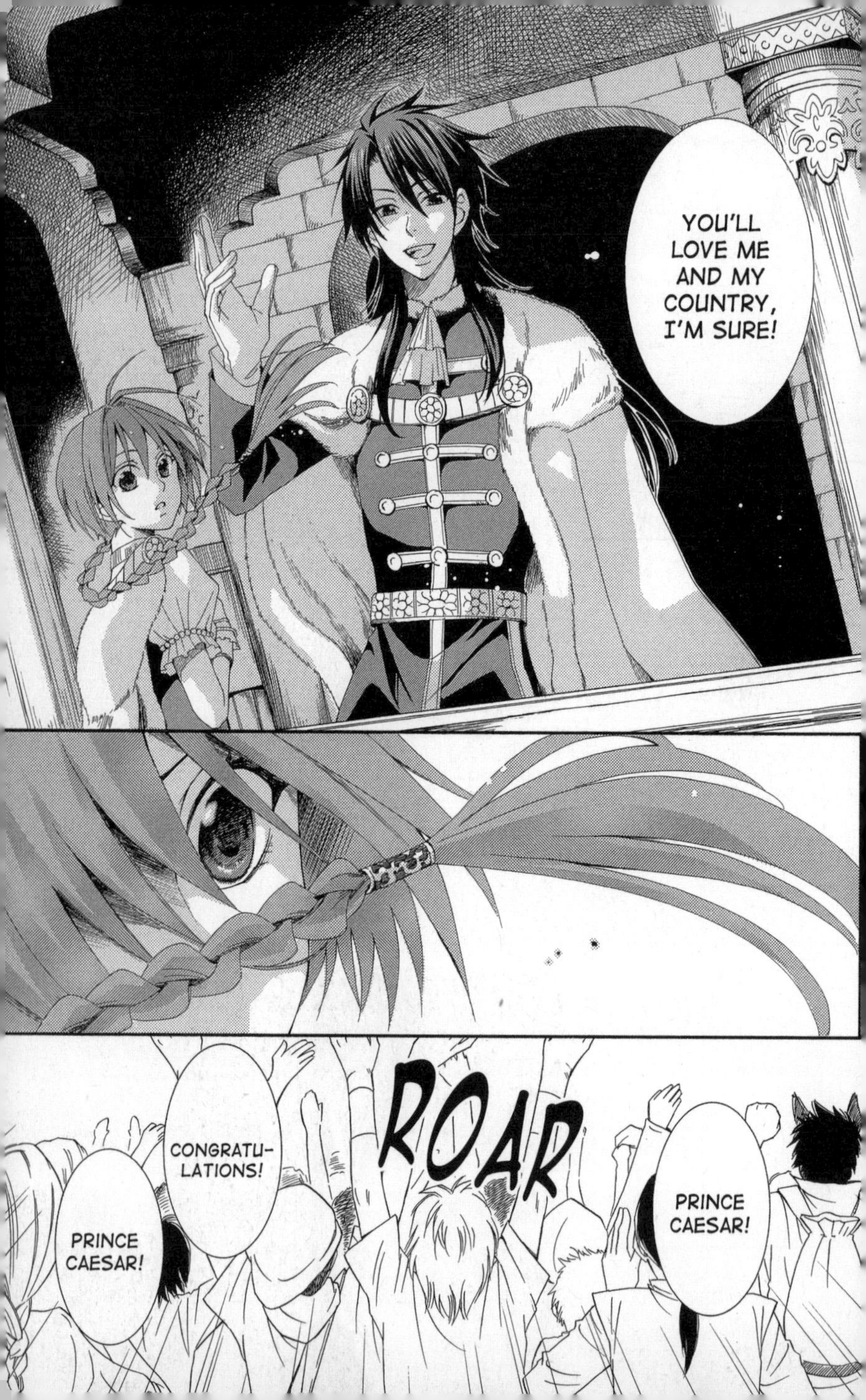
YOU'LL LOVE ME AND MY COUNTRY, I'M SURE!
PRINCE CAESAR!
ROAR
CONGRATU-LATIONS!
PRINCE CAESAR!

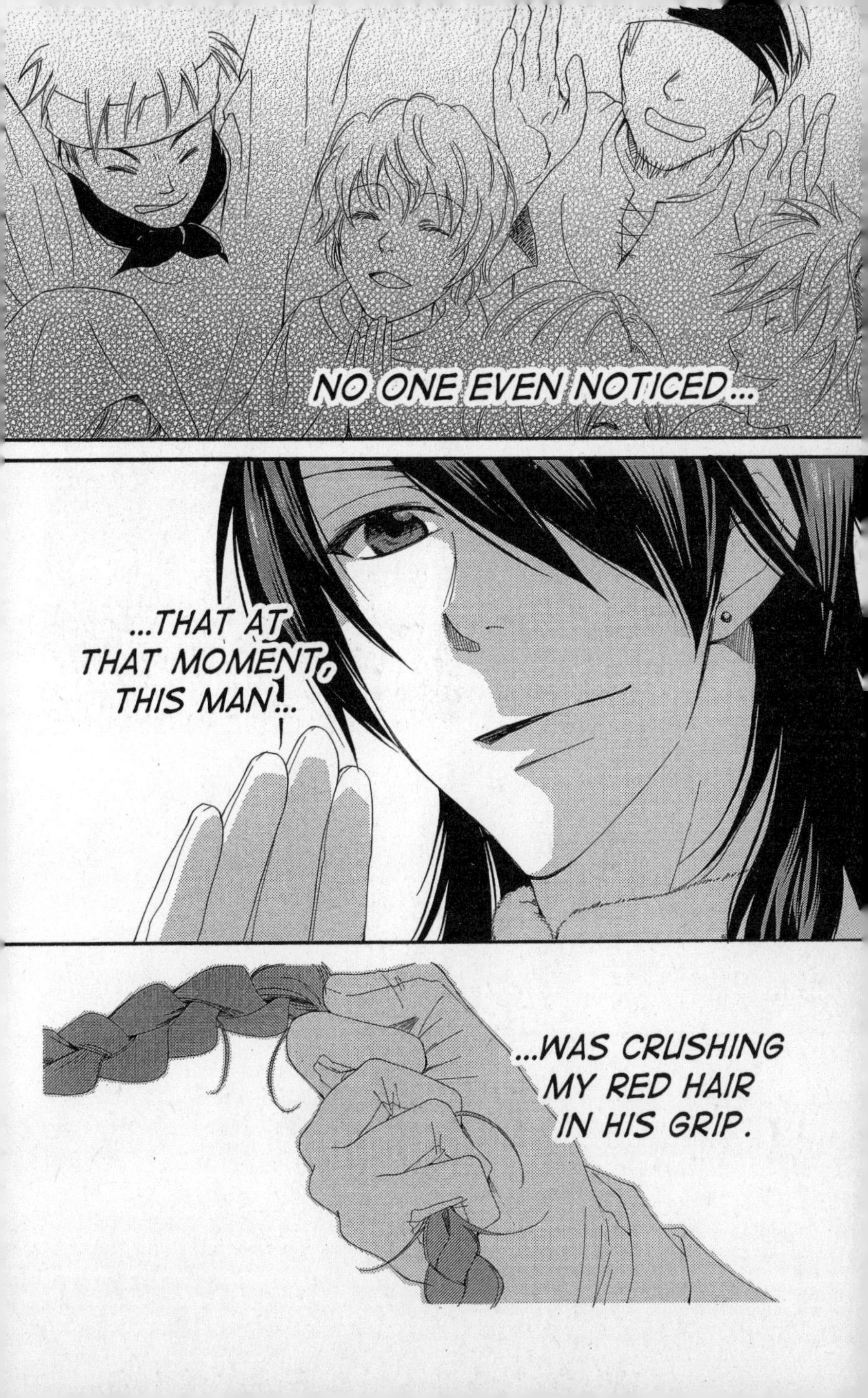
NO ONE EVEN NOTICED...
...THAT AT THAT MOMENT, THIS MAN...
...WAS CRUSHING MY RED HAIR IN HIS GRIP.

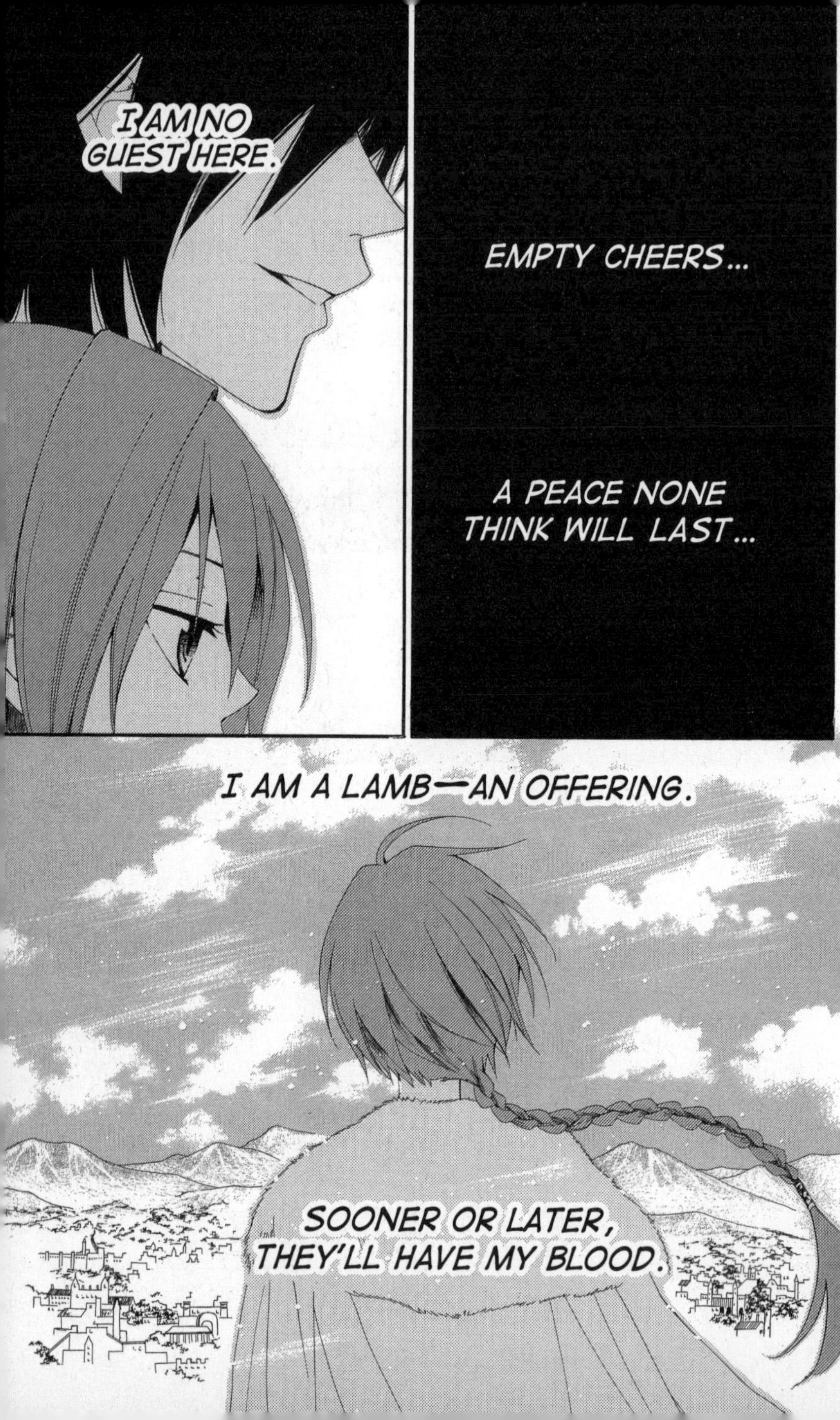
EMPTY CHEERS...
A PEACE NONE THINK WILL LAST...
I AM NO GUEST HERE.
I AM A LAMB—AN OFFERING.
SOONER OR LATER, THEY'LL HAVE MY BLOOD.

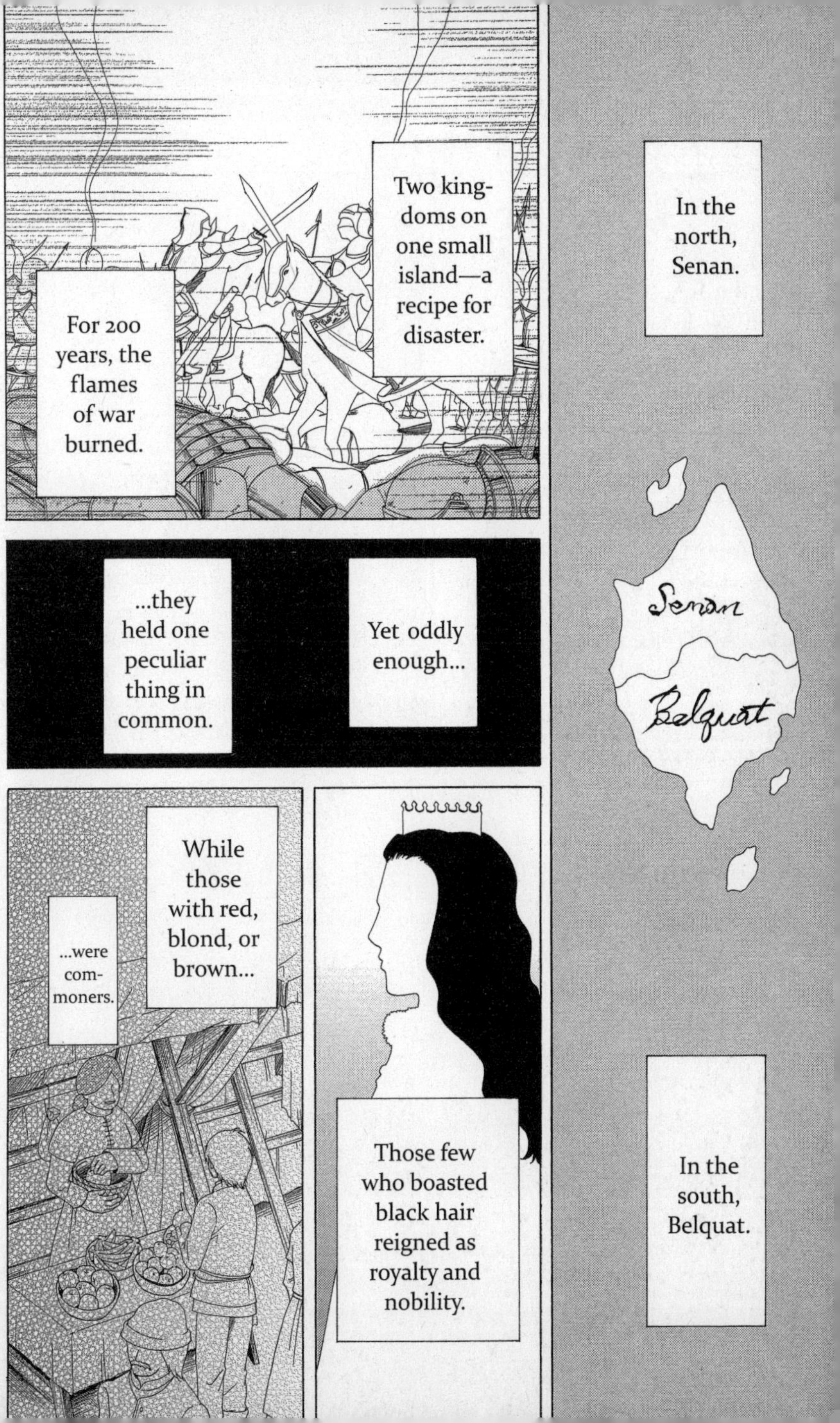
In the north, Senan.
Senan
Belquat
In the south, Belquat.
Two kingdoms on one small island—a recipe for disaster.
For 200 years, the flames of war burned.
Yet oddly enough...
...they held one peculiar thing in common.
Those few who boasted black hair reigned as royalty and nobility.
While those with red, blond, or brown...
...were commoners.

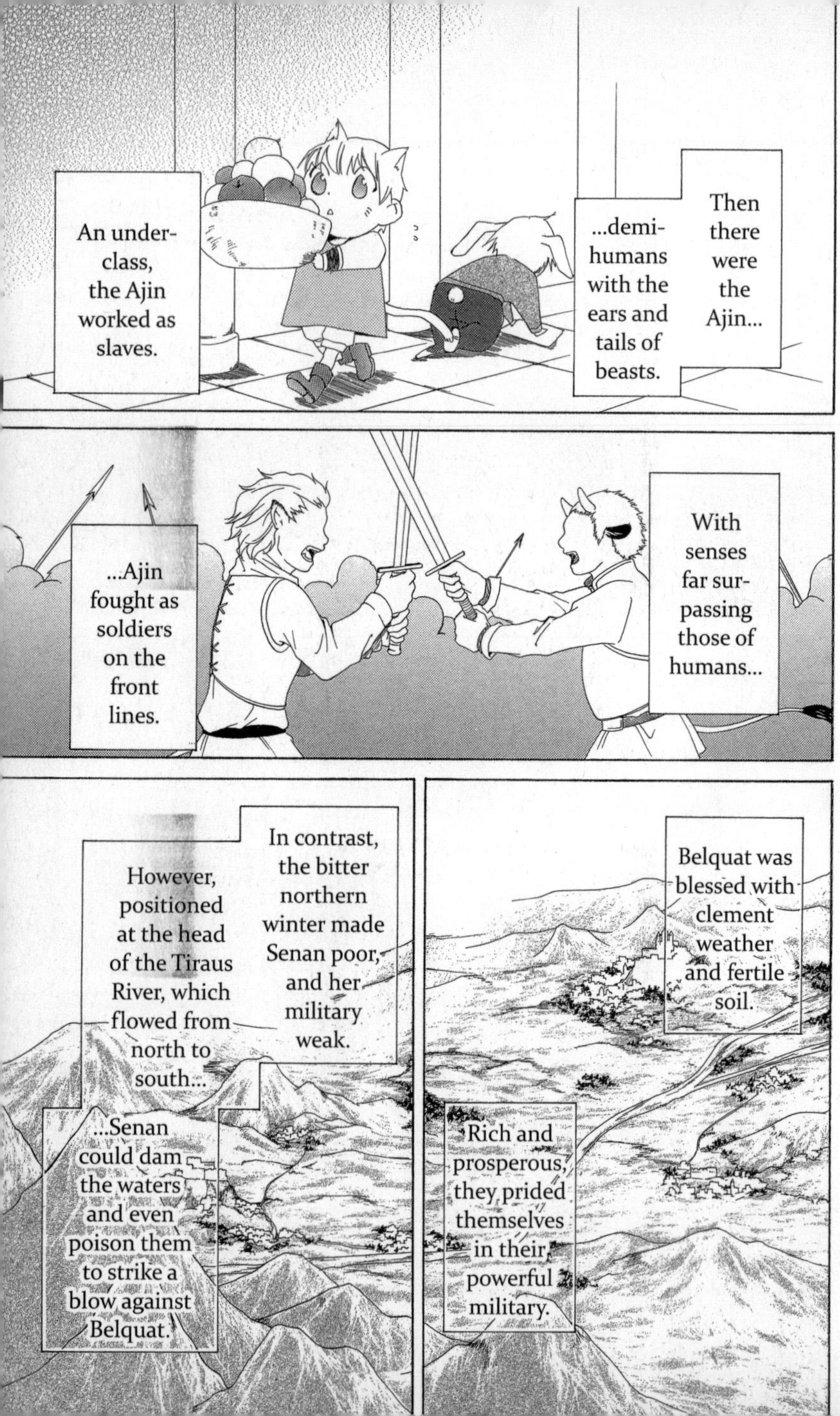
Then there were the Ajin...
...demi-humans with the ears and tails of beasts.
An under-class, the Ajin worked as slaves.
With senses far surpassing those of humans...
...Ajin fought as soldiers on the front lines.
Belquat was blessed with clement weather and fertile soil.
Rich and prosperous, they prided themselves in their powerful military.
In contrast, the bitter northern winter made Senan poor, and her military weak.
However, positioned at the head of the Tiraus River, which flowed from north to south...
...Senan could dam the waters and even poison them to strike a blow against Belquat.

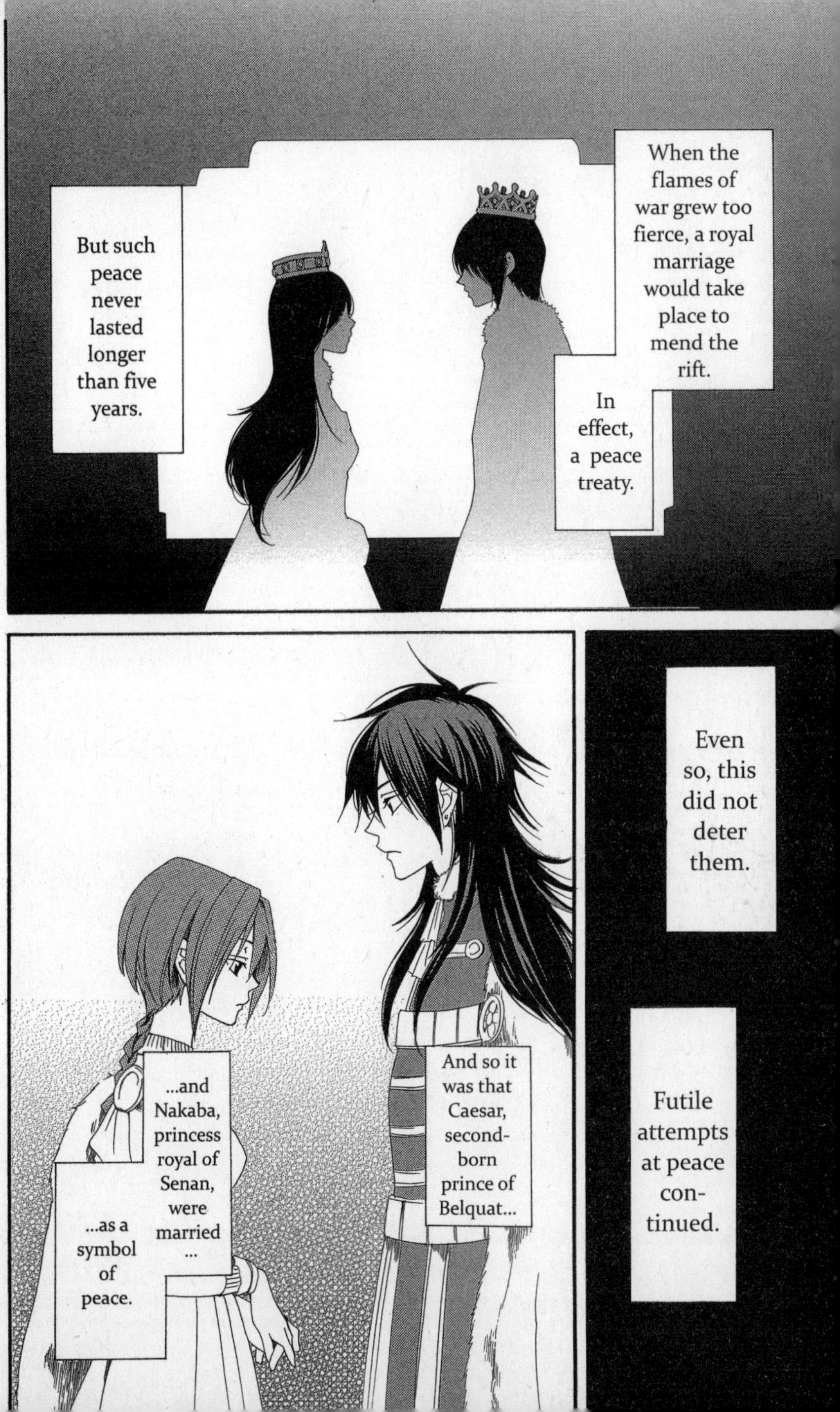
When the flames of war grew too fierce, a royal marriage would take place to mend the rift.
In effect, a peace treaty.
But such peace never lasted longer than five years.
Even so, this did not deter them.
Futile attempts at peace con-tinued.
And so it was that Caesar, second-born prince of Belquat...
...and Nakaba, princess royal of Senan, were married ...
...as a symbol of peace.

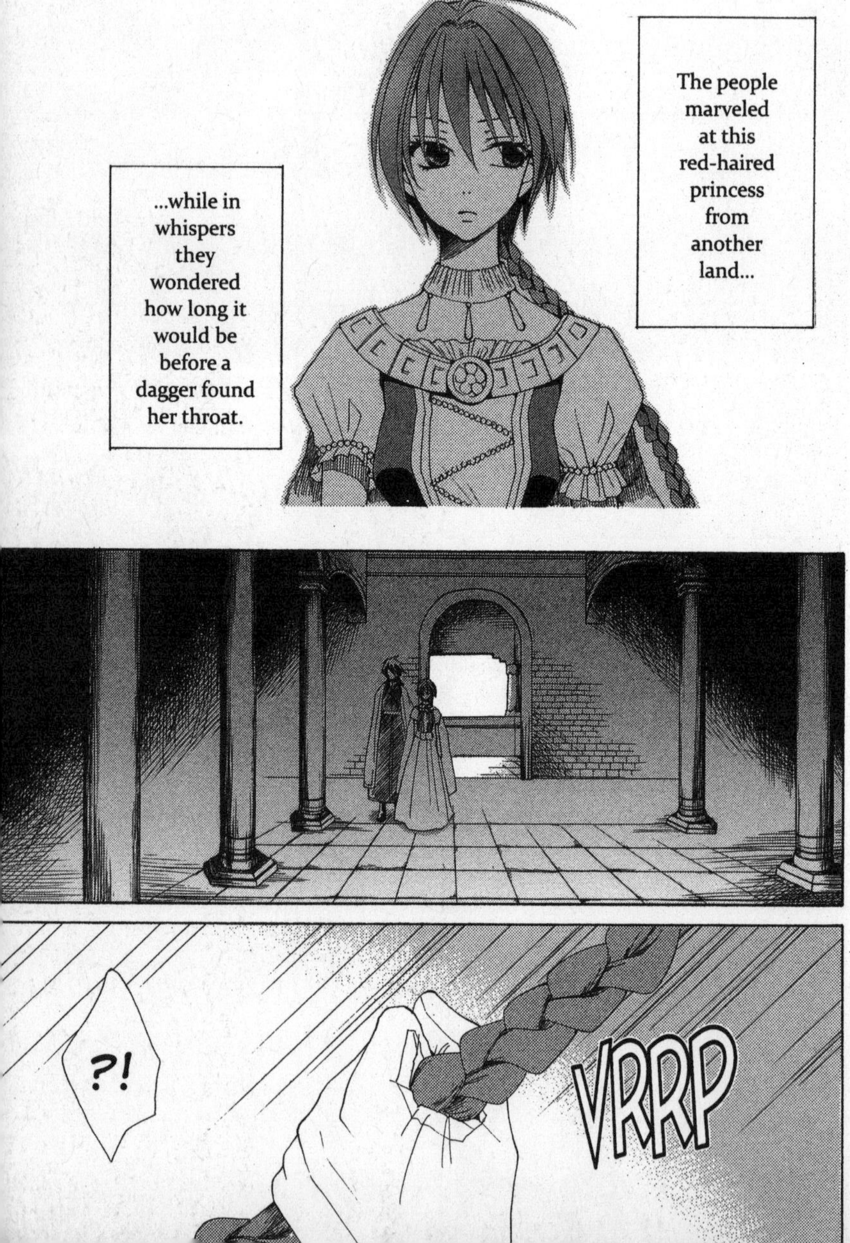
The people marveled at this red-haired princess from another land...
...while in whispers they wondered how long it would be before a dagger found her throat.
VRRP
?!

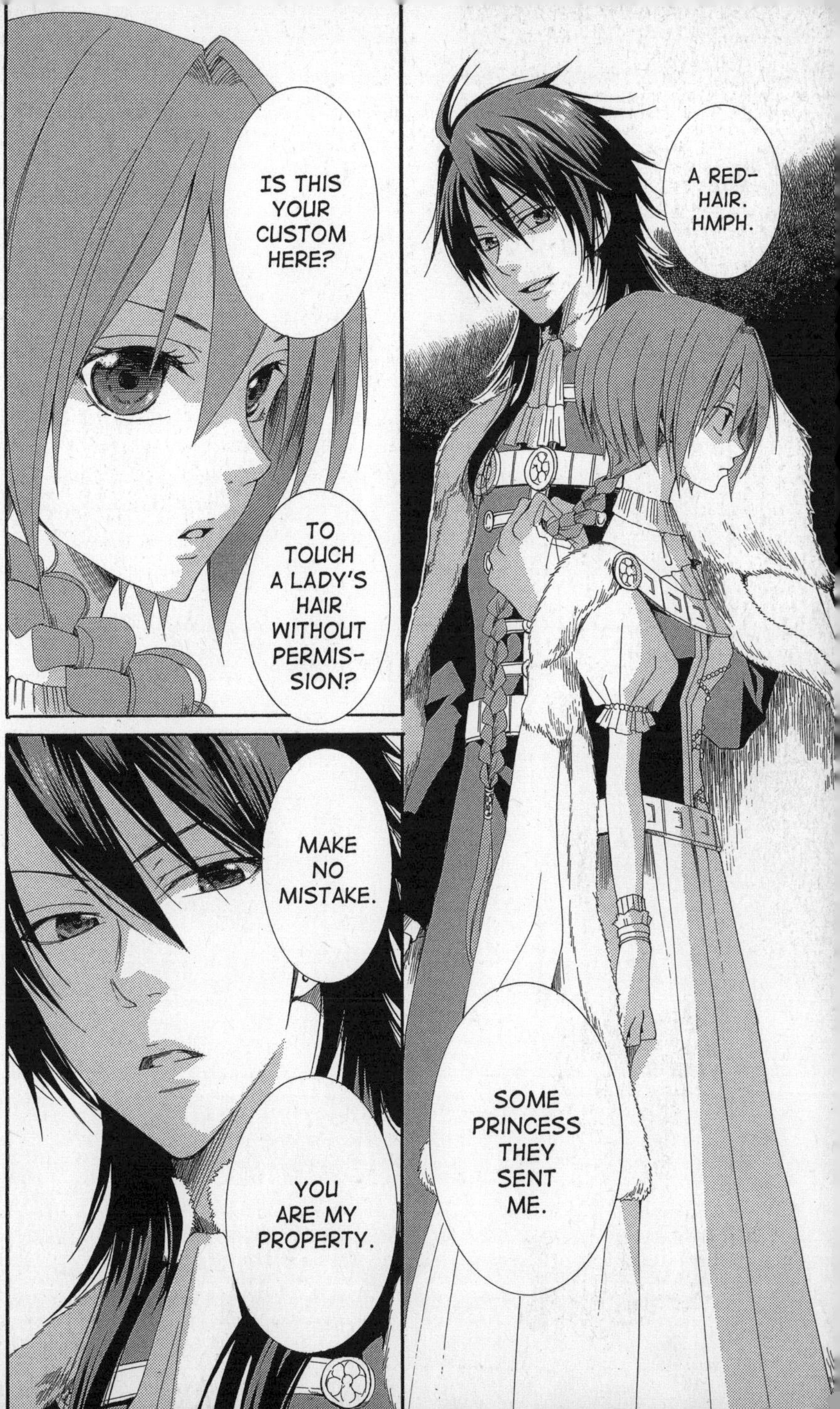
A RED-HAIR. HMPH.
SOME PRINCESS THEY SENT ME.
IS THIS YOUR CUSTOM HERE?
TO TOUCH A LADY'S HAIR WITHOUT PERMISSION?
MAKE NO MISTAKE.
YOU ARE MY PROPERTY.

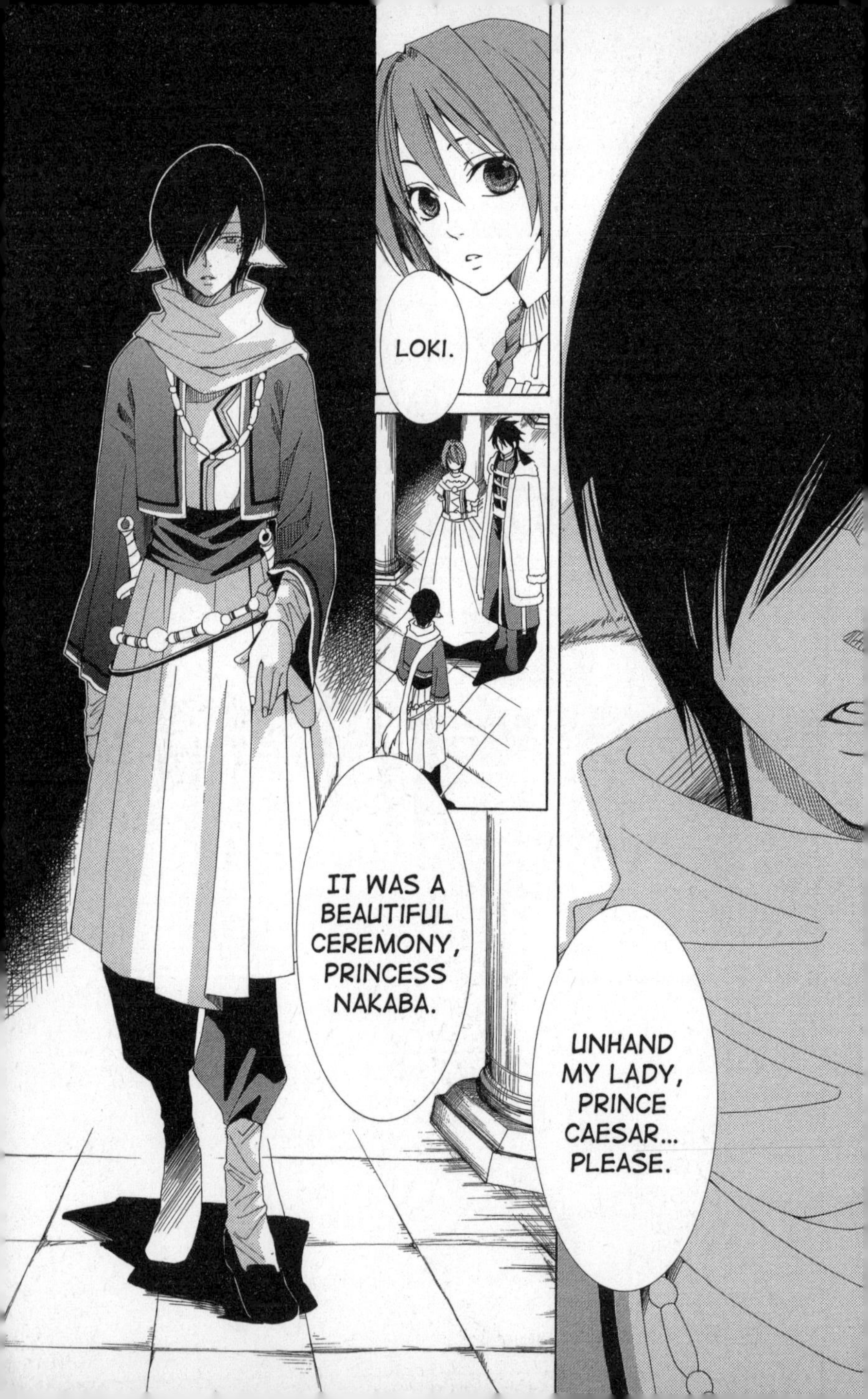
UNHAND MY LADY, PRINCE CAESAR... PLEASE.
LOKI.
IT WAS A BEAUTIFUL CEREMONY, PRINCESS NAKABA.

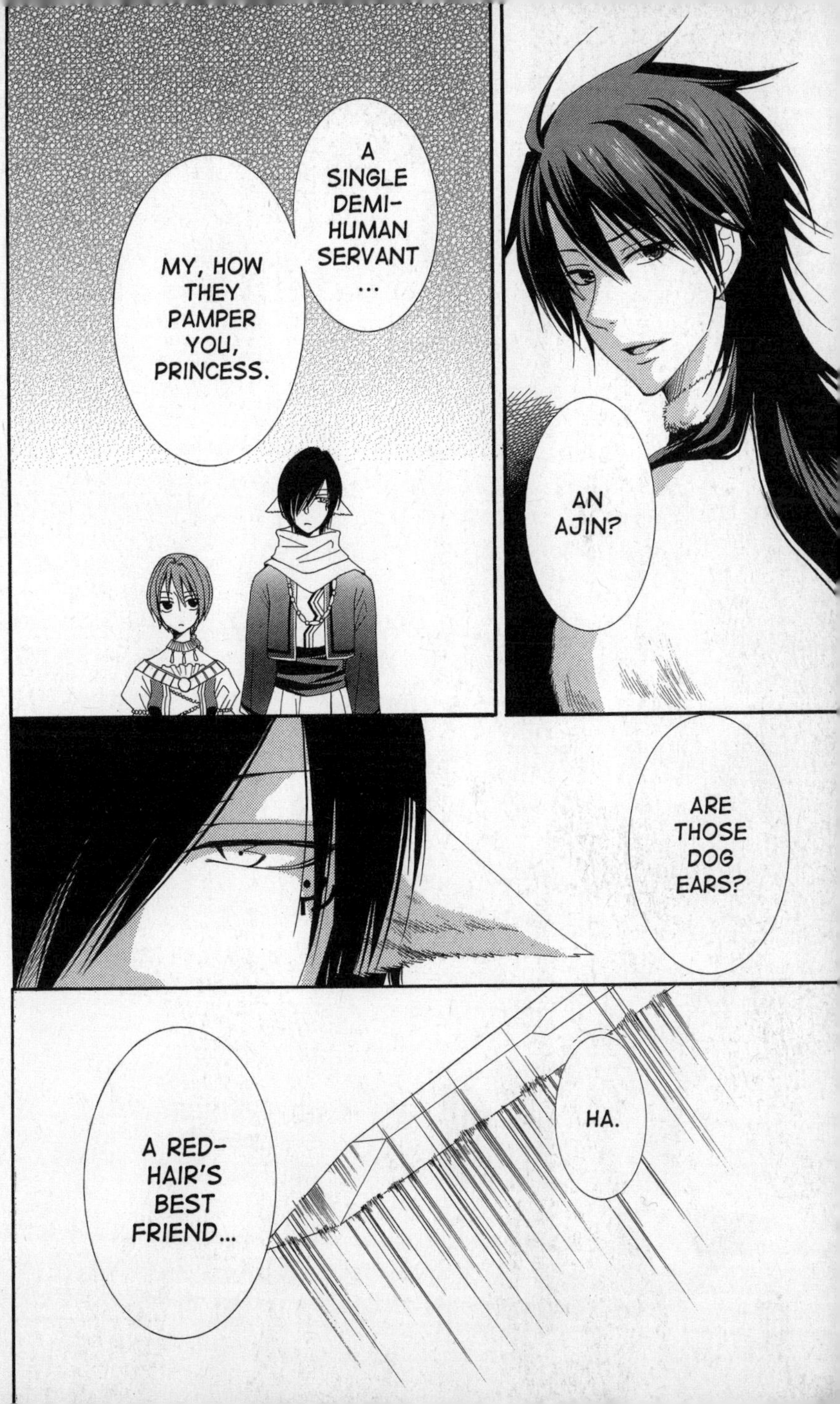
AN AJIN?
A SINGLE DEMI-HUMAN SERVANT ...
MY, HOW THEY PAMPER YOU, PRINCESS.
ARE THOSE DOG EARS?
HA.
A RED-HAIR'S BEST FRIEND...

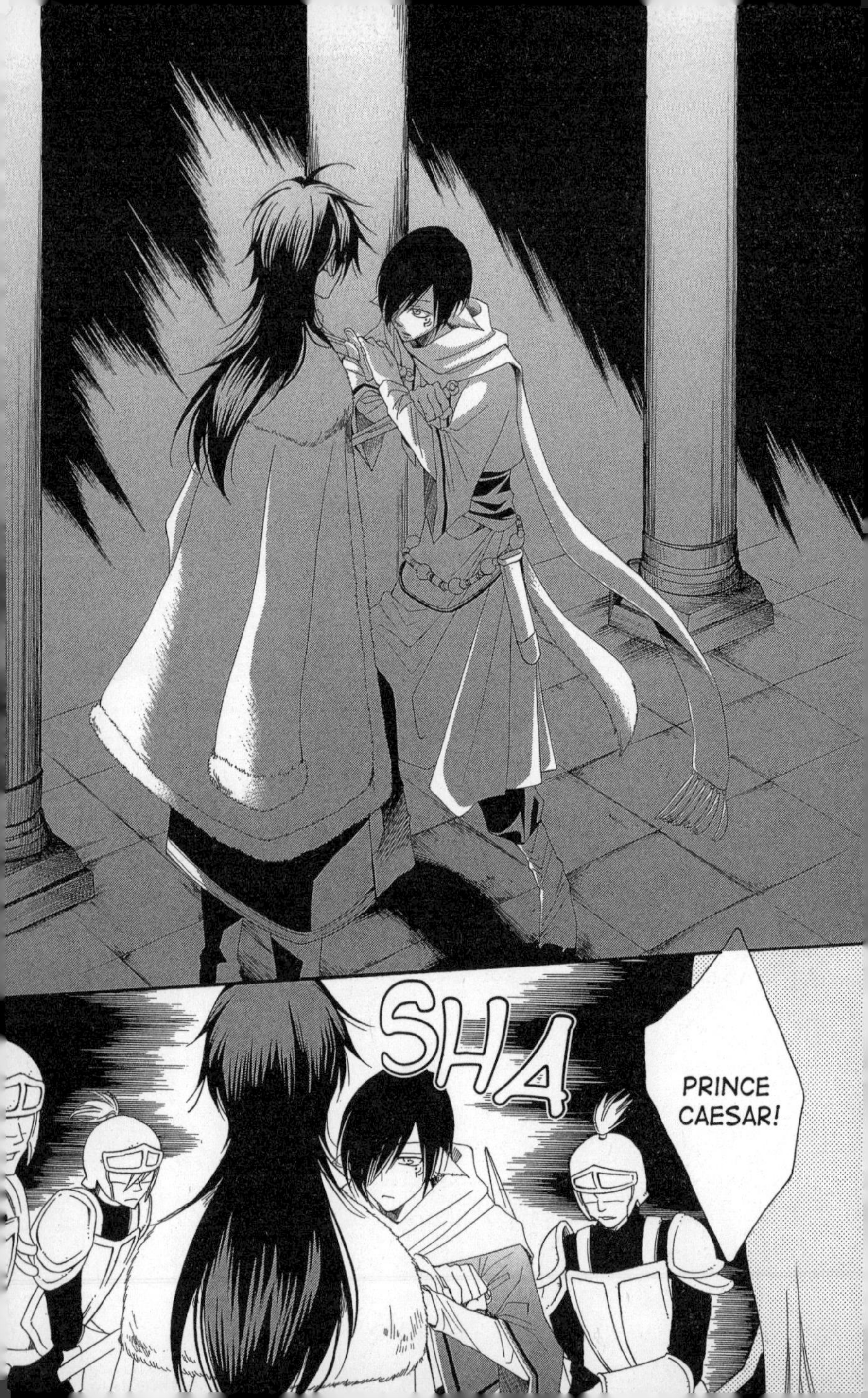
SHA
PRINCE CAESAR!

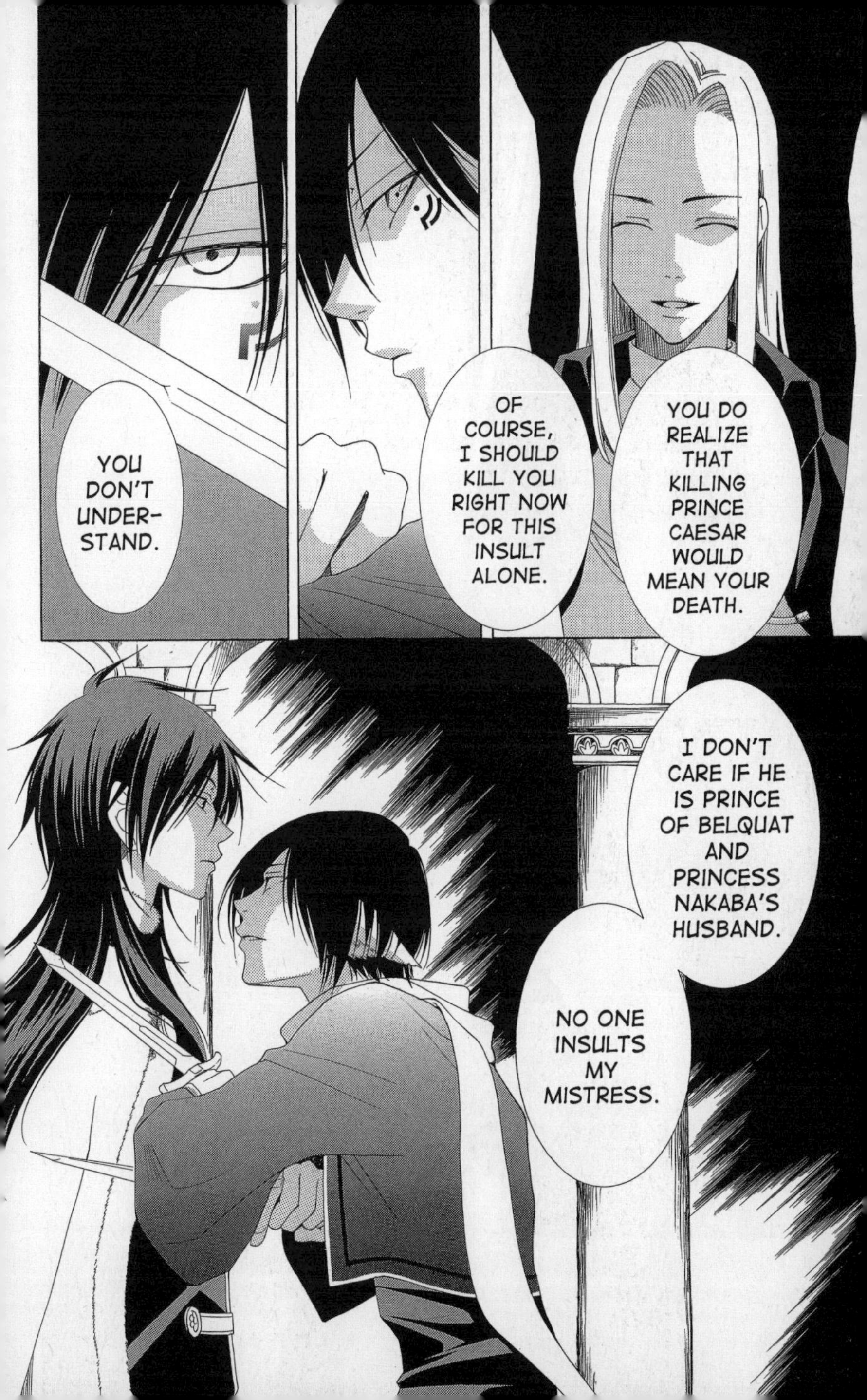
YOU DO REALIZE THAT KILLING PRINCE CAESAR WOULD MEAN YOUR DEATH.
OF COURSE, I SHOULD KILL YOU RIGHT NOW FOR THIS INSULT ALONE.
YOU DON'T UNDER-STAND.
I DON'T CARE IF HE IS PRINCE OF BELQUAT AND PRINCESS NAKABA'S HUSBAND.
NO ONE INSULTS MY MISTRESS.

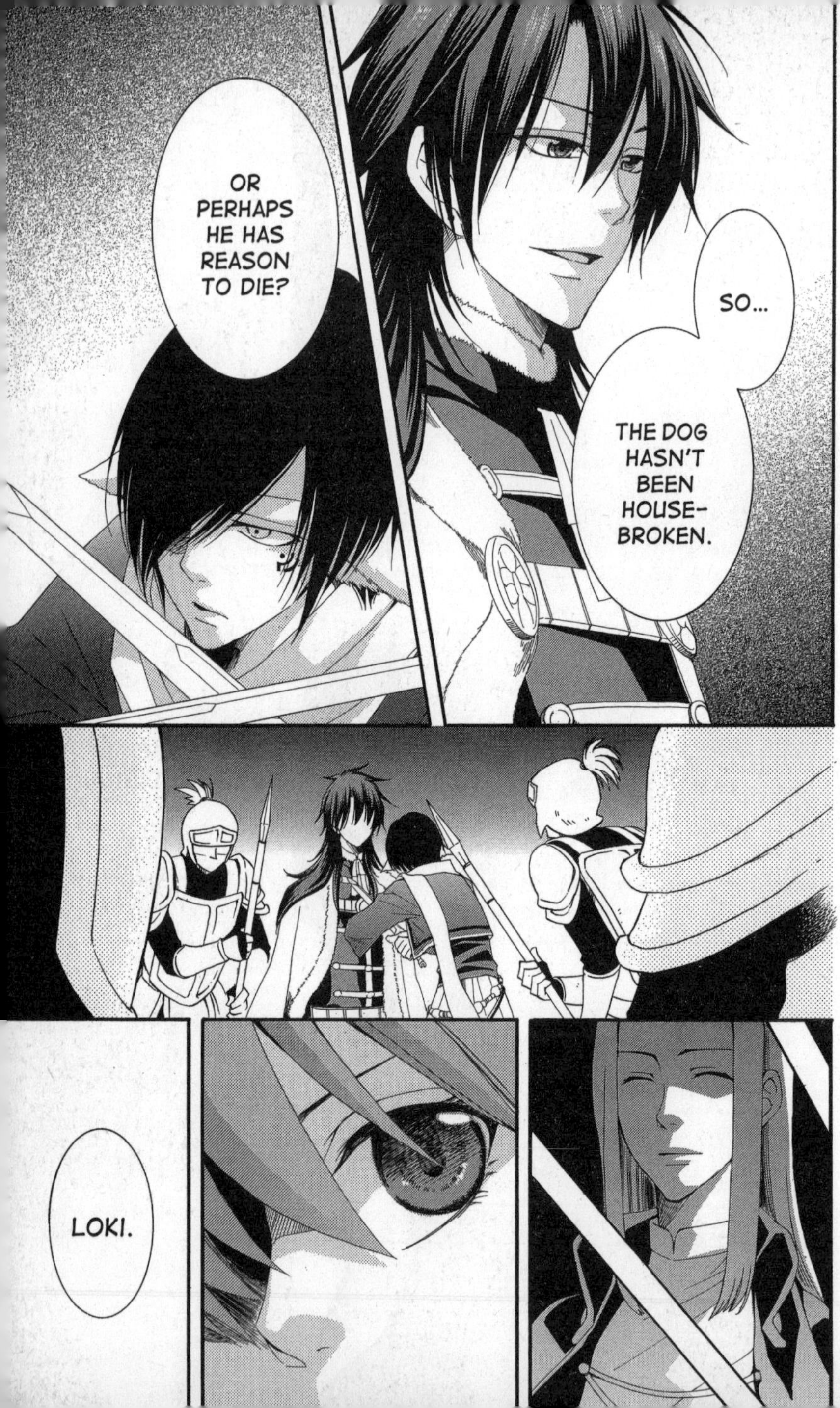
SO...
THE DOG HASN'T BEEN HOUSE-BROKEN.
OR PERHAPS HE HAS REASON TO DIE?
LOKI.

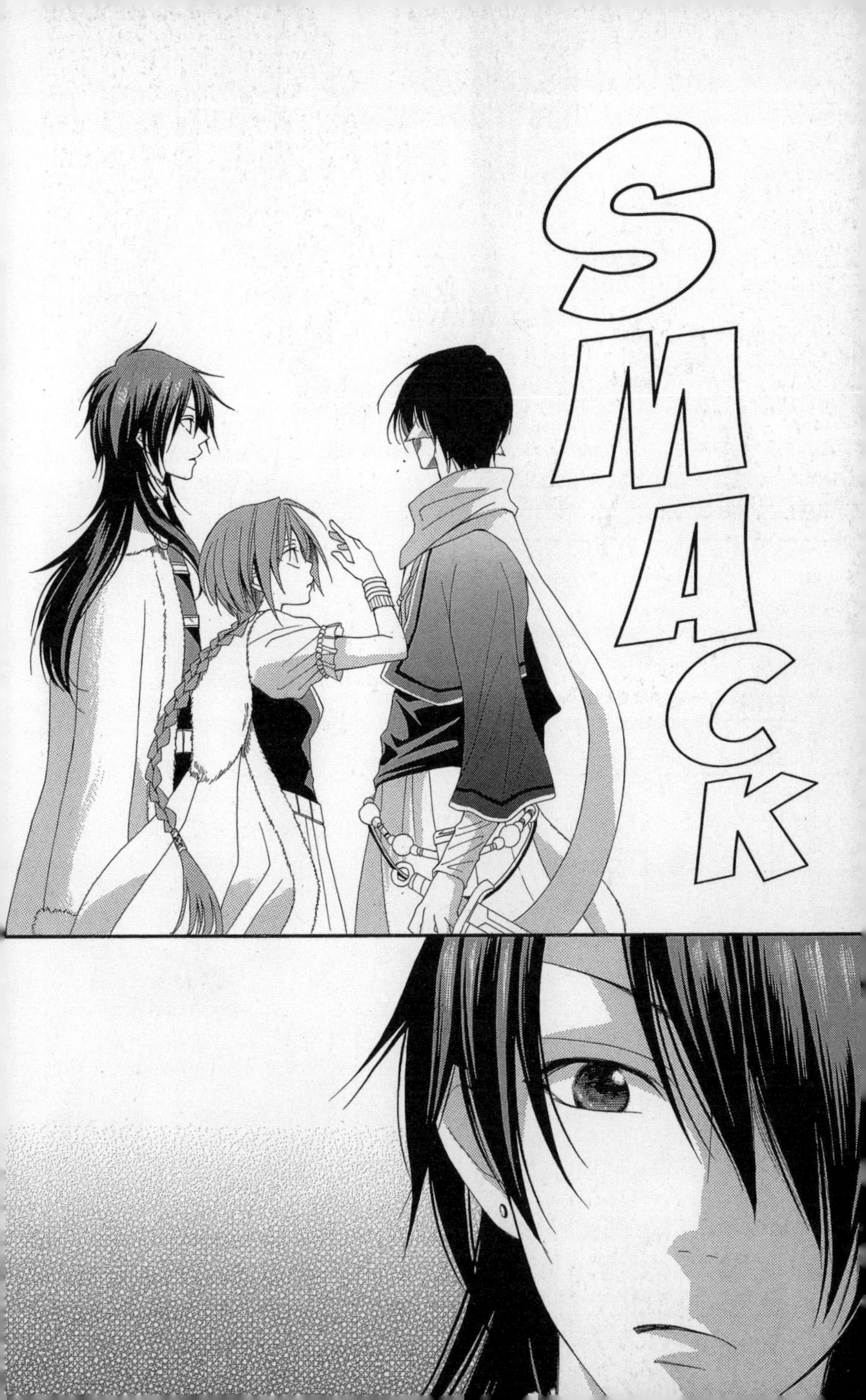
SMACK

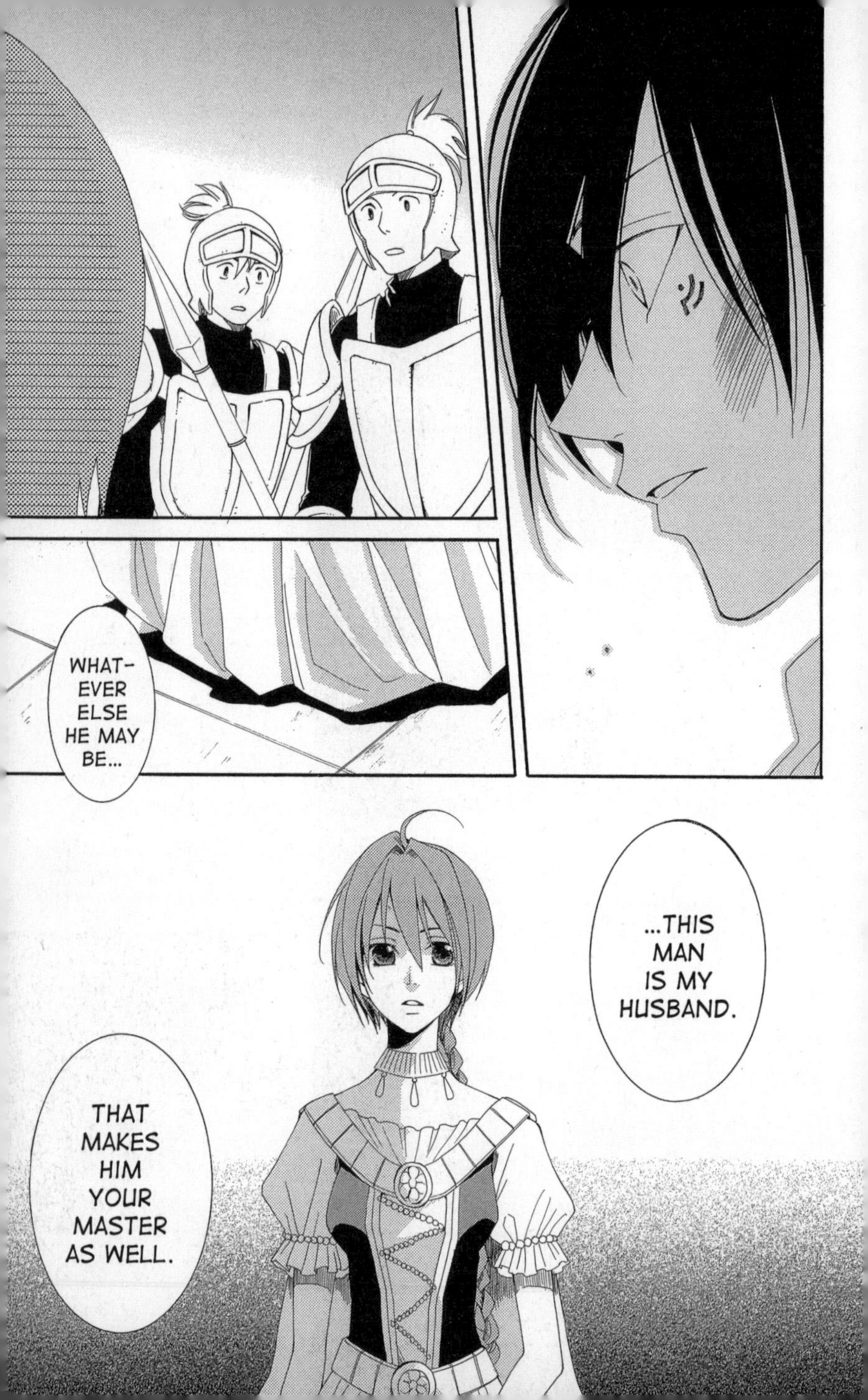
WHATEVER ELSE HE MAY BE...
...THIS MAN IS MY HUSBAND.
THAT MAKES HIM YOUR MASTER AS WELL.

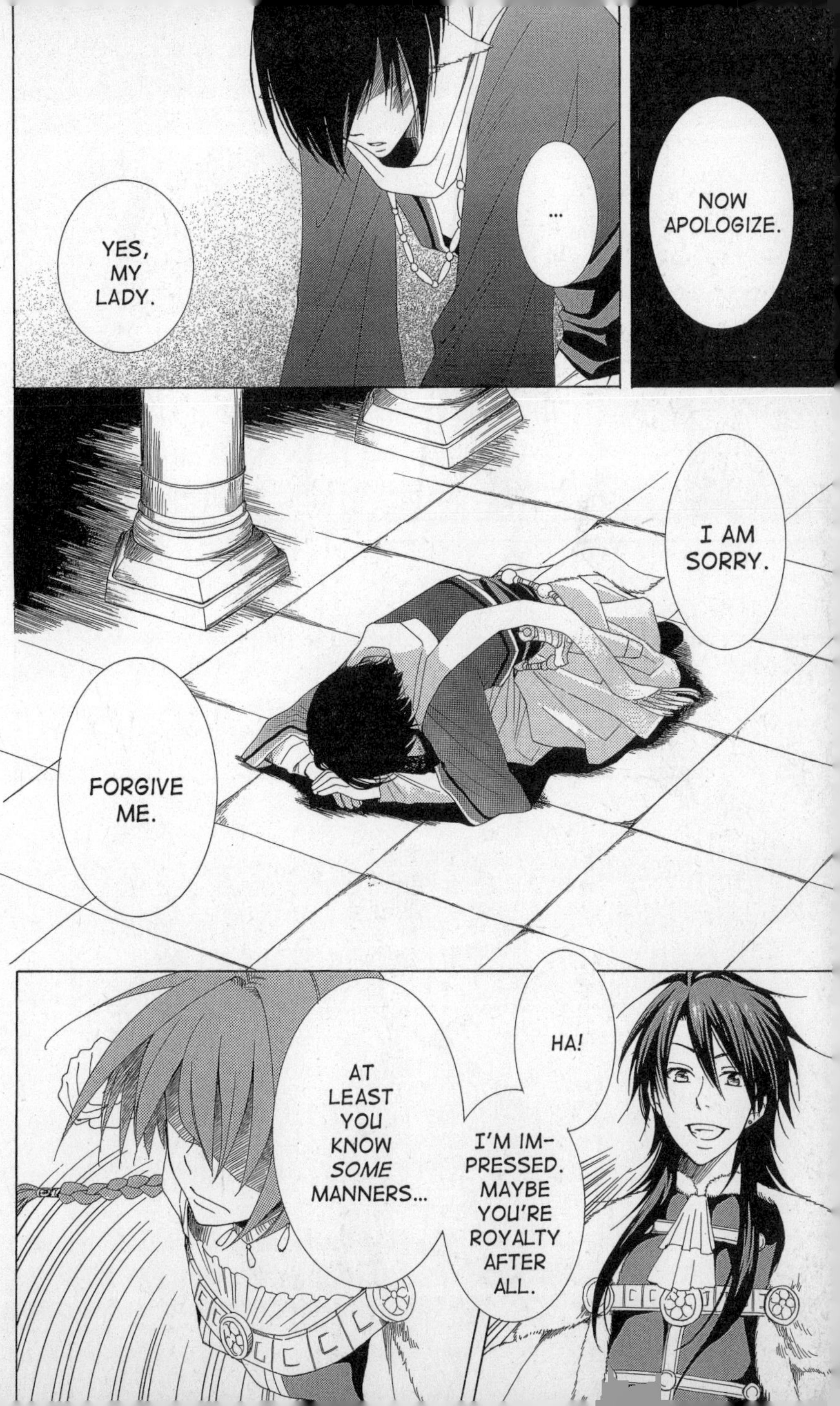
NOW APOLOGIZE.
...
YES, MY LADY.
I AM SORRY.
FORGIVE ME.
HA!
AT LEAST YOU KNOW *SOME* MANNERS...
I'M IM-PRESSED. MAYBE YOU'RE ROYALTY AFTER ALL.

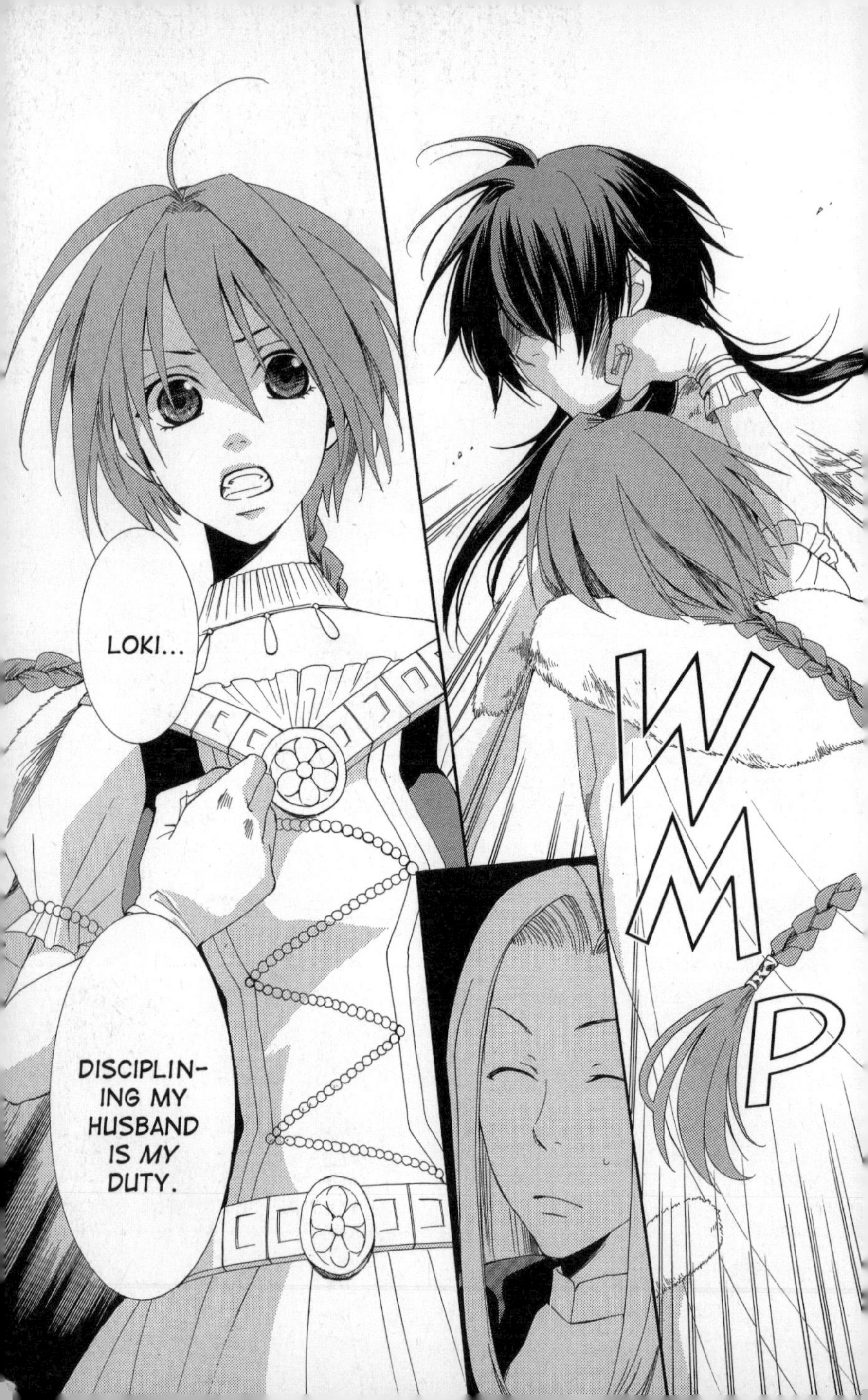
WMMP
LOKI...
DISCIPLIN-ING MY HUSBAND IS MY DUTY.

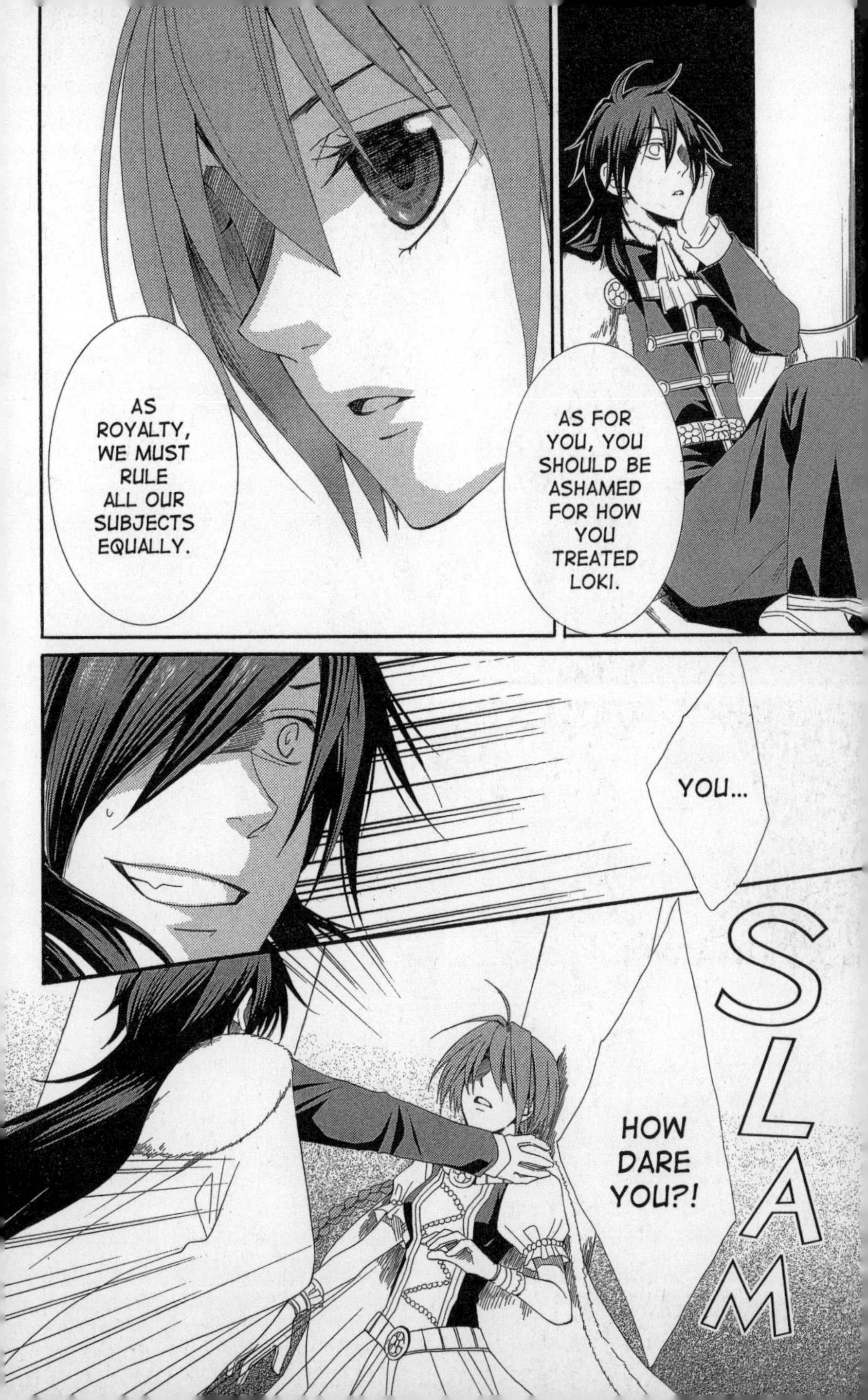
AS FOR YOU, YOU SHOULD BE ASHAMED FOR HOW YOU TREATED LOKI.
AS ROYALTY, WE MUST RULE ALL OUR SUBJECTS EQUALLY.
YOU...
SLAM
HOW DARE YOU?!

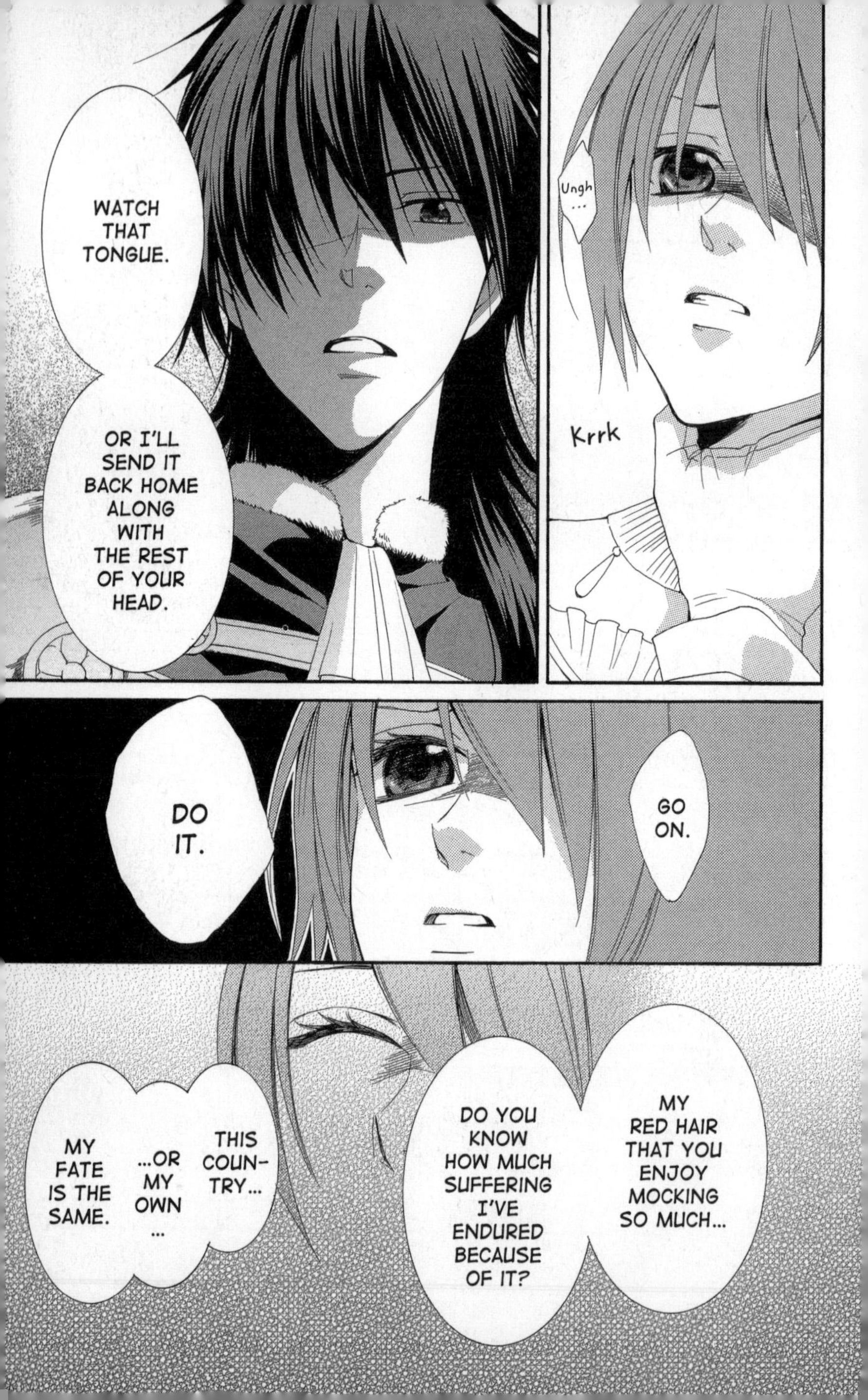
Ungh...
Krrk
WATCH THAT TONGUE.
OR I'LL SEND IT BACK HOME ALONG WITH THE REST OF YOUR HEAD.
GO ON.
DO IT.
MY RED HAIR THAT YOU ENJOY MOCKING SO MUCH...
DO YOU KNOW HOW MUCH SUFFERING I'VE ENDURED BECAUSE OF IT?
THIS COUN-TRY...
...OR MY OWN...
MY FATE IS THE SAME.

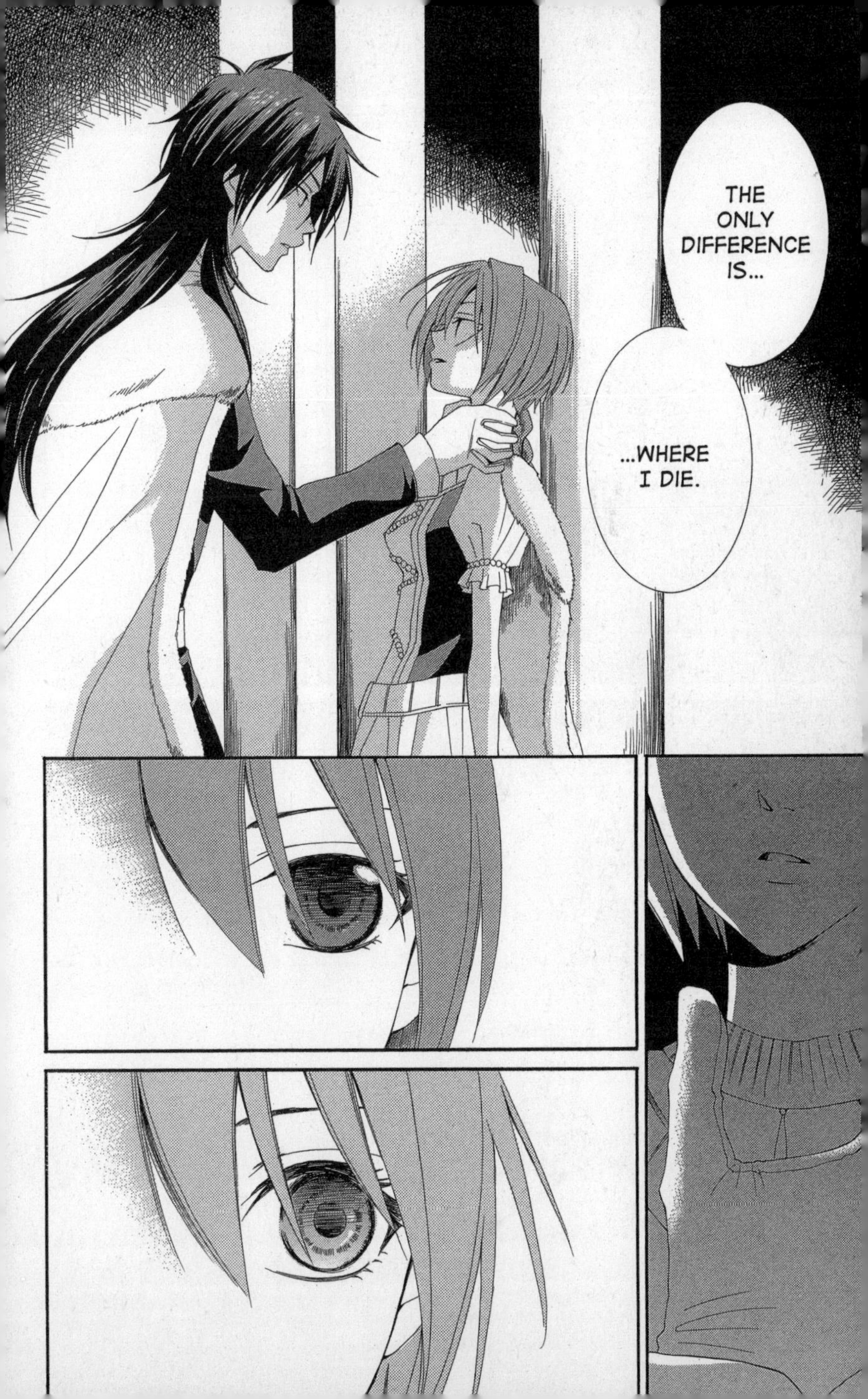
THE ONLY DIFFERENCE IS...
...WHERE I DIE.

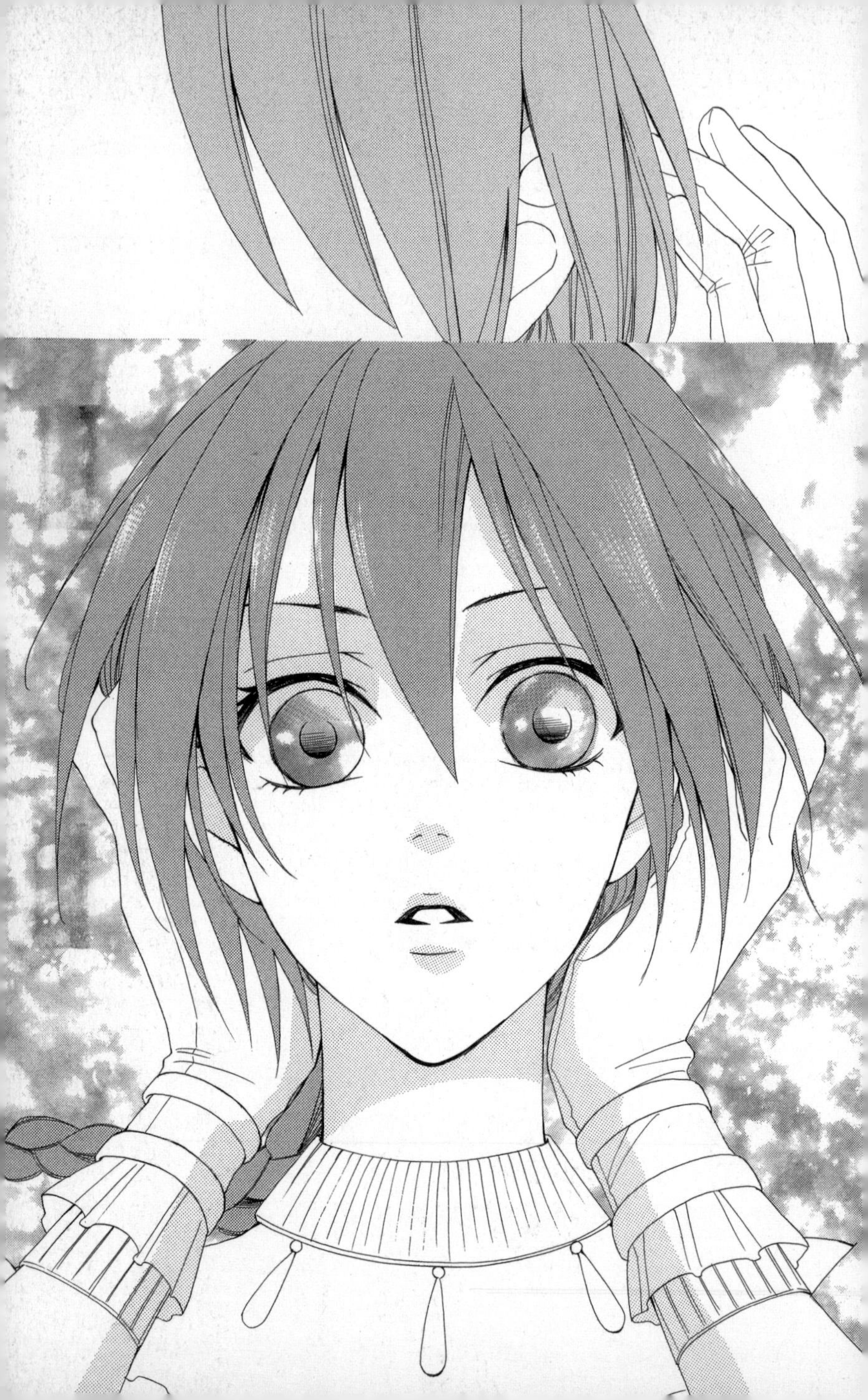

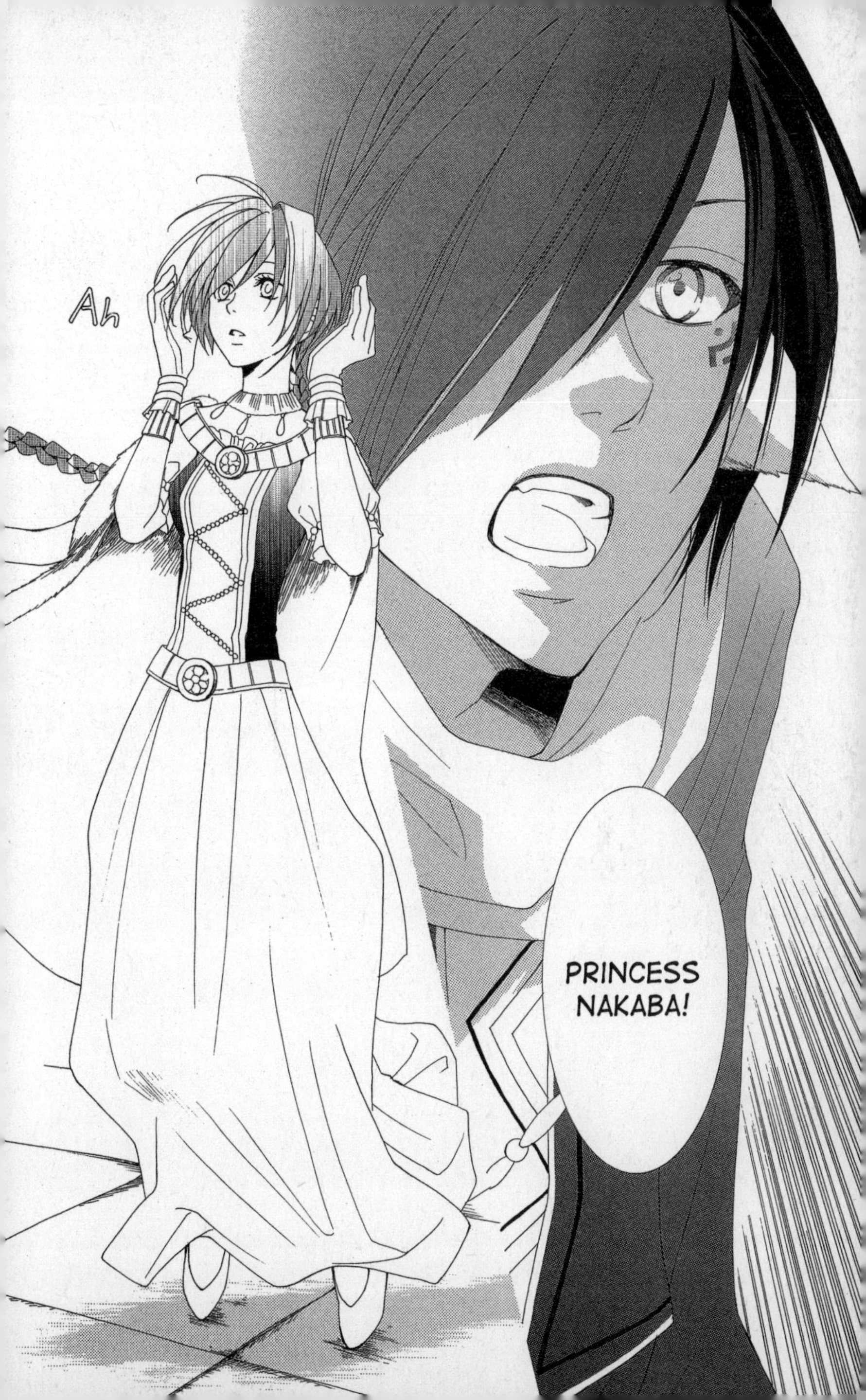
PRINCESS NAKABA!
Ah

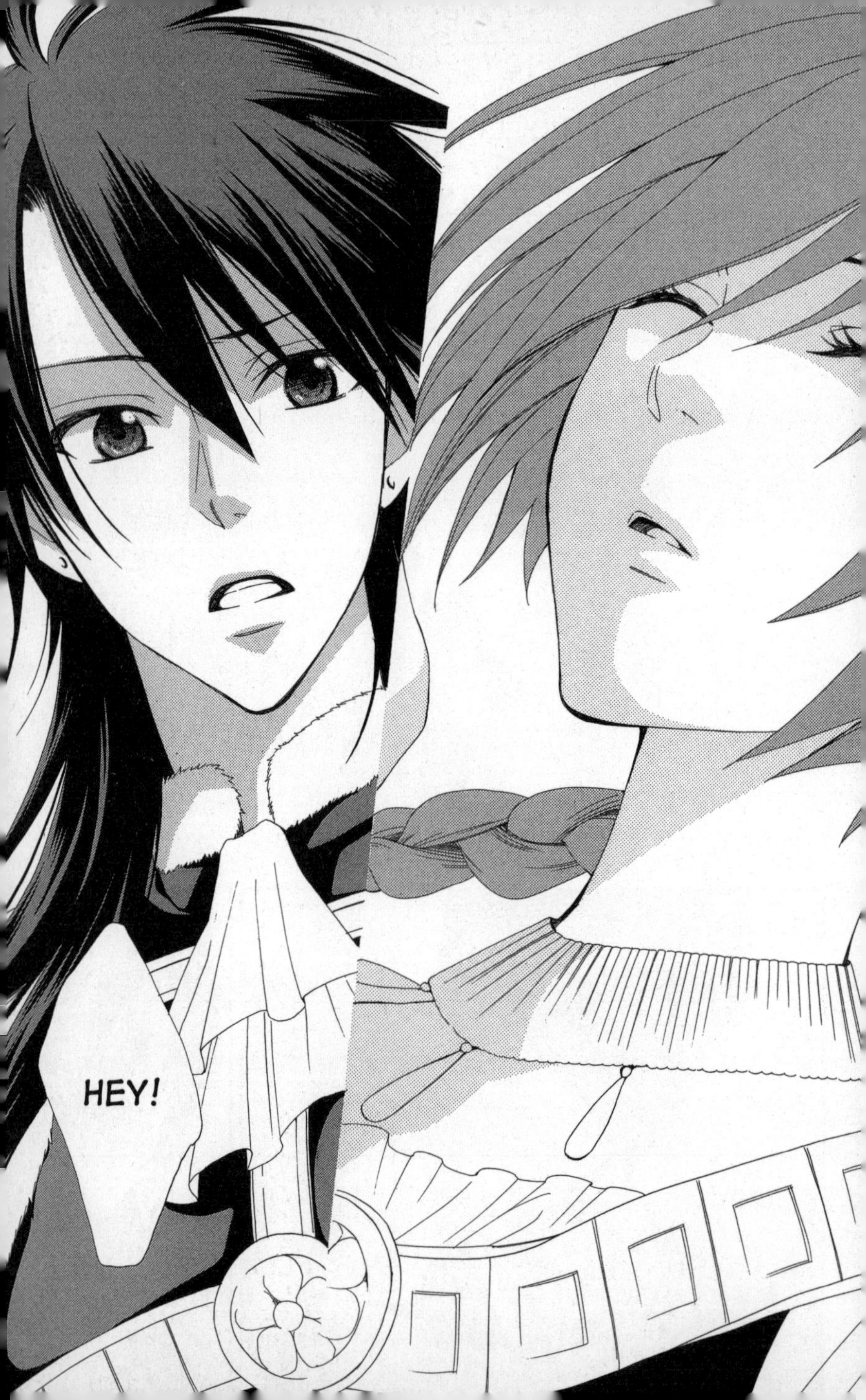
HEY!

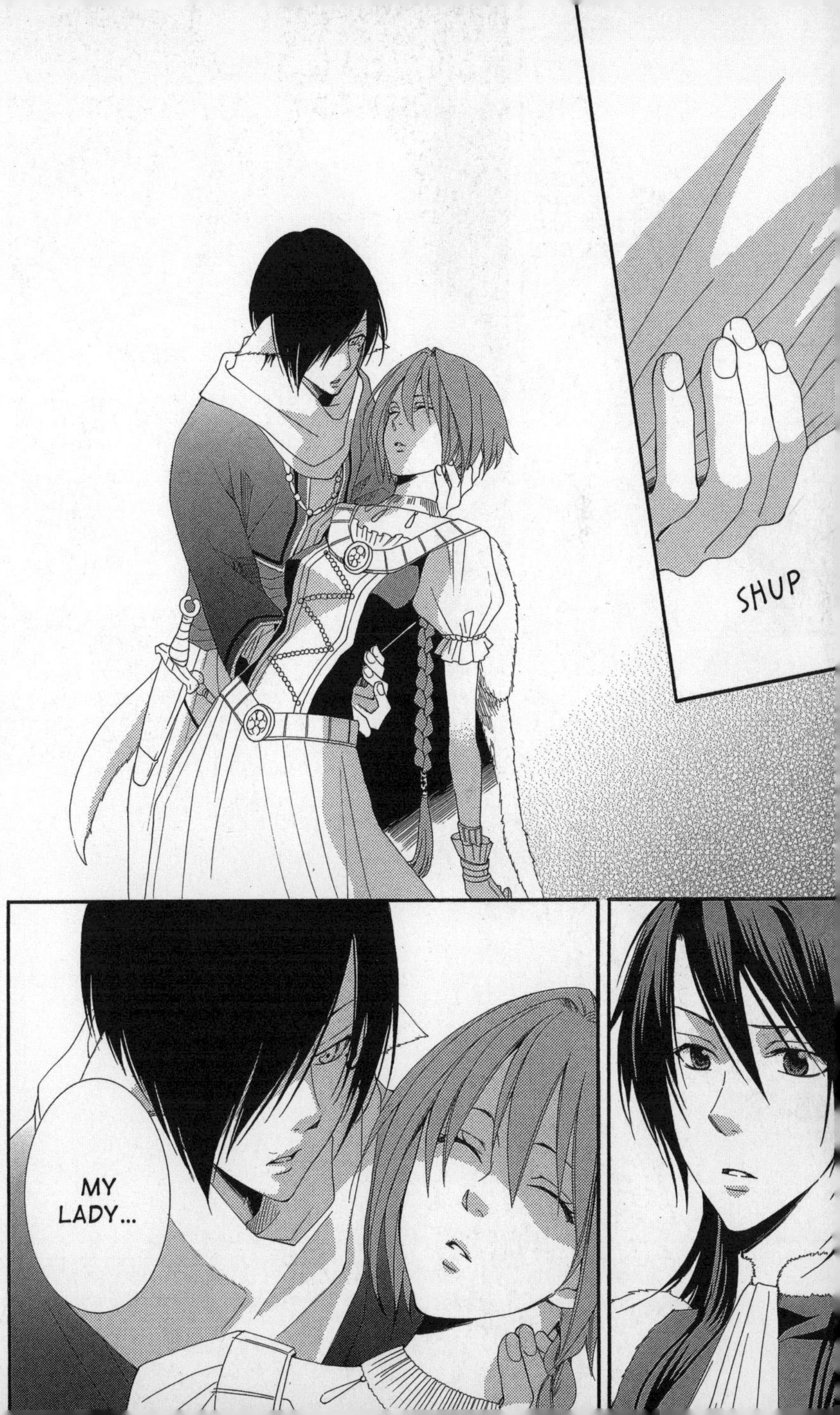
SHUP
MY LADY...

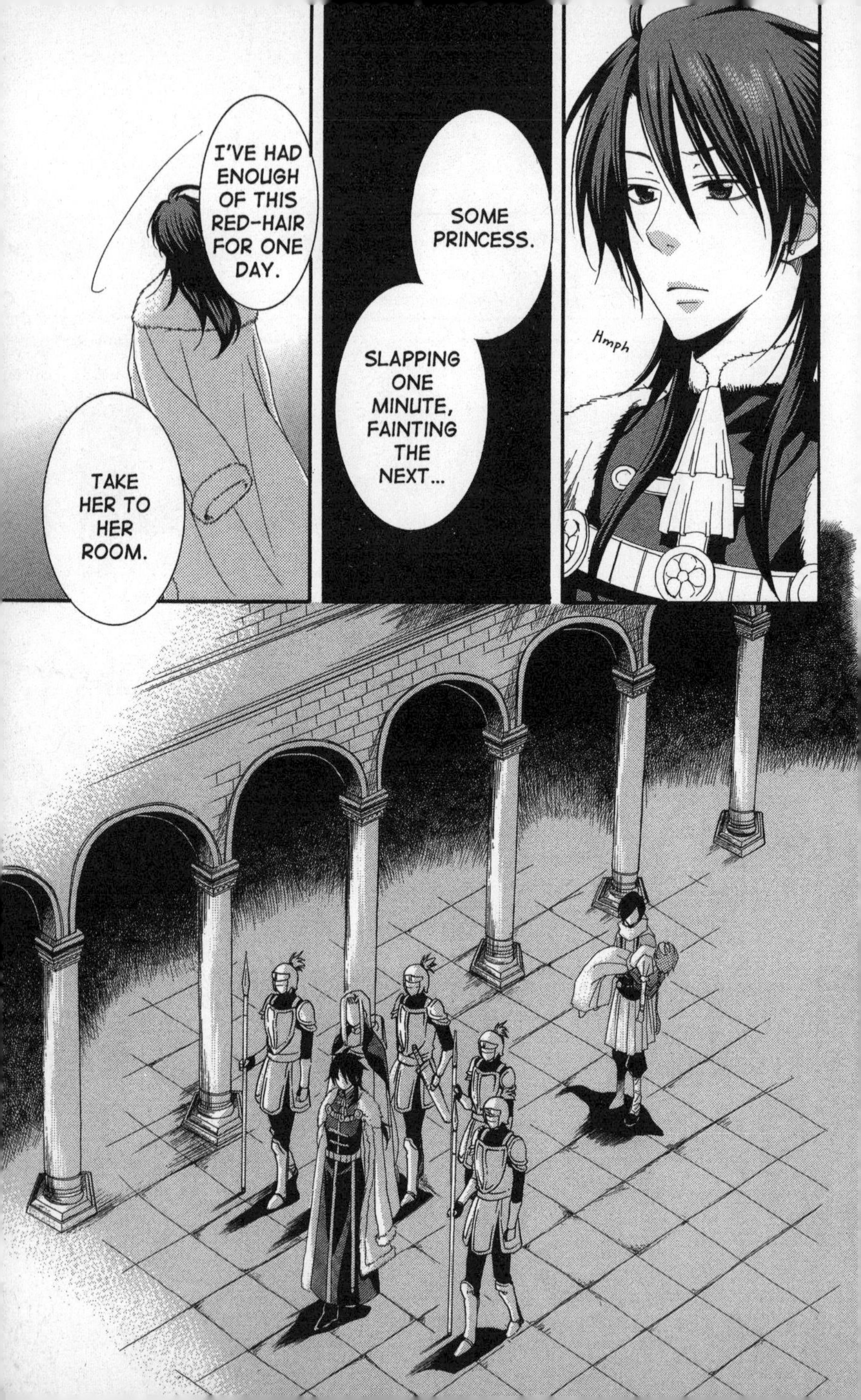
Hmph
SOME PRINCESS.
SLAPPING ONE MINUTE, FAINTING THE NEXT...
I'VE HAD ENOUGH OF THIS RED-HAIR FOR ONE DAY.
TAKE HER TO HER ROOM.

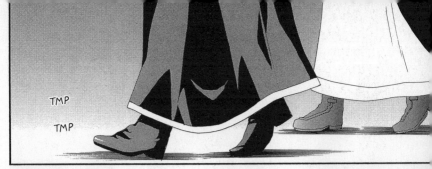

TMP

TMP

PFFT
...

HA
HA
HA
...

HA
HA
HA
...

HA
HA
....

BELLI-
NUS!

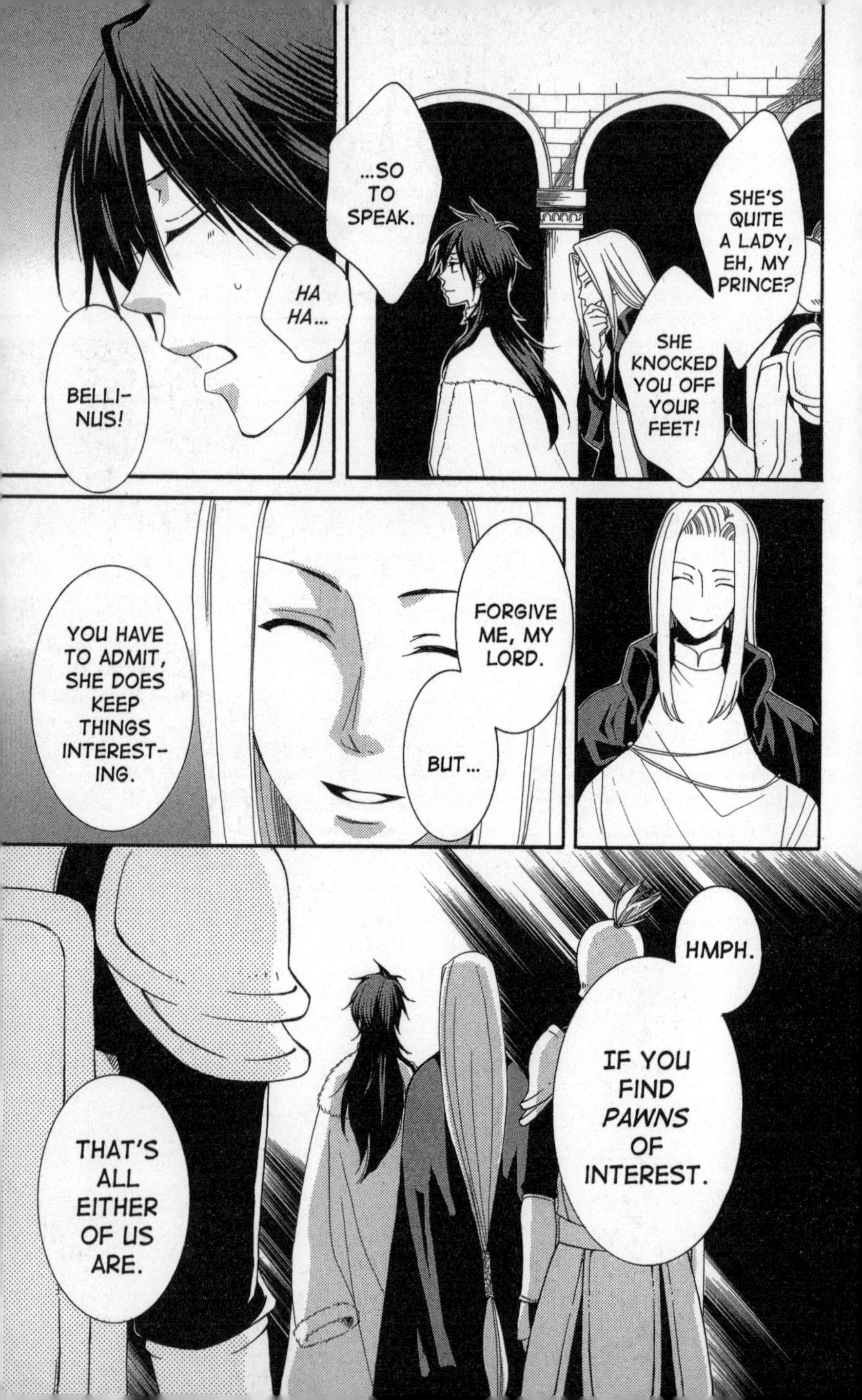
SHE'S QUITE A LADY, EH, MY PRINCE?
SHE KNOCKED YOU OFF YOUR FEET!
...SO TO SPEAK.
HA HA...
BELLI-NUS!
FORGIVE ME, MY LORD.
BUT...
YOU HAVE TO ADMIT, SHE DOES KEEP THINGS INTEREST-ING.
HMPH.
IF YOU FIND *PAWNS* OF INTEREST.
THAT'S ALL EITHER OF US ARE.

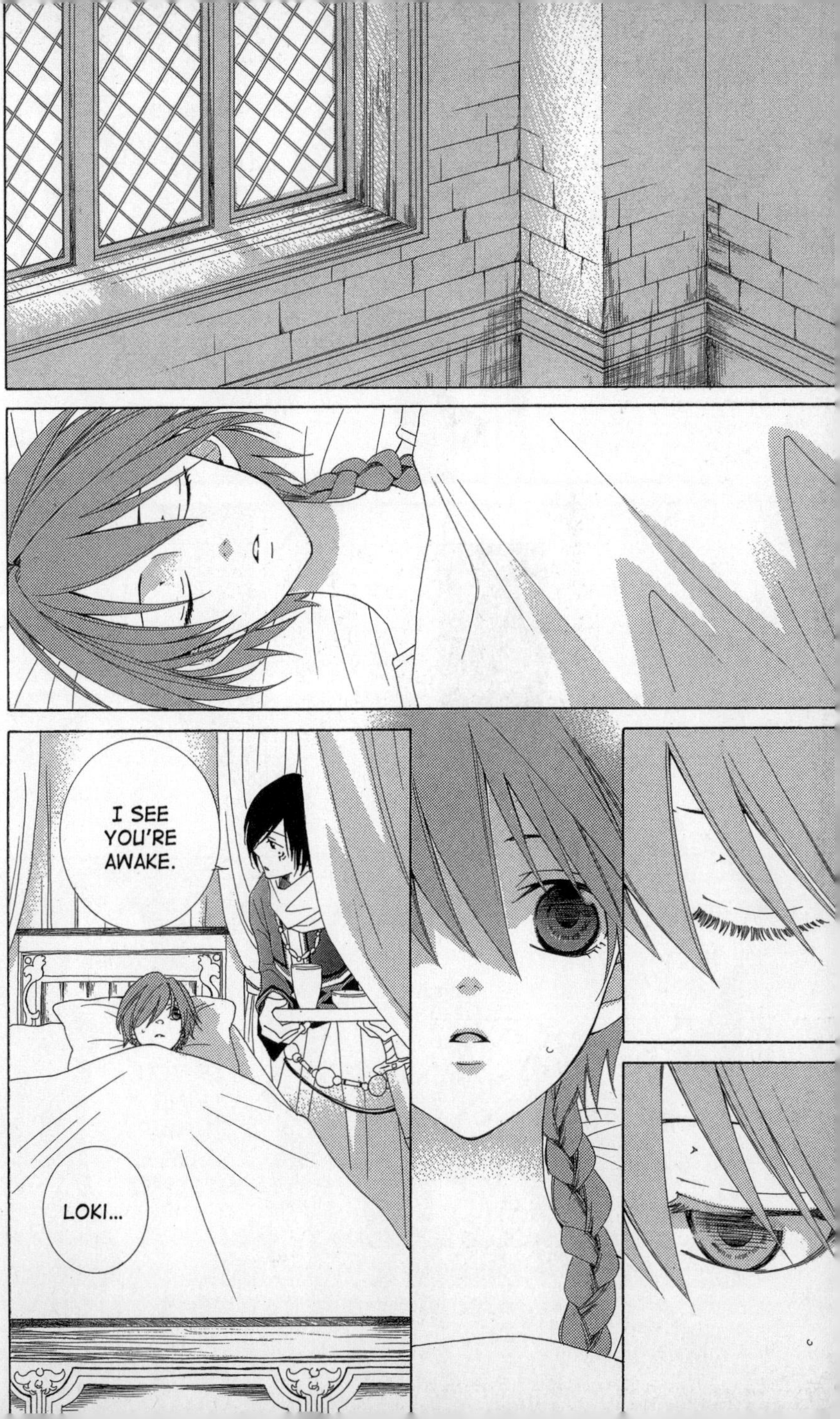
I SEE YOU'RE AWAKE.
LOKI...

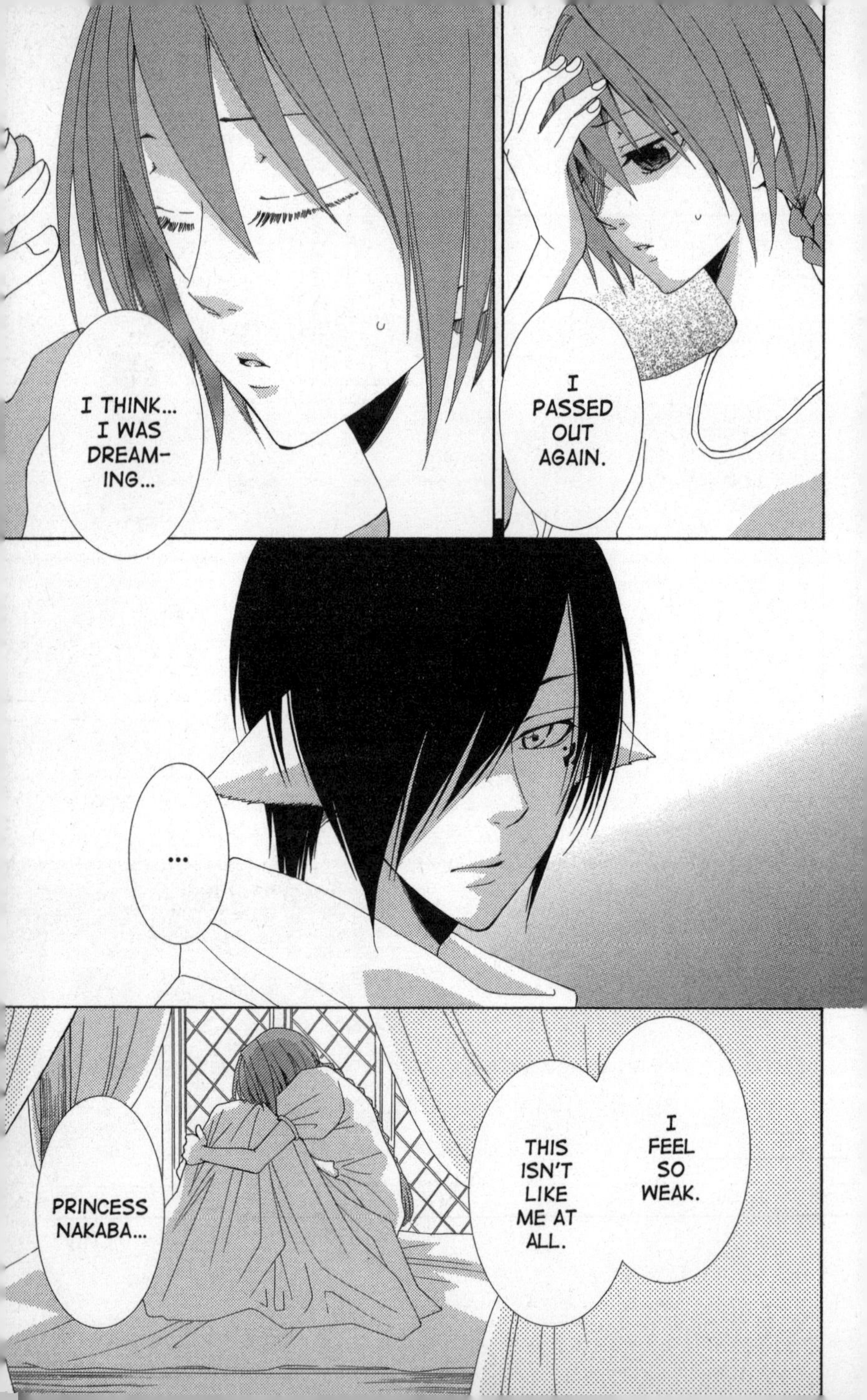
I PASSED OUT AGAIN.
I THINK... I WAS DREAM-ING...
...
I FEEL SO WEAK.
THIS ISN'T LIKE ME AT ALL.
PRINCESS NAKABA...

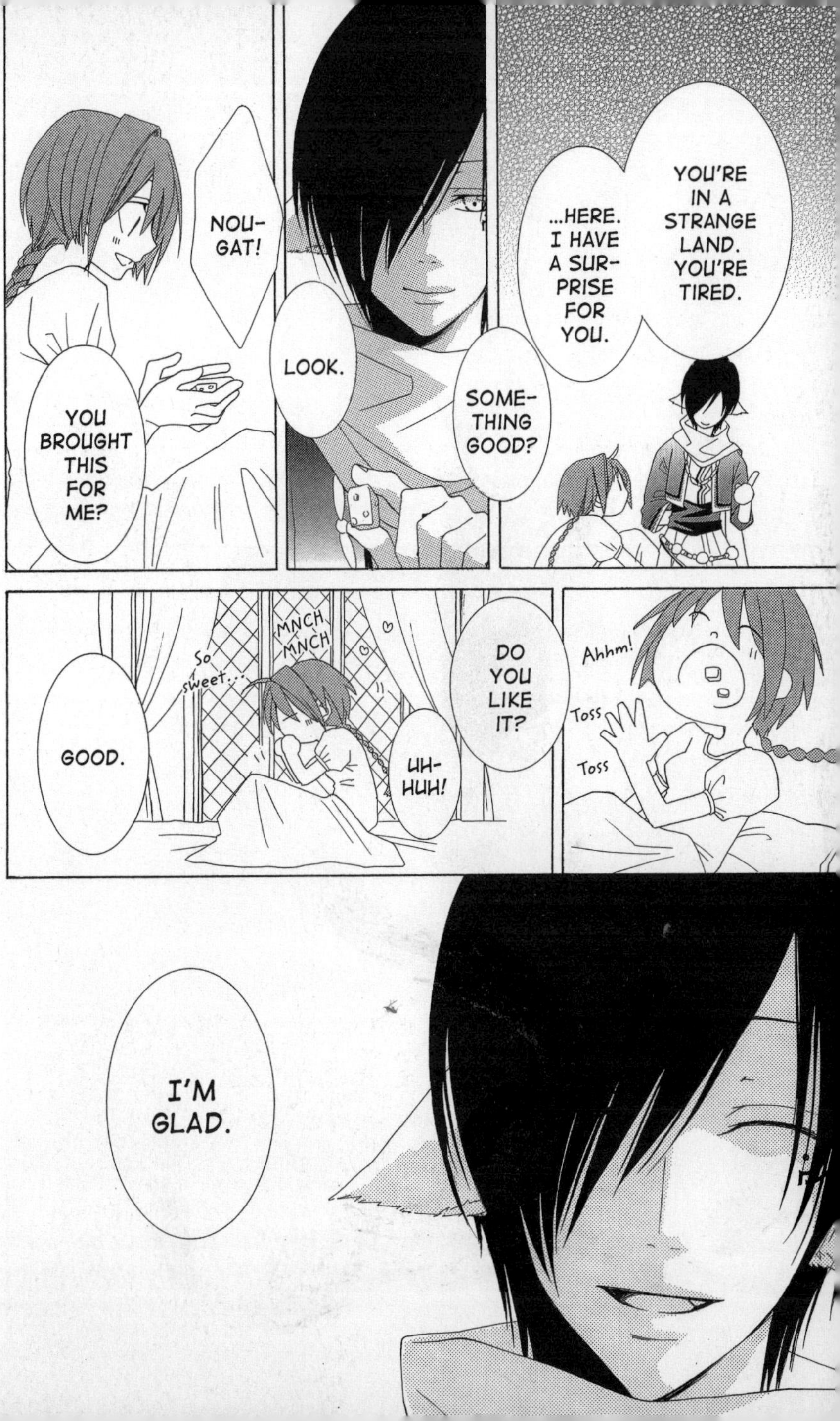
YOU'RE IN A STRANGE LAND. YOU'RE TIRED.
...HERE. I HAVE A SURPRISE FOR YOU.
SOMETHING GOOD?
LOOK.
NOUGAT!
YOU BROUGHT THIS FOR ME?
Ahhm!
Toss
Toss
DO YOU LIKE IT?
UH-HUH!
MNCH MNCH
So sweet...
GOOD.
I'M GLAD.

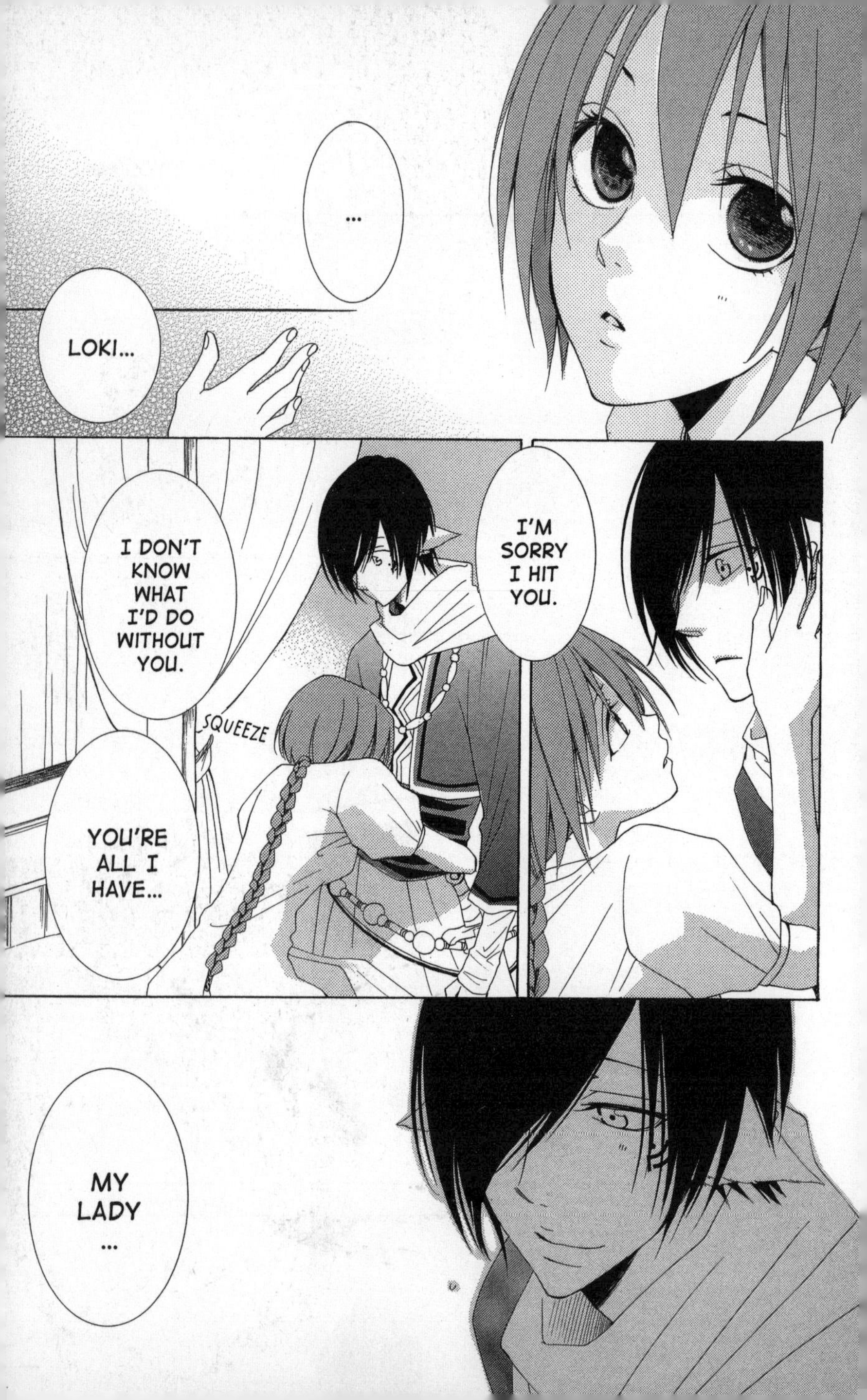
...
LOKI...
I'M SORRY I HIT YOU.
I DON'T KNOW WHAT I'D DO WITHOUT YOU.
SQUEEZE
YOU'RE ALL I HAVE...
MY LADY ...

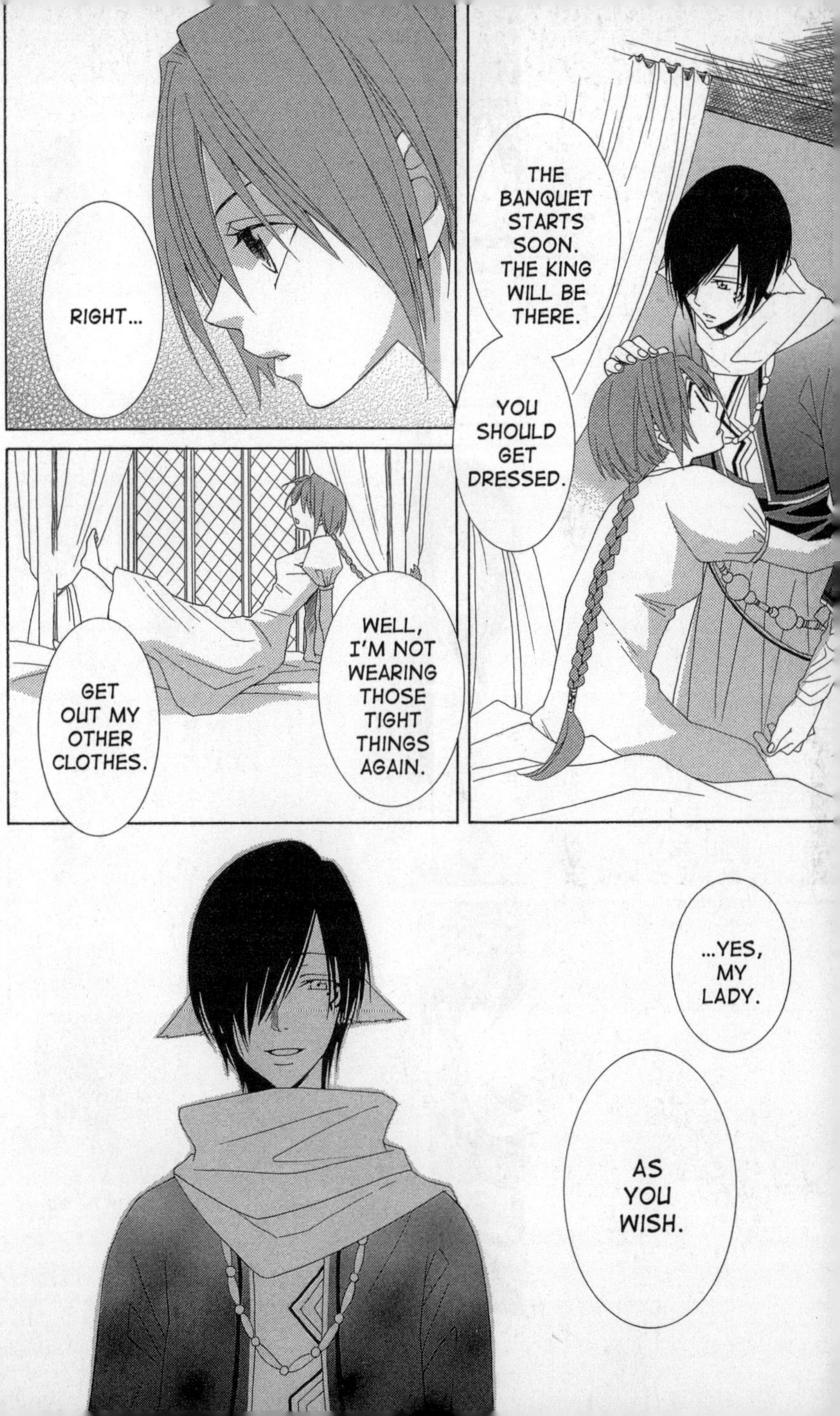
THE BANQUET STARTS SOON. THE KING WILL BE THERE.
YOU SHOULD GET DRESSED.
RIGHT...
WELL, I'M NOT WEARING THOSE TIGHT THINGS AGAIN.
GET OUT MY OTHER CLOTHES.
...YES, MY LADY.
AS YOU WISH.

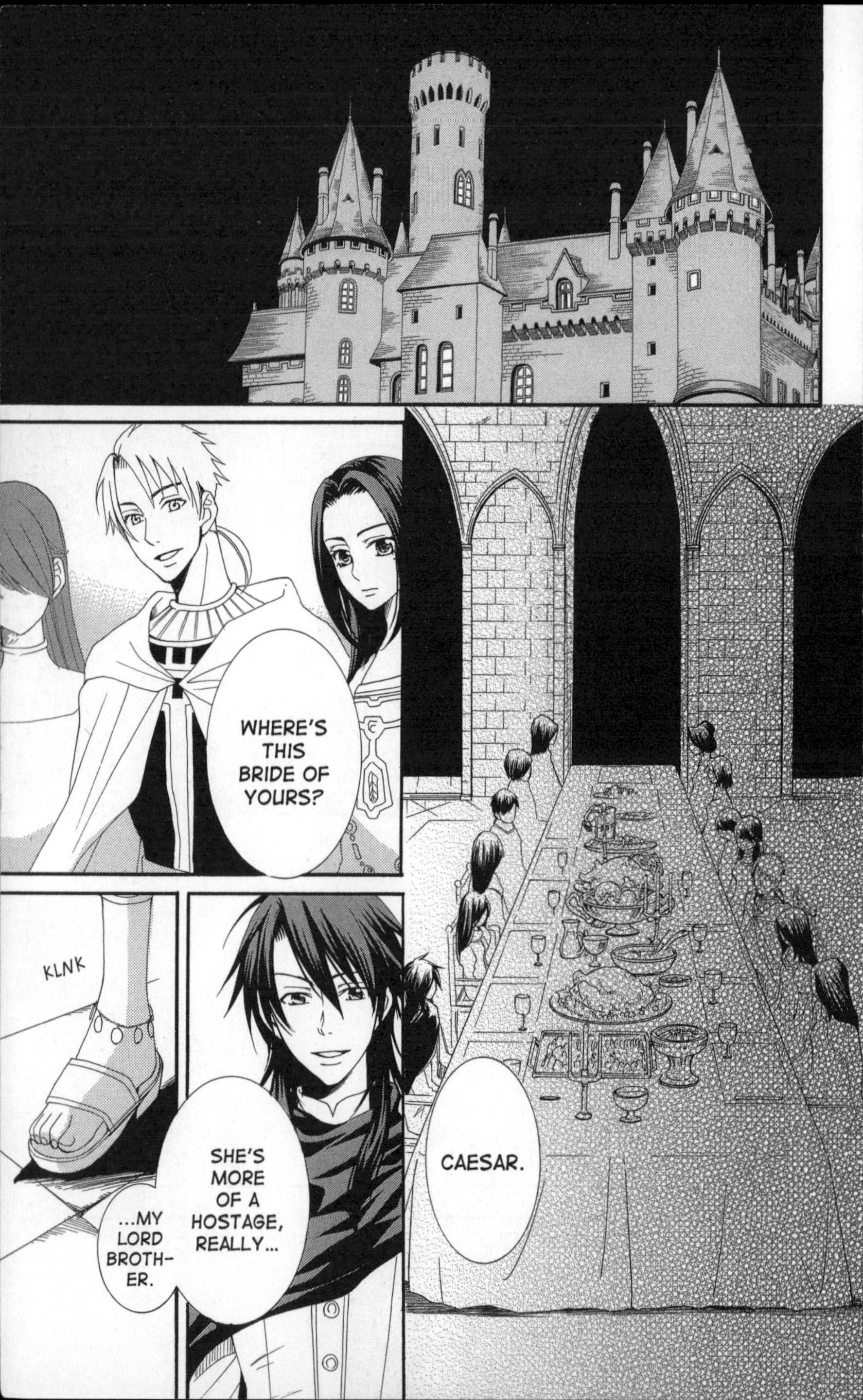
CAESAR.
WHERE'S THIS BRIDE OF YOURS?
SHE'S MORE OF A HOSTAGE, REALLY...
...MY LORD BROTH-ER.
KLNK

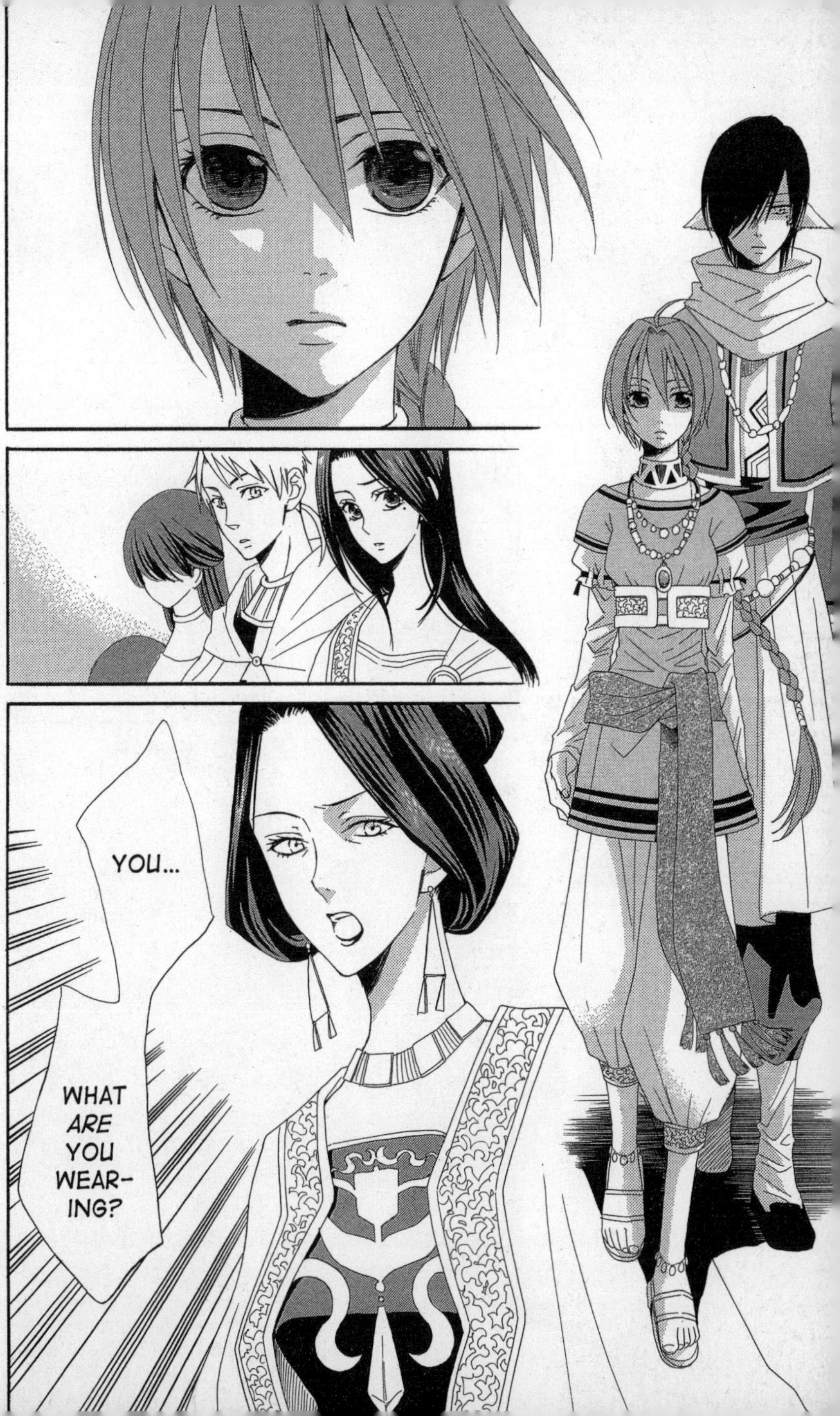
YOU...
WHAT *ARE* YOU WEAR-ING?

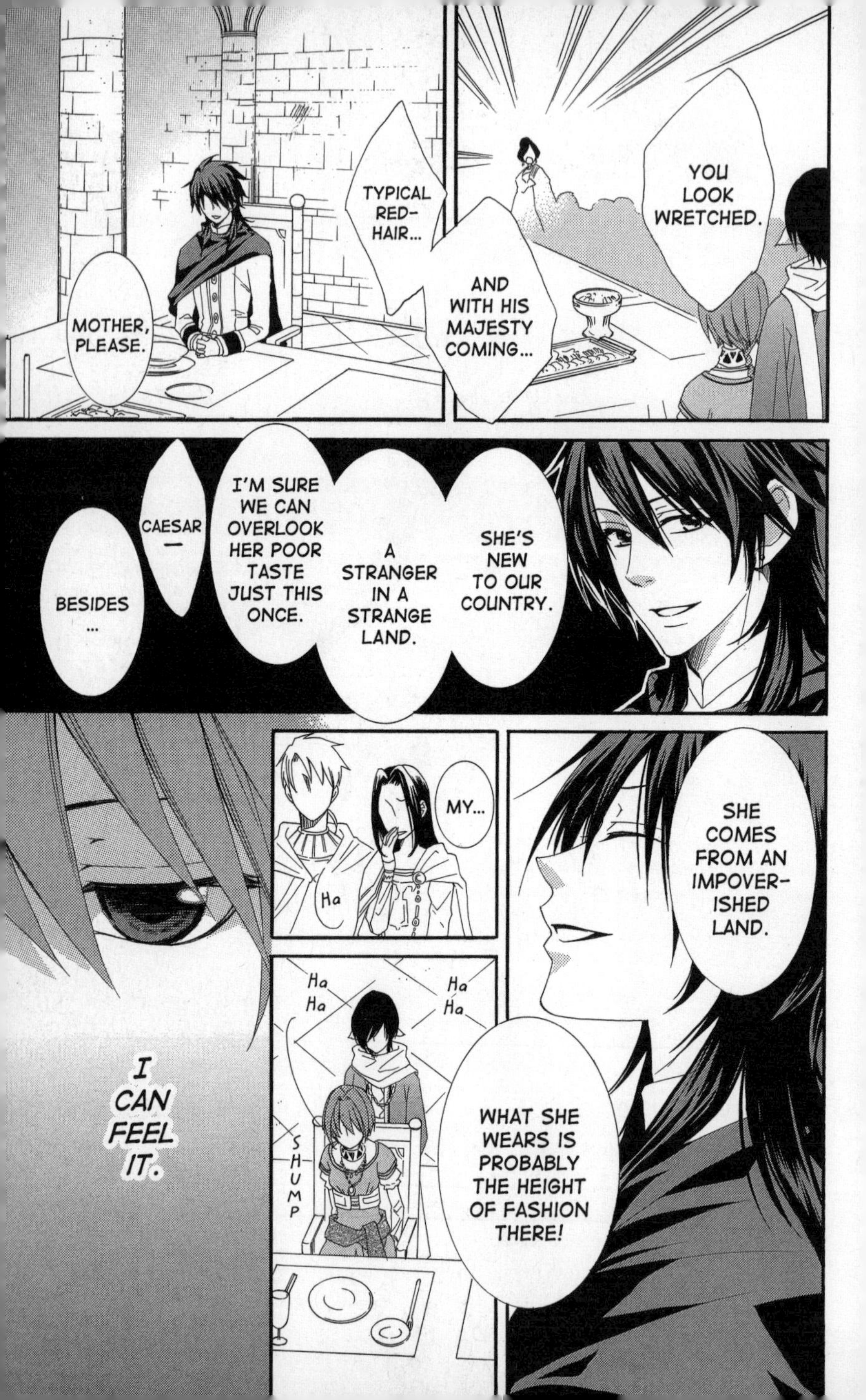
YOU LOOK WRETCHED.
TYPICAL RED-HAIR...
AND WITH HIS MAJESTY COMING...
MOTHER, PLEASE.
SHE'S NEW TO OUR COUNTRY.
A STRANGER IN A STRANGE LAND.
I'M SURE WE CAN OVERLOOK HER POOR TASTE JUST THIS ONCE.
CAESAR—
BESIDES...
SHE COMES FROM AN IMPOVERISHED LAND.
WHAT SHE WEARS IS PROBABLY THE HEIGHT OF FASHION THERE!
MY...
Ha
Ha Ha
Ha Ha
SHUMP
I CAN FEEL IT.

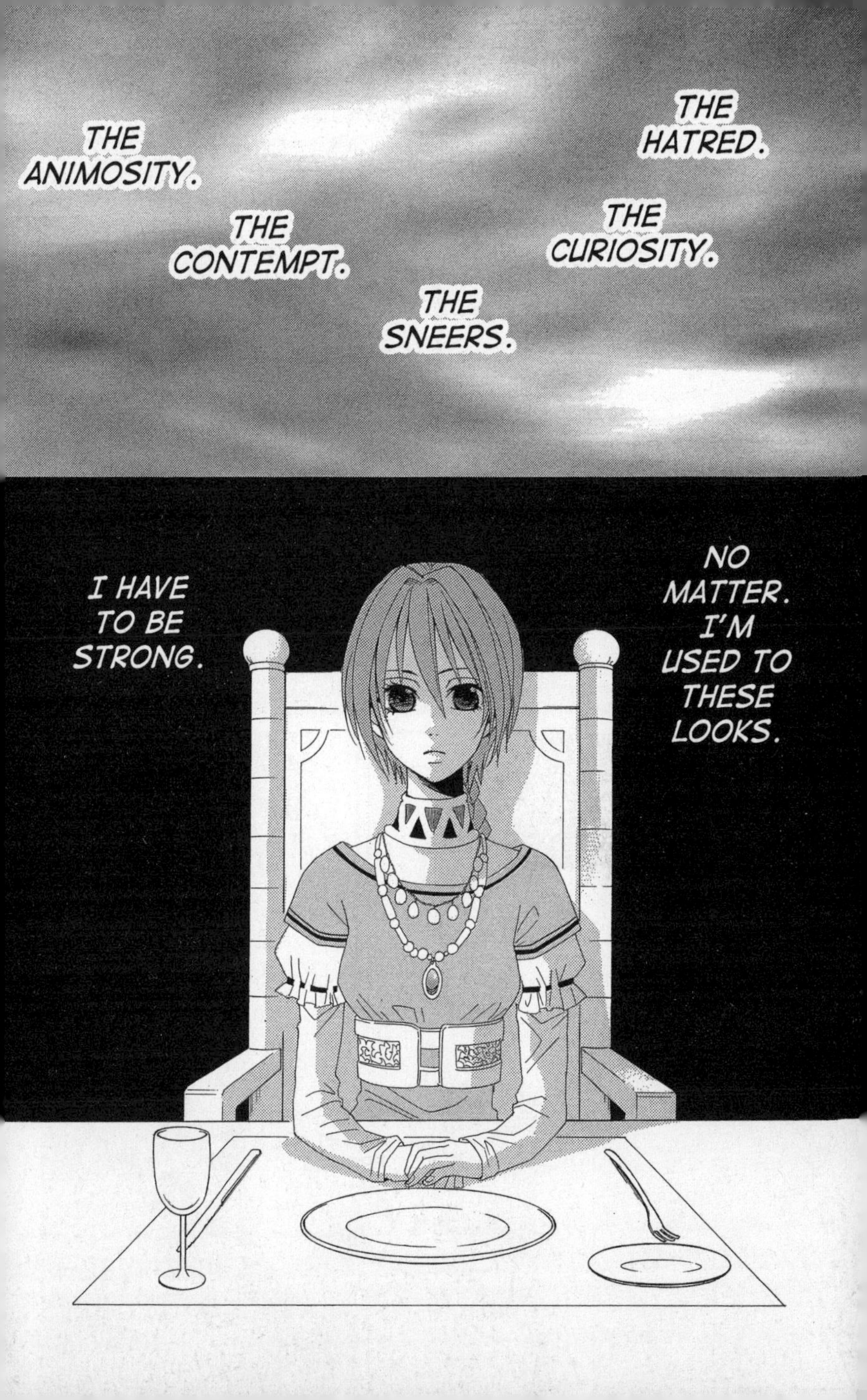
THE HATRED.
THE ANIMOSITY.
THE CURIOSITY.
THE CONTEMPT.
THE SNEERS.
NO MATTER. I'M USED TO THESE LOOKS.
I HAVE TO BE STRONG.

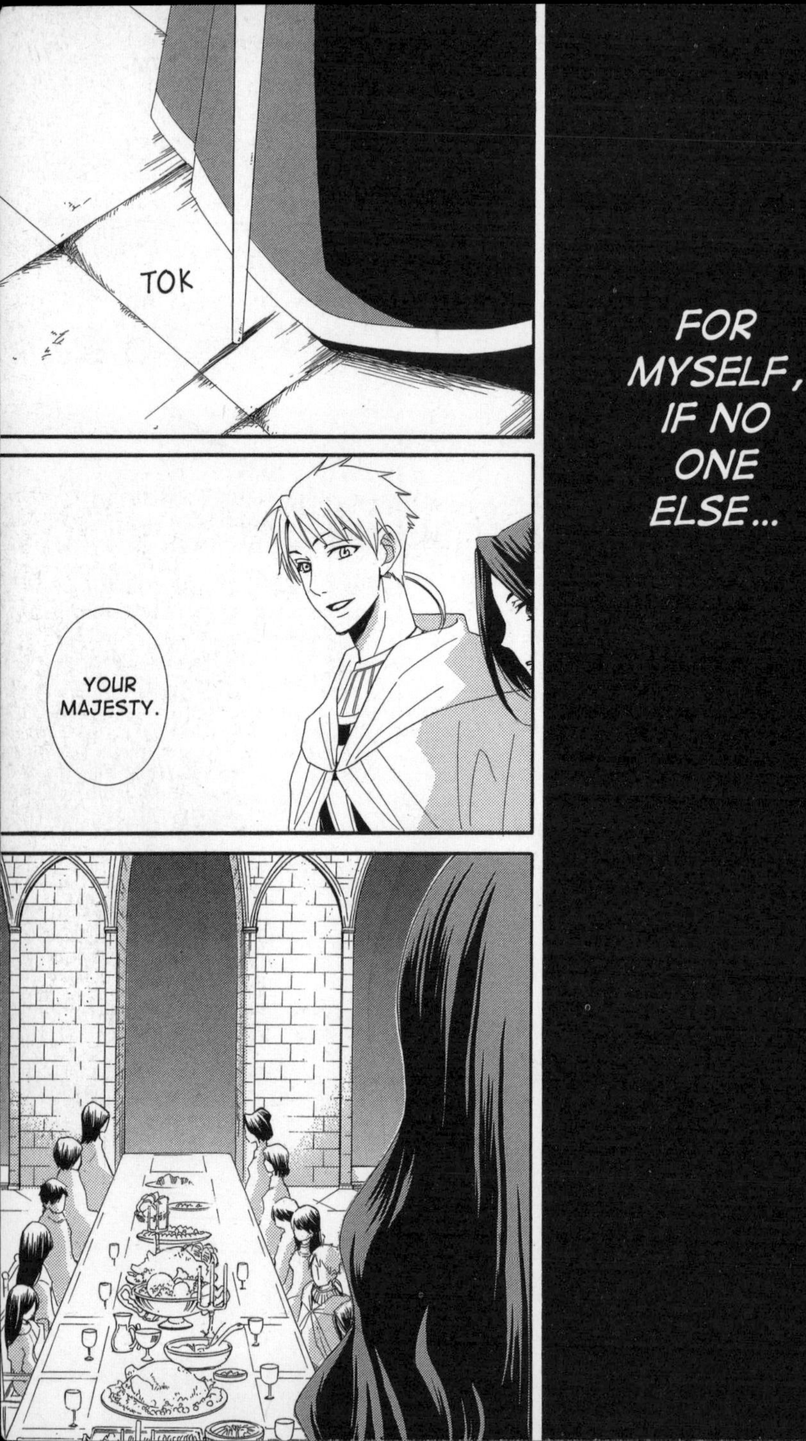
FOR MYSELF, IF NO ONE ELSE...
TOK
YOUR MAJESTY.

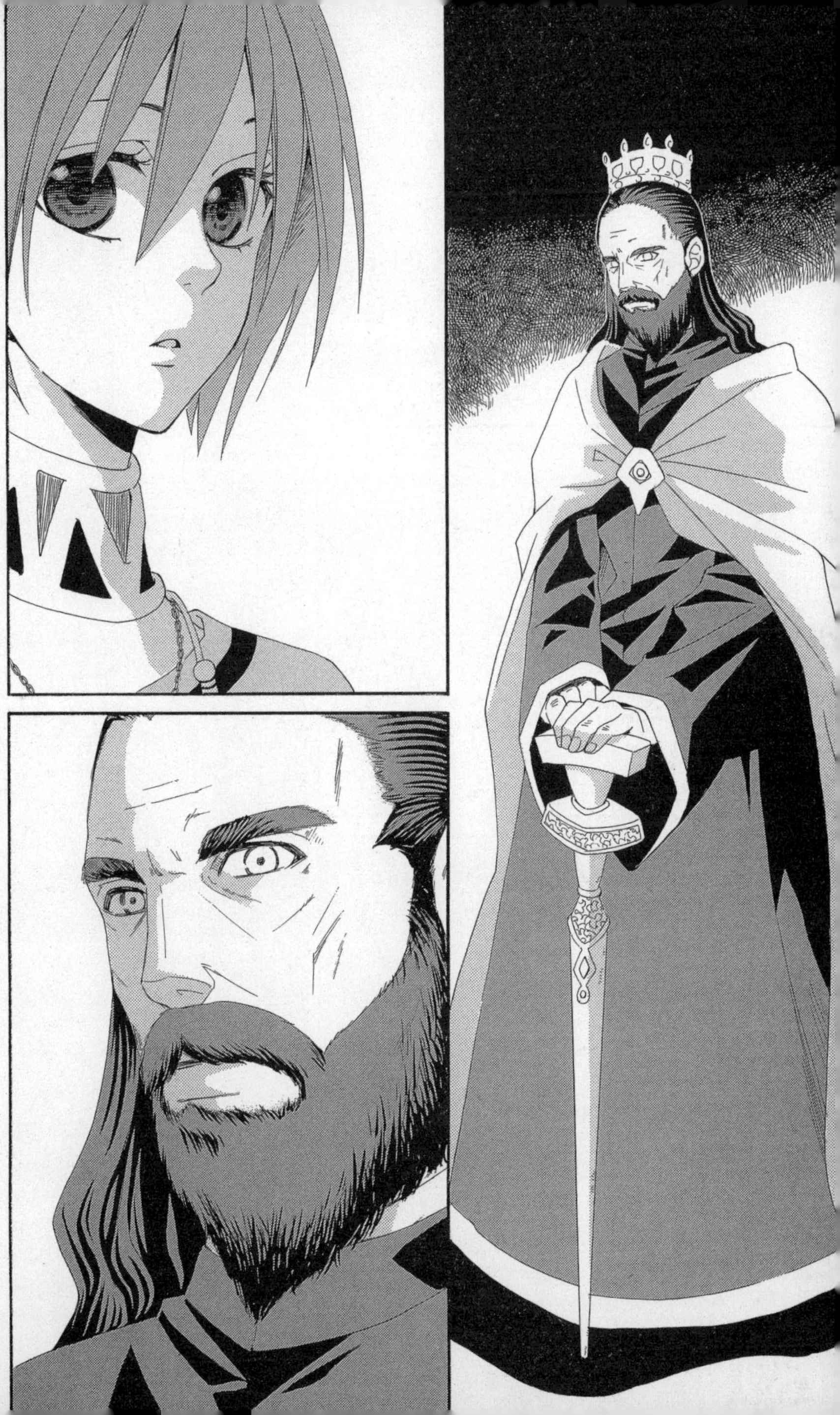

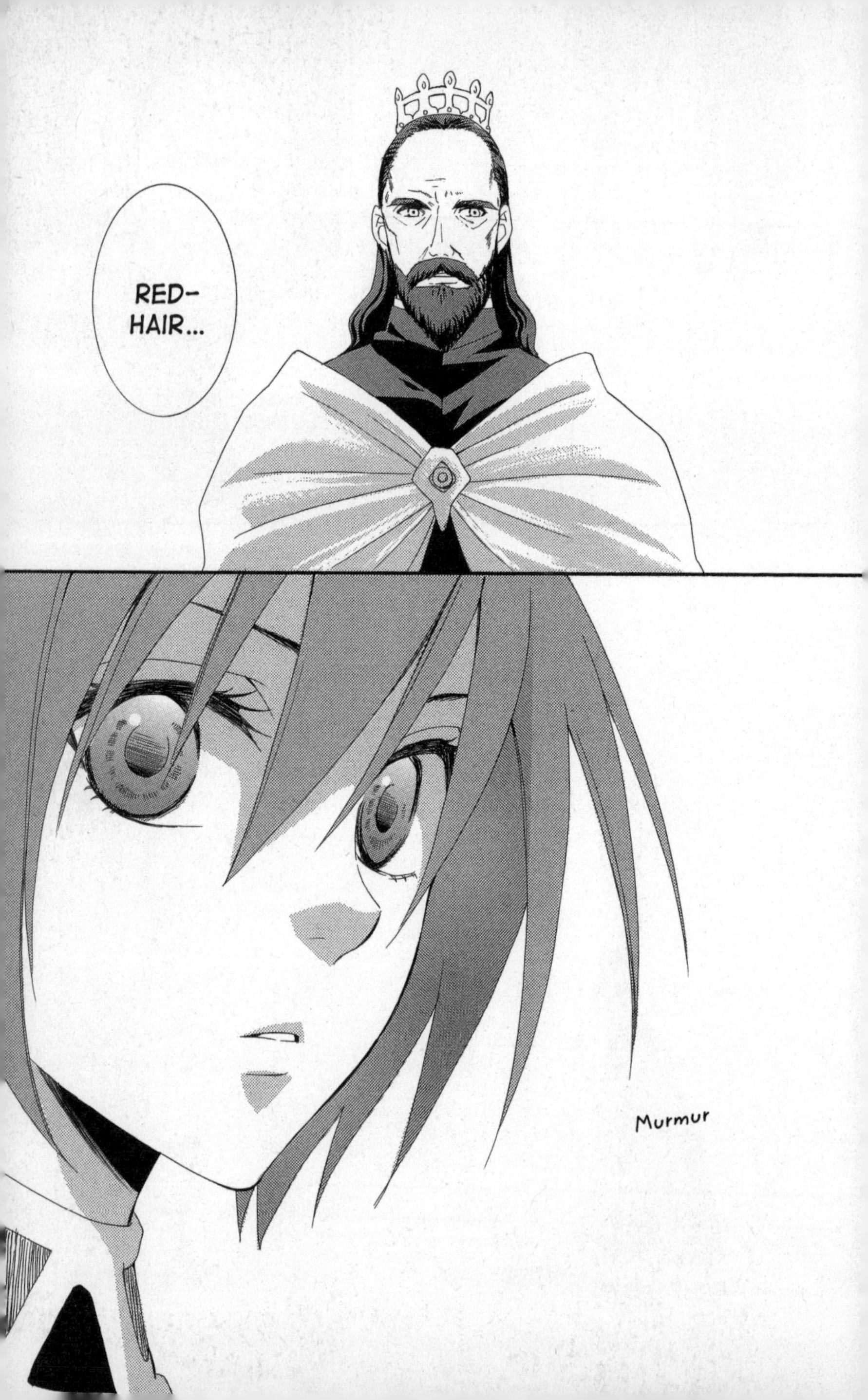
RED-HAIR...
Murmur

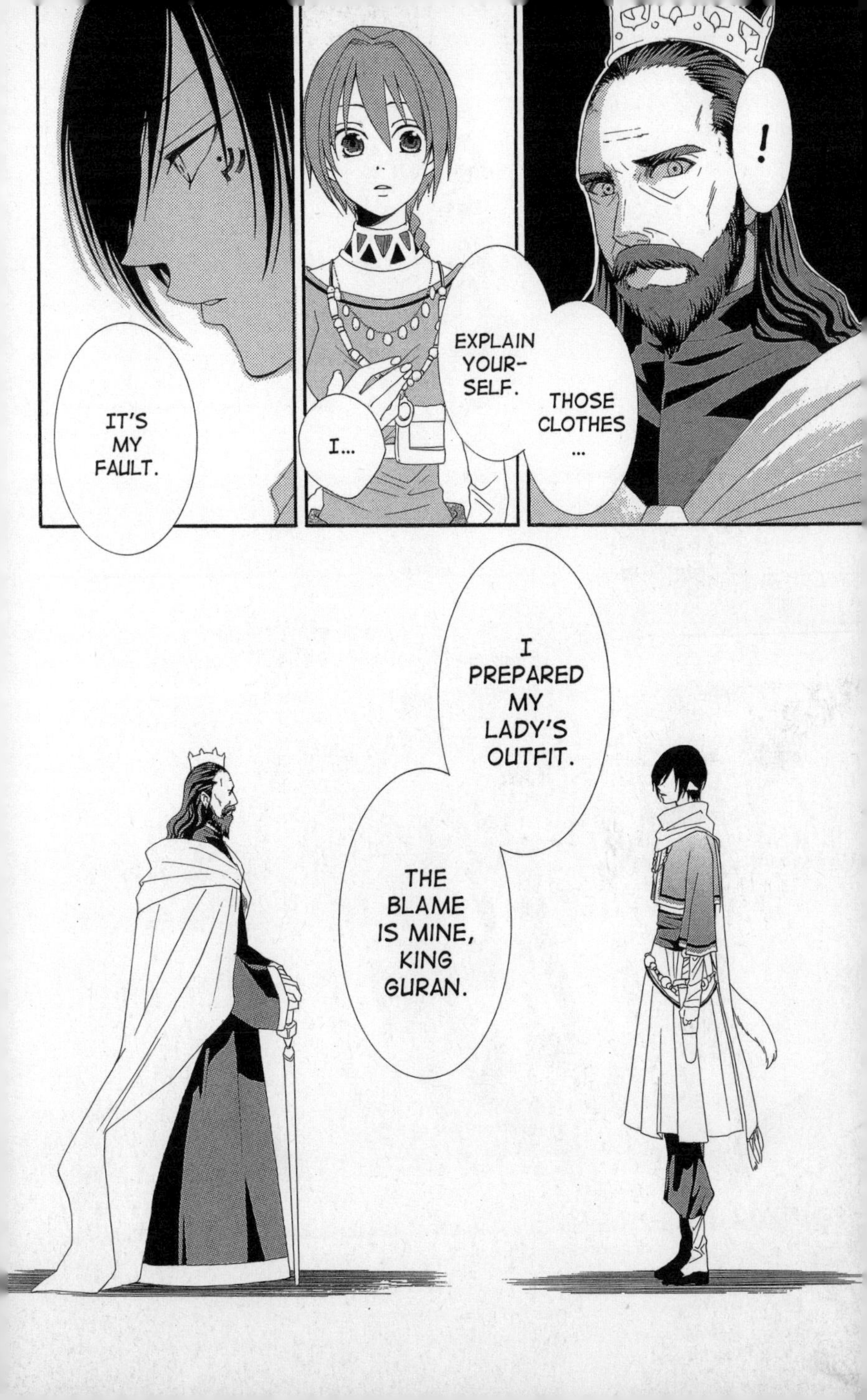
!
THOSE CLOTHES ...
EXPLAIN YOUR-SELF.
I...
IT'S MY FAULT.
I PREPARED MY LADY'S OUTFIT.
THE BLAME IS MINE, KING GURAN.

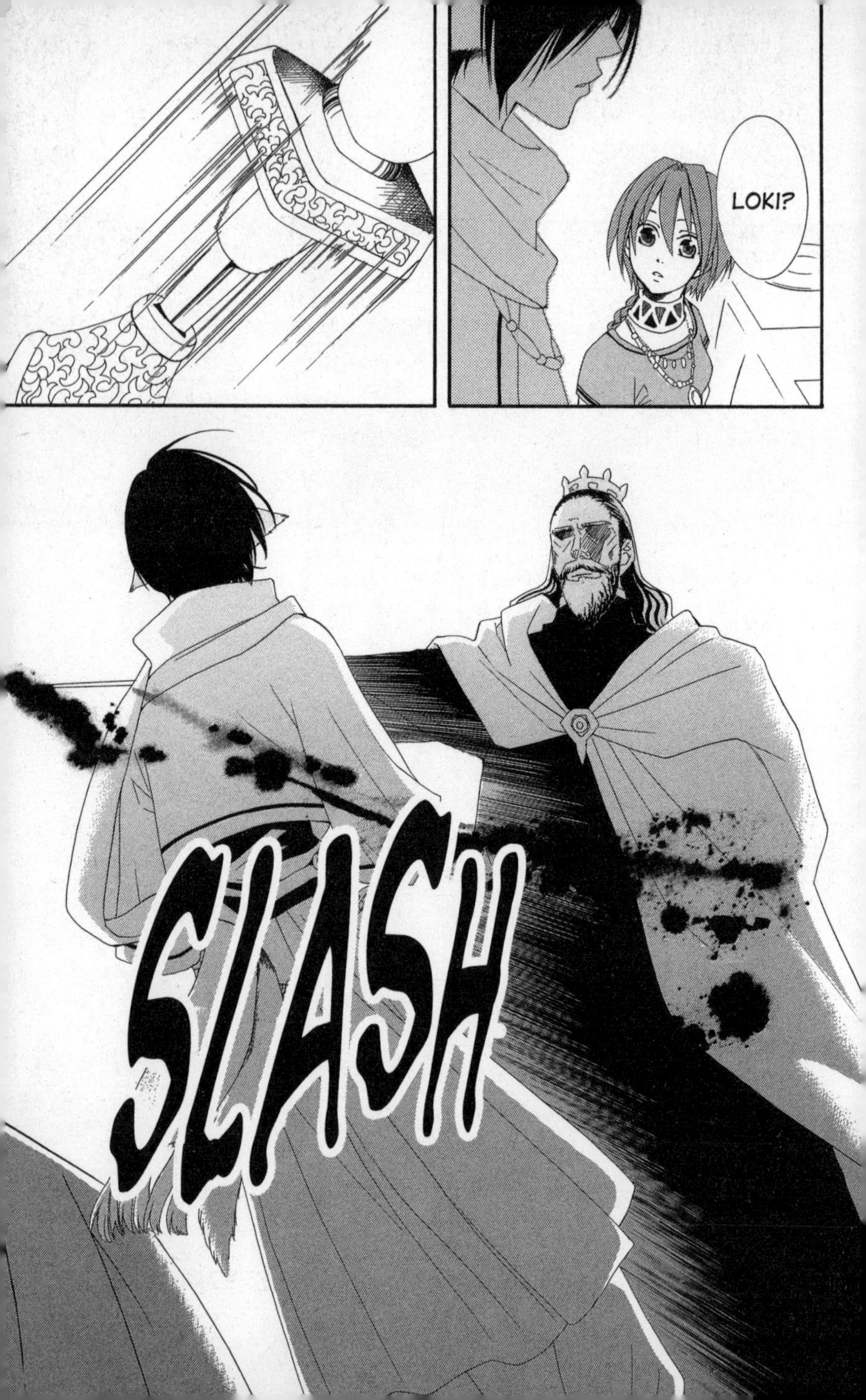
LOKI?
SLASH

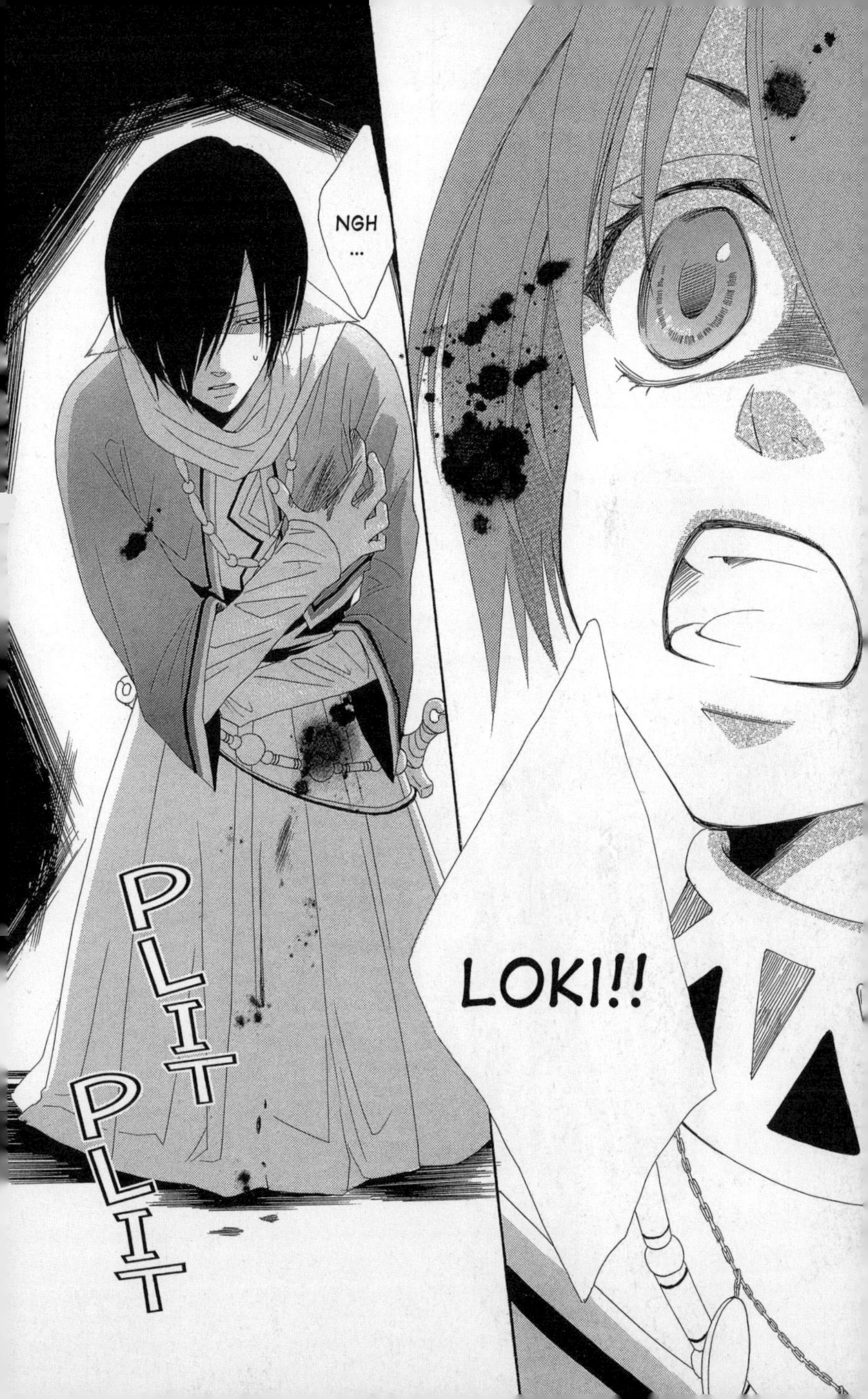
LOKI!!
NGH
...
PLIT
PLIT

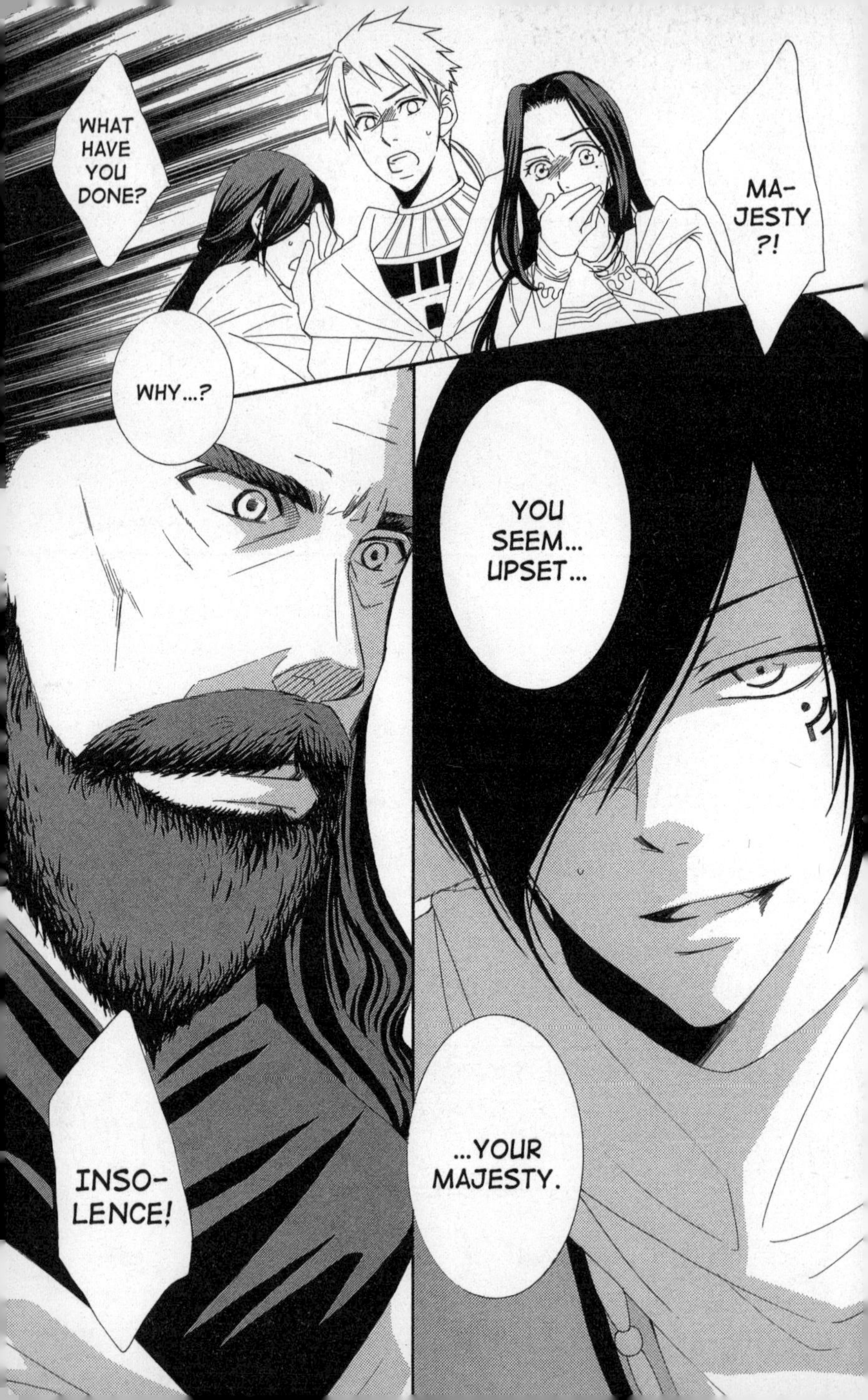
MA-JESTY?!
WHAT HAVE YOU DONE?
WHY...?
YOU SEEM... UPSET...
...YOUR MAJESTY.
INSO-LENCE!

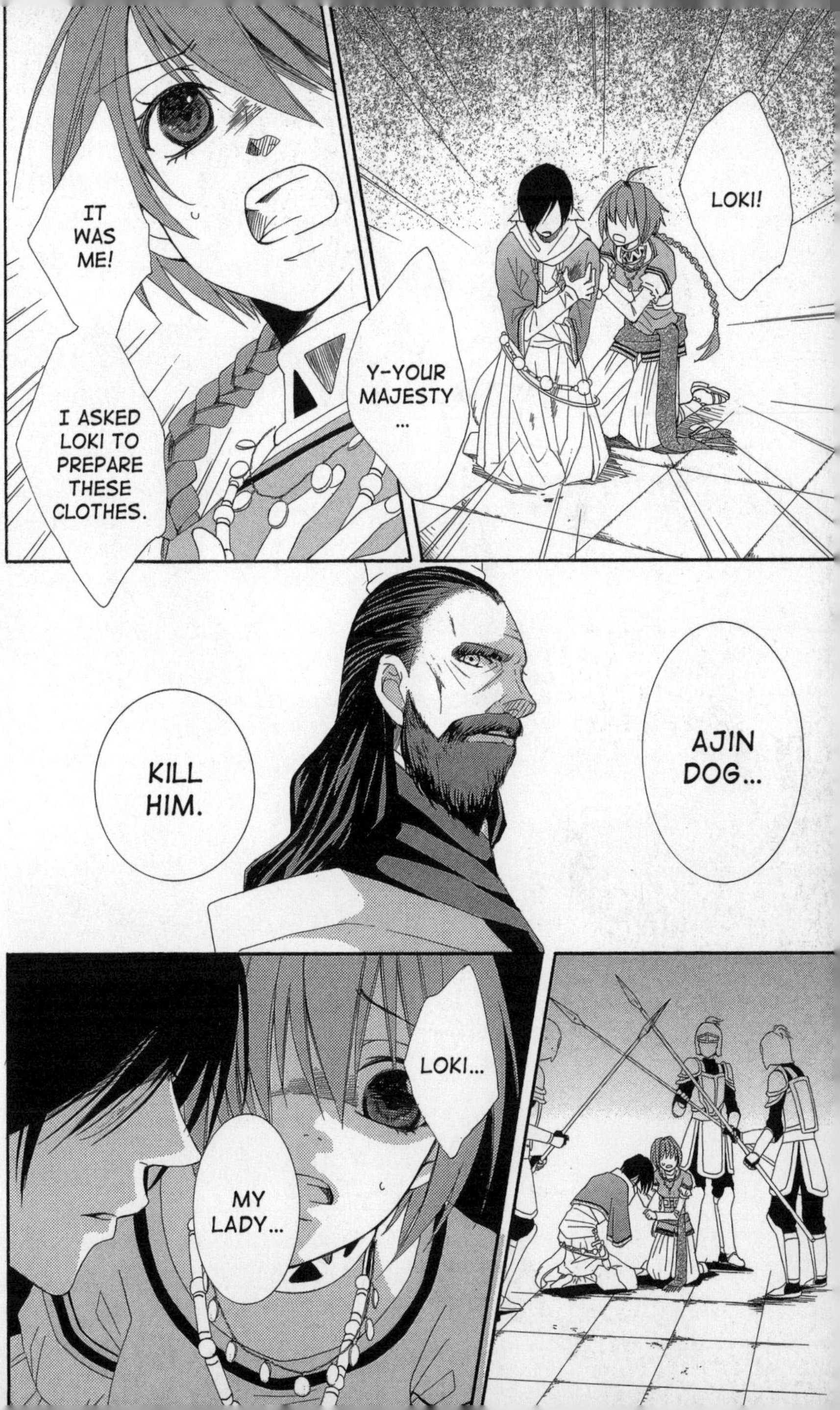
LOKI!
Y-YOUR MAJESTY ...
IT WAS ME!
I ASKED LOKI TO PREPARE THESE CLOTHES.
AJIN DOG...
KILL HIM.
LOKI...
MY LADY...

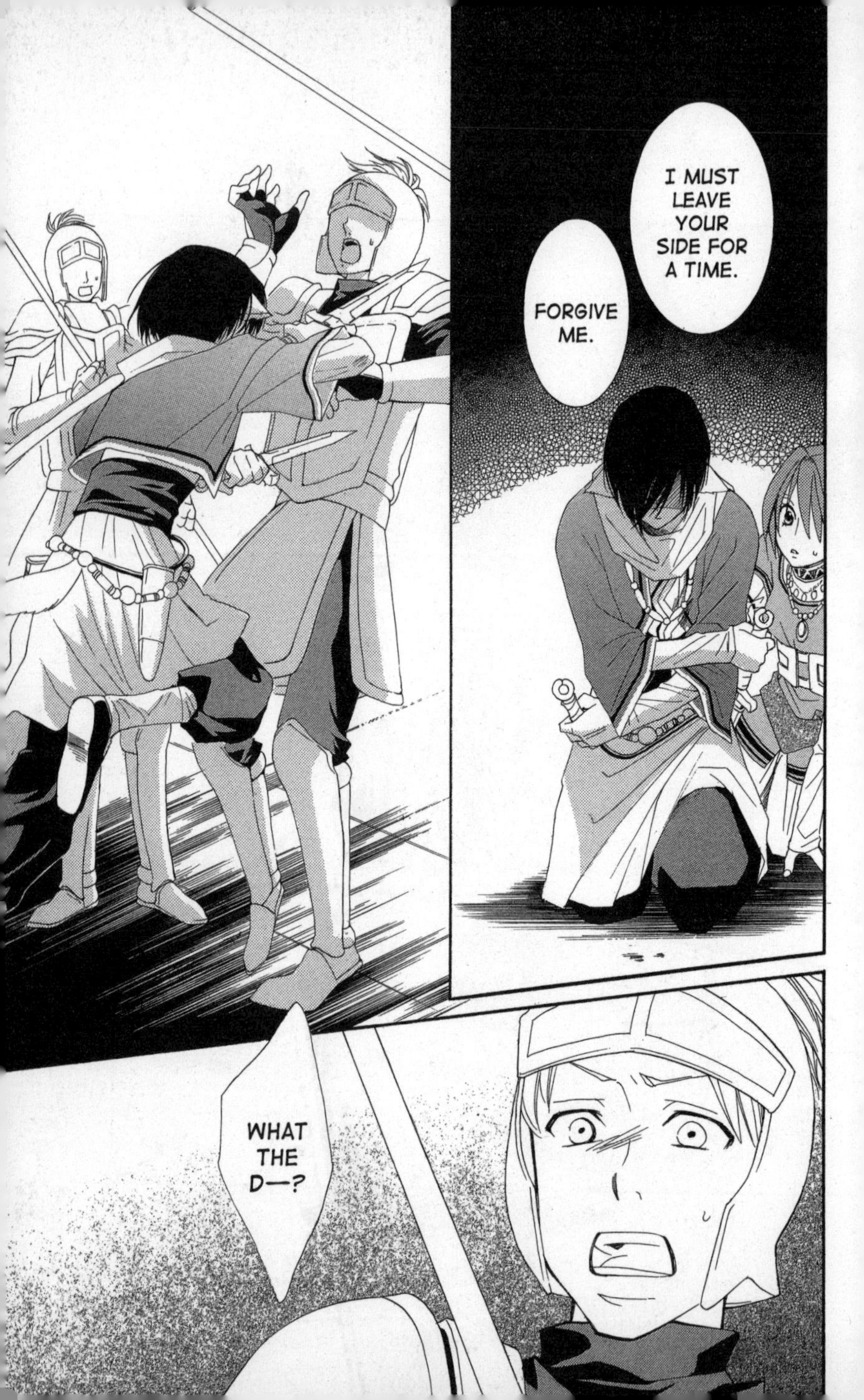
I MUST LEAVE YOUR SIDE FOR A TIME.
FORGIVE ME.
WHAT THE D—?

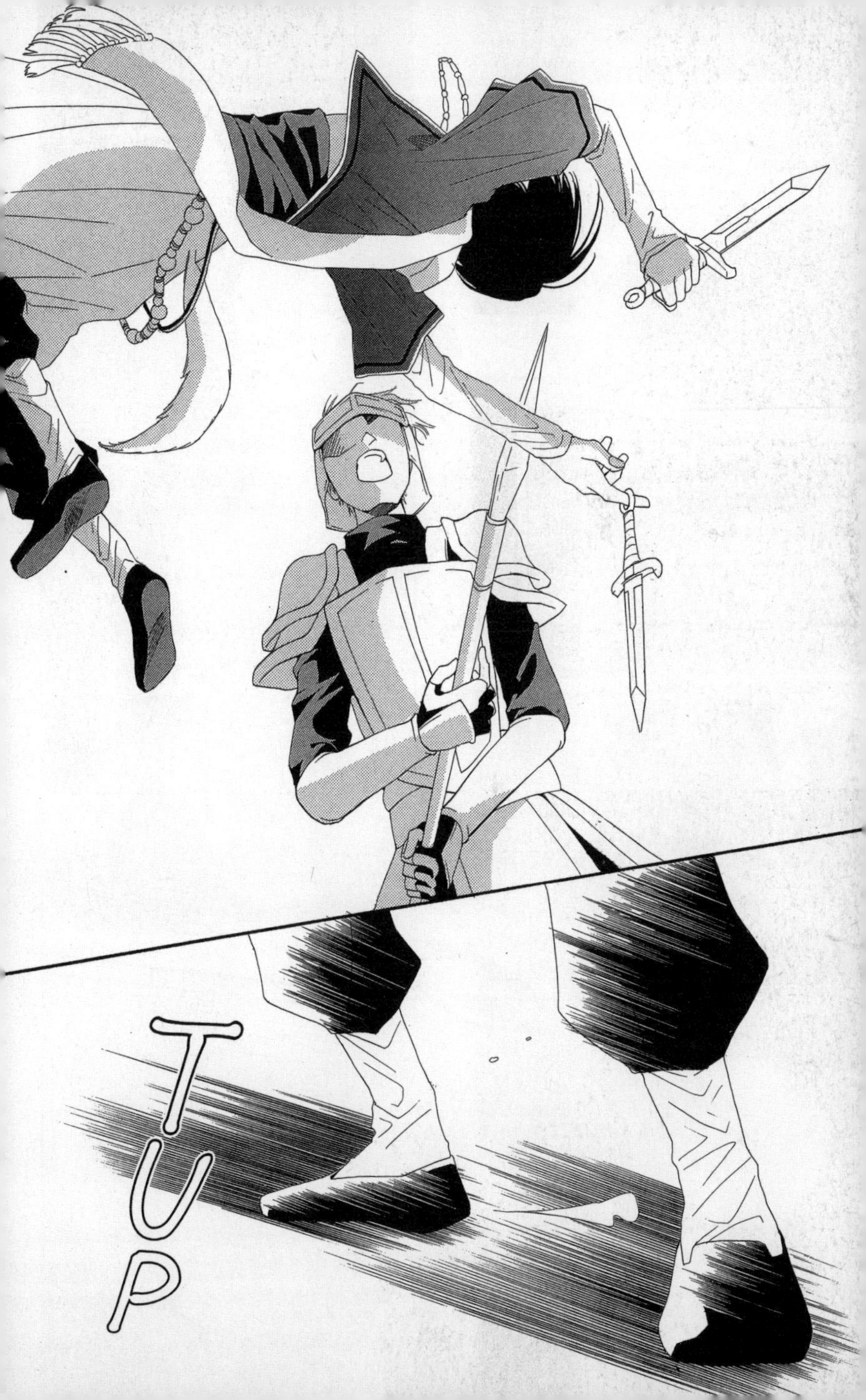
TUP

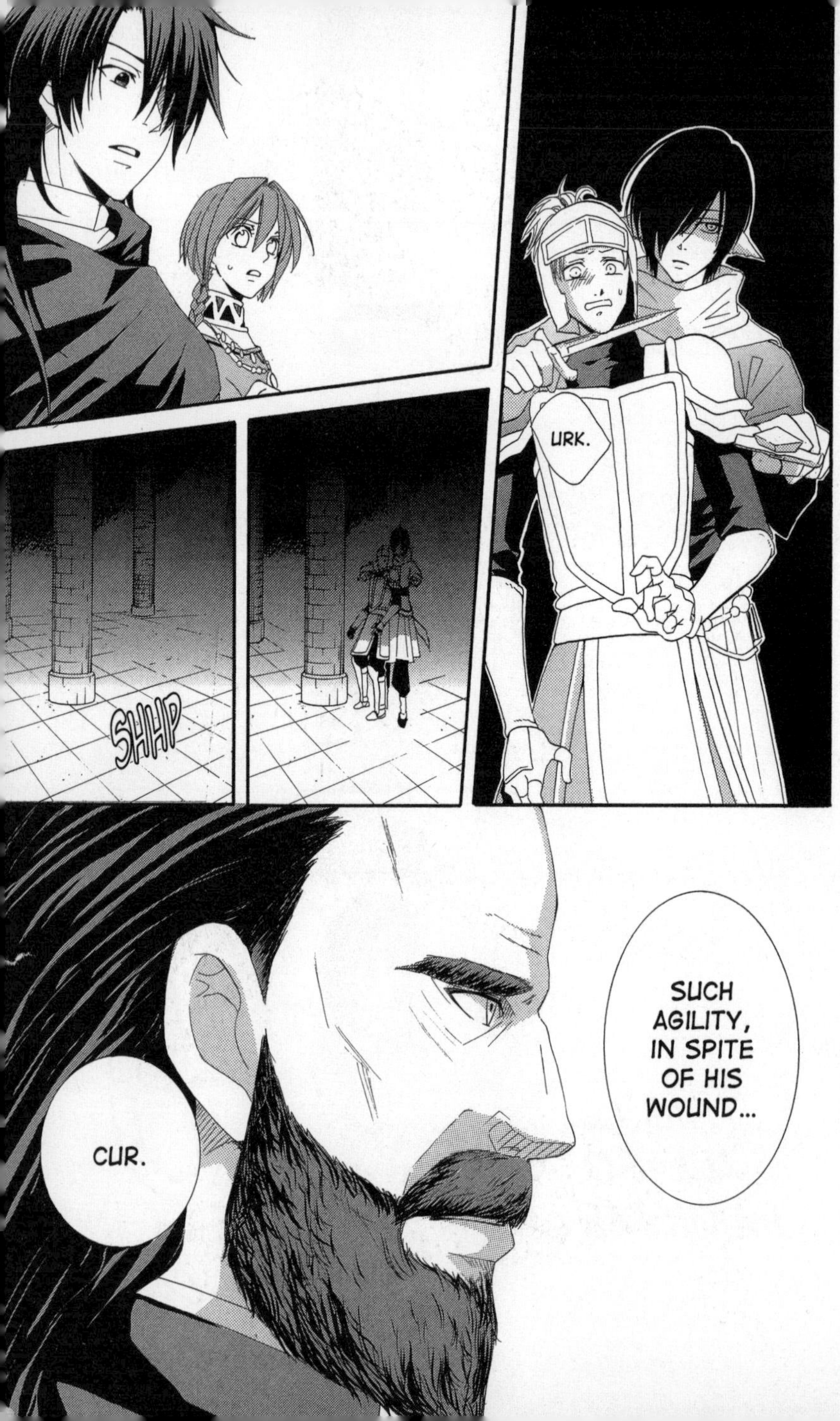
URK.
SHHP
SUCH AGILITY, IN SPITE OF HIS WOUND...
CUR.

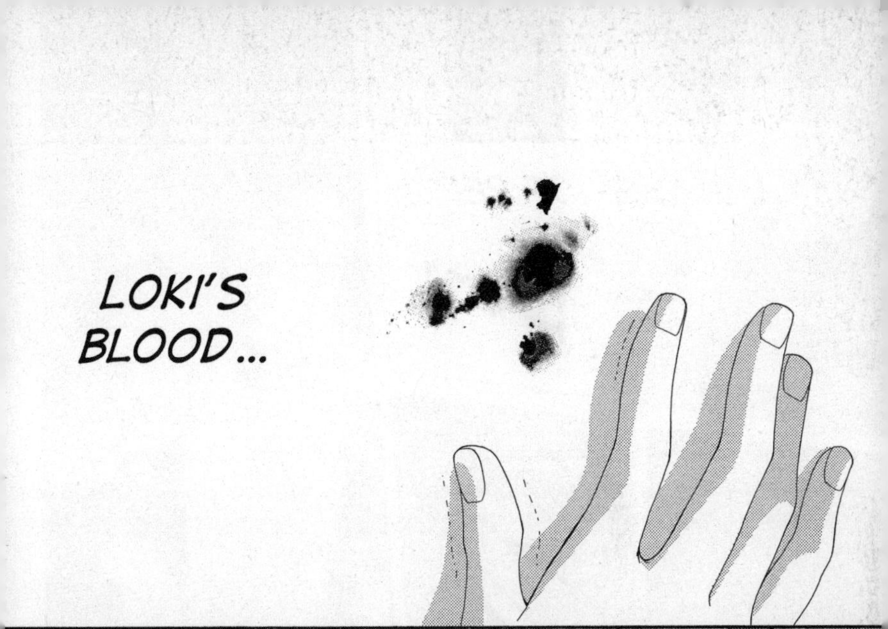
LOKI'S BLOOD...
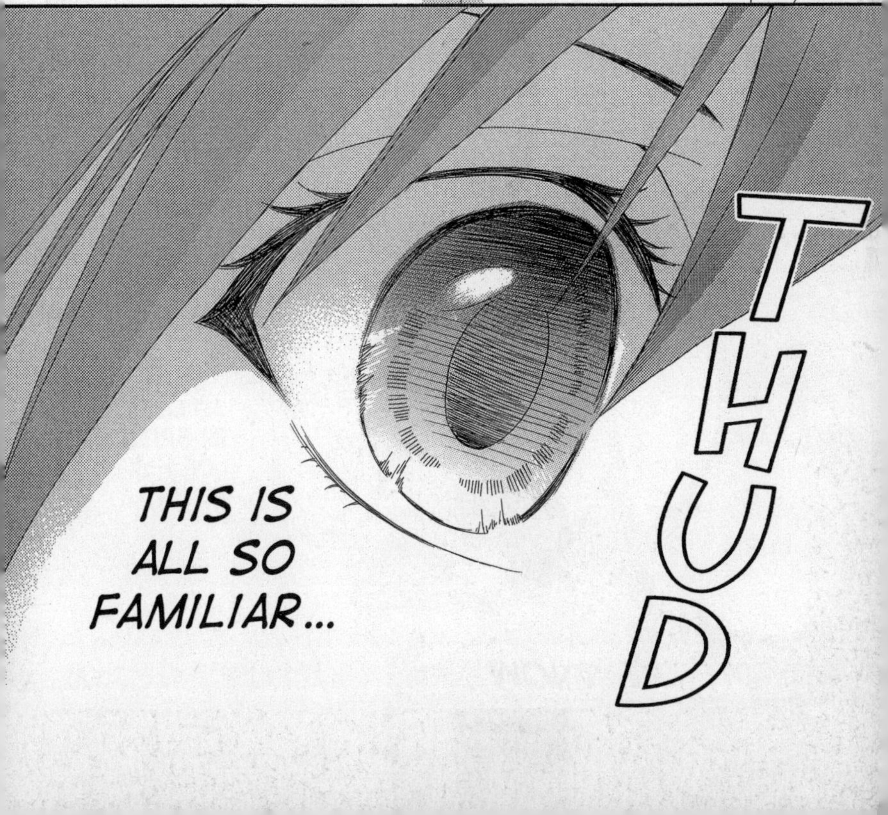
THUD
THIS IS ALL SO FAMILIAR...

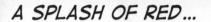

A SPLASH OF RED...

...BEFORE MY EYES...

sss

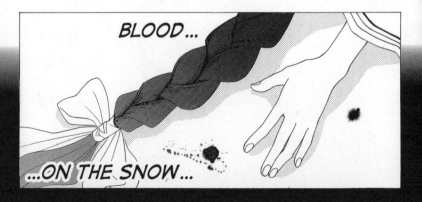

BLOOD...

...ON THE SNOW...

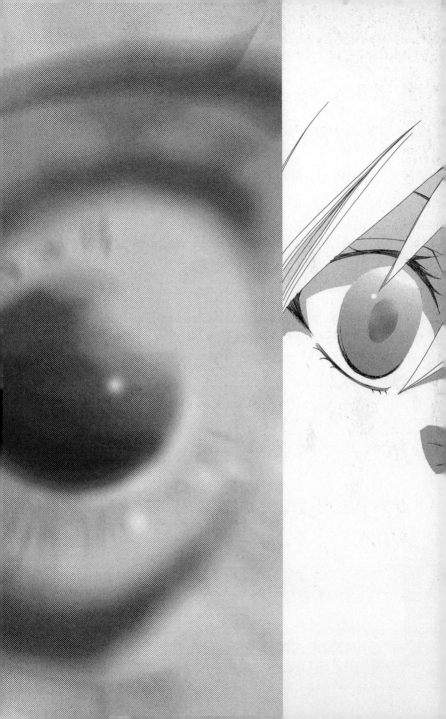

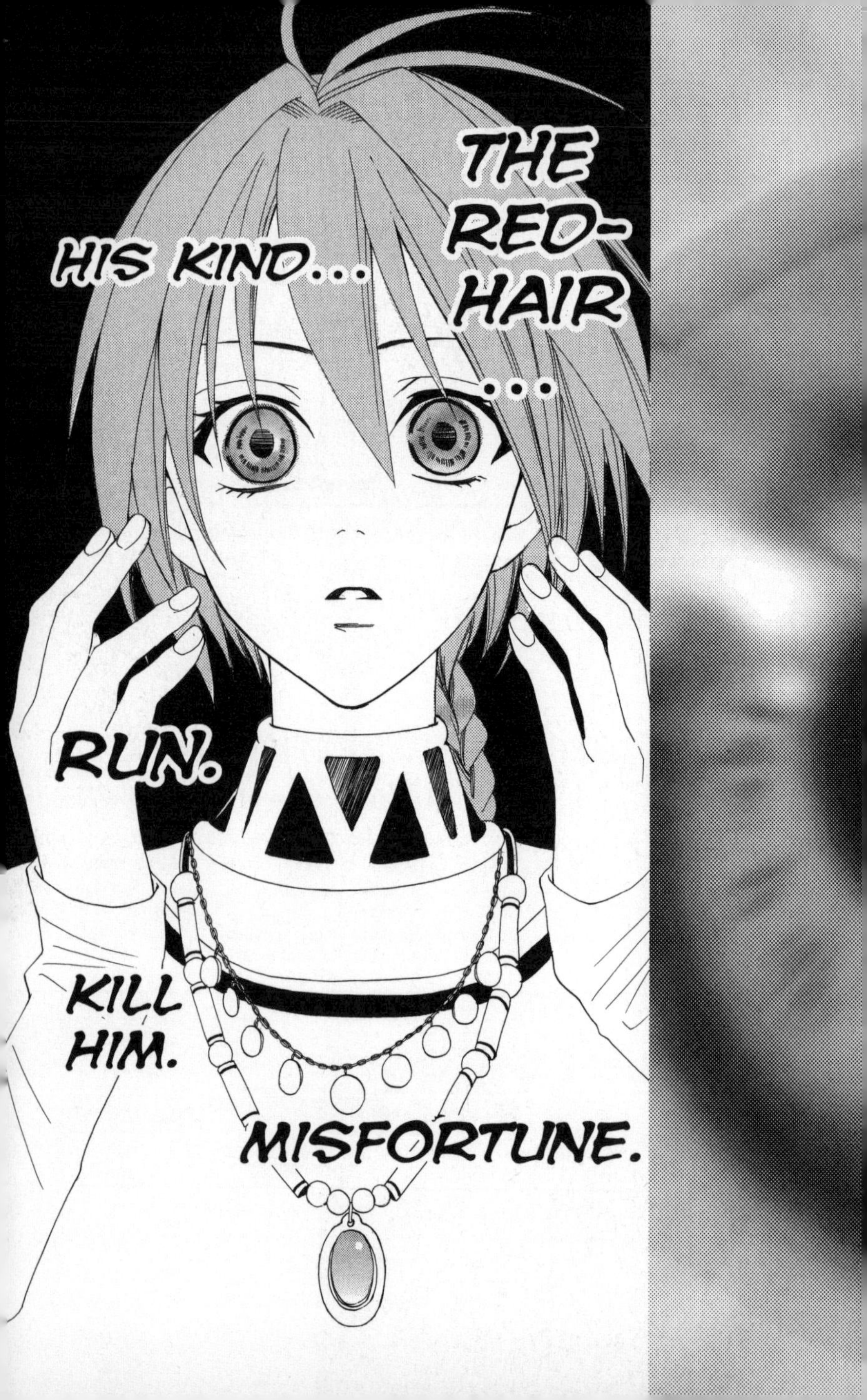
THE RED-HAIR...
HIS KIND...
RUN.
KILL HIM.
MISFORTUNE.

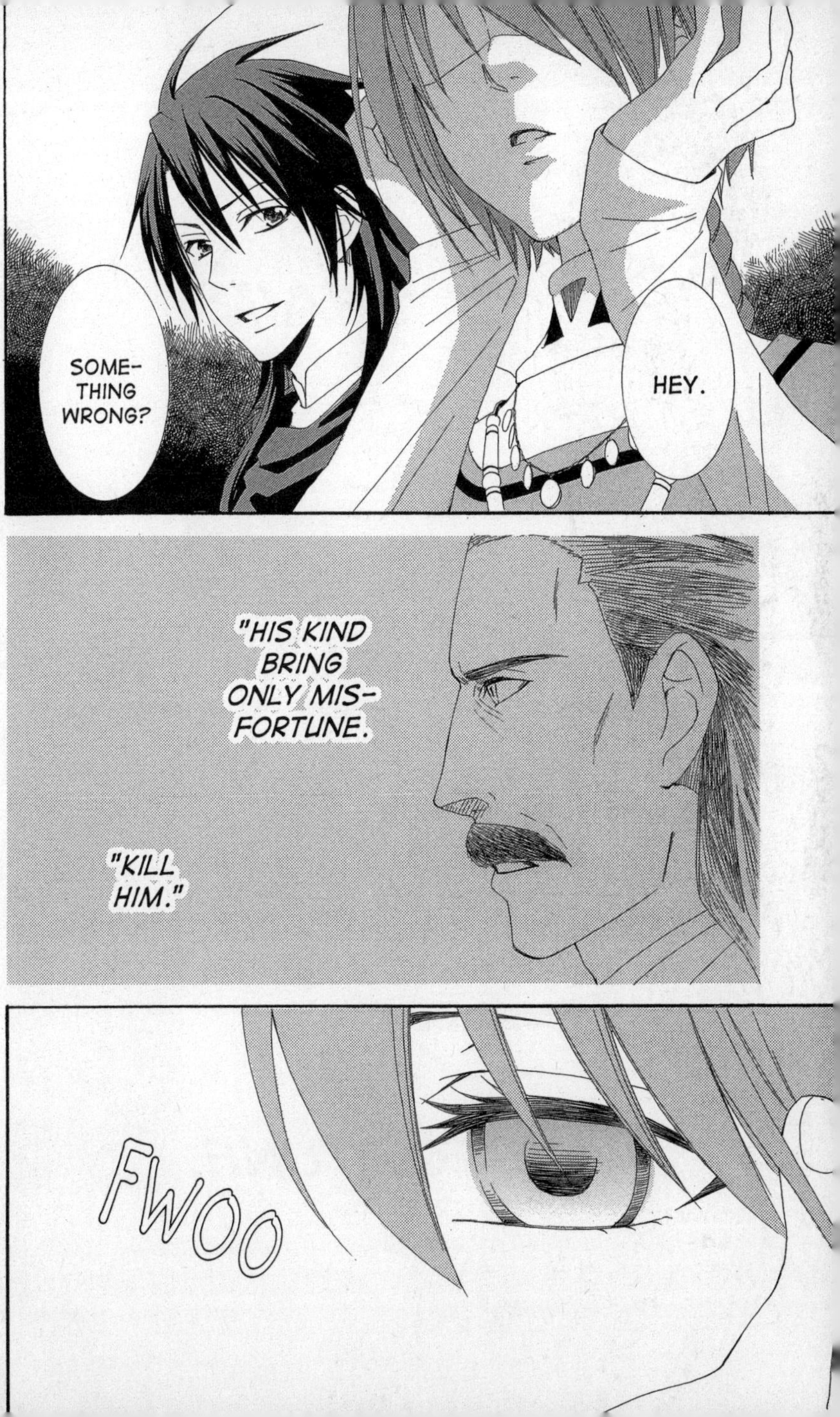
HEY.
SOME-THING WRONG?
"HIS KIND BRING ONLY MIS-FORTUNE.
"KILL HIM."
FWOO

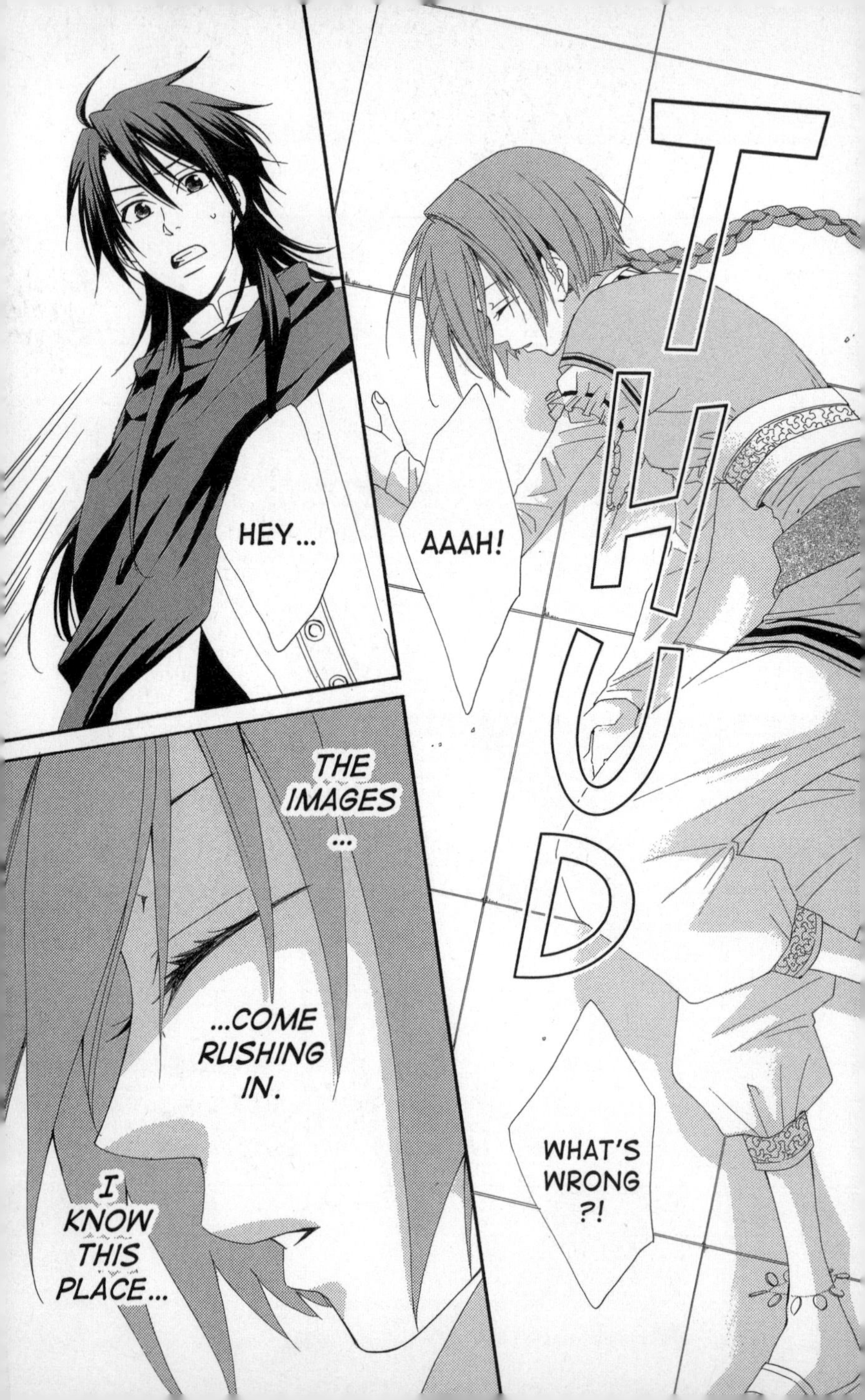
THUD
AAAH!
WHAT'S WRONG ?!
HEY...
THE IMAGES ...
...COME RUSHING IN.
I KNOW THIS PLACE...

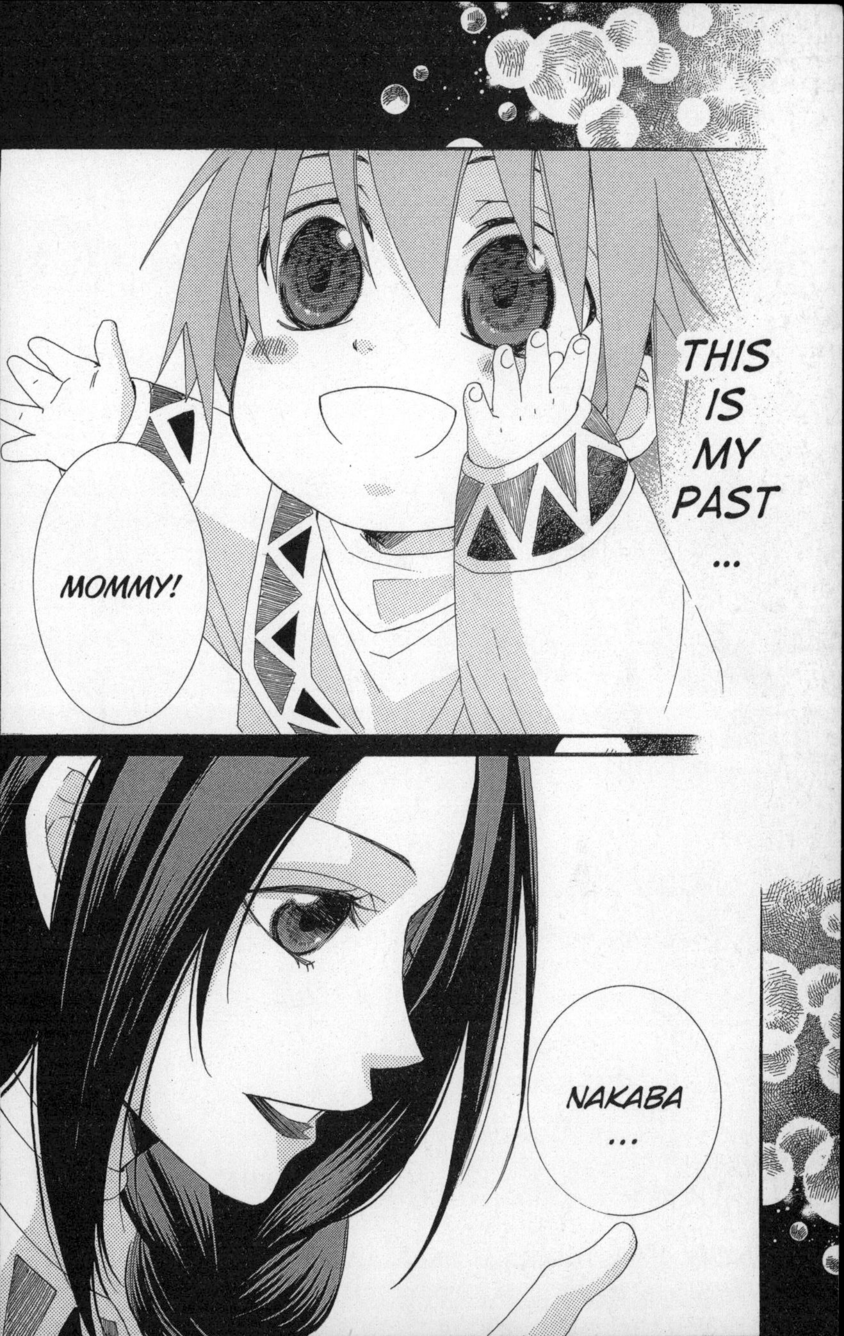
THIS IS MY PAST ...
MOMMY!
NAKABA ...

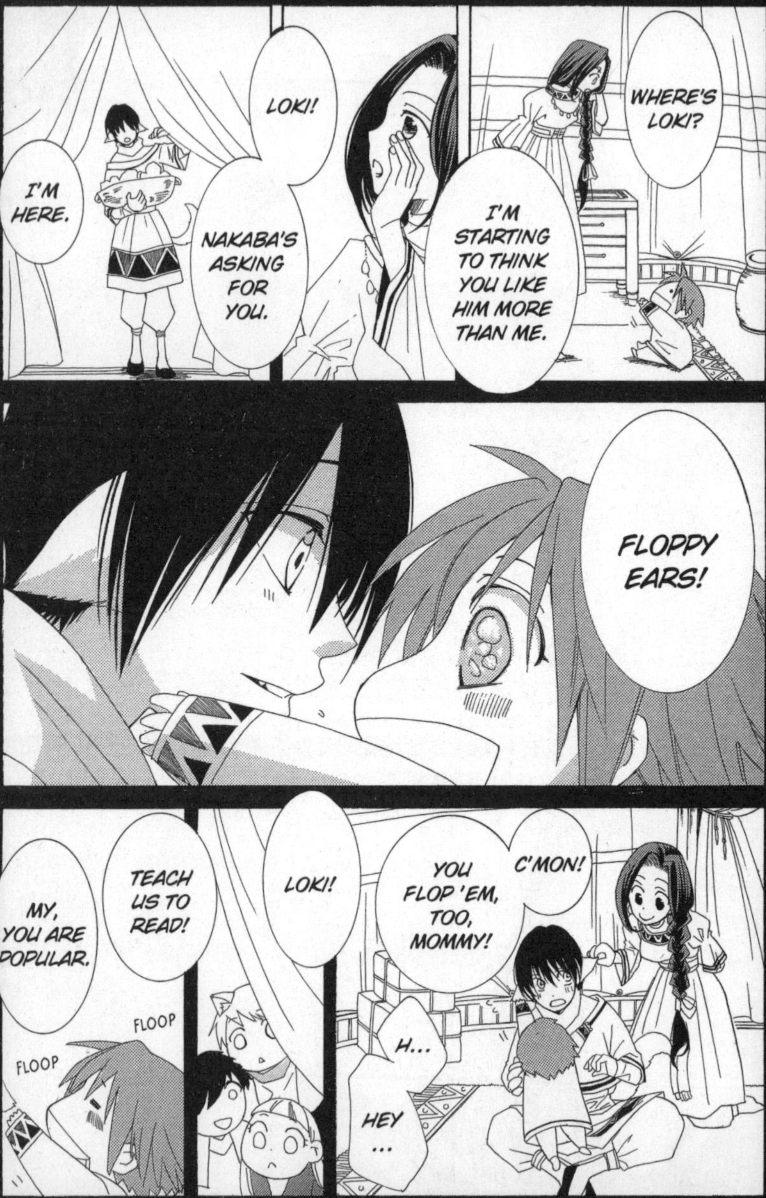
WHERE'S LOKI?
I'M STARTING TO THINK YOU LIKE HIM MORE THAN ME.
LOKI!
NAKABA'S ASKING FOR YOU.
I'M HERE.
FLOPPY EARS!
C'MON!
YOU FLOP 'EM, TOO, MOMMY!
H...
HEY ...
LOKI!
TEACH US TO READ!
MY, YOU ARE POPULAR.
FLOOP
FLOOP

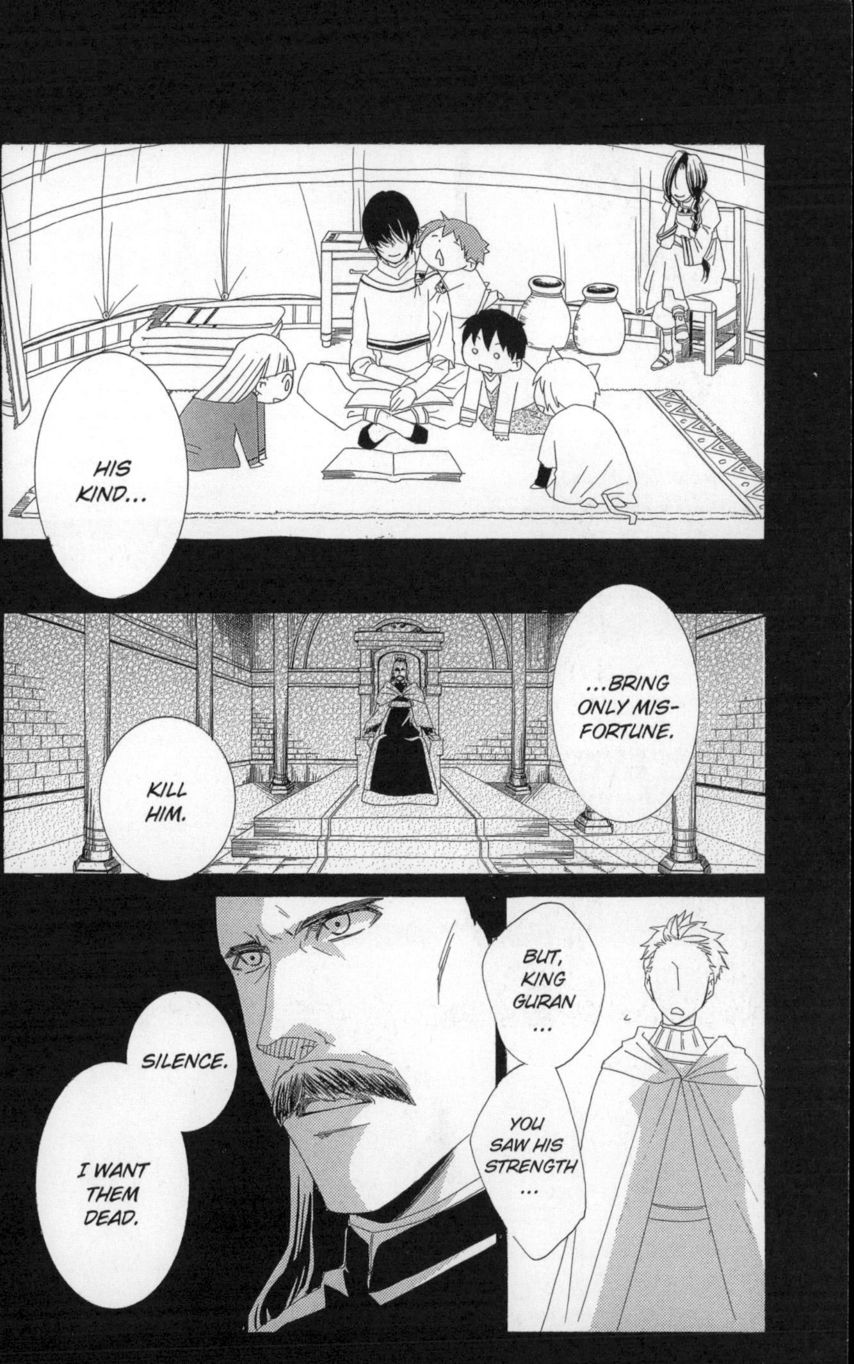
HIS KIND...
...BRING ONLY MIS-FORTUNE.
KILL HIM.
BUT, KING GURAN ...
YOU SAW HIS STRENGTH ...
SILENCE.
I WANT THEM DEAD.

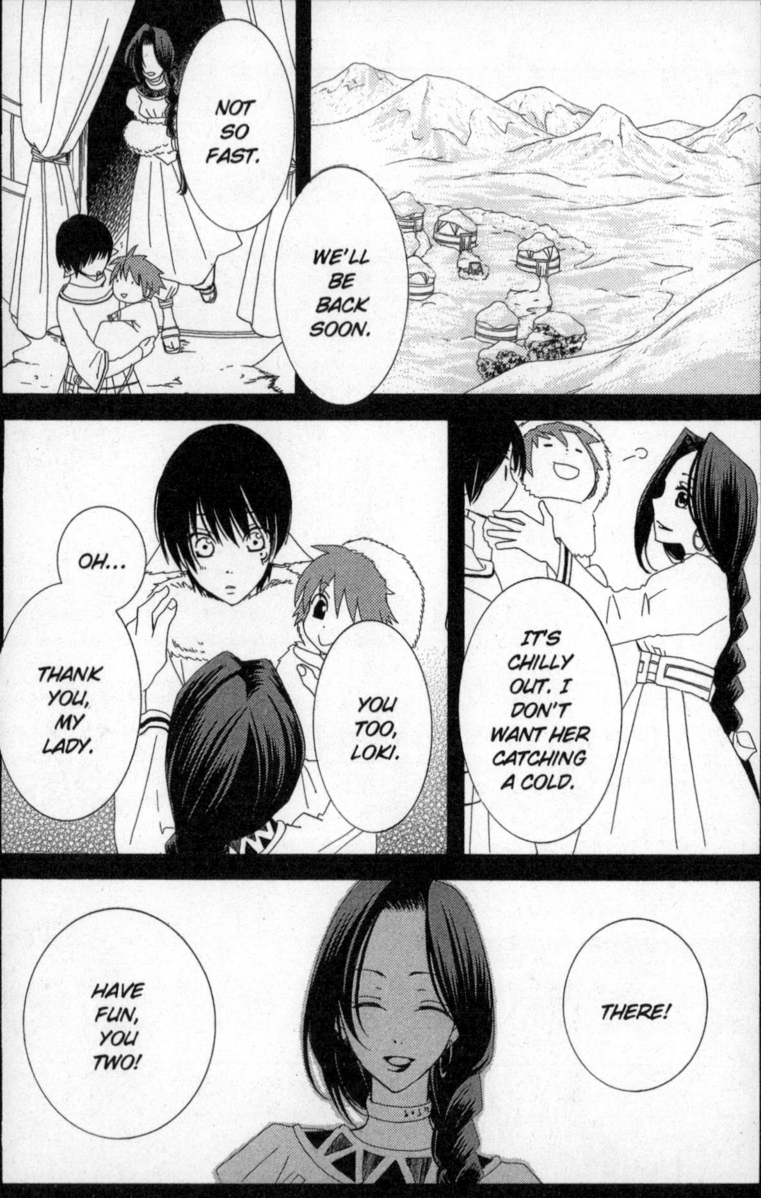
WE'LL BE BACK SOON.
NOT SO FAST.
IT'S CHILLY OUT. I DON'T WANT HER CATCHING A COLD.
OH...
THANK YOU, MY LADY.
YOU TOO, LOKI.
THERE!
HAVE FUN, YOU TWO!

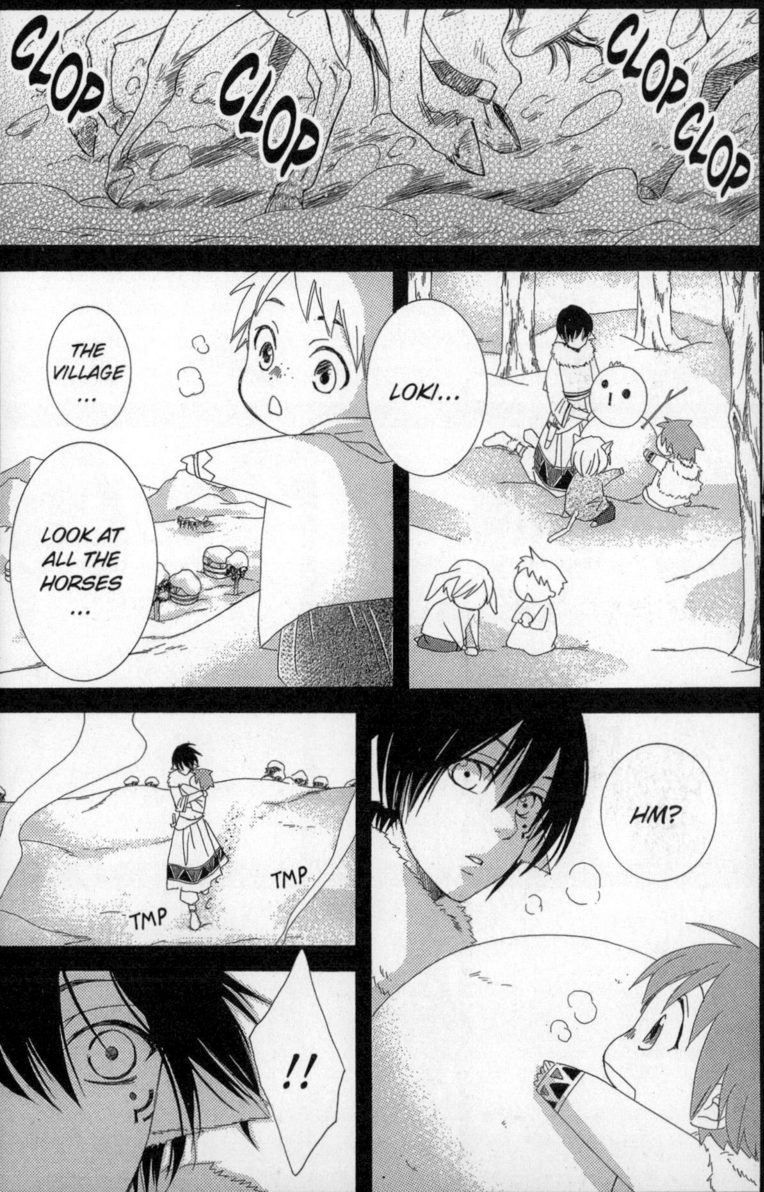
CLOP CLOP
CLOP
CLOP
LOKI...
THE VILLAGE ...
LOOK AT ALL THE HORSES ...
HM?
TMP
TMP
!!

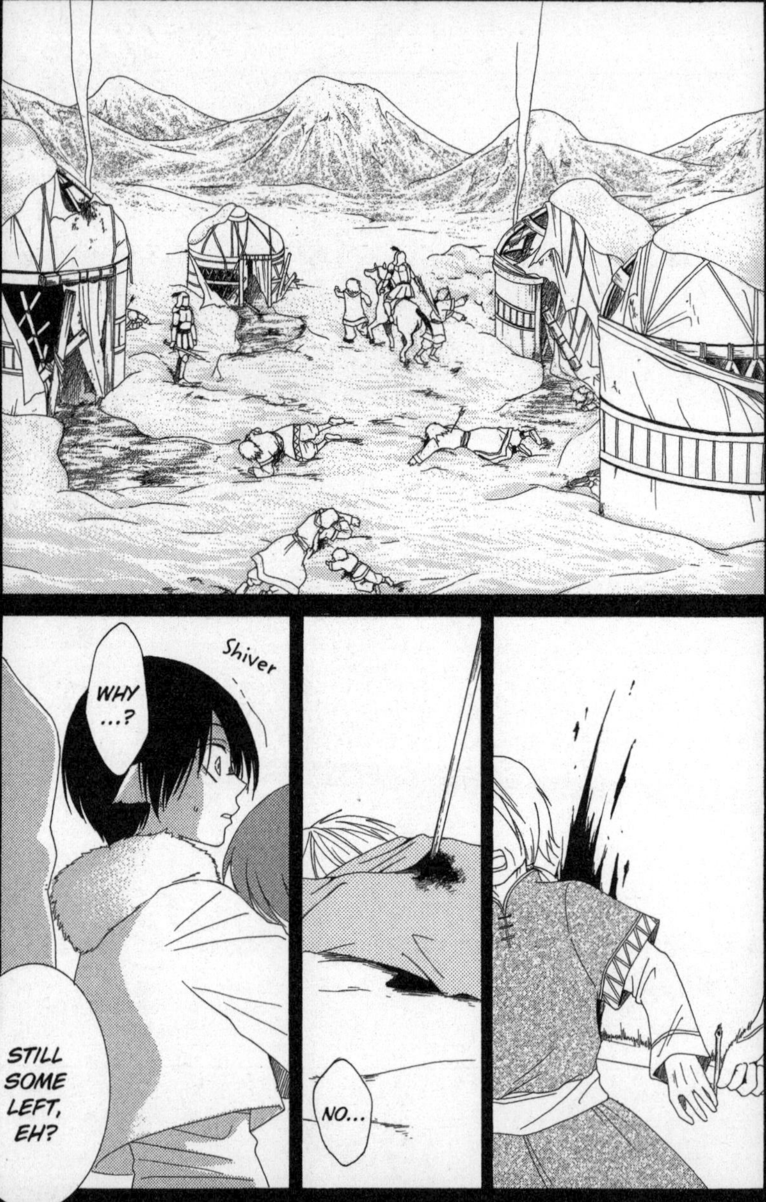
NO...
Shiver
WHY ...?
STILL SOME LEFT, EH?

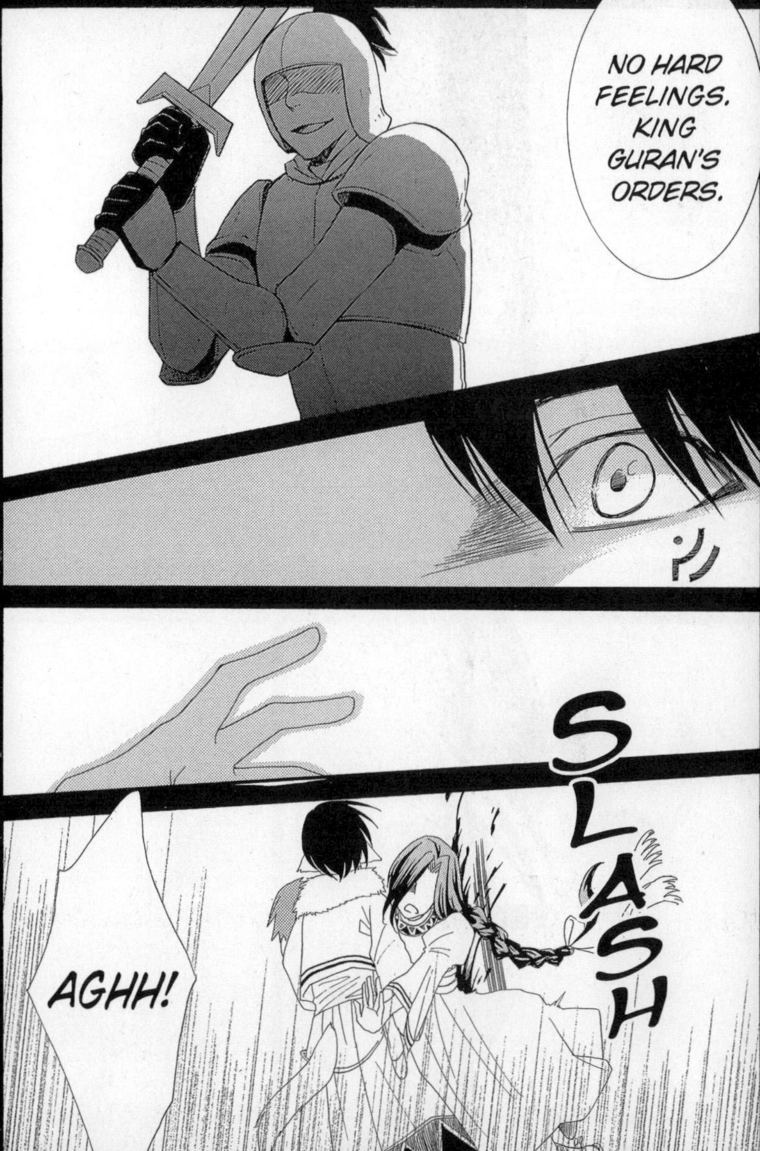
NO HARD FEELINGS. KING GURAN'S ORDERS.
SLASH
AGHH!

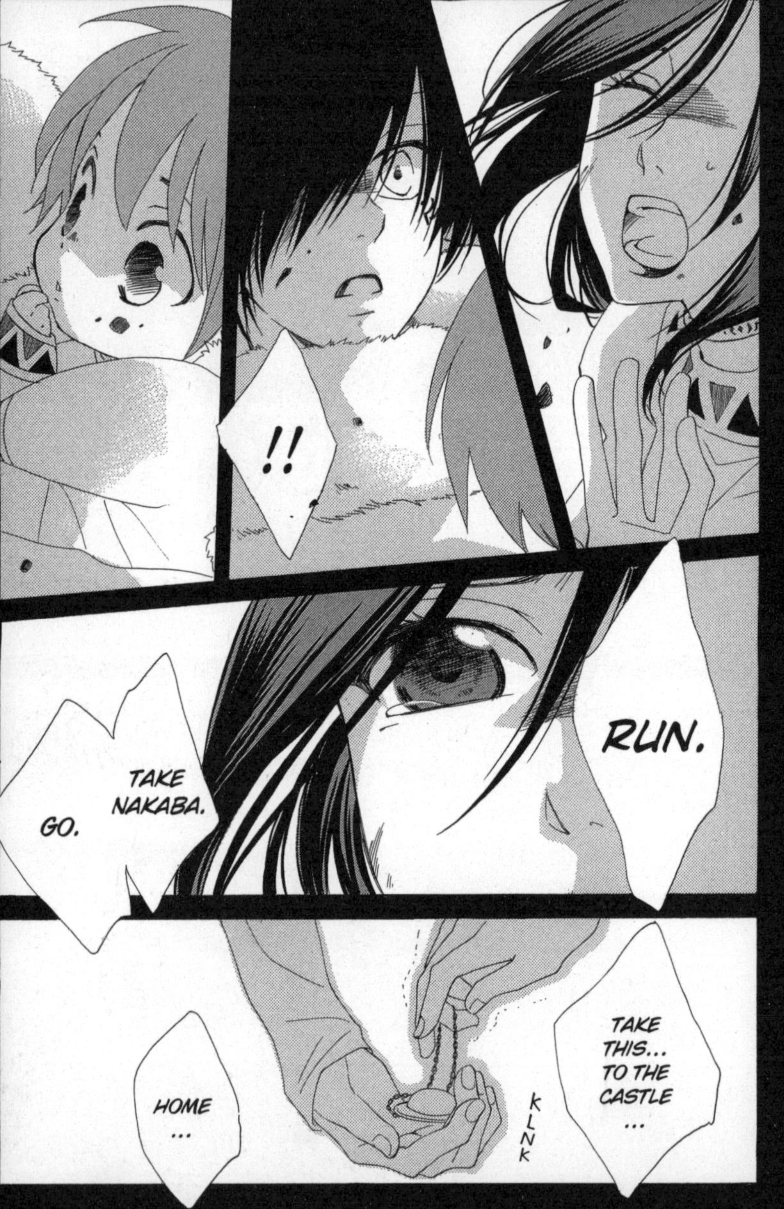
!!
RUN.
TAKE NAKABA.
GO.
TAKE THIS... TO THE CASTLE ...
KLNK
HOME ...

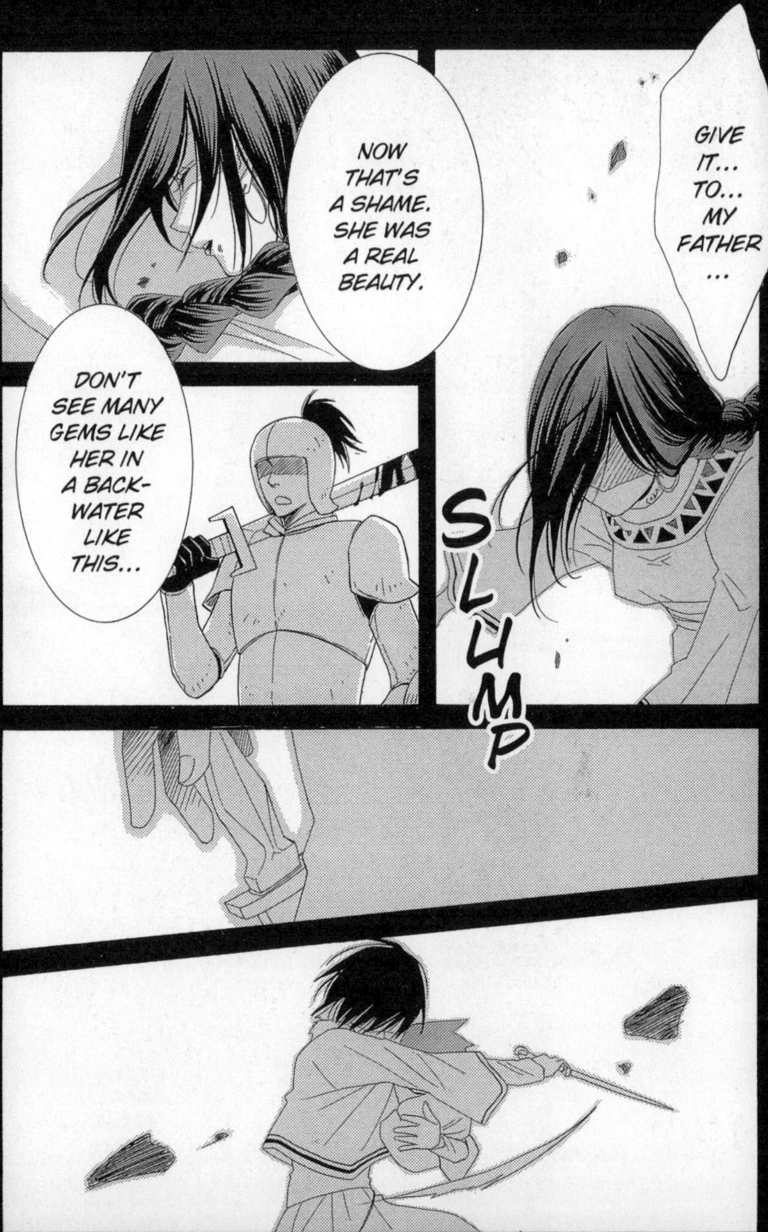
GIVE IT... TO... MY FATHER ...
SLUMP
NOW THAT'S A SHAME. SHE WAS A REAL BEAUTY.
DON'T SEE MANY GEMS LIKE HER IN A BACK-WATER LIKE THIS...

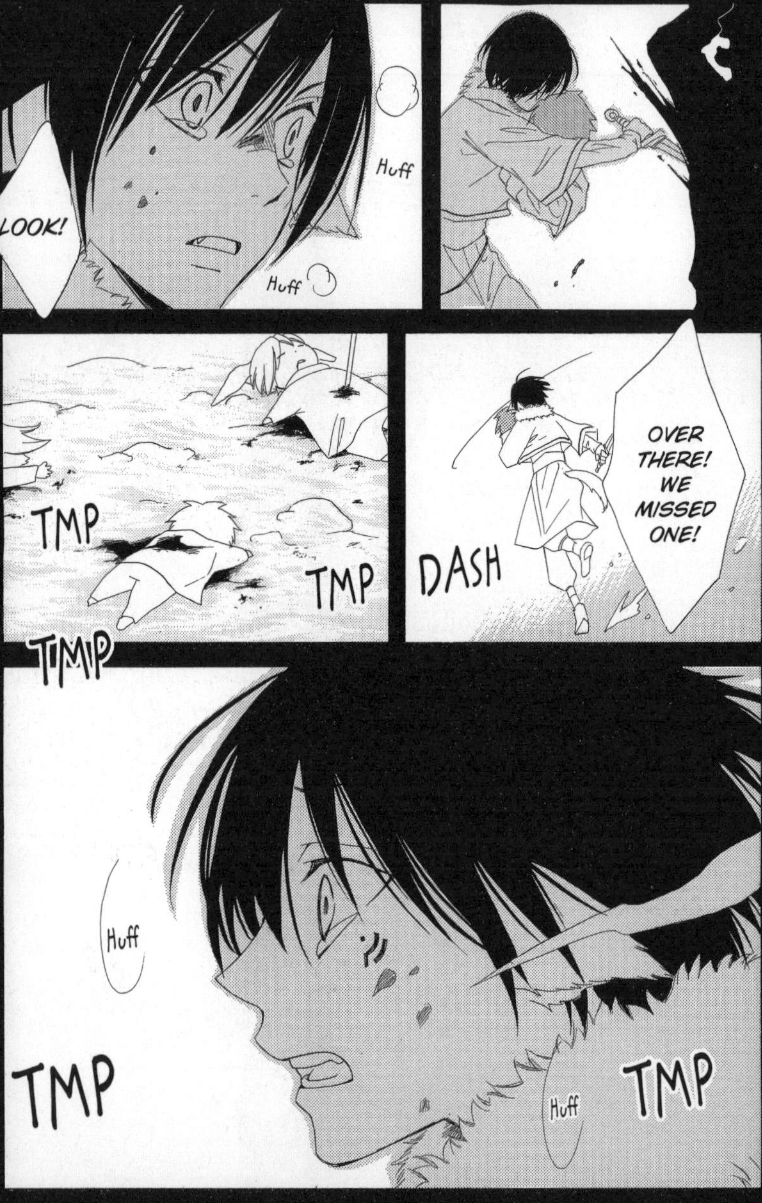
Huff
LOOK!
Huff
OVER THERE! WE MISSED ONE!
DASH
TMP
TMP
TMP
TMP
Huff
Huff
TMP

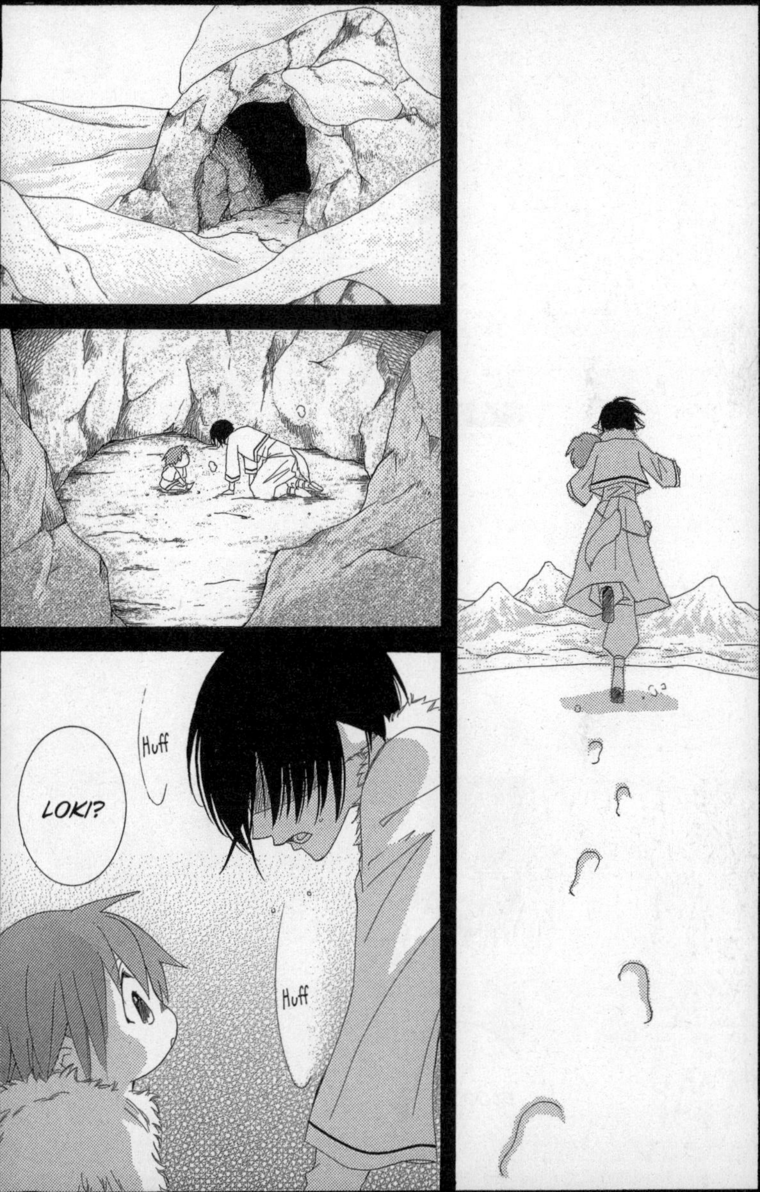
Huff
LOKI?
Huff

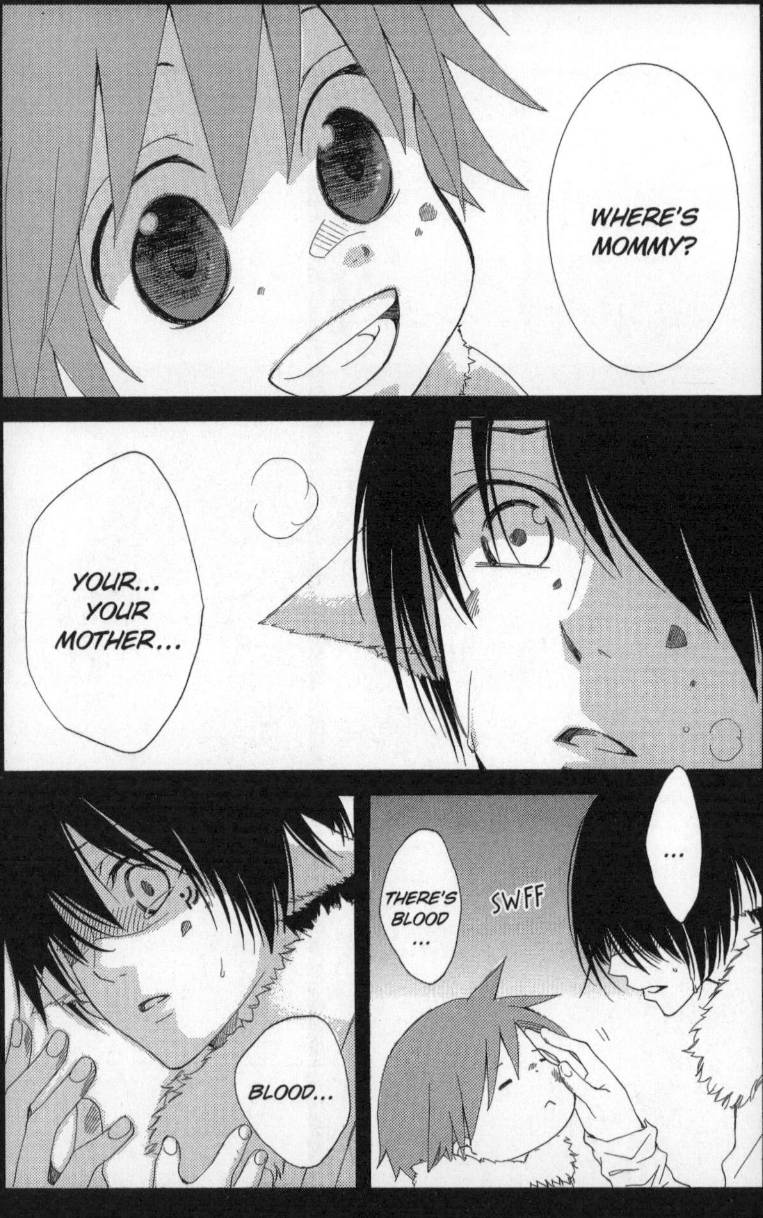
WHERE'S MOMMY?
YOUR... YOUR MOTHER...
...
SWFF
THERE'S BLOOD ...
BLOOD...

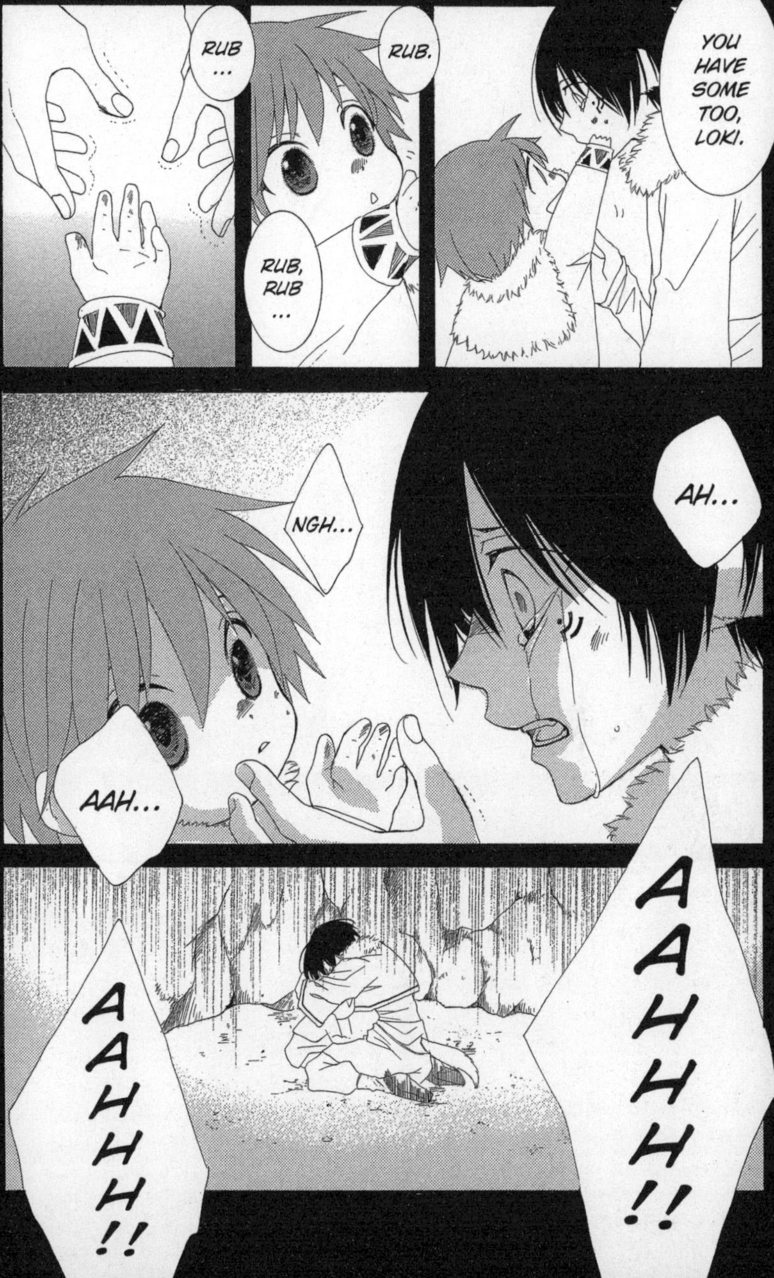
YOU HAVE SOME TOO, LOKI.
RUB.
RUB, RUB ...
RUB ...
AH...
NGH...
AAH...
AAHHH!!
AAHHH!!

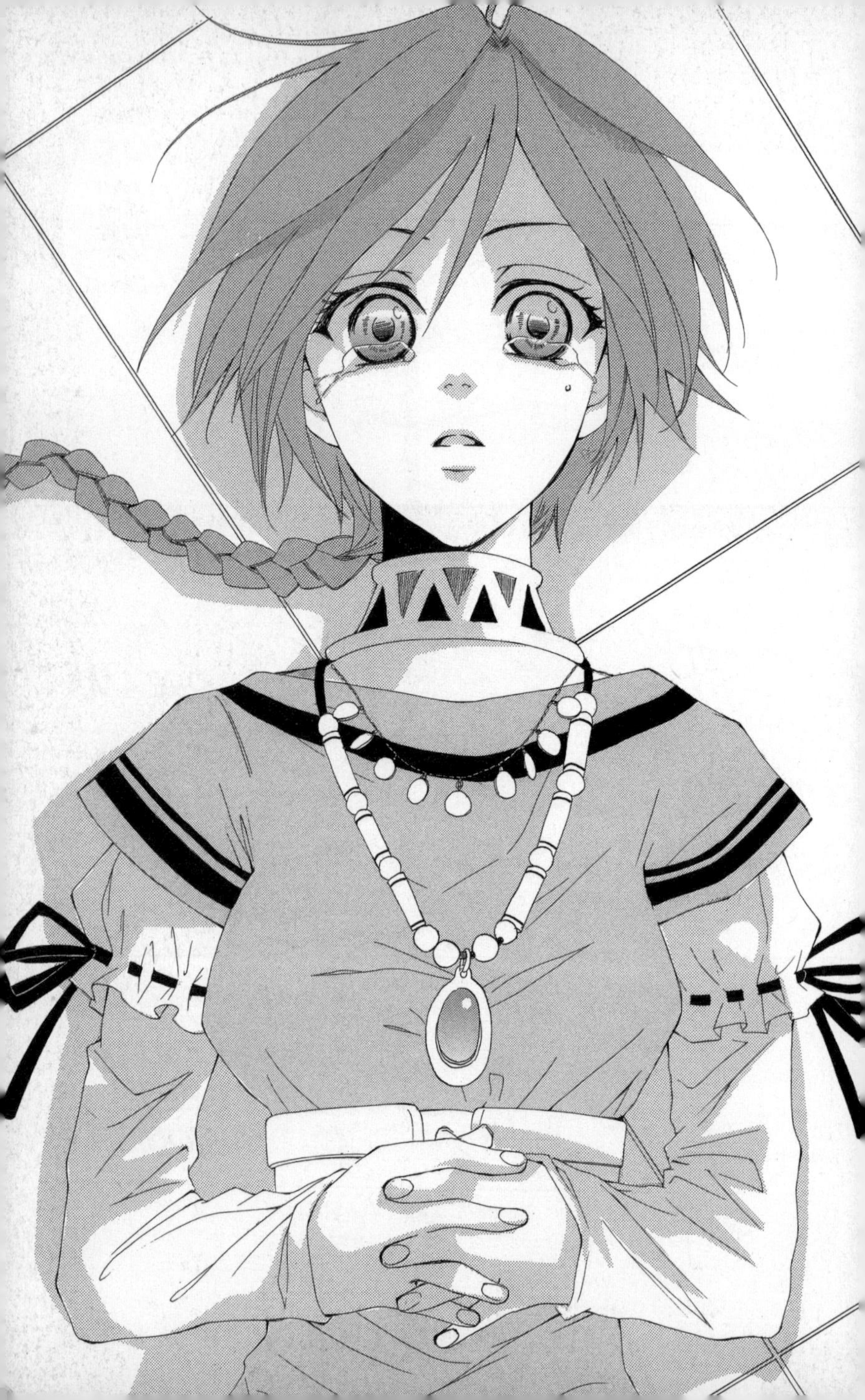

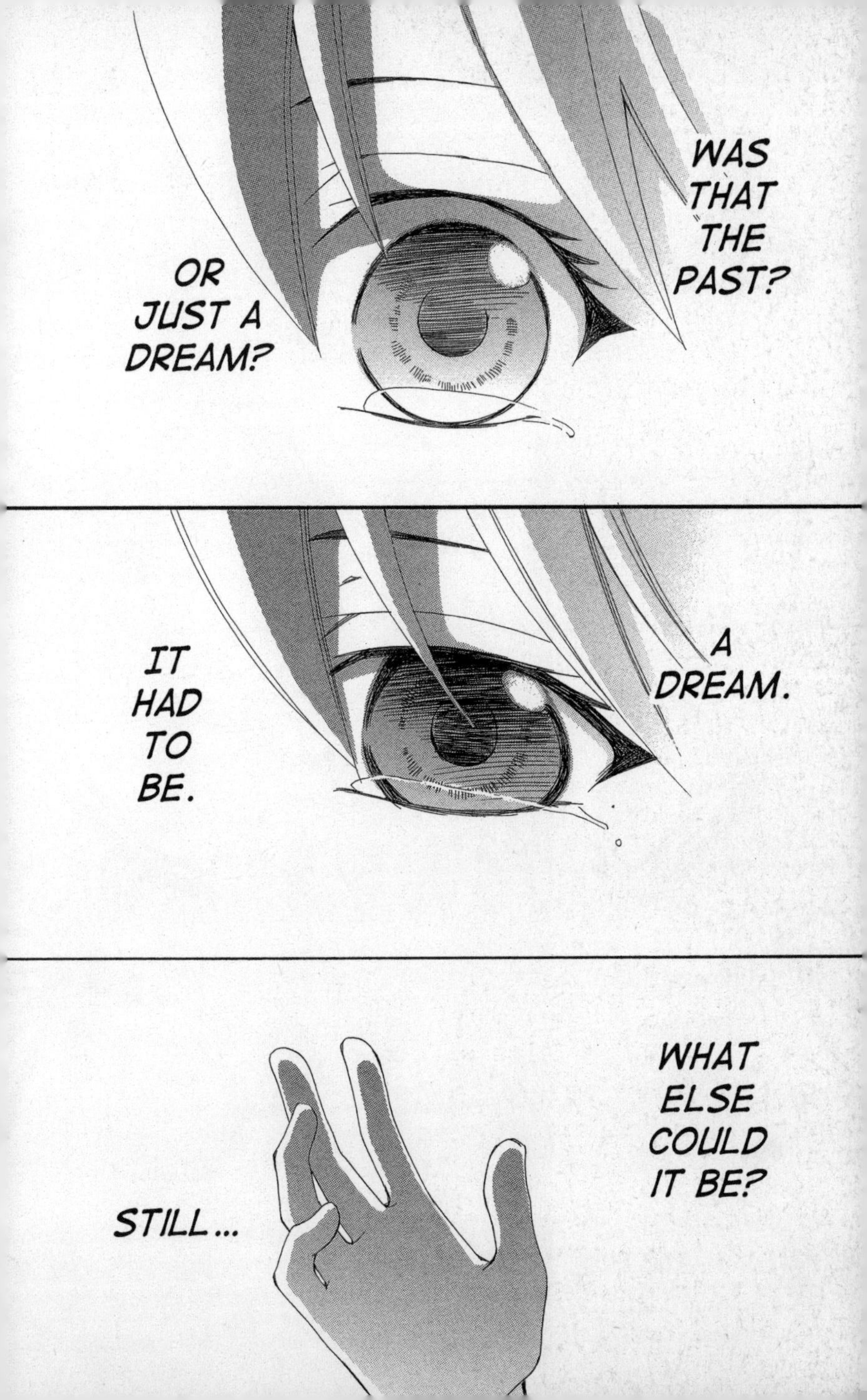
WAS THAT THE PAST?
OR JUST A DREAM?
A DREAM.
IT HAD TO BE.
WHAT ELSE COULD IT BE?
STILL...

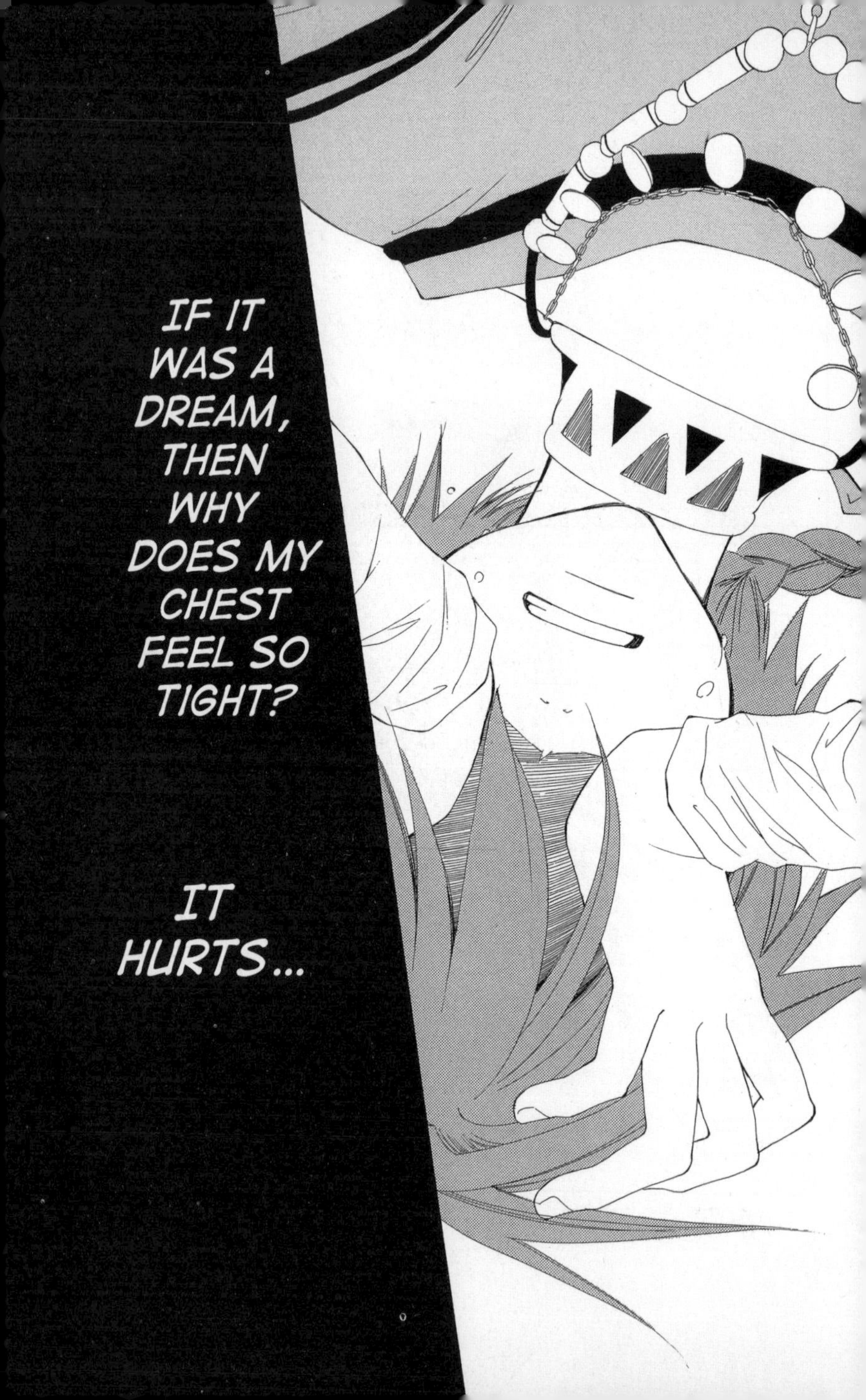
IF IT WAS A DREAM, THEN WHY DOES MY CHEST FEEL SO TIGHT?
IT HURTS...

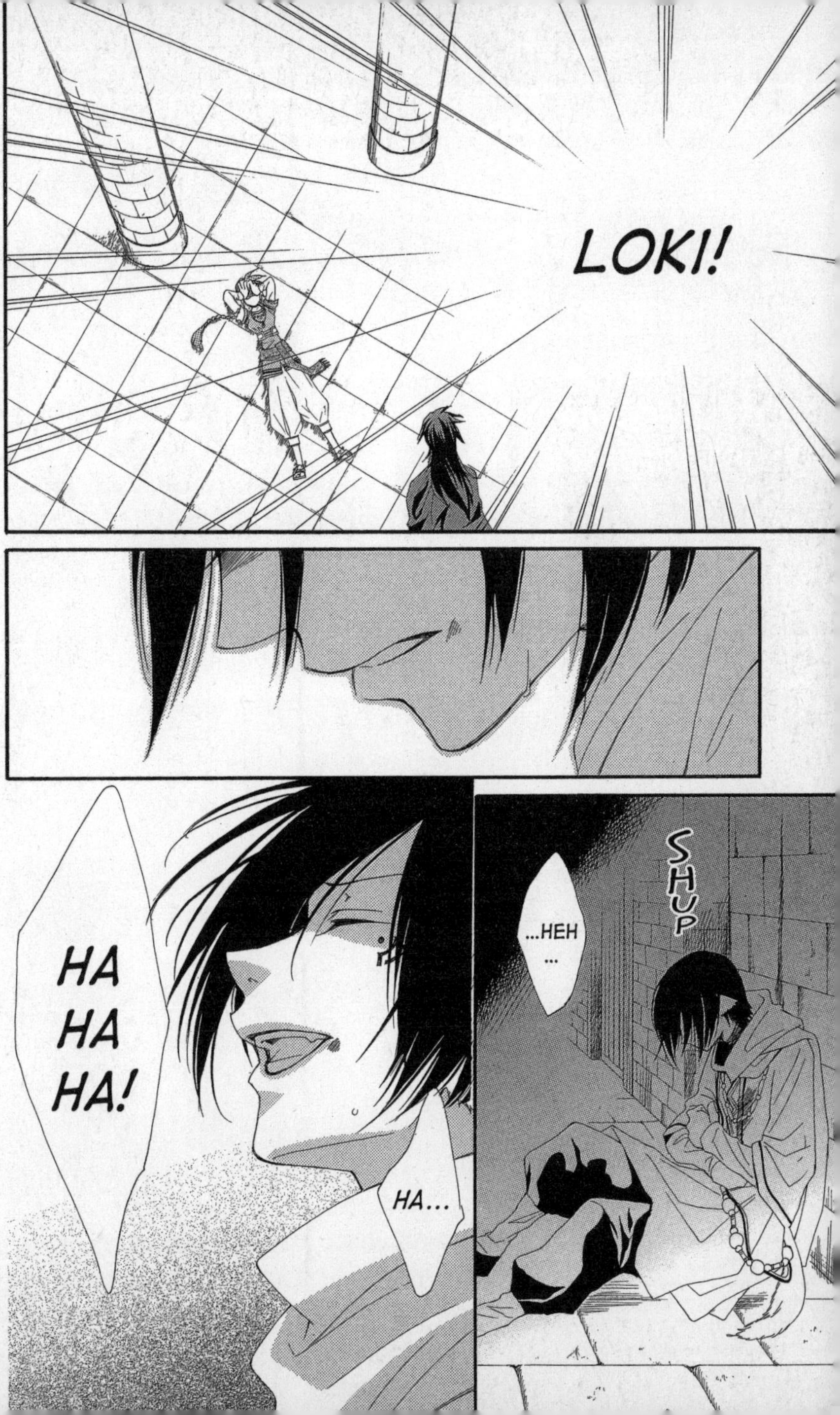
LOKI!
SHUP
...HEH ...
HA HA HA!
HA...

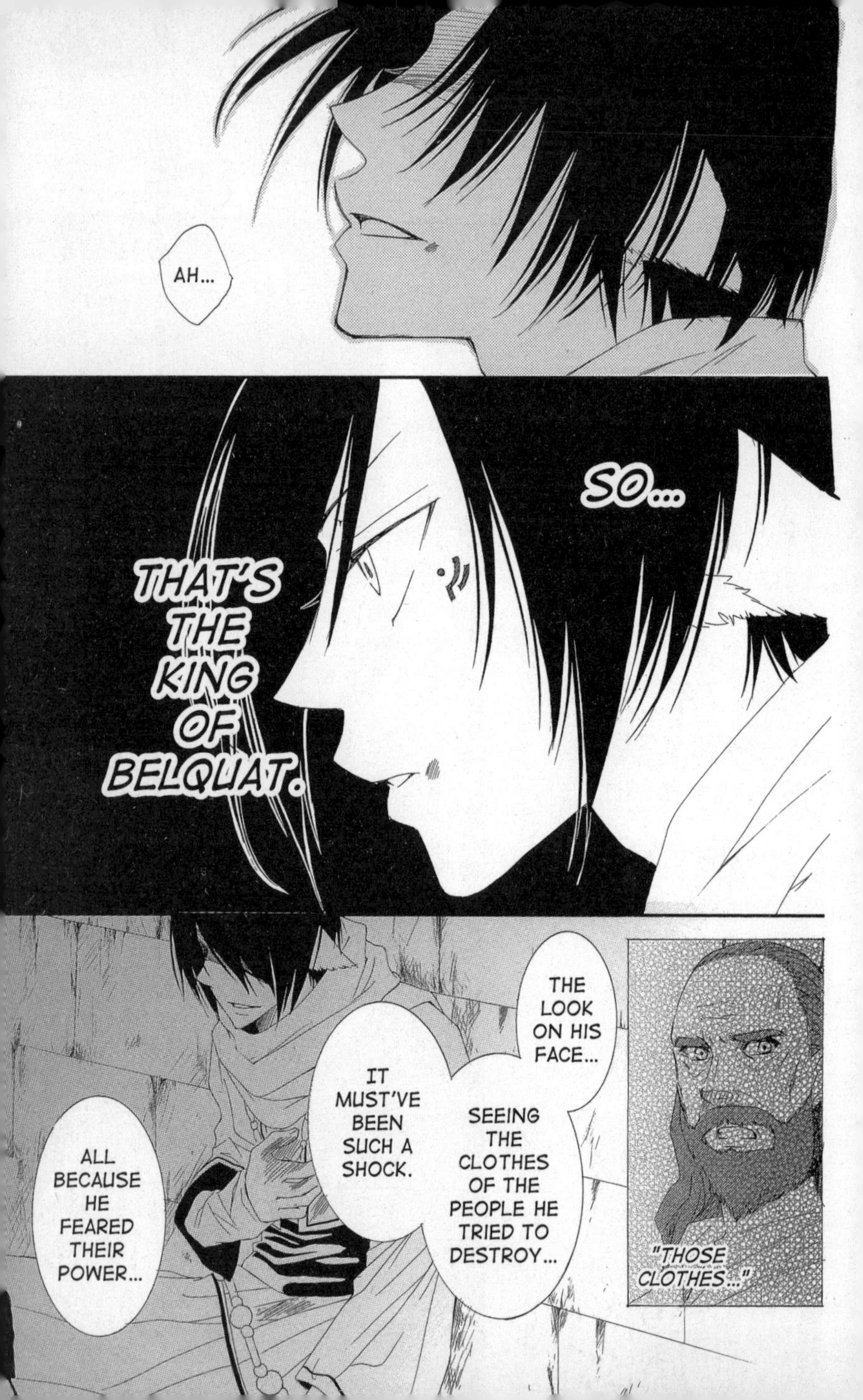
AH...
SO...
THAT'S THE KING OF BELQUAT.
"THOSE CLOTHES..."
THE LOOK ON HIS FACE...
SEEING THE CLOTHES OF THE PEOPLE HE TRIED TO DESTROY...
IT MUST'VE BEEN SUCH A SHOCK.
ALL BECAUSE HE FEARED THEIR POWER...

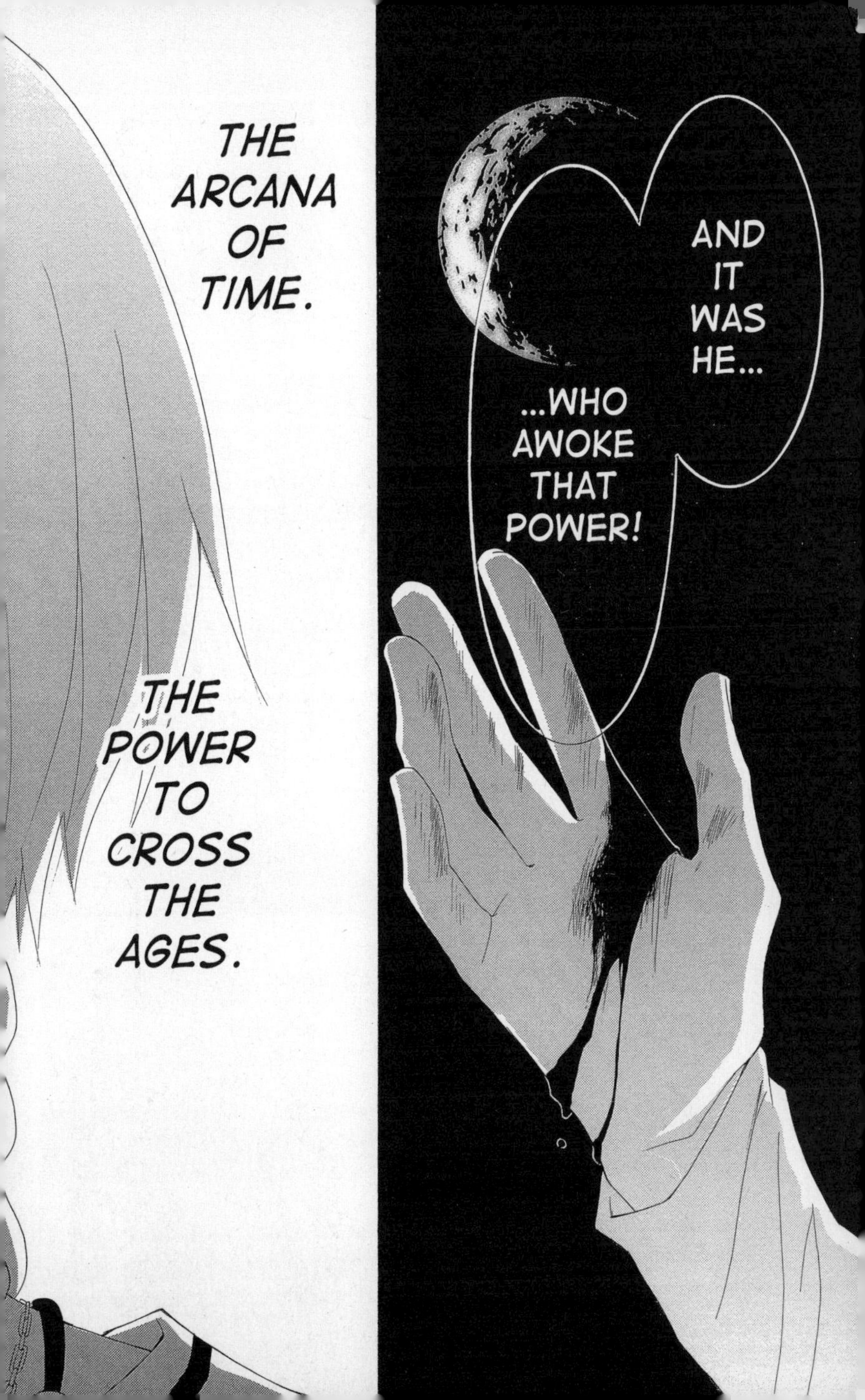
AND IT WAS HE...
...WHO AWOKE THAT POWER!
THE ARCANA OF TIME.
THE POWER TO CROSS THE AGES.

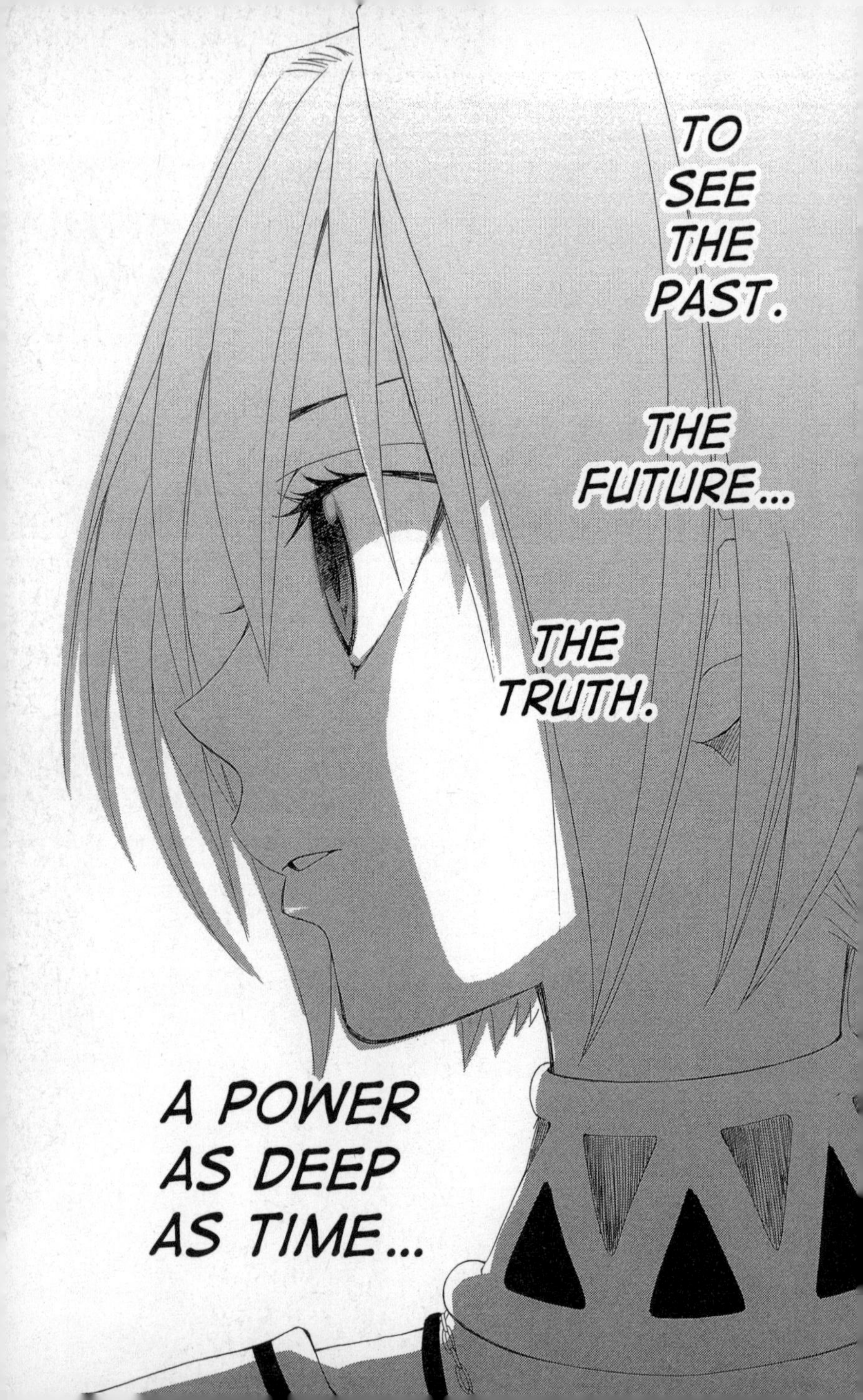
TO SEE THE PAST.
THE FUTURE...
THE TRUTH.
A POWER AS DEEP AS TIME...

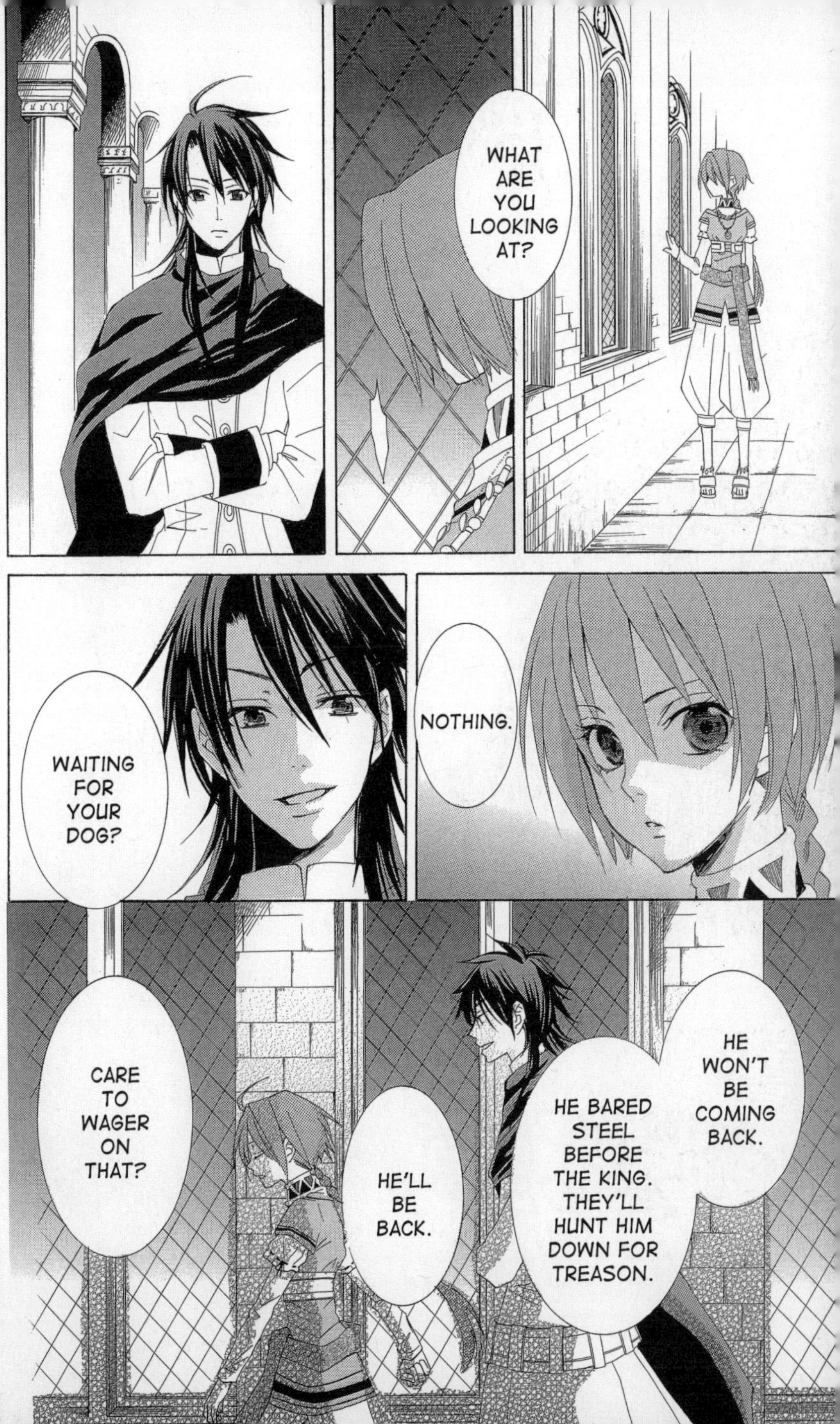
WHAT ARE YOU LOOKING AT?
NOTHING.
WAITING FOR YOUR DOG?
HE WON'T BE COMING BACK.
HE BARED STEEL BEFORE THE KING. THEY'LL HUNT HIM DOWN FOR TREASON.
HE'LL BE BACK.
CARE TO WAGER ON THAT?

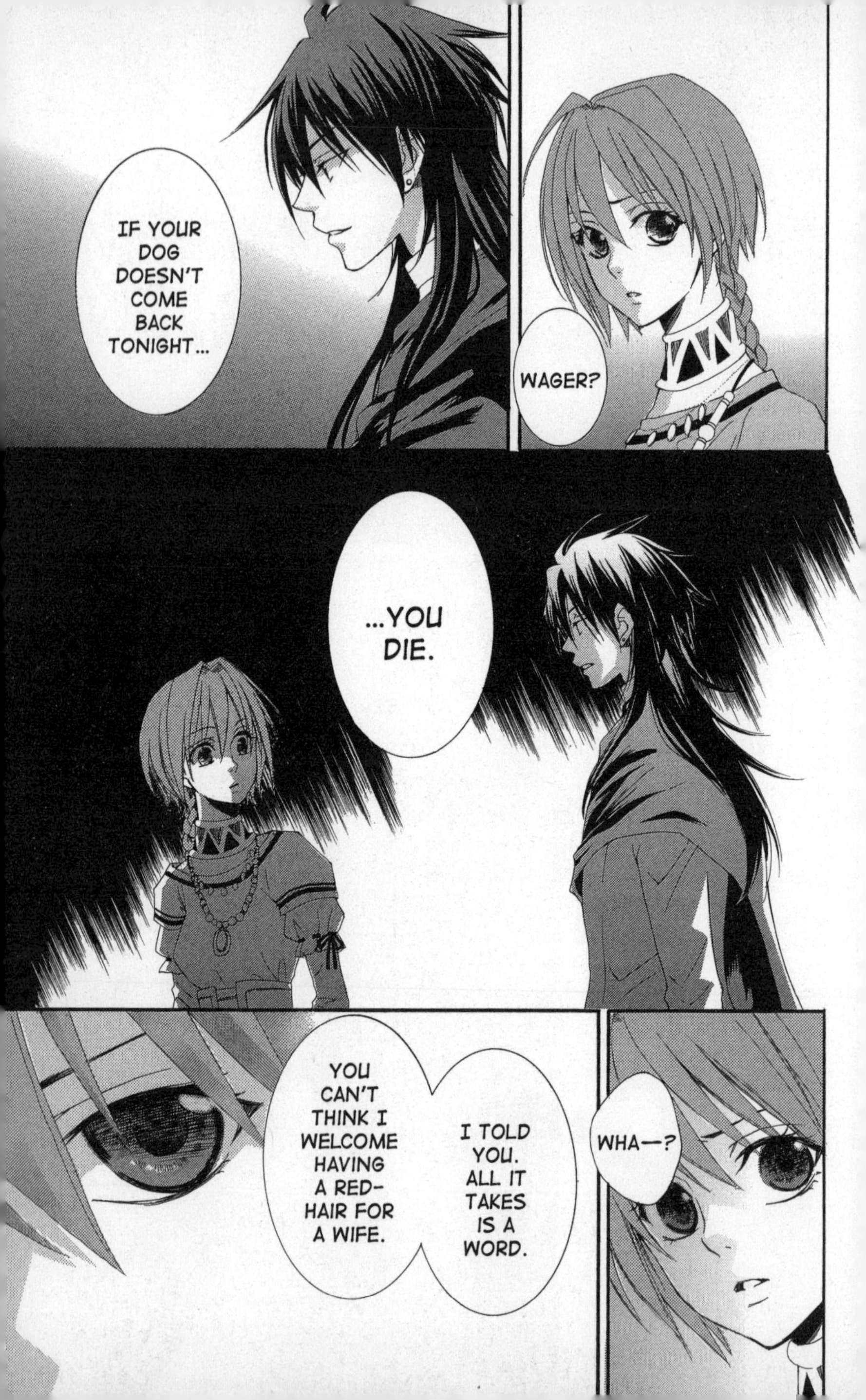
WAGER?
IF YOUR DOG DOESN'T COME BACK TONIGHT...
...YOU DIE.
WHA—?
I TOLD YOU. ALL IT TAKES IS A WORD.
YOU CAN'T THINK I WELCOME HAVING A RED-HAIR FOR A WIFE.

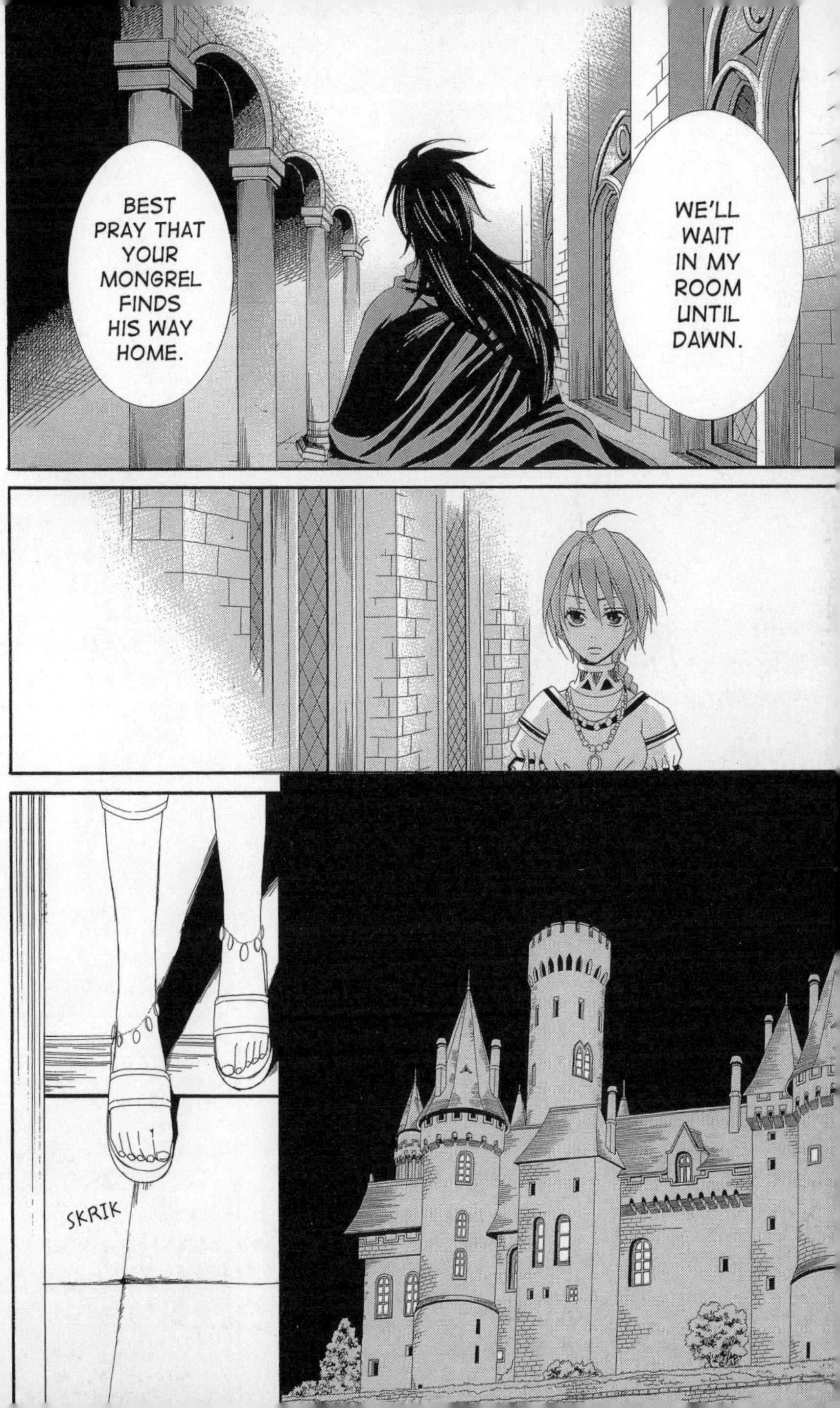
WE'LL WAIT IN MY ROOM UNTIL DAWN.
BEST PRAY THAT YOUR MONGREL FINDS HIS WAY HOME.
SKRIK

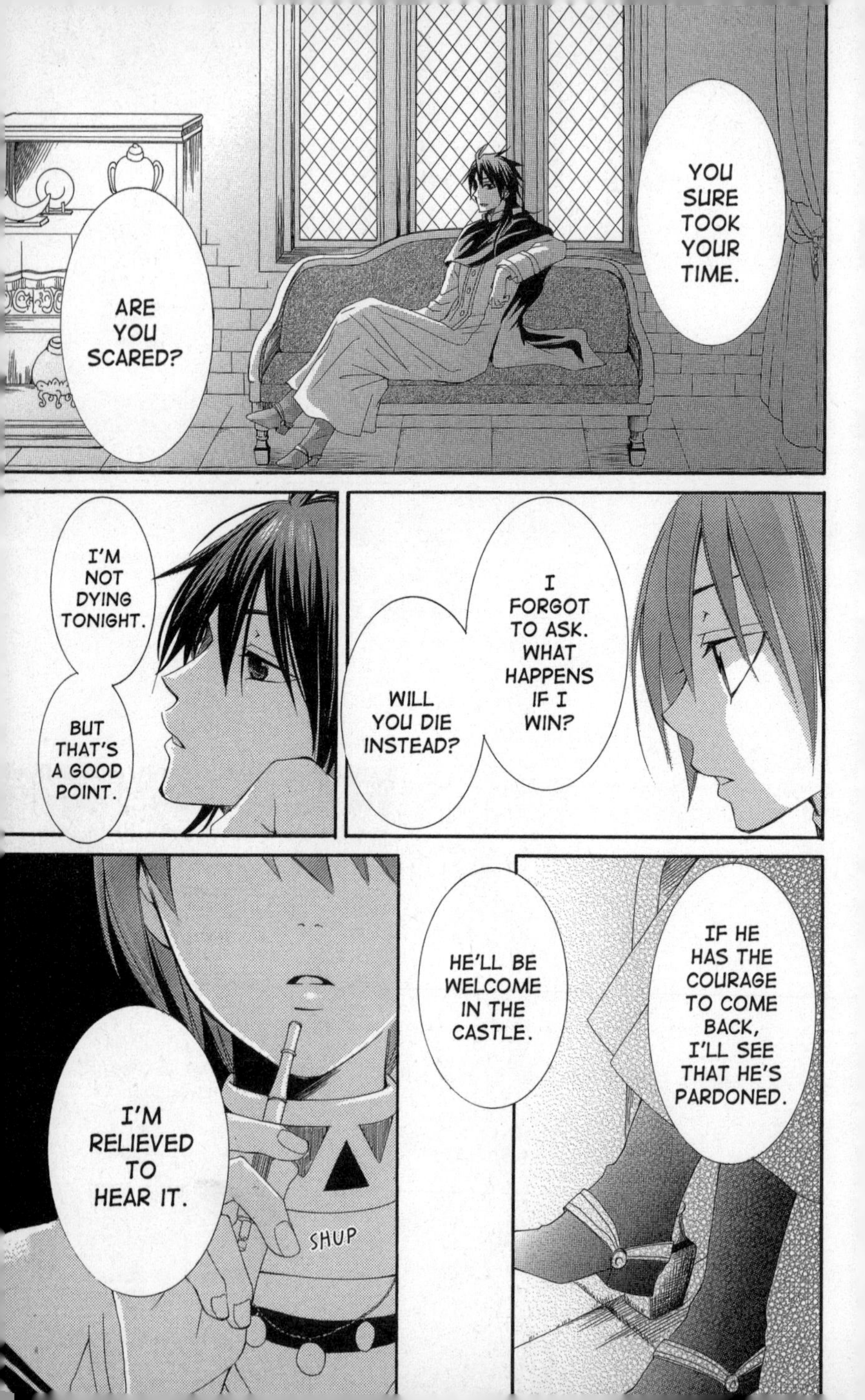
YOU SURE TOOK YOUR TIME.
ARE YOU SCARED?
I FORGOT TO ASK. WHAT HAPPENS IF I WIN?
WILL YOU DIE INSTEAD?
I'M NOT DYING TONIGHT.
BUT THAT'S A GOOD POINT.
IF HE HAS THE COURAGE TO COME BACK, I'LL SEE THAT HE'S PARDONED.
HE'LL BE WELCOME IN THE CASTLE.
I'M RELIEVED TO HEAR IT.
SHUP

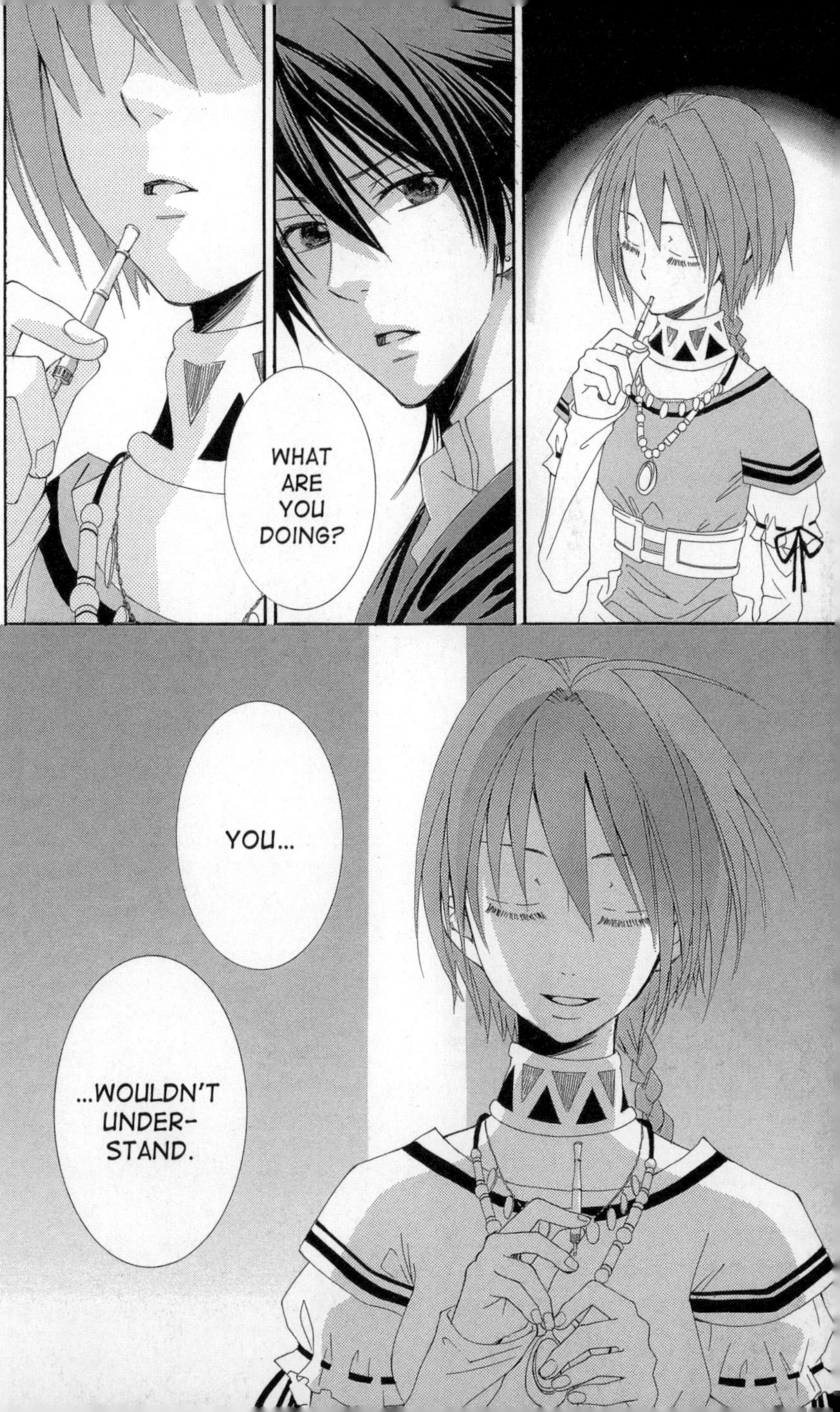
WHAT ARE YOU DOING?
YOU...
...WOULDN'T UNDER-STAND.

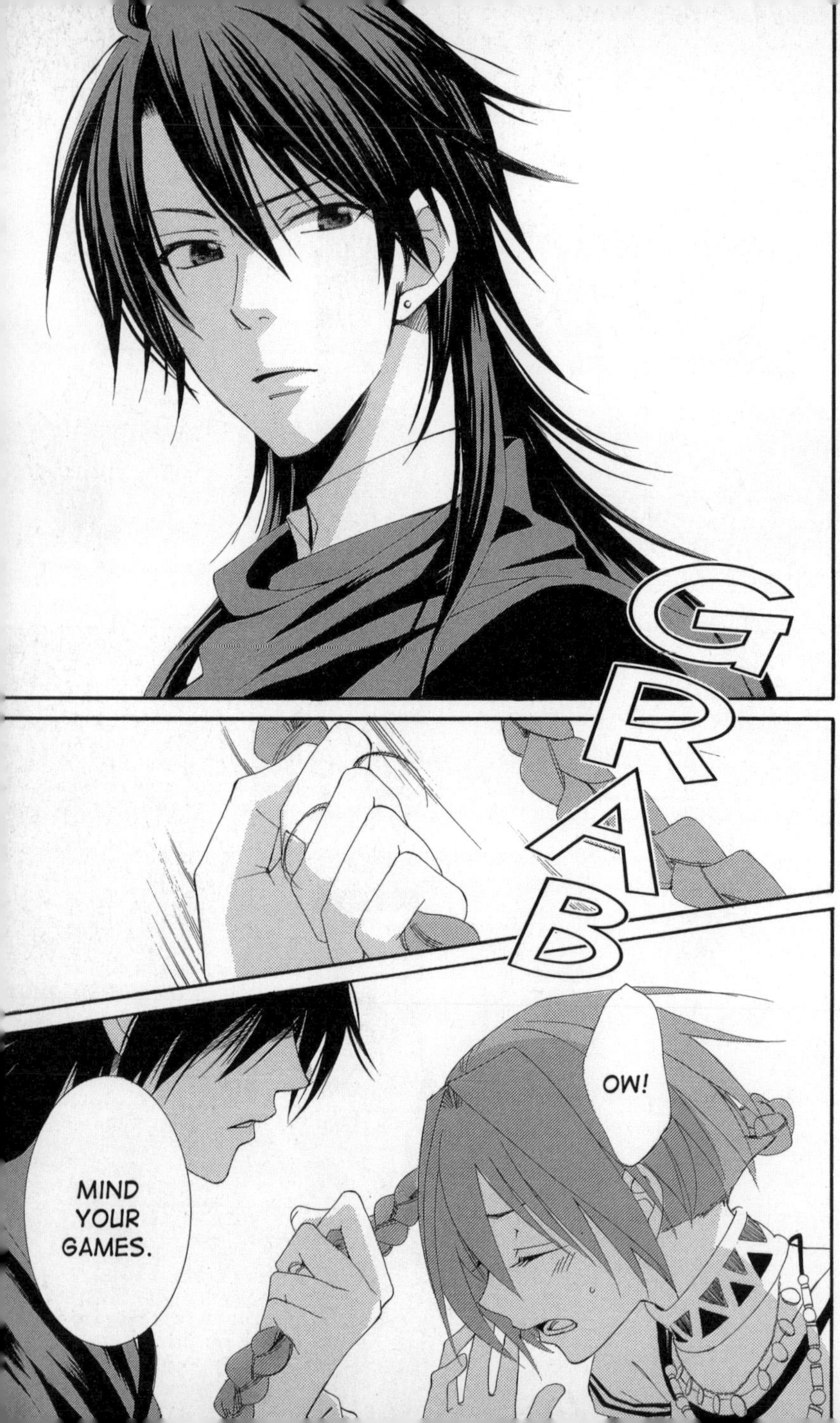
GRAB
OW!
MIND YOUR GAMES.

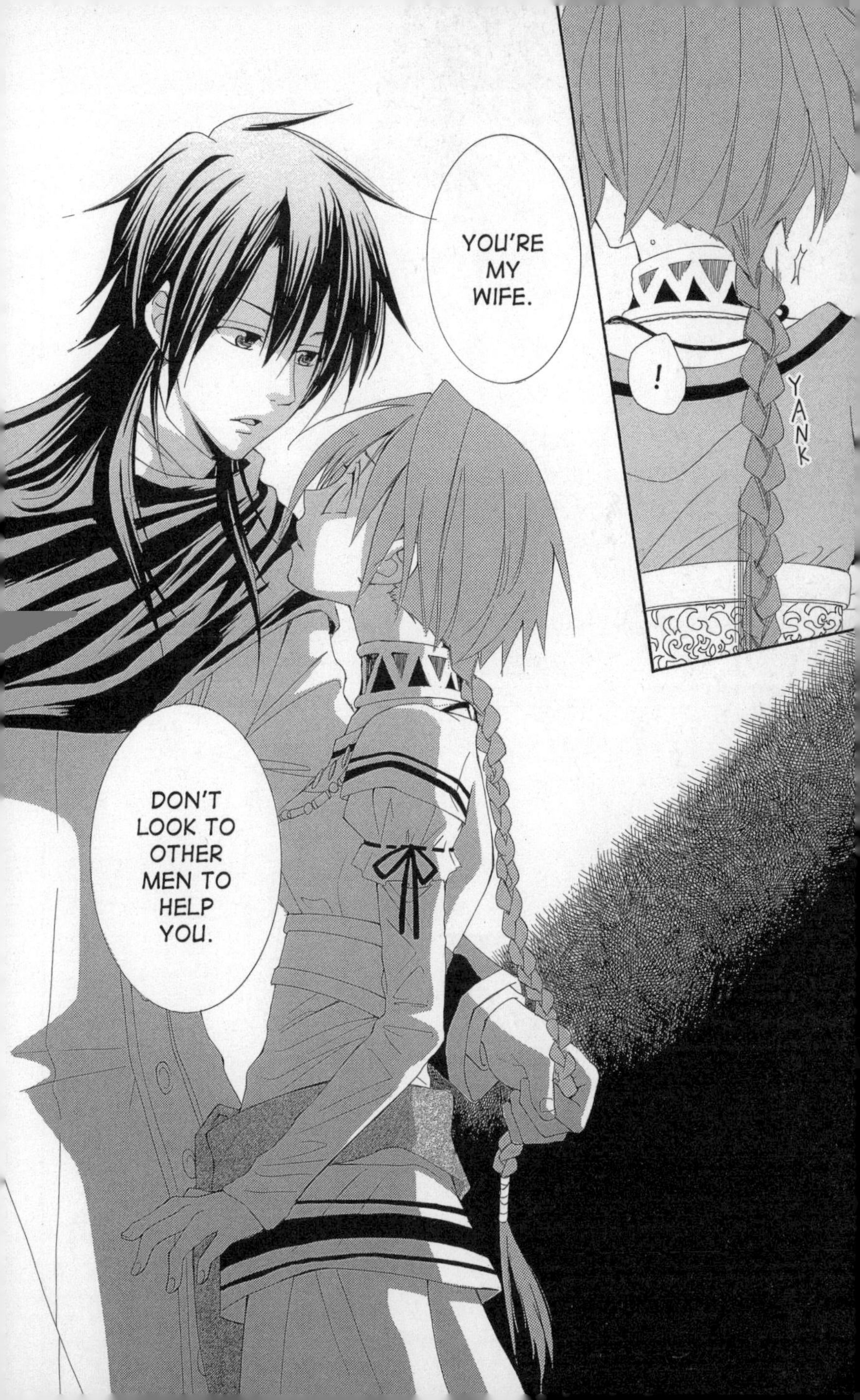
!
YANK
YOU'RE MY WIFE.
DON'T LOOK TO OTHER MEN TO HELP YOU.

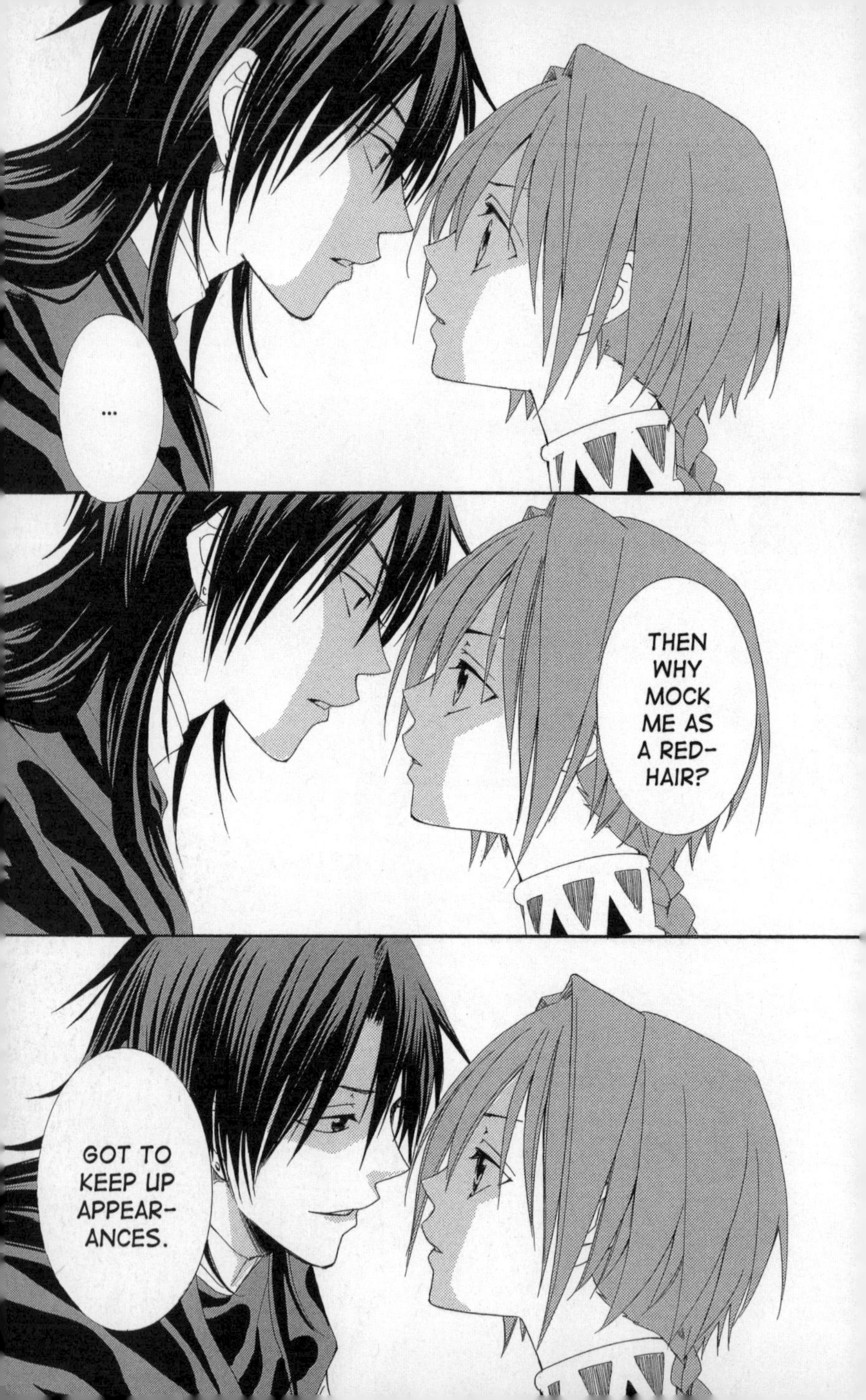
...
THEN WHY MOCK ME AS A RED-HAIR?
GOT TO KEEP UP APPEAR-ANCES.

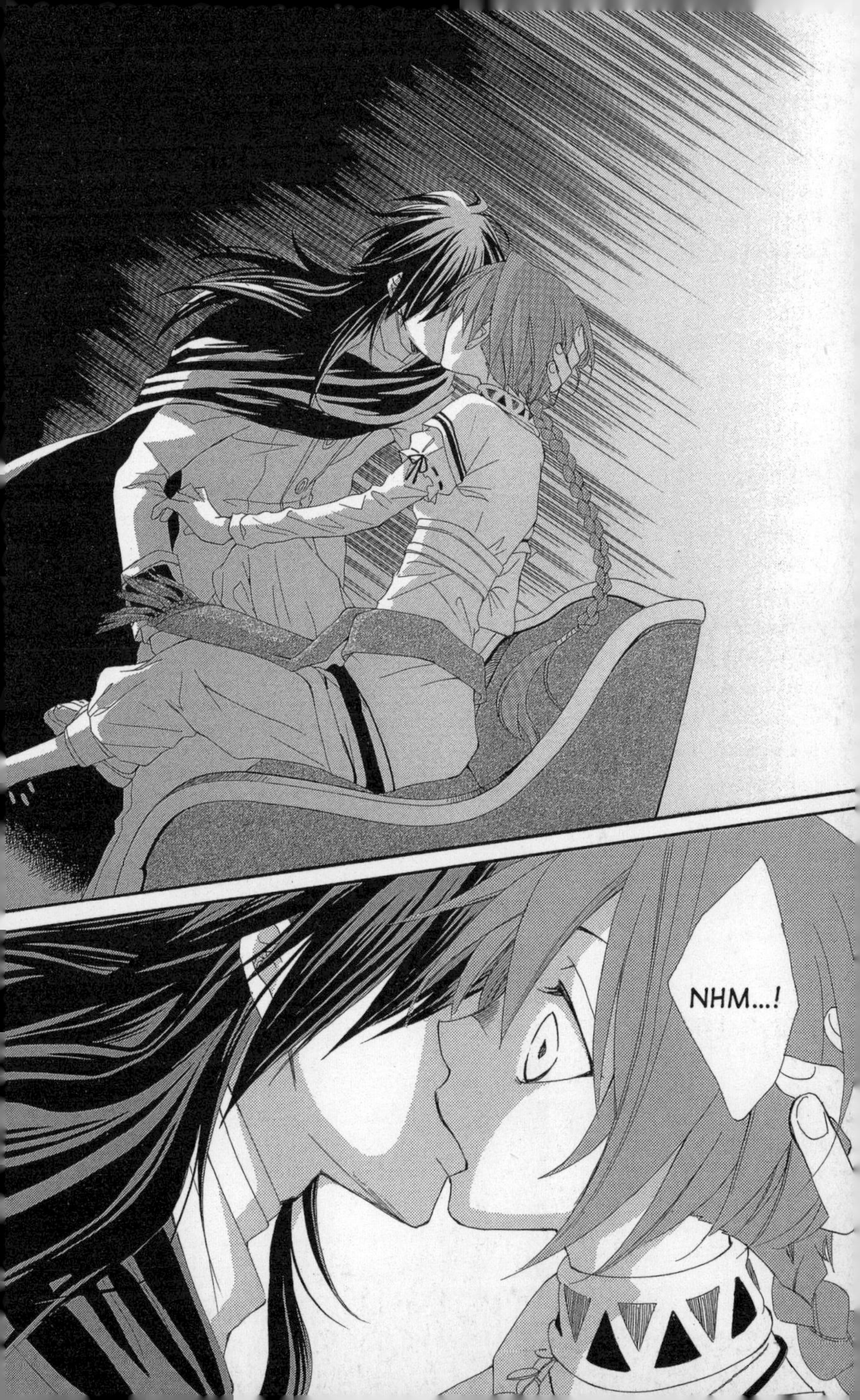
NHM...!

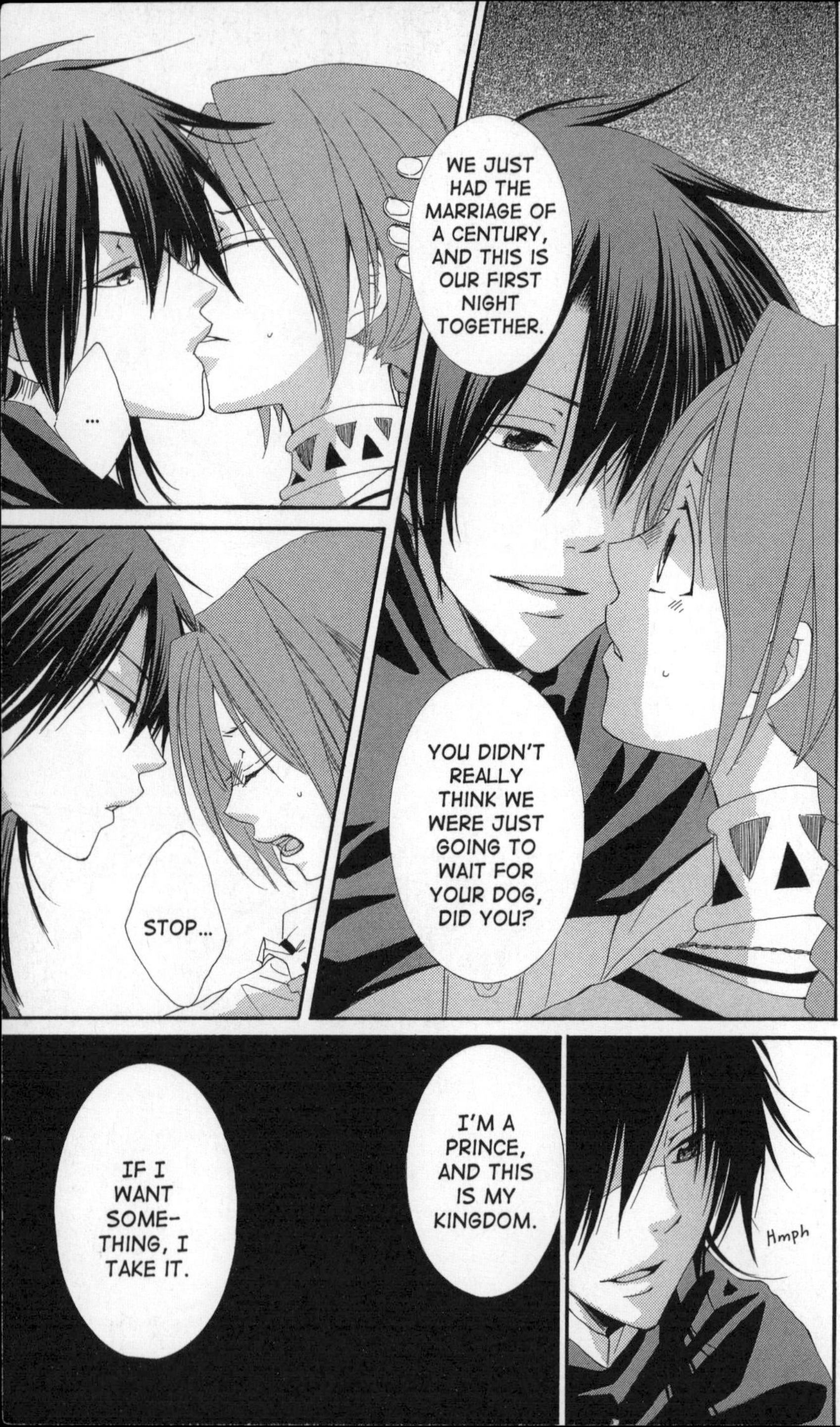
WE JUST HAD THE MARRIAGE OF A CENTURY, AND THIS IS OUR FIRST NIGHT TOGETHER.
YOU DIDN'T REALLY THINK WE WERE JUST GOING TO WAIT FOR YOUR DOG, DID YOU?
...
STOP...
Hmph
I'M A PRINCE, AND THIS IS MY KINGDOM.
IF I WANT SOME-THING, I TAKE IT.

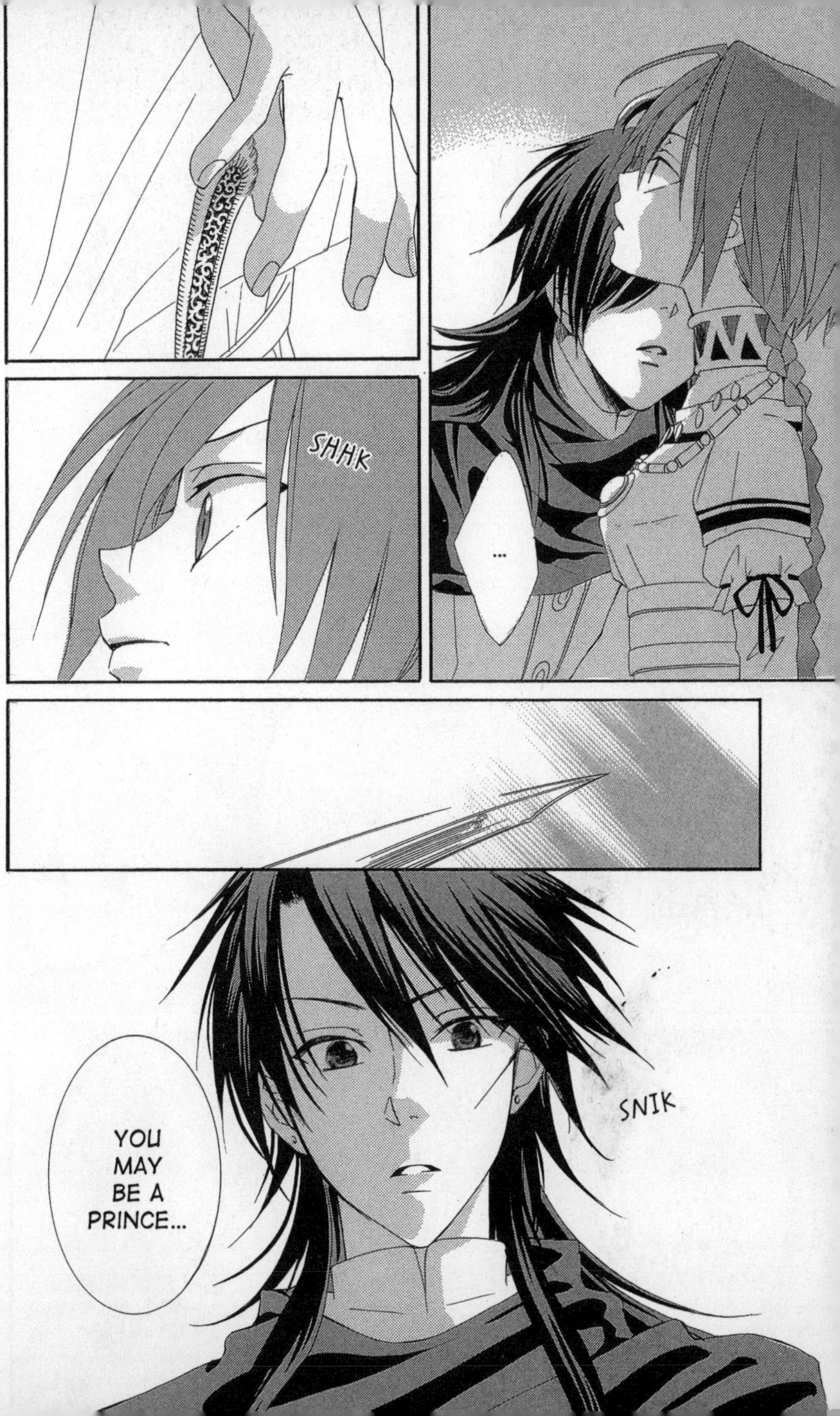
...
SHHK
SNIK
YOU MAY BE A PRINCE...

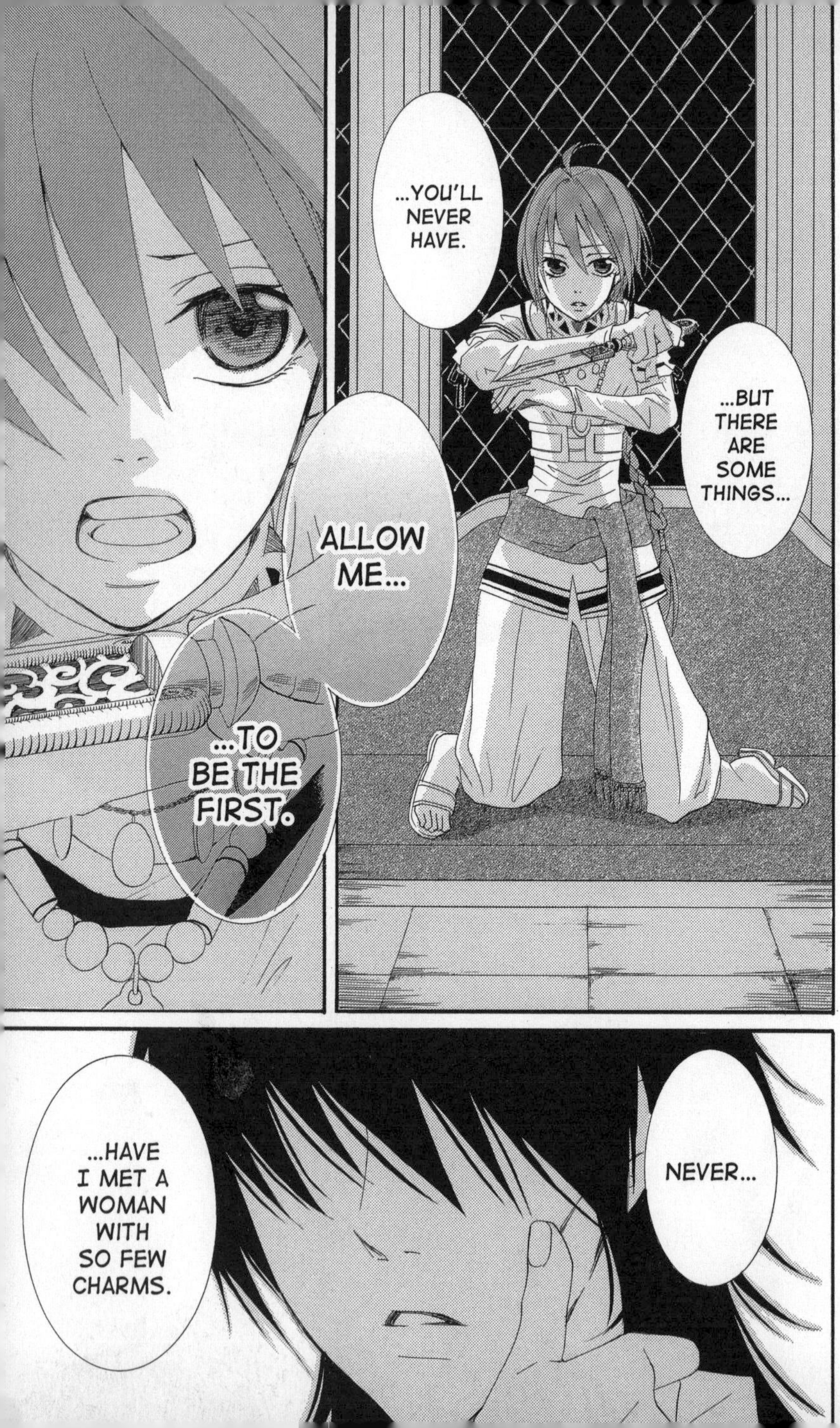
...BUT THERE ARE SOME THINGS...
...YOU'LL NEVER HAVE.
ALLOW ME...
...TO BE THE FIRST.
NEVER...
...HAVE I MET A WOMAN WITH SO FEW CHARMS.

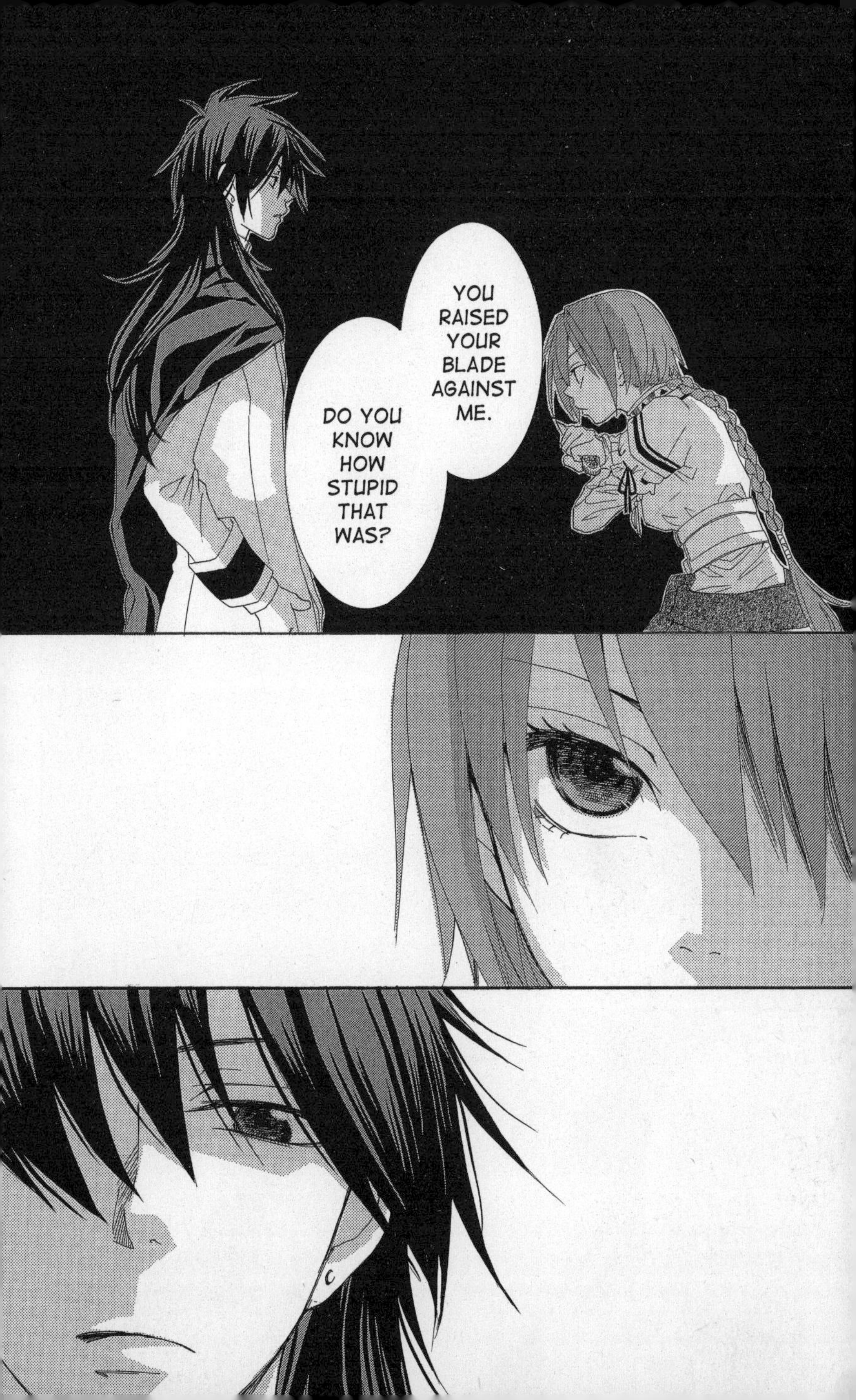
YOU RAISED YOUR BLADE AGAINST ME.
DO YOU KNOW HOW STUPID THAT WAS?

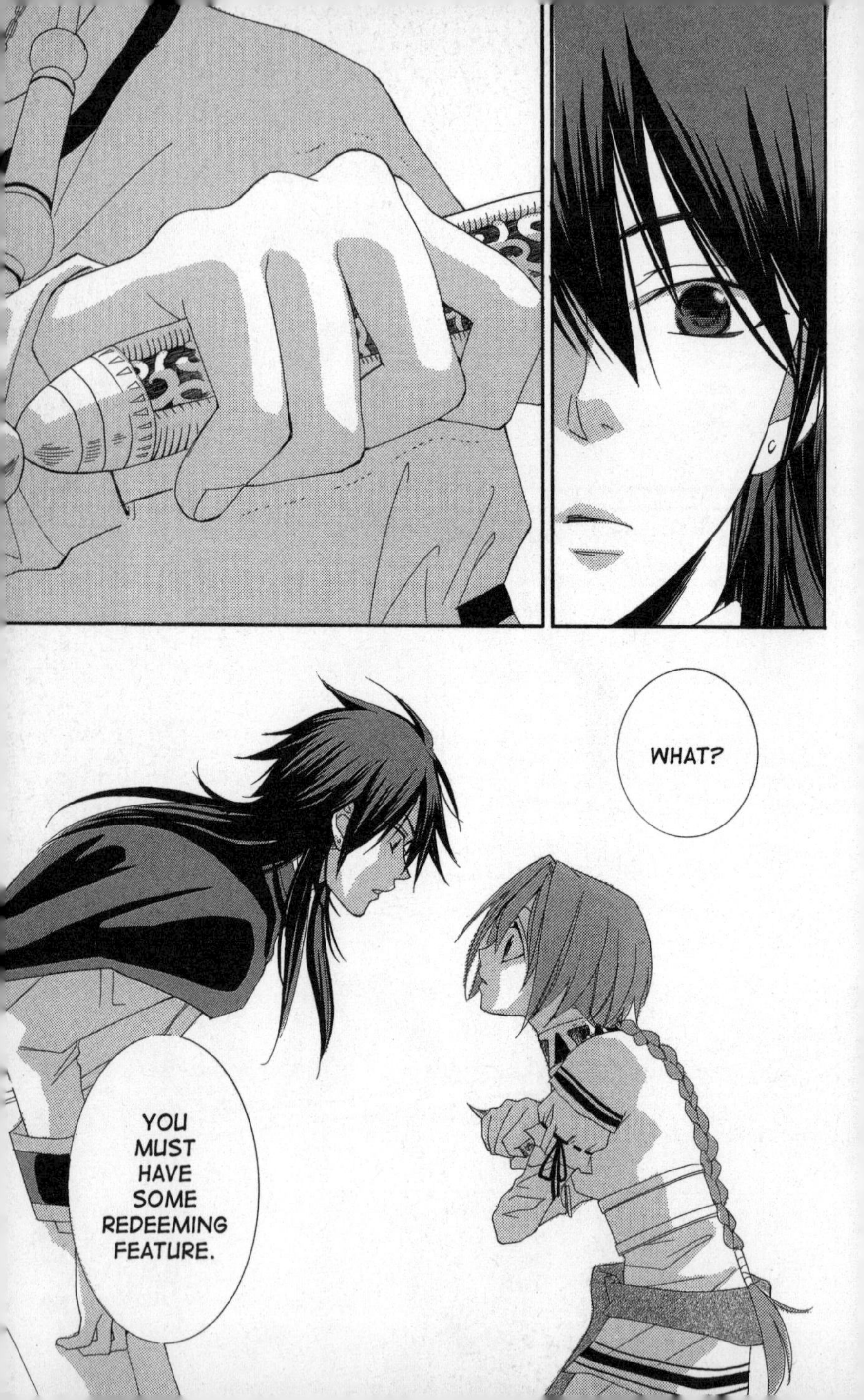
WHAT?
YOU MUST HAVE SOME REDEEMING FEATURE.

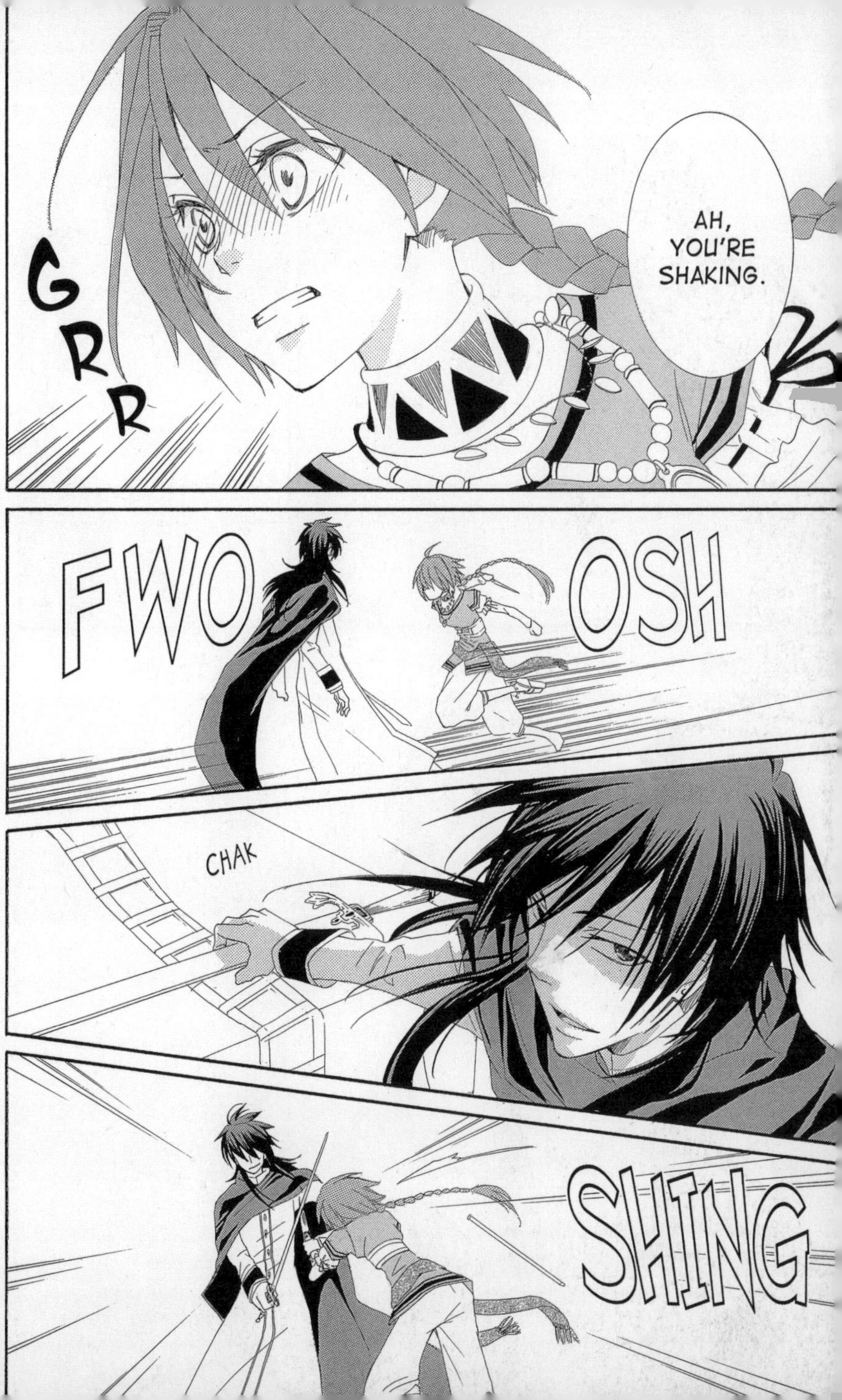
AH, YOU'RE SHAKING.
GRR
FWOOSH
CHAK
SHING

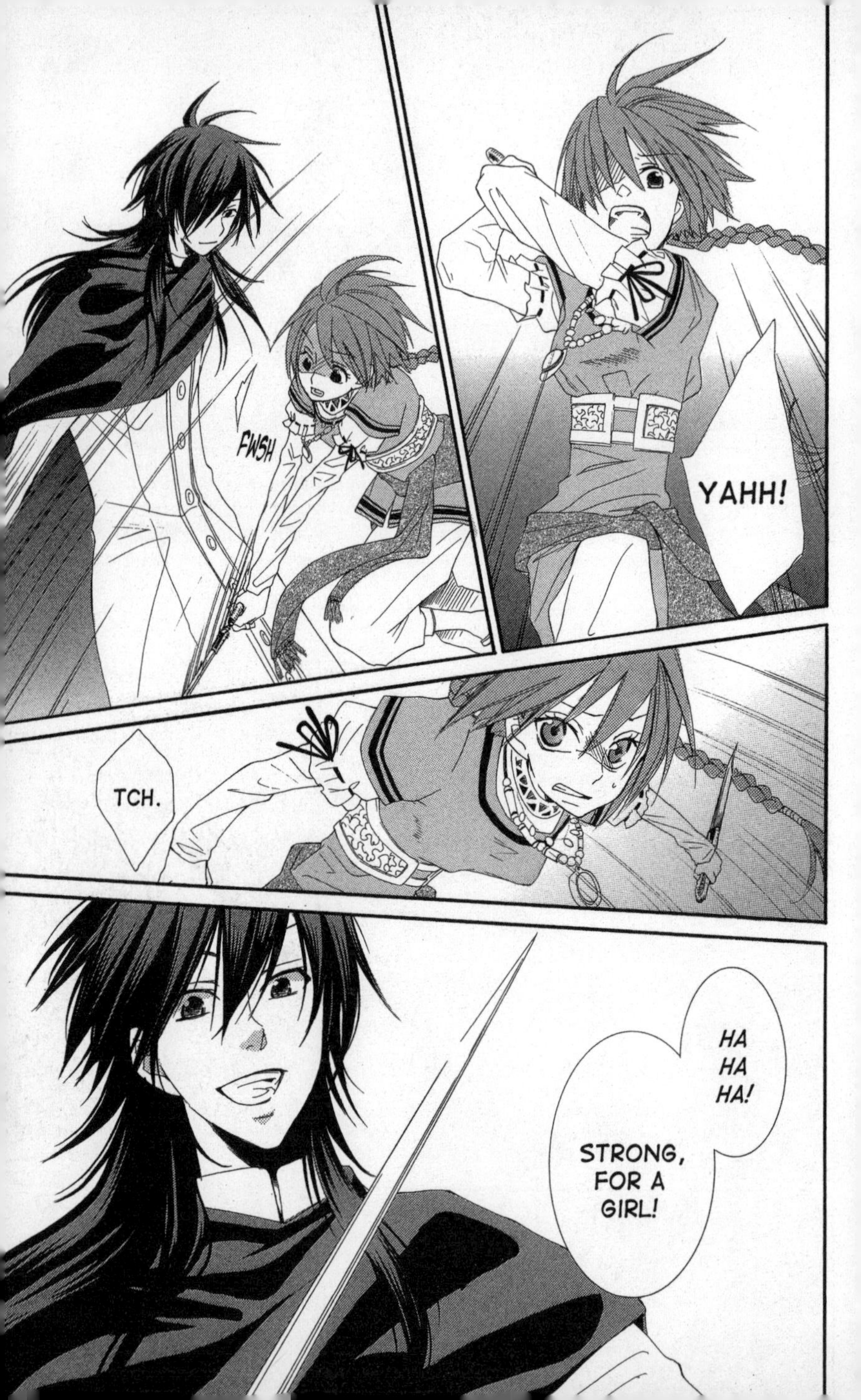
YAHH!
FWSH
TCH.
HA HA HA!
STRONG, FOR A GIRL!

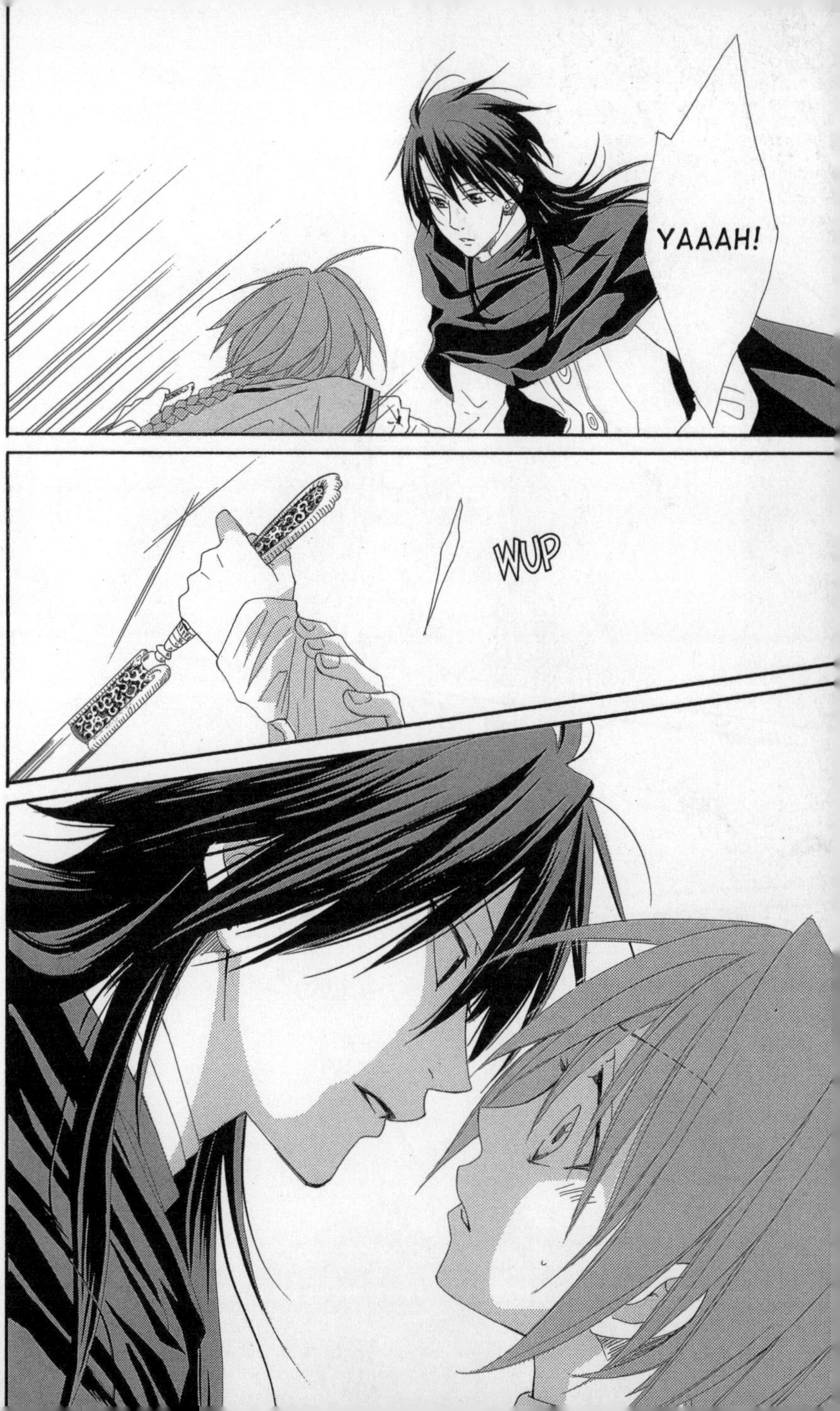
YAAAH!
WUP

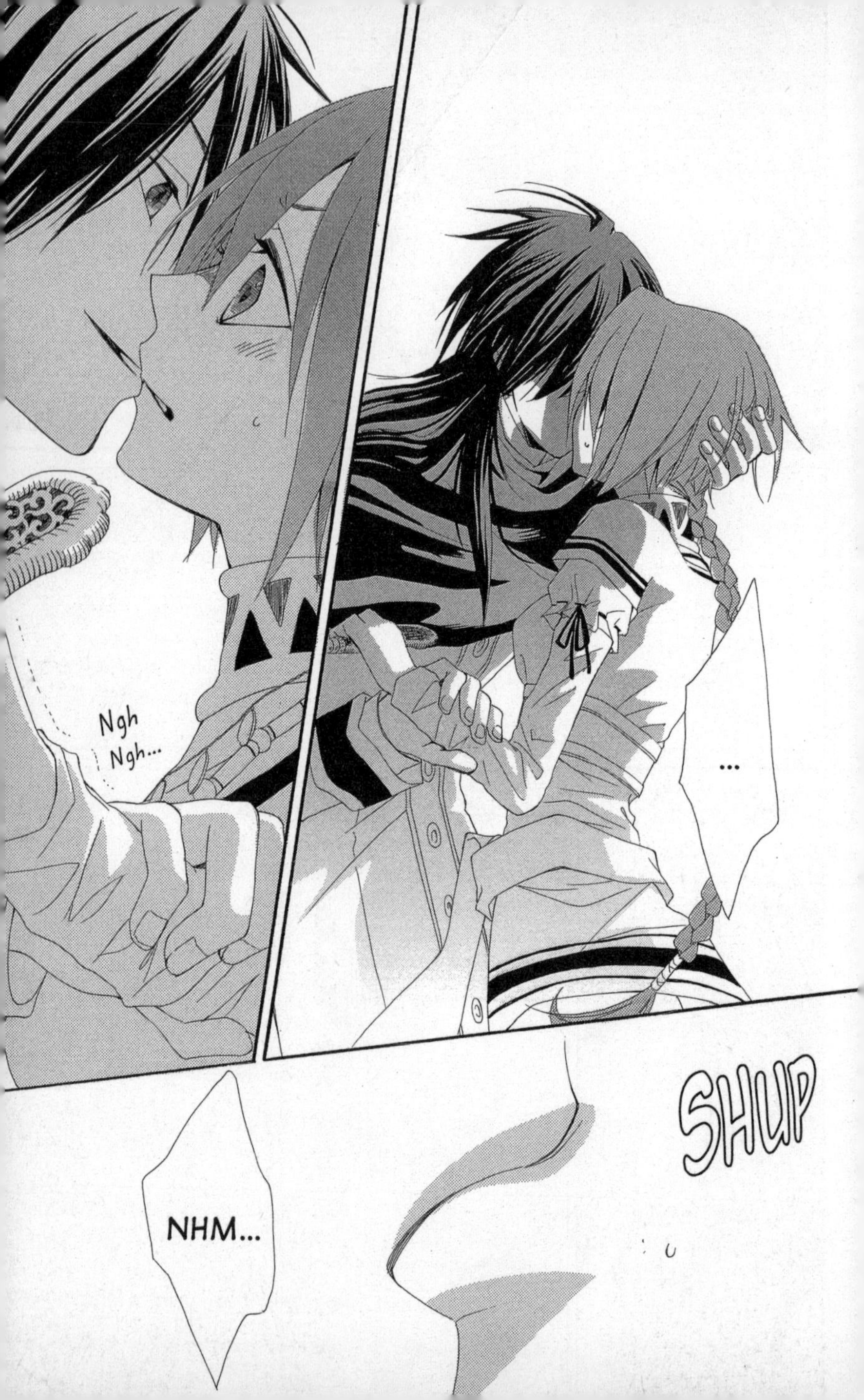
...
Ngh
Ngh...
SHUP
NHM...

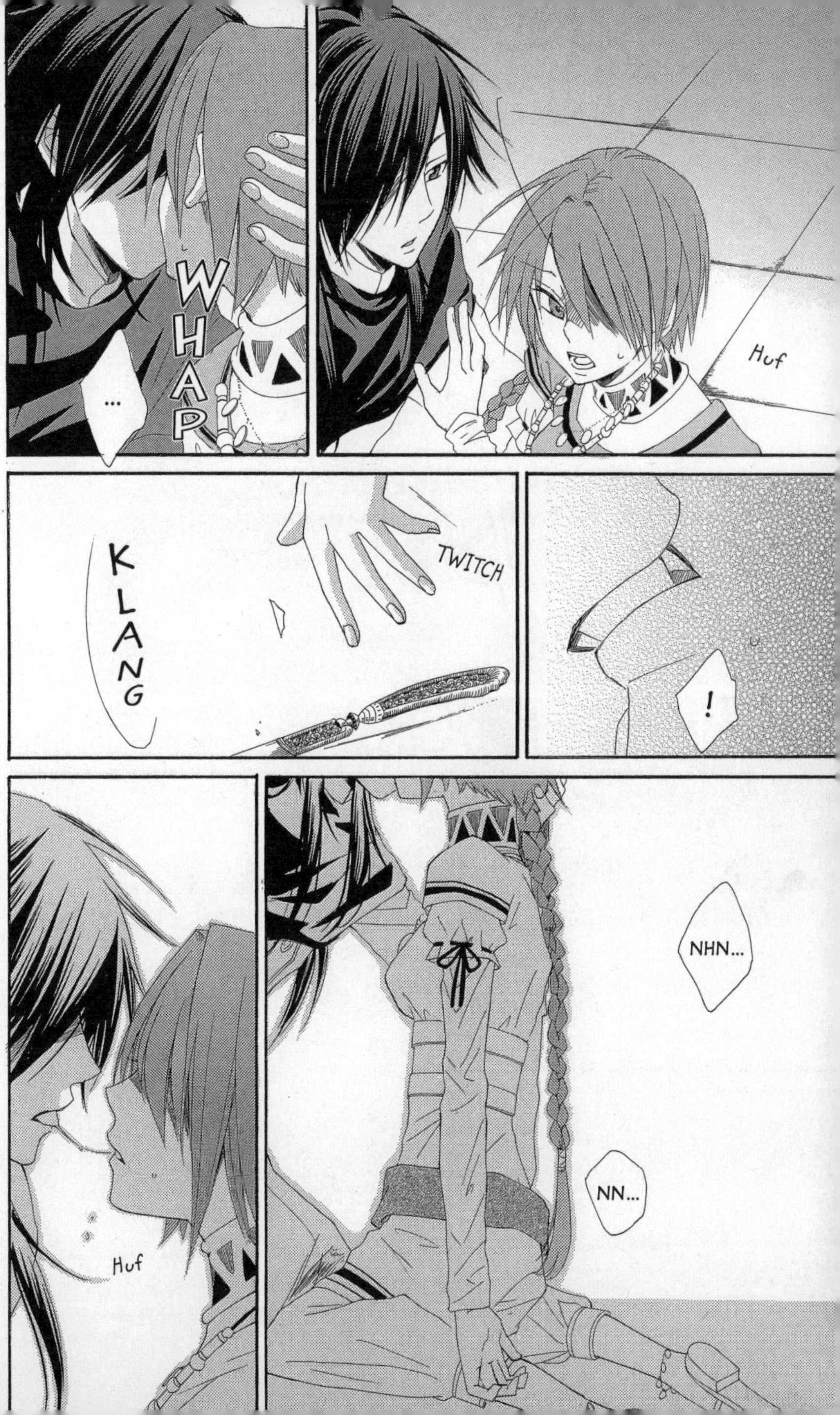
Huf
WHAP
...
!
TWITCH
KLANG
NHN...
NN...
Huf

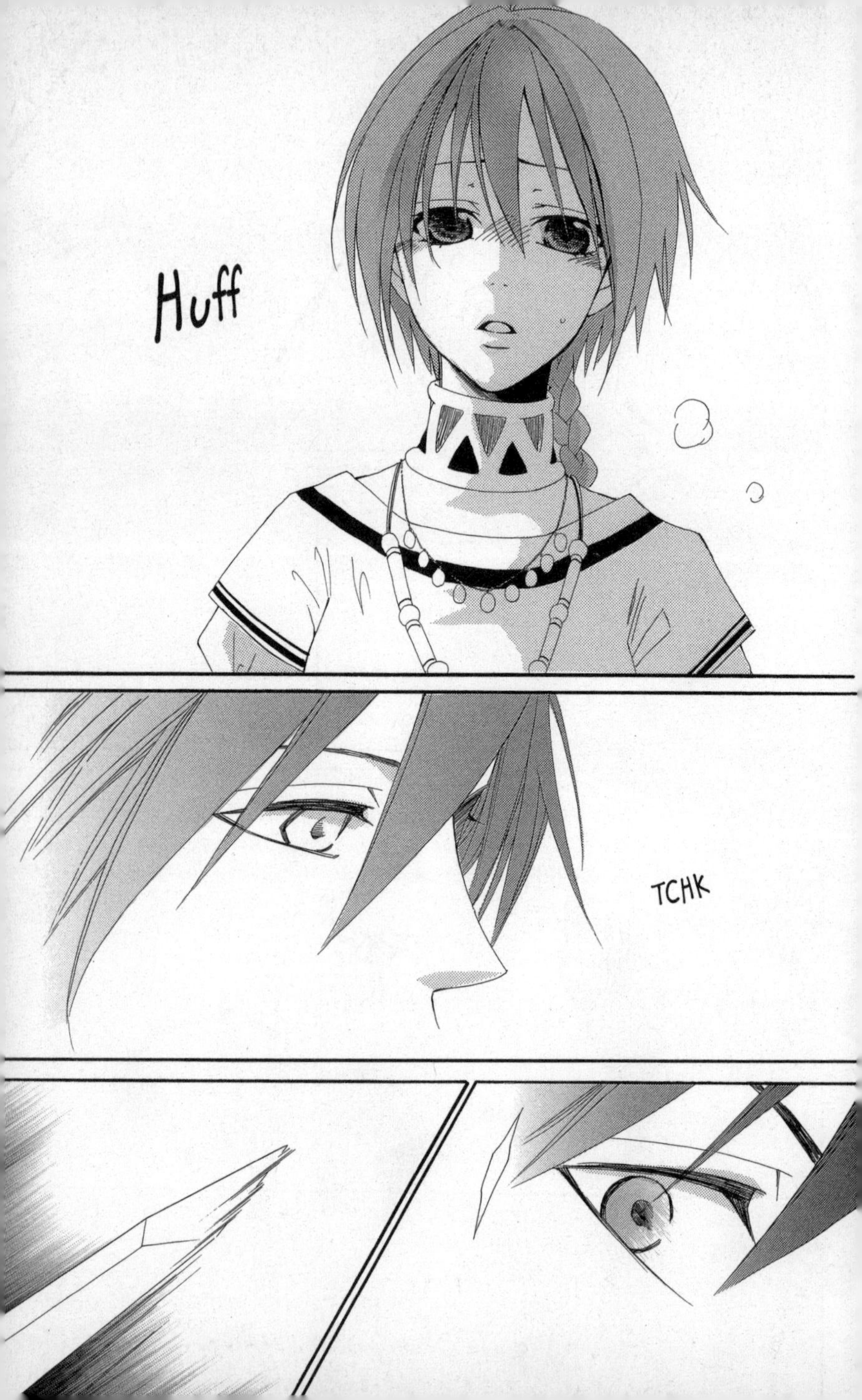
Huff
TCHK

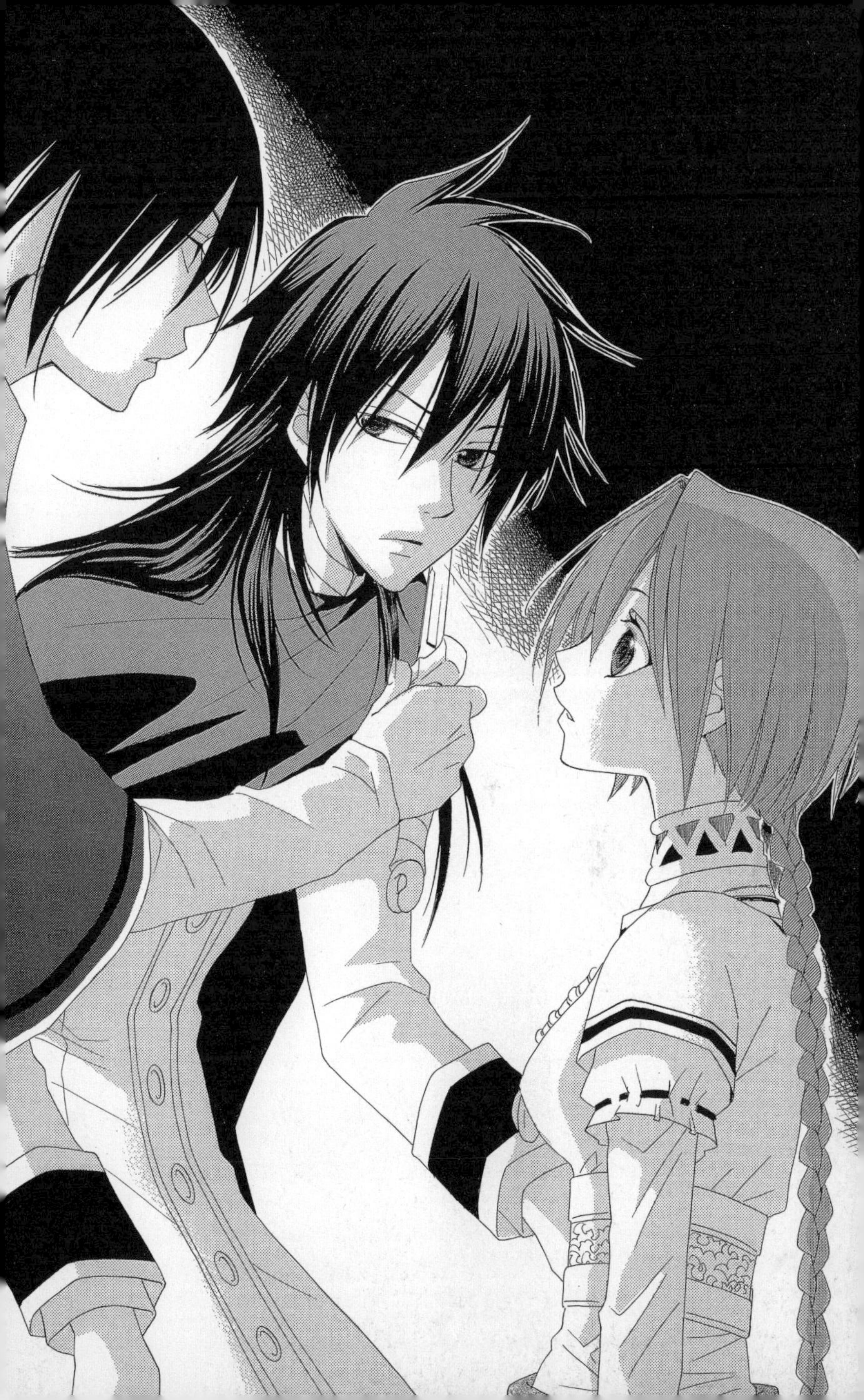

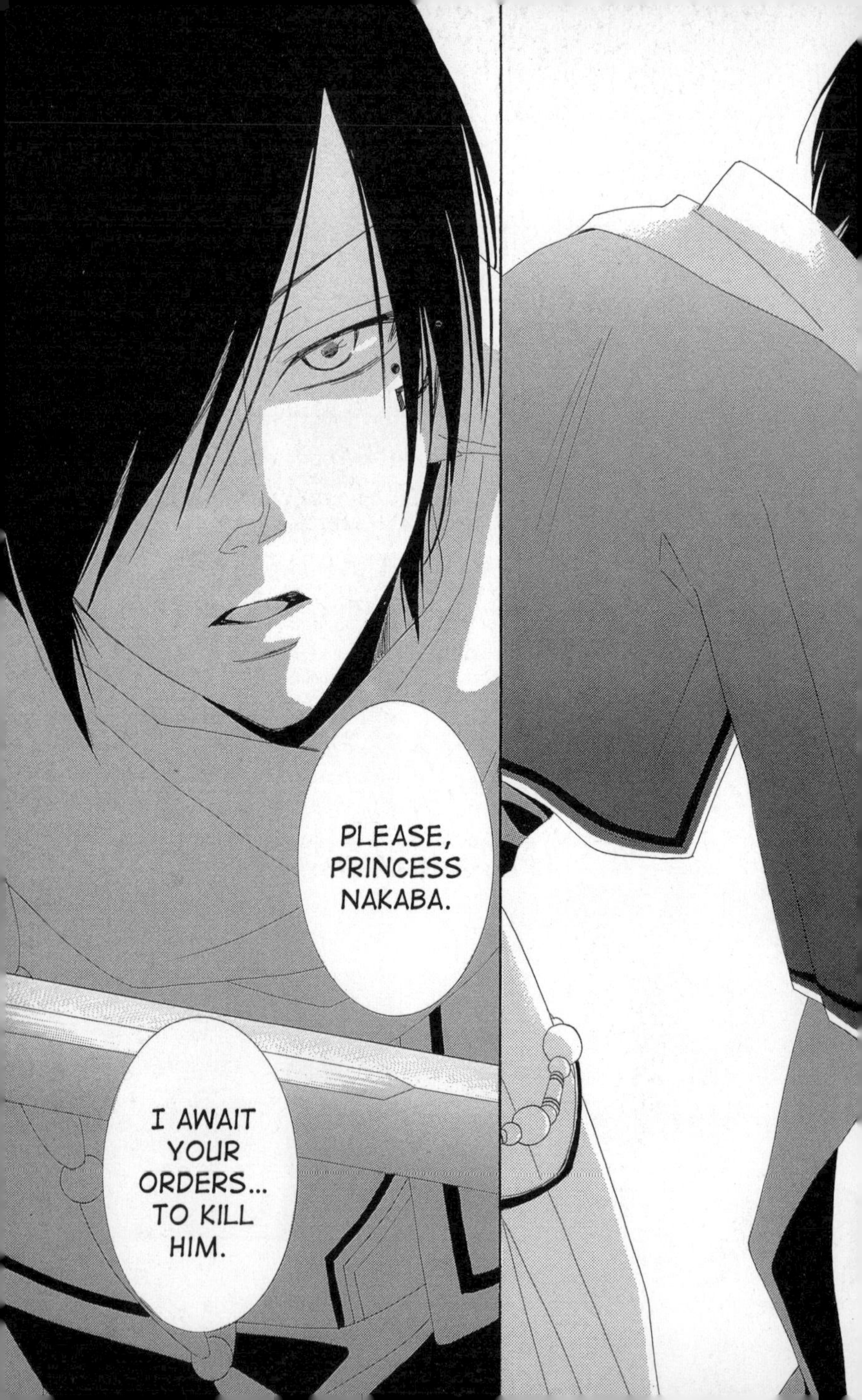
PLEASE, PRINCESS NAKABA.
I AWAIT YOUR ORDERS... TO KILL HIM.

Author's Rambling Space No. 2 (-ish)

So…this is the second one of my ramblings. For *Dawn of the Arcana*,
I had 100 pages when I first started the serialization. But because this is a
fantasy, I found that describing the world and the events within it difficult.
I was unable to get everything I had planned onto the pages, so as I wrote the
next issue and the next, I completed the first volume before I knew it. (*Laugh*)
When the series started, they let me do the cover for *Cheese!* magazine, but
I was unable to get one of the tiny demi-humans that appeared on that cover
into the first volume… They even made some tarot cards as a premium with
the first issue, but quite a few of the characters on the cards didn't even
show up in volume 1. (*Laugh*) Oops! Er, that is to say...
All according to plan. Right.

Our small demi-human friend made it into the second volume, so don't
worry. (*Laugh*) There are still a lot of characters and stories I want
to get out there, so I intend to keep on writing! Wish me luck.

Summer's just around the corner, and when I look up at the summer sky,
all I can say is, "Wow!" It really makes me want to draw a summer sky.
I want Nakaba and everyone standing beneath a broad blue sky and
billowing white clouds.
If I get the chance, I'd love to draw that in color.

…And that's the end of my second ramble!

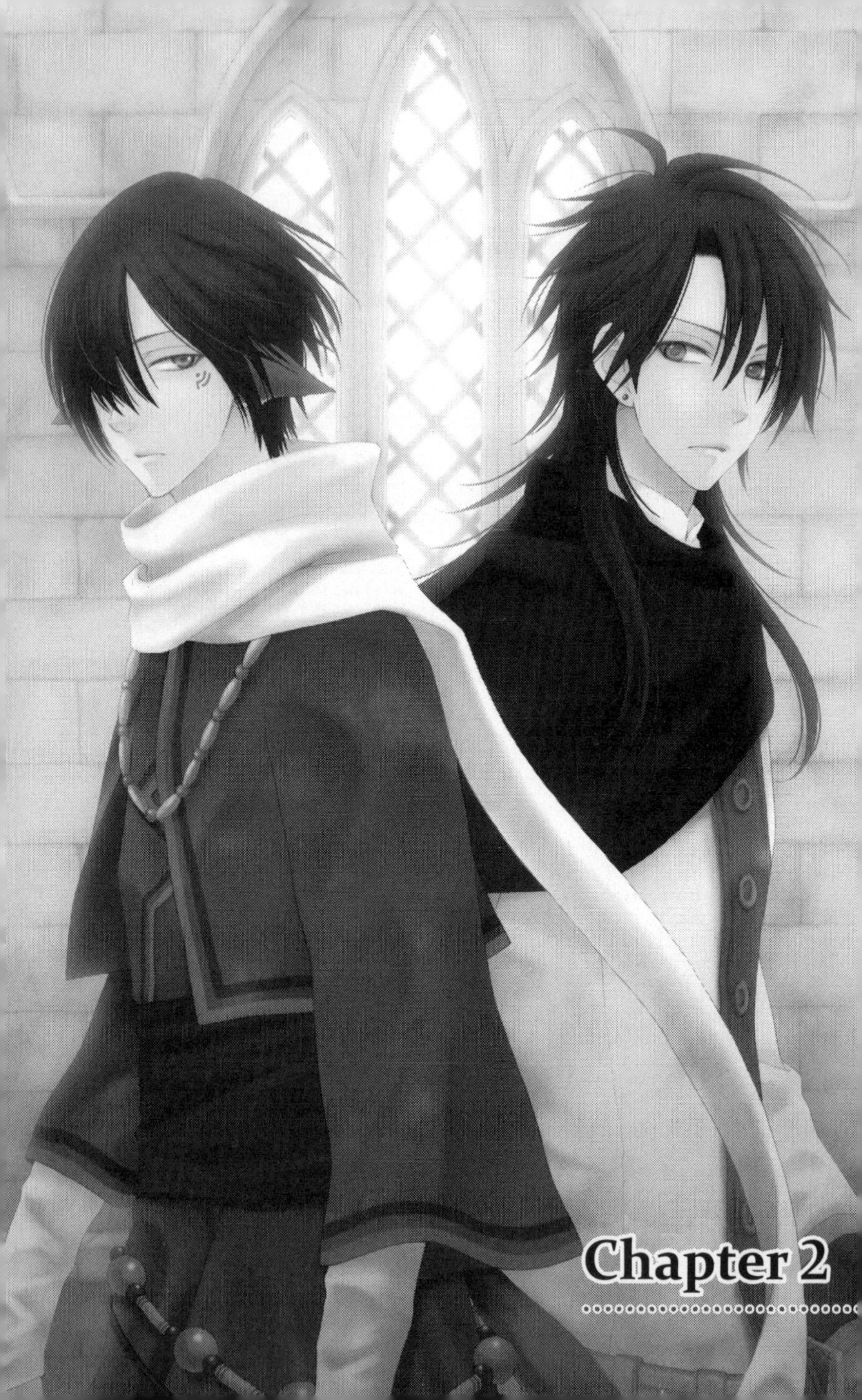

Chapter 2

Author's Rambling Space No. 3 (Uh-huh)

Here we are at number three. Some of the letters I get ask what
kind of music I like, so I thought I'd go ahead and draw up a list.
And no, this is not filler! So there!

Music: Mostly Western rock, with a few Japanese artists thrown in.
But while I'm working, Teresa Teng and Akira Kobayashi show up on shuffle
in my iTunes playlist. My favorite AniSong (Anime Song) is Akuma-kun.
Novels: Mystery
TV: Comedy, Dramas with murder cases
Food: Spring Rolls, Ramen, Sushi
Movies: Shunji Iwai
Drinks: Coca-Cola, Aquarius, Coffee, Tea, Green Tea
Mascot: Doala
Emoticon: (´ · ω · `) Dejected

Okay, out of filler… (*Laugh*) But this is almost over anyway, so who cares.
Either way, thanks to everyone for reading!
Thanks to everyone in Editorial, my editor, everyone who helped me,
everyone who supported me, and of course, Mother Earth…

This was Rei Toma.

Send feedback to:
Rei Toma
c/o Dawn of the Arcana Editor
Viz Media
P.O. Box 77010
San Francisco, CA 94107

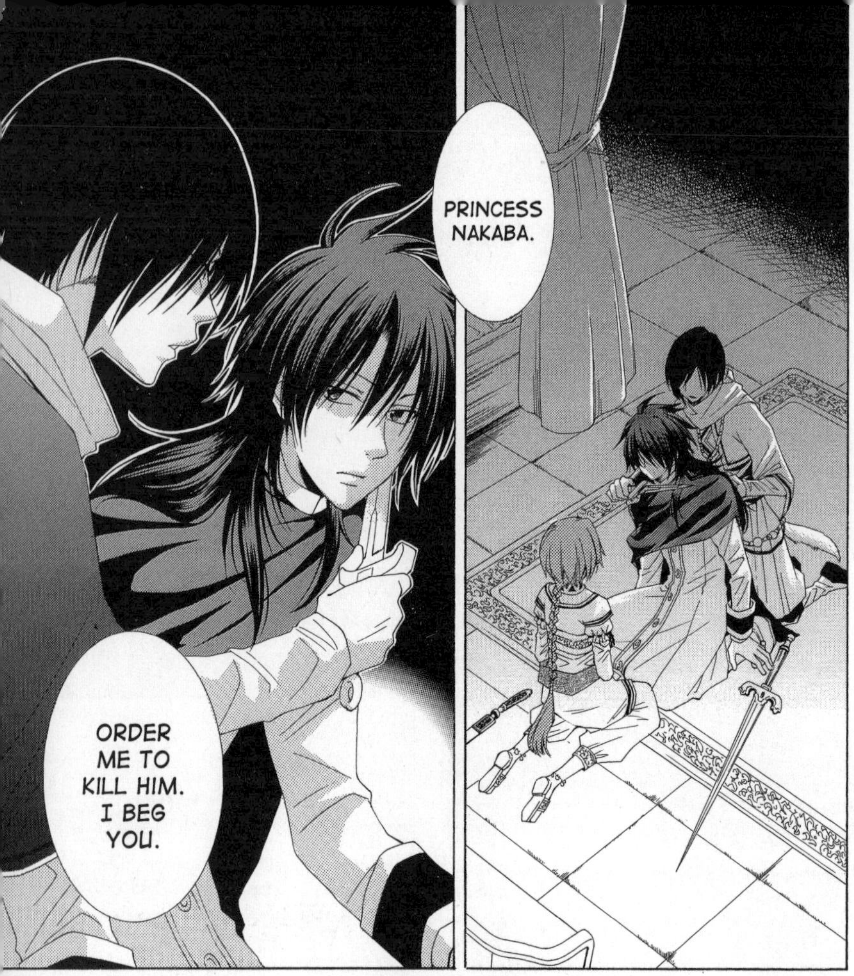
PRINCESS NAKABA.
ORDER ME TO KILL HIM. I BEG YOU.

Dawn of the Arcana

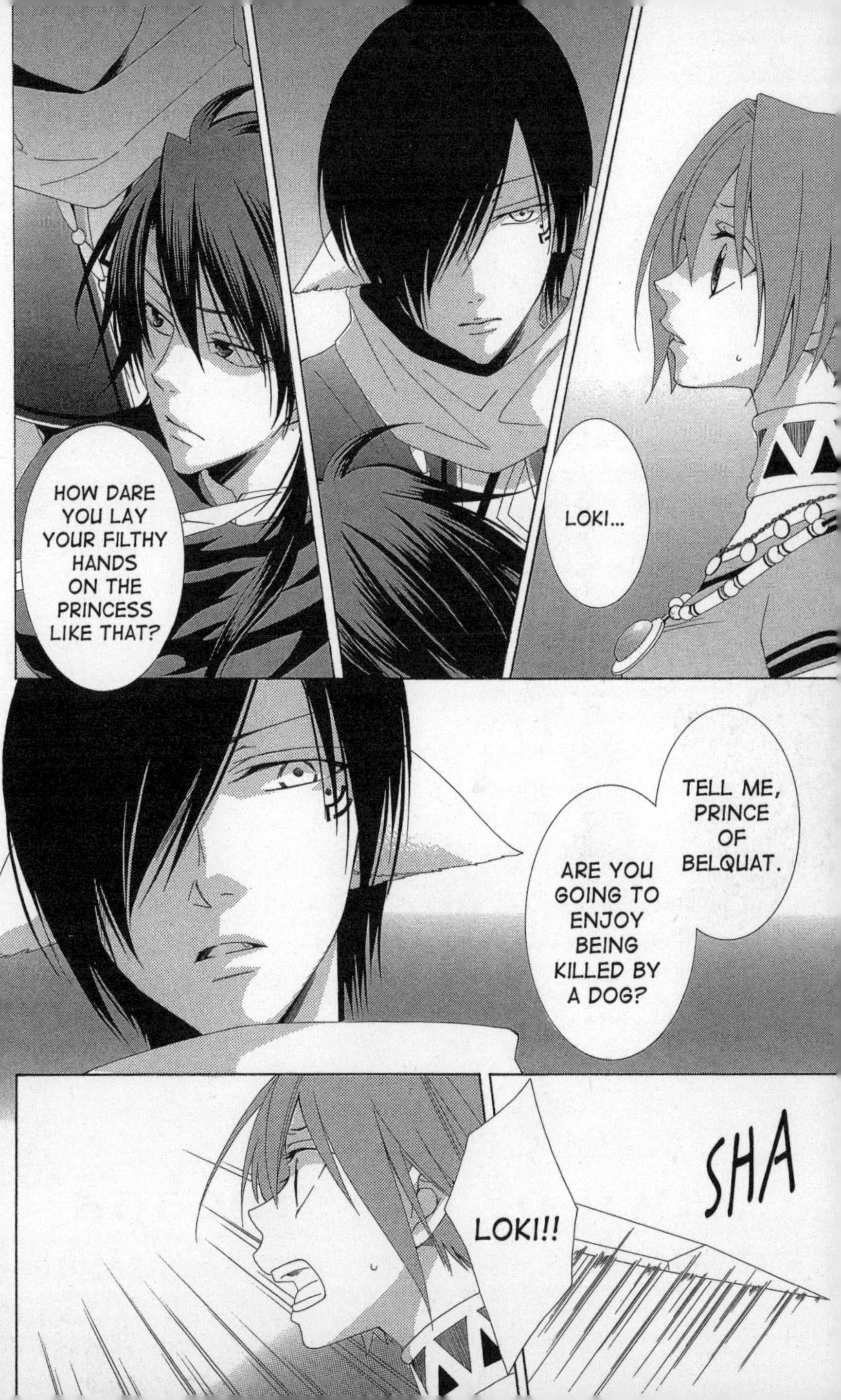
LOKI...
HOW DARE YOU LAY YOUR FILTHY HANDS ON THE PRINCESS LIKE THAT?
TELL ME, PRINCE OF BELQUAT.
ARE YOU GOING TO ENJOY BEING KILLED BY A DOG?
SHA
LOKI!!

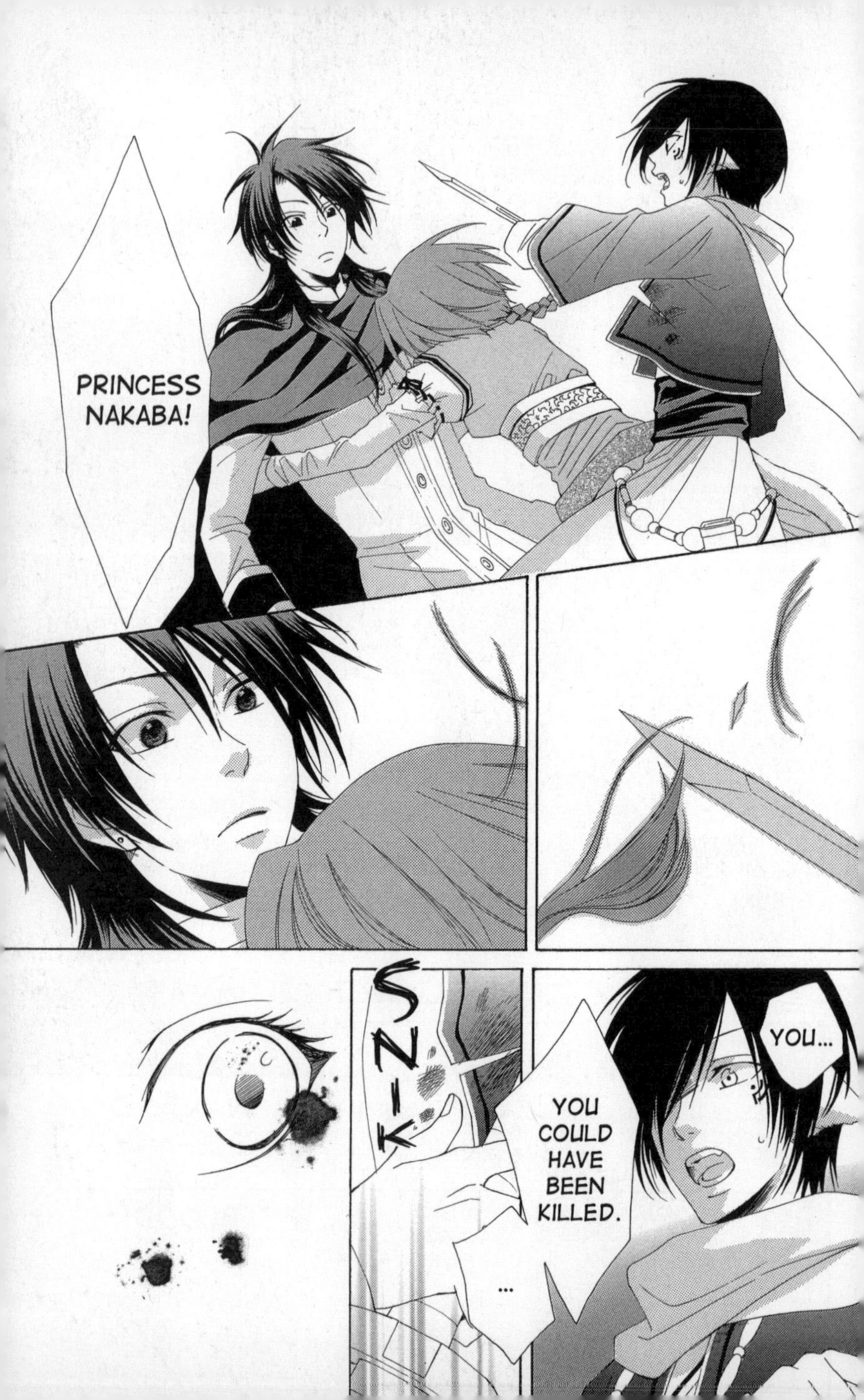
PRINCESS NAKABA!
YOU...
YOU COULD HAVE BEEN KILLED.
...
SNIK

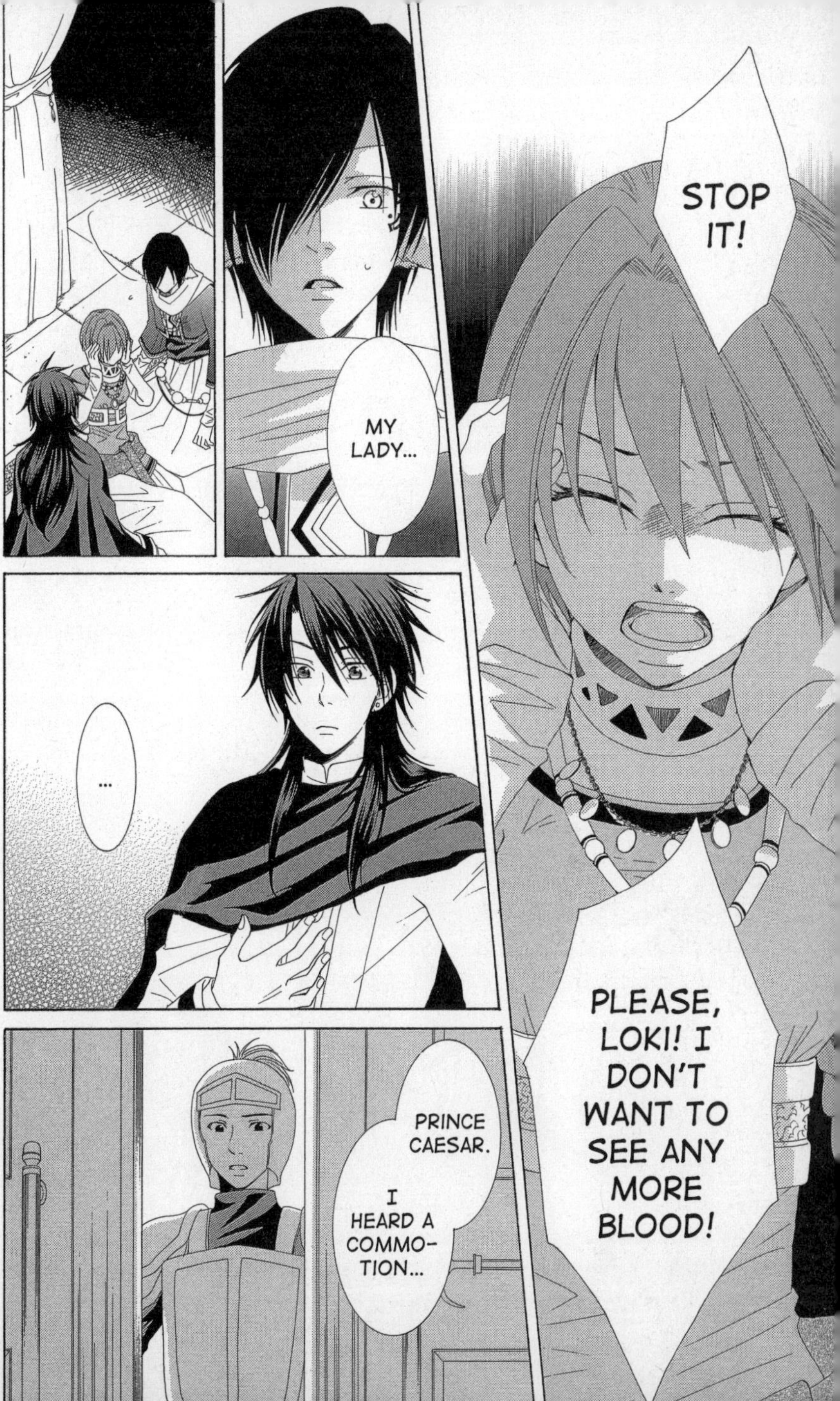
STOP IT!
PLEASE, LOKI! I DON'T WANT TO SEE ANY MORE BLOOD!
MY LADY...
...
PRINCE CAESAR.
I HEARD A COMMOTION...

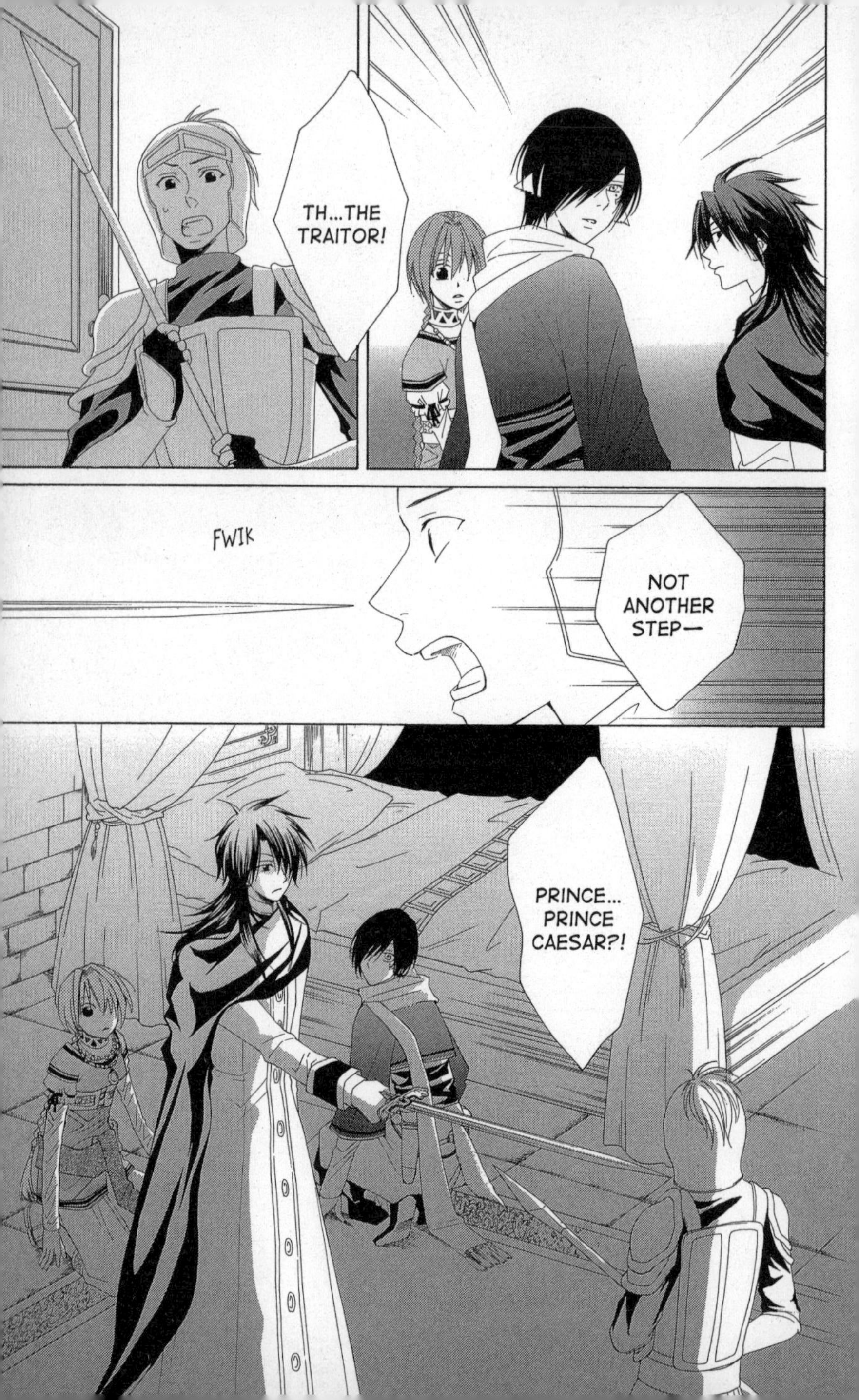
TH...THE TRAITOR!
NOT ANOTHER STEP—
FWIK
PRINCE... PRINCE CAESAR?!

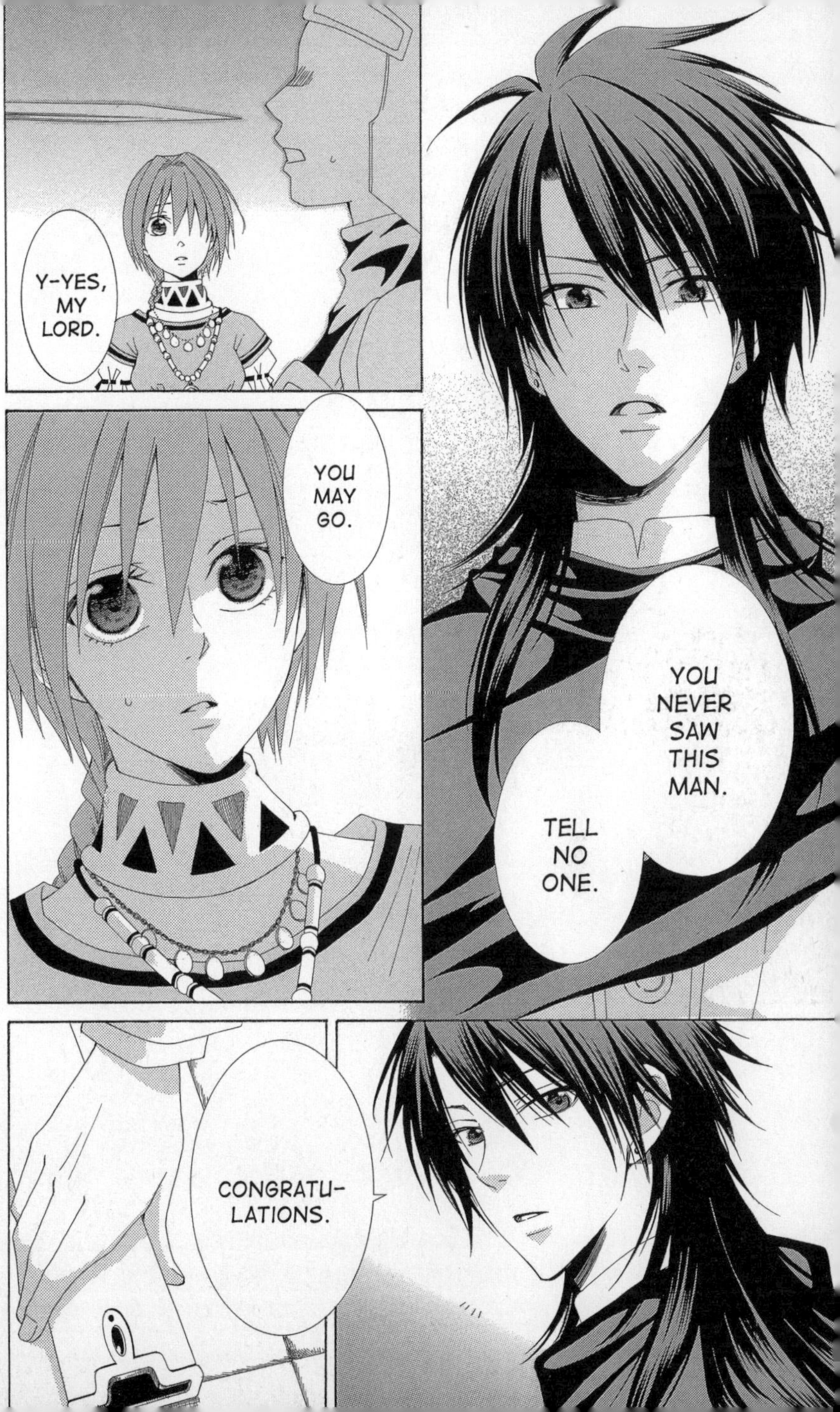
YOU NEVER SAW THIS MAN.
TELL NO ONE.
Y-YES, MY LORD.
YOU MAY GO.
CONGRATU-LATIONS.

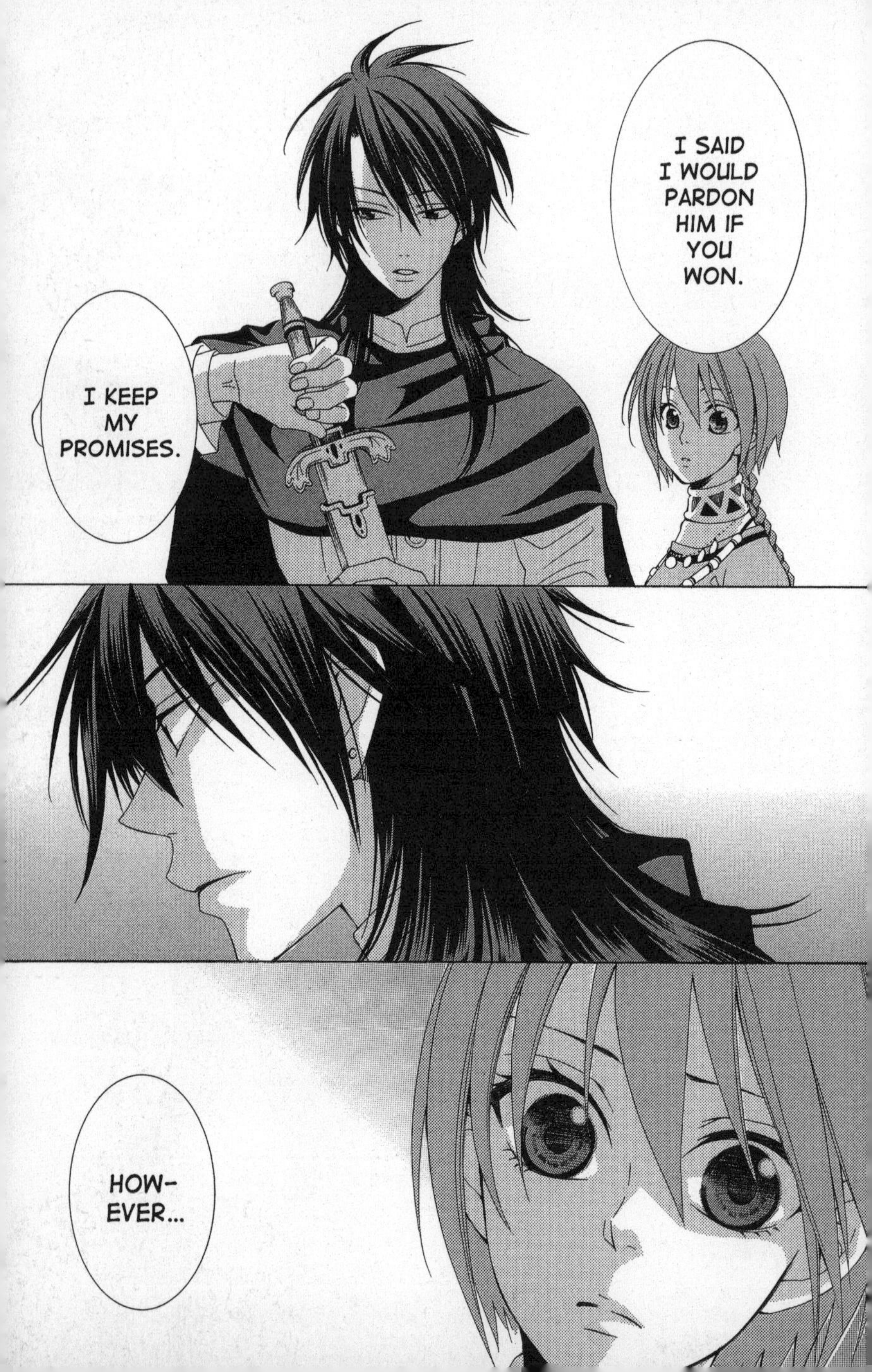
I SAID I WOULD PARDON HIM IF YOU WON.
I KEEP MY PROMISES.
HOW-EVER...

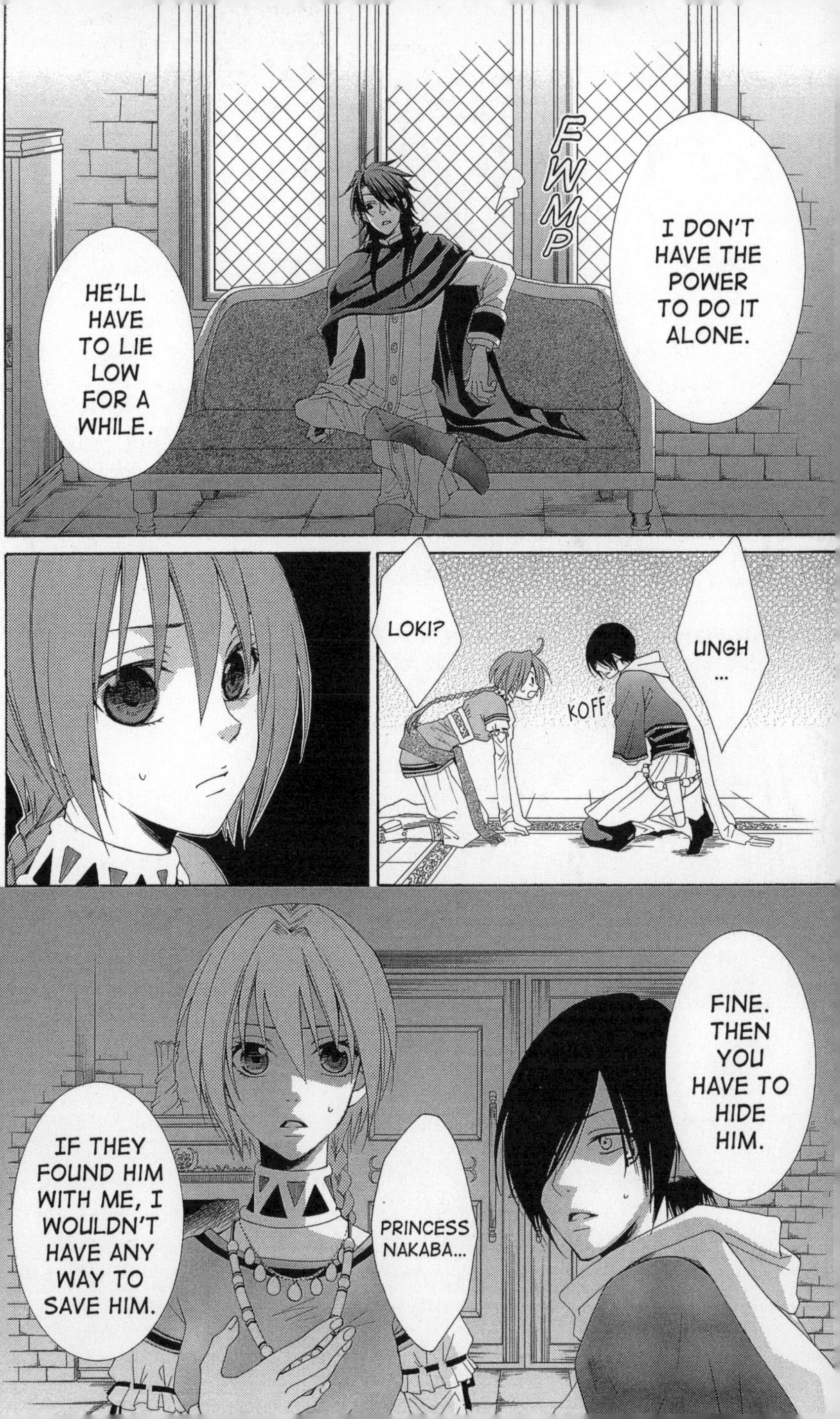
I DON'T HAVE THE POWER TO DO IT ALONE.
FWMP
HE'LL HAVE TO LIE LOW FOR A WHILE.
UNGH ...
KOFF
LOKI?
FINE. THEN YOU HAVE TO HIDE HIM.
PRINCESS NAKABA...
IF THEY FOUND HIM WITH ME, I WOULDN'T HAVE ANY WAY TO SAVE HIM.

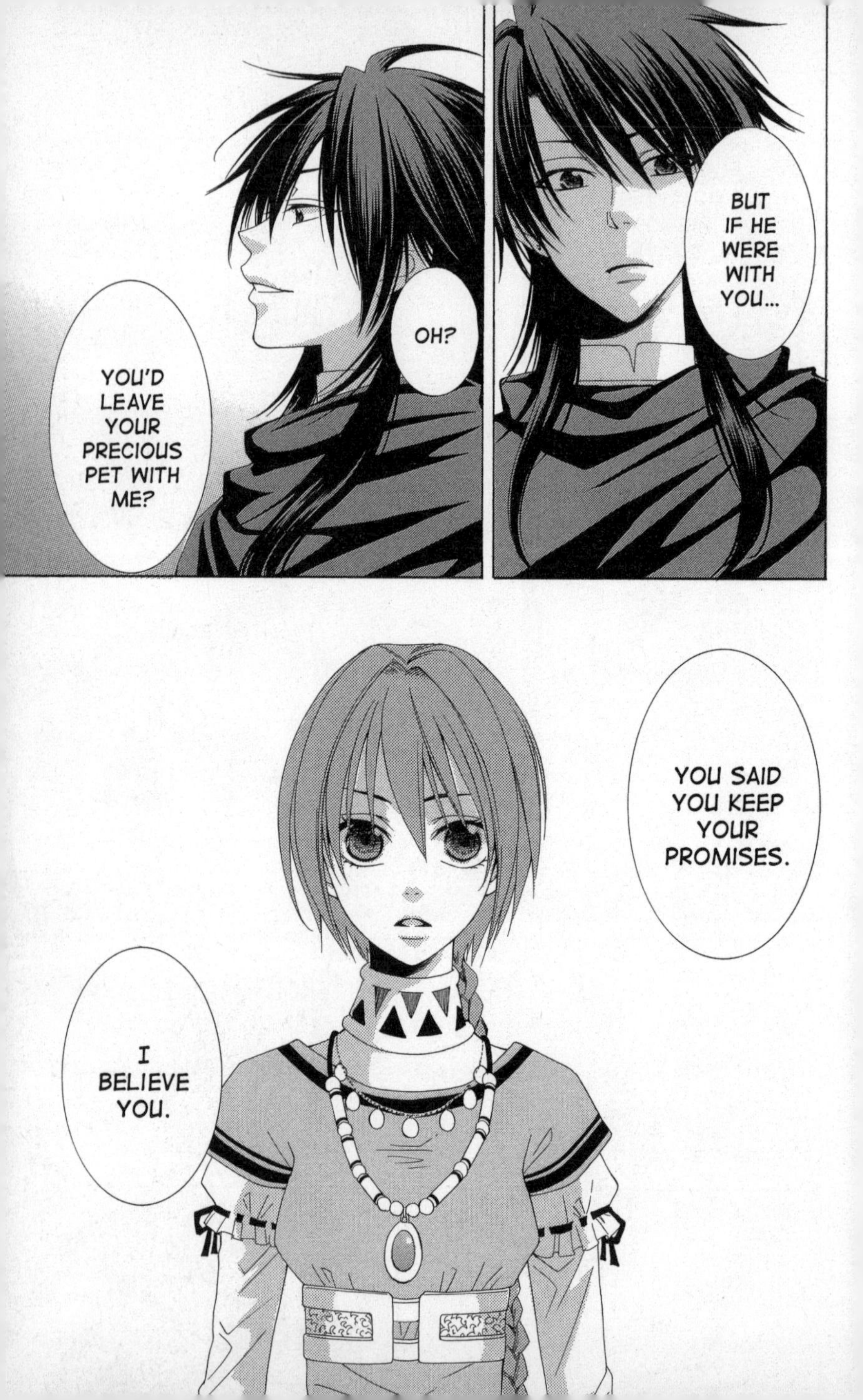
BUT IF HE WERE WITH YOU...
OH?
YOU'D LEAVE YOUR PRECIOUS PET WITH ME?
YOU SAID YOU KEEP YOUR PROMISES.
I BELIEVE YOU.

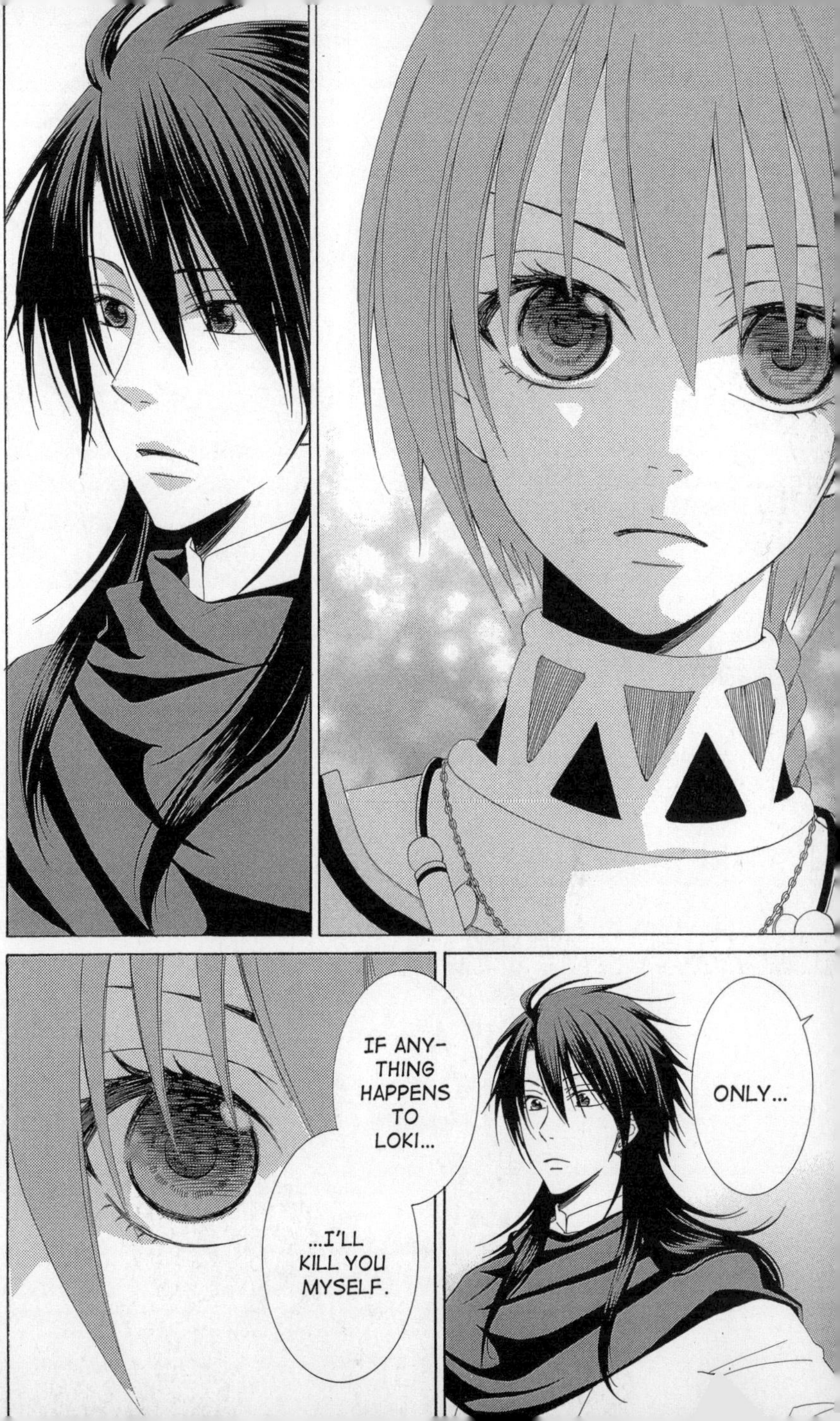
ONLY...
IF ANY-THING HAPPENS TO LOKI...
...I'LL KILL YOU MYSELF.

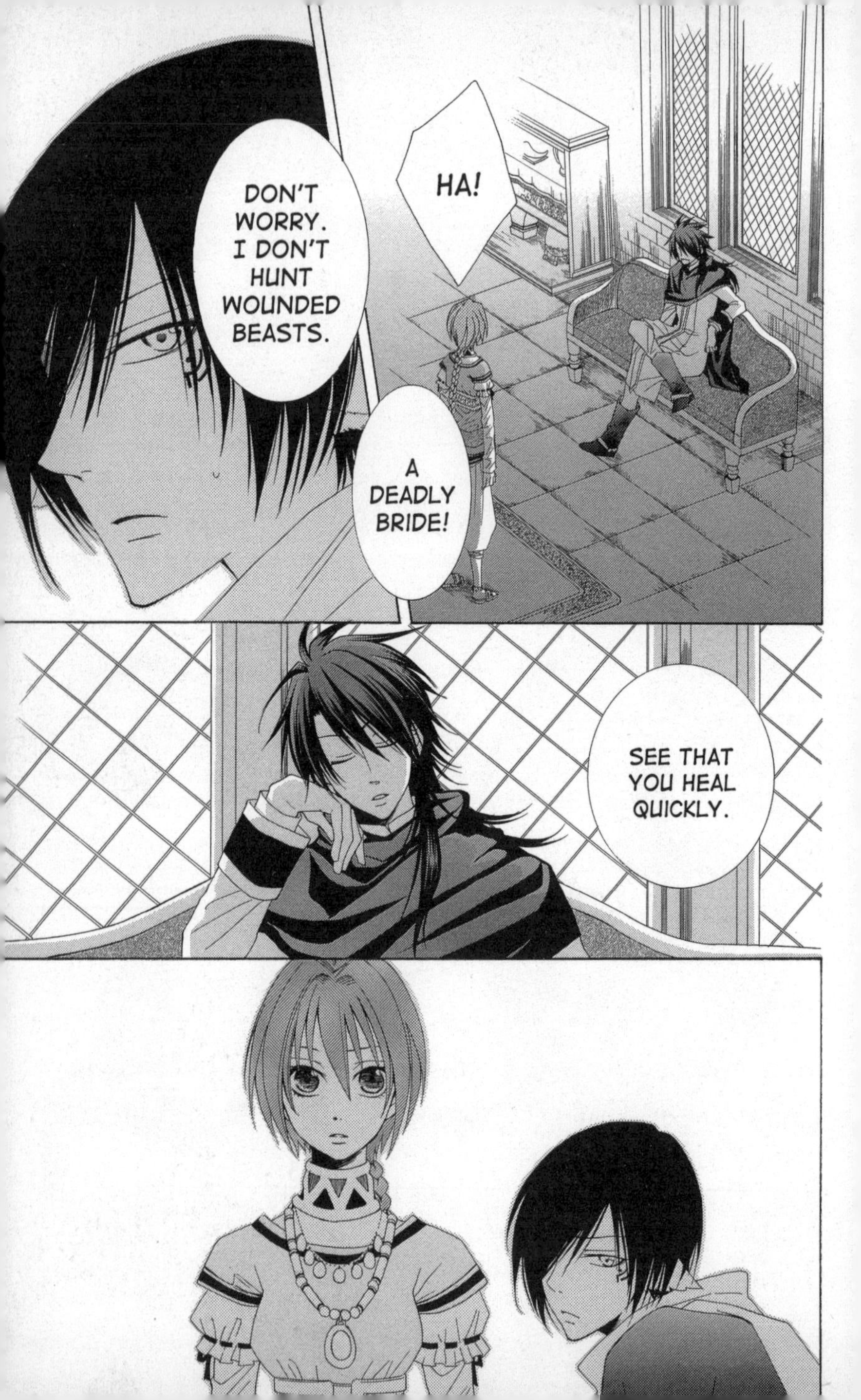
HA!
A DEADLY BRIDE!
DON'T WORRY. I DON'T HUNT WOUNDED BEASTS.
SEE THAT YOU HEAL QUICKLY.

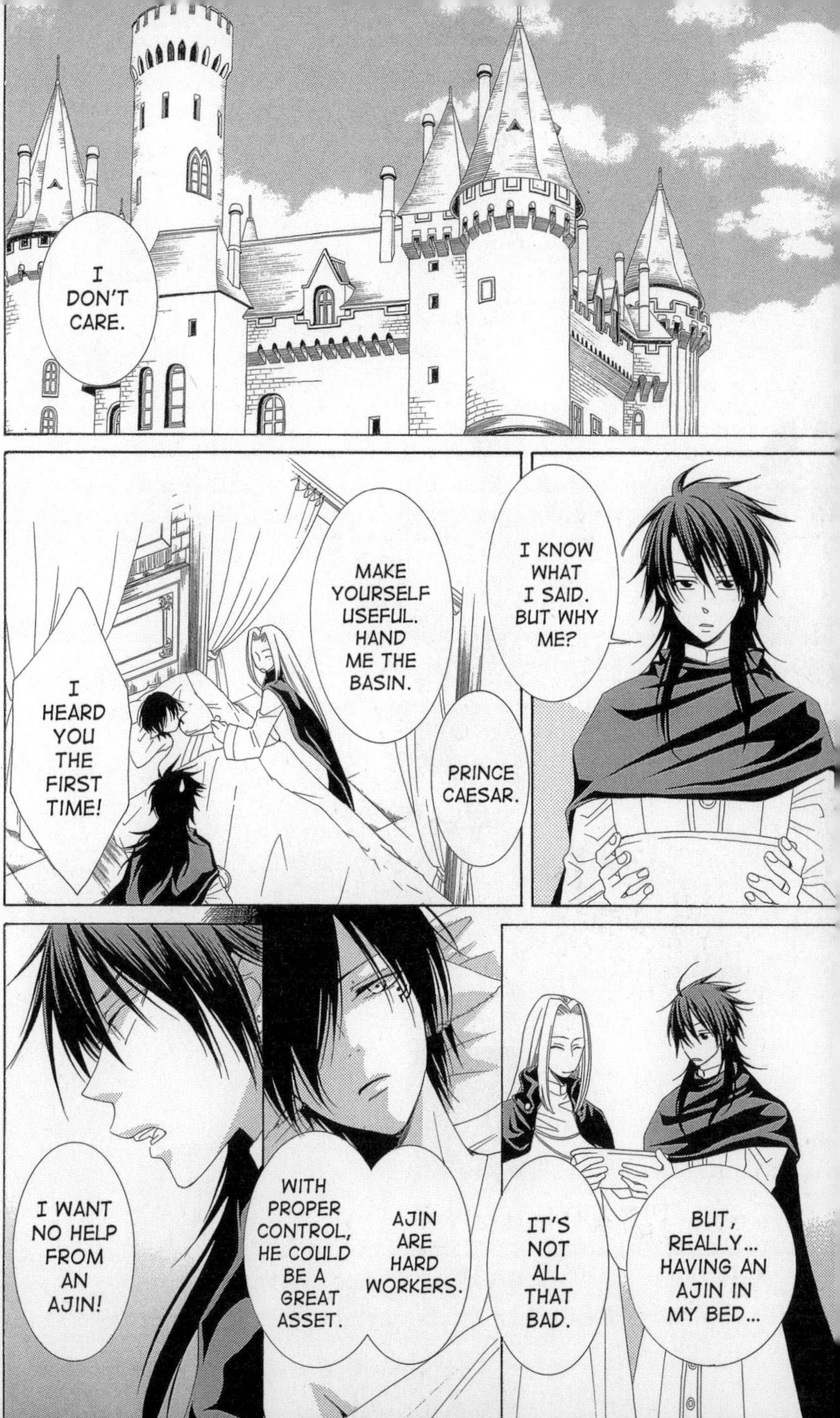
I DON'T CARE.
I KNOW WHAT I SAID. BUT WHY ME?
MAKE YOURSELF USEFUL. HAND ME THE BASIN.
PRINCE CAESAR.
I HEARD YOU THE FIRST TIME!
BUT, REALLY... HAVING AN AJIN IN MY BED...
IT'S NOT ALL THAT BAD.
AJIN ARE HARD WORKERS.
WITH PROPER CONTROL, HE COULD BE A GREAT ASSET.
I WANT NO HELP FROM AN AJIN!

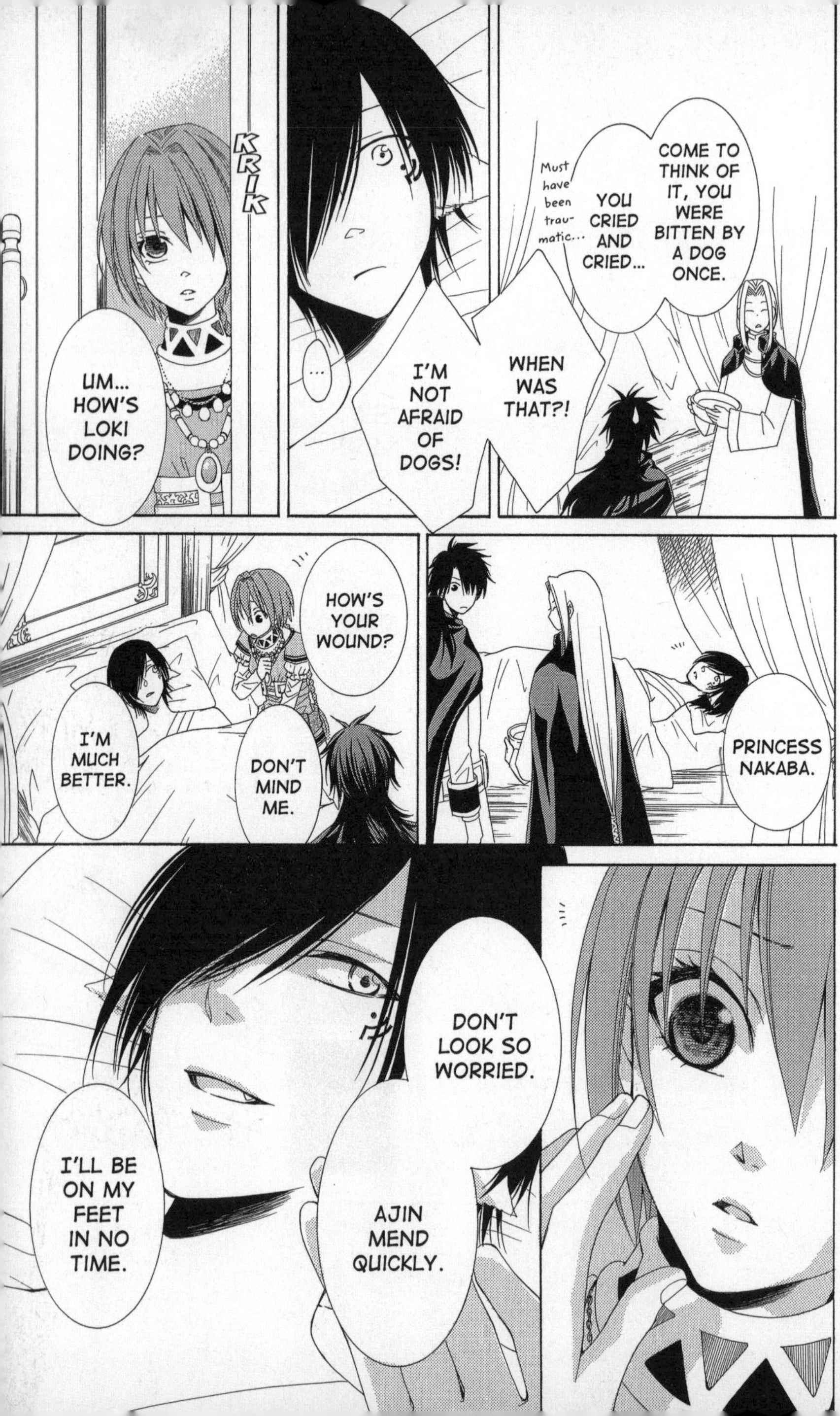
COME TO THINK OF IT, YOU WERE BITTEN BY A DOG ONCE.
YOU CRIED AND CRIED...
Must have been trau-matic...
WHEN WAS THAT?!
I'M NOT AFRAID OF DOGS!
...
KRIK
UM... HOW'S LOKI DOING?
PRINCESS NAKABA.
HOW'S YOUR WOUND?
DON'T MIND ME.
I'M MUCH BETTER.
DON'T LOOK SO WORRIED.
AJIN MEND QUICKLY.
I'LL BE ON MY FEET IN NO TIME.

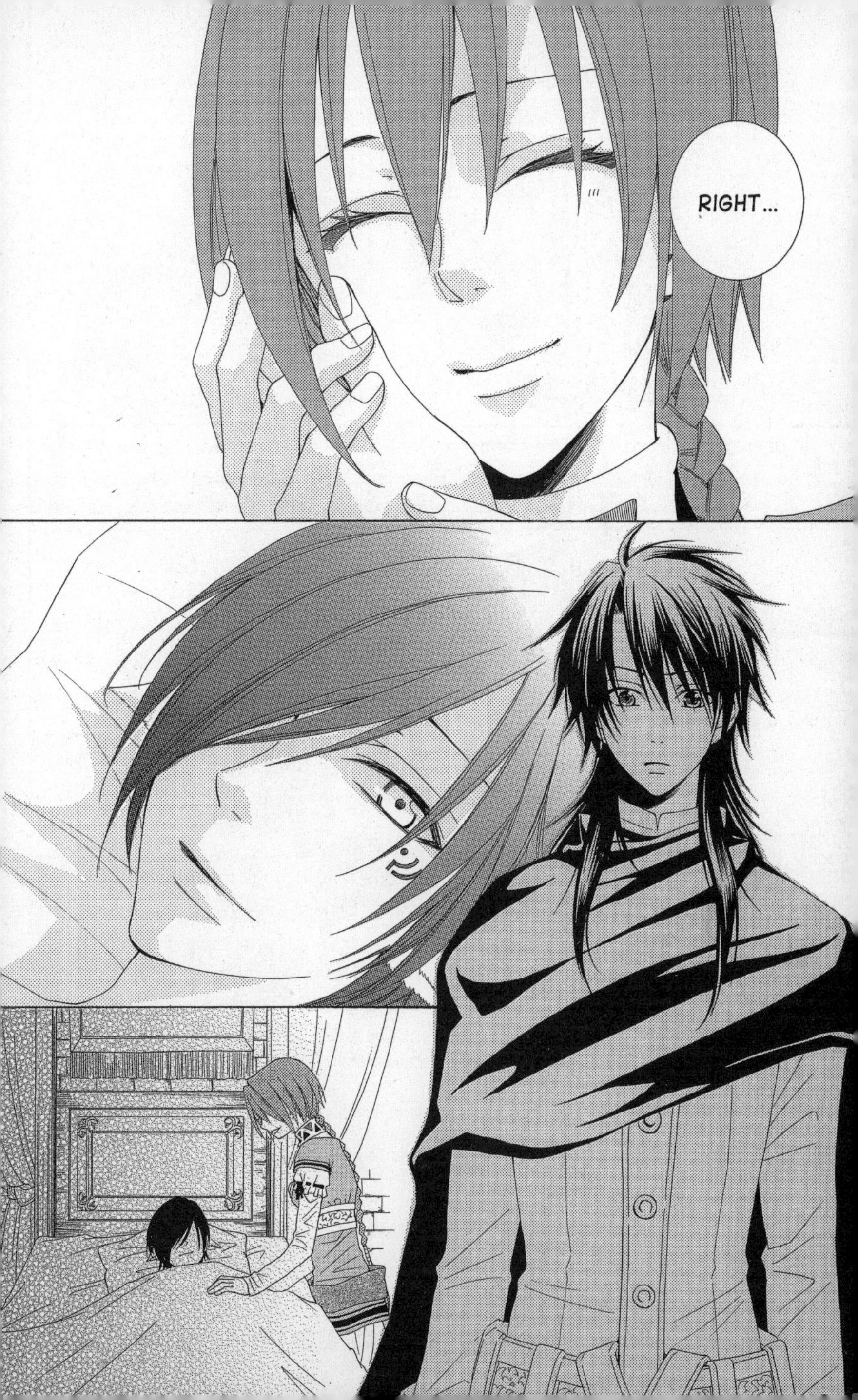
RIGHT...

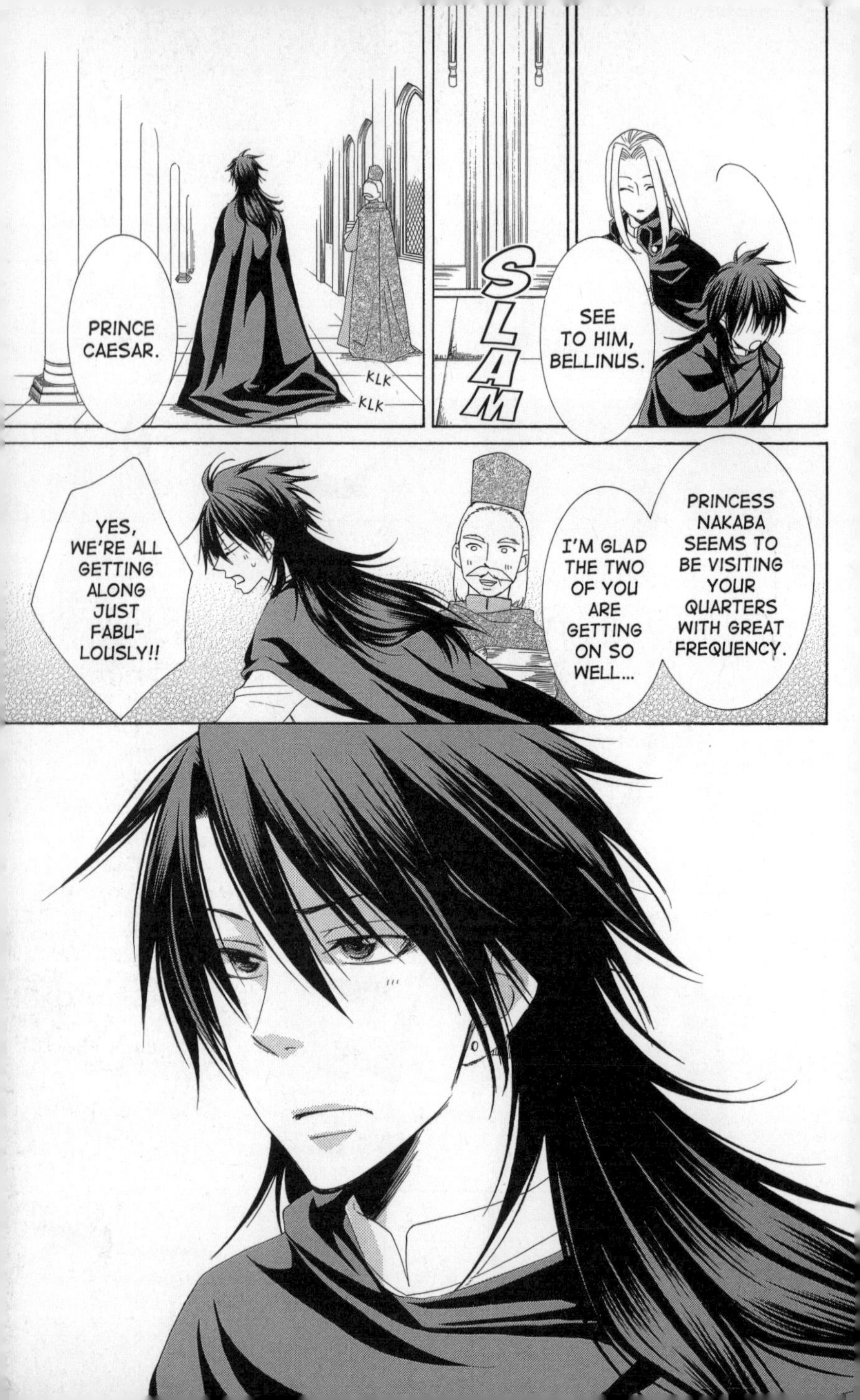
SEE TO HIM, BELLINUS.
SLAM
PRINCE CAESAR.
KLK
KLK
PRINCESS NAKABA SEEMS TO BE VISITING YOUR QUARTERS WITH GREAT FREQUENCY.
I'M GLAD THE TWO OF YOU ARE GETTING ON SO WELL...
YES, WE'RE ALL GETTING ALONG JUST FABU-LOUSLY!!

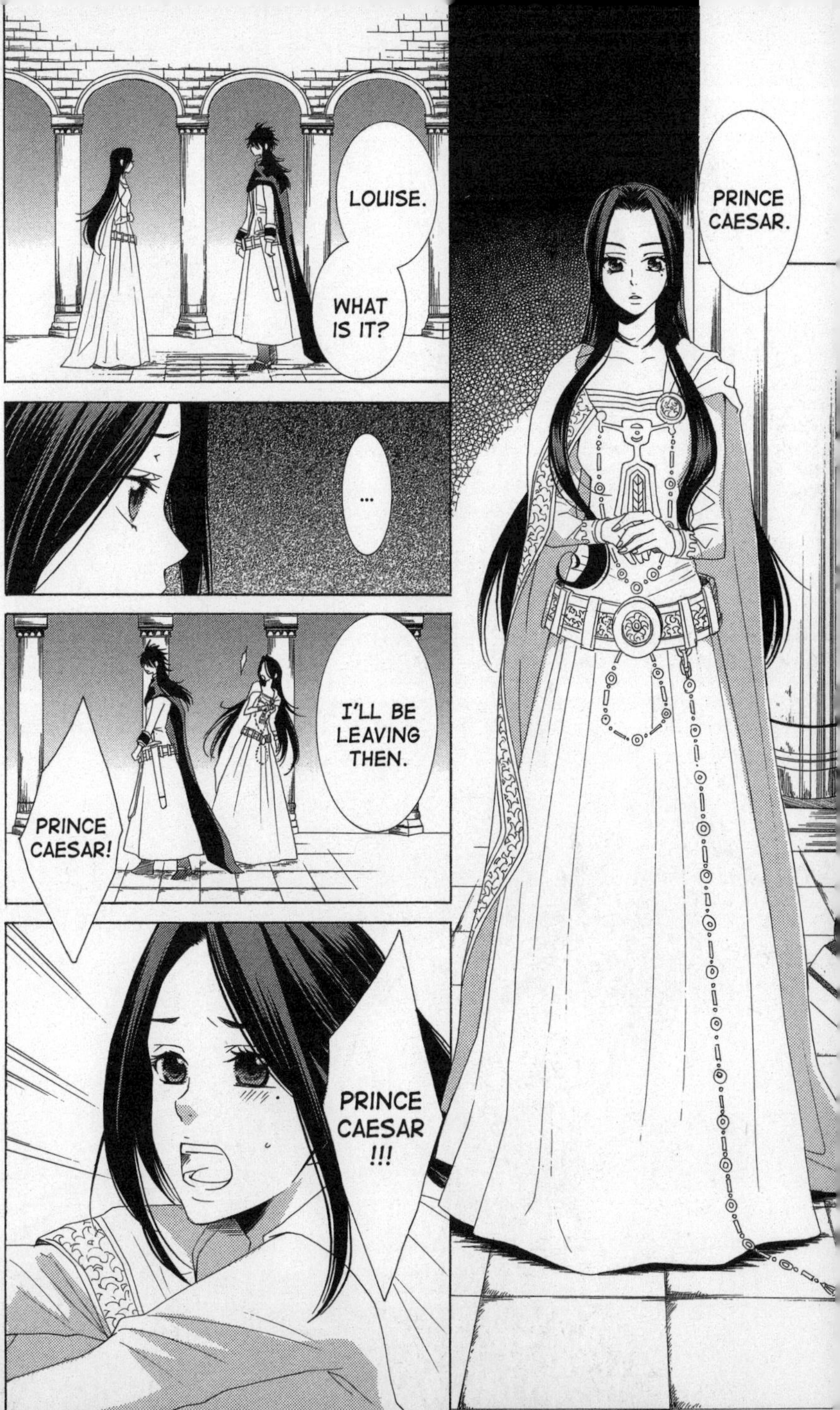
PRINCE CAESAR.
LOUISE.
WHAT IS IT?
...
I'LL BE LEAVING THEN.
PRINCE CAESAR!
PRINCE CAESAR !!!

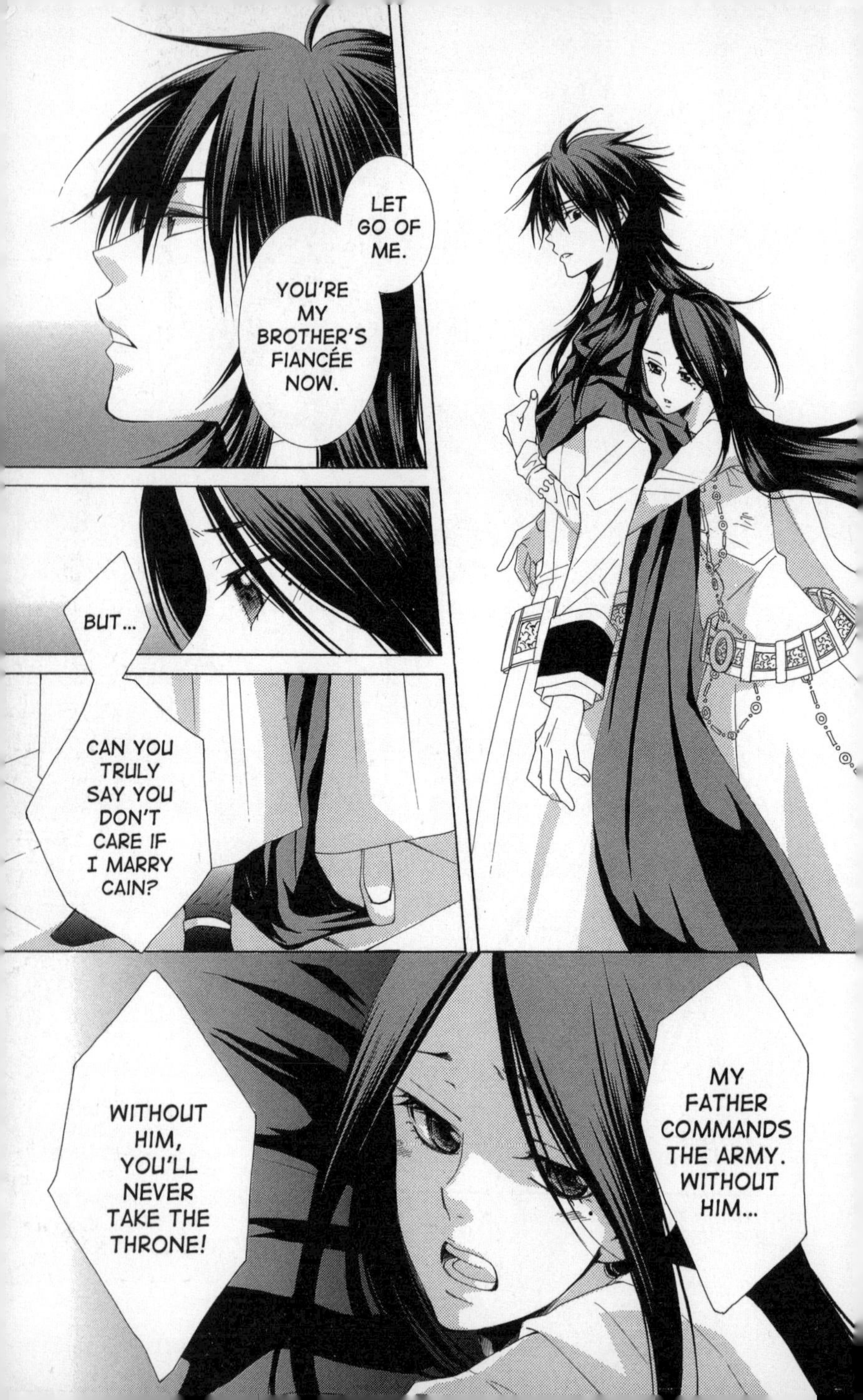
LET GO OF ME.
YOU'RE MY BROTHER'S FIANCÉE NOW.
BUT...
CAN YOU TRULY SAY YOU DON'T CARE IF I MARRY CAIN?
MY FATHER COMMANDS THE ARMY. WITHOUT HIM...
WITHOUT HIM, YOU'LL NEVER TAKE THE THRONE!

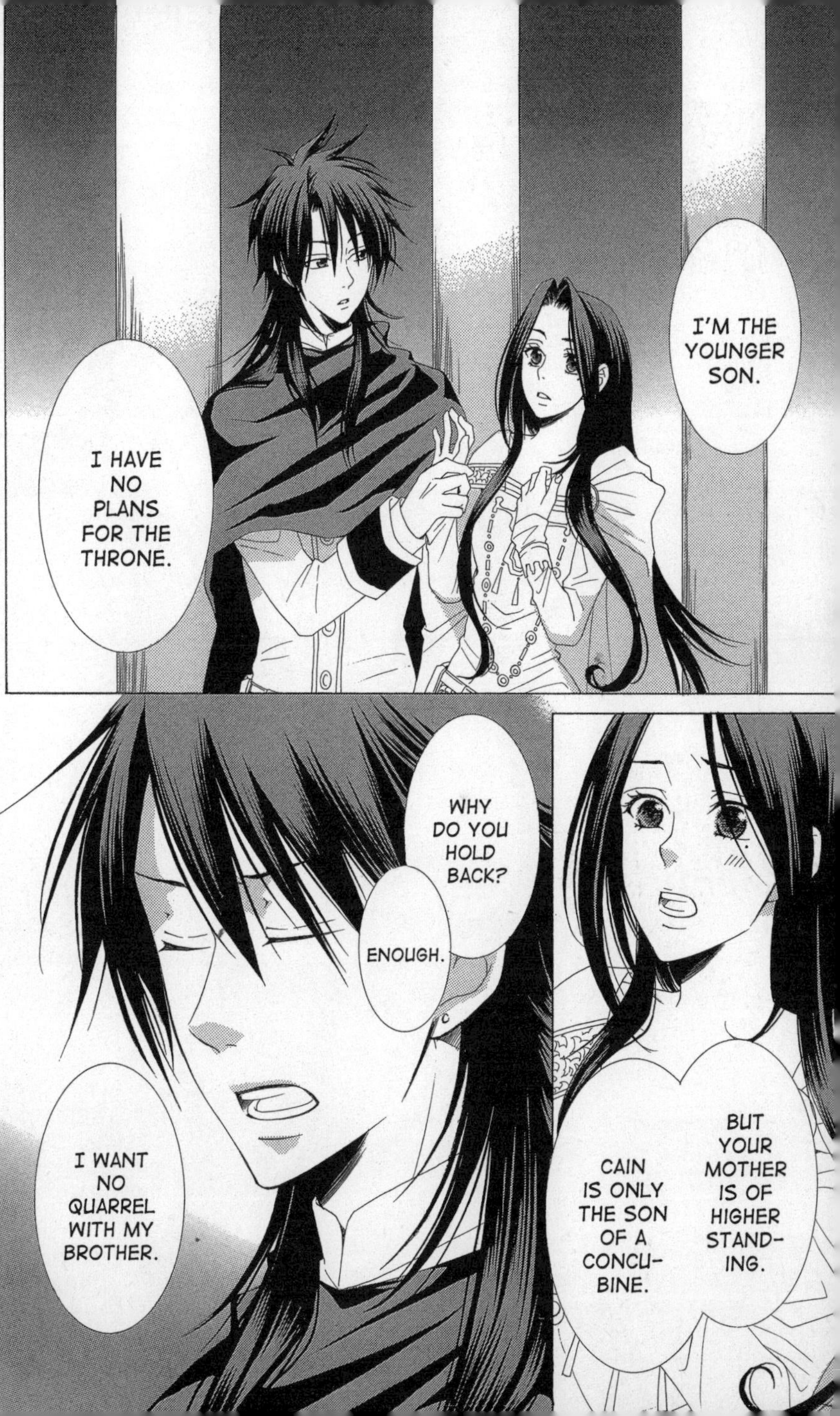
I'M THE YOUNGER SON.
I HAVE NO PLANS FOR THE THRONE.
WHY DO YOU HOLD BACK?
BUT YOUR MOTHER IS OF HIGHER STANDING.
CAIN IS ONLY THE SON OF A CONCUBINE.
ENOUGH.
I WANT NO QUARREL WITH MY BROTHER.

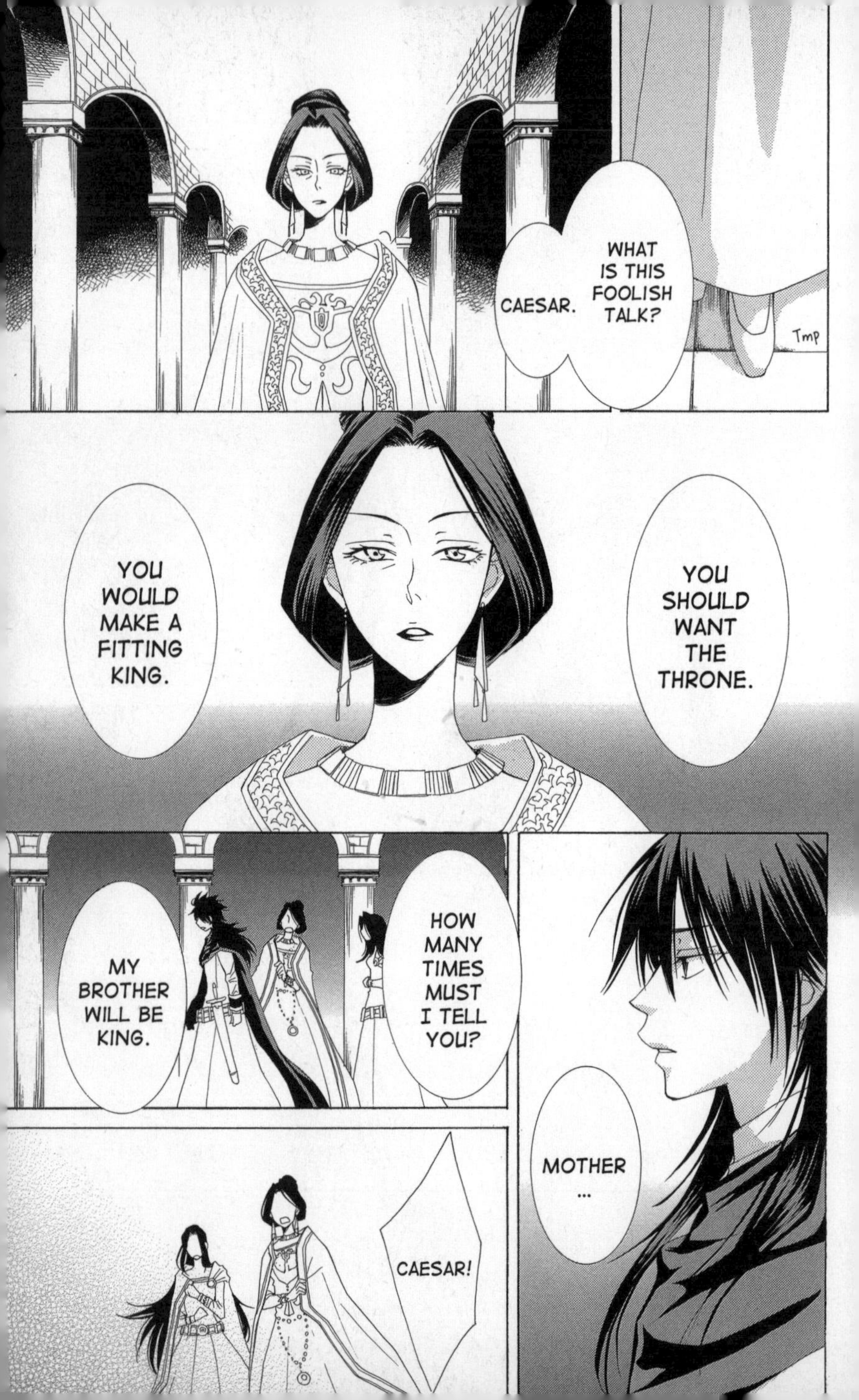

Tmp
WHAT IS THIS FOOLISH TALK?
CAESAR.
YOU SHOULD WANT THE THRONE.
YOU WOULD MAKE A FITTING KING.
MOTHER ...
HOW MANY TIMES MUST I TELL YOU?
MY BROTHER WILL BE KING.
CAESAR!

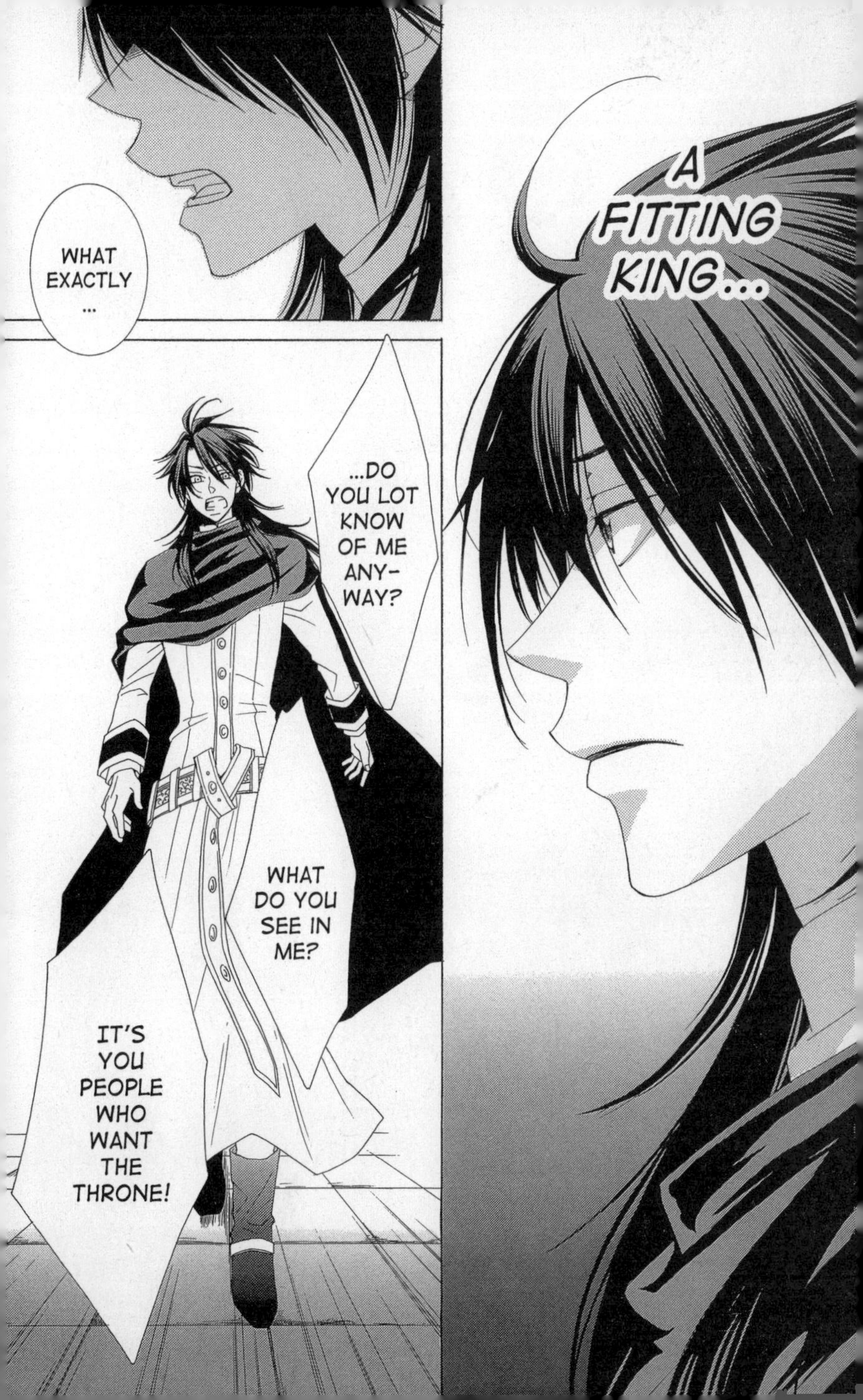
A FITTING KING...
WHAT EXACTLY ...
...DO YOU LOT KNOW OF ME ANY-WAY?
WHAT DO YOU SEE IN ME?
IT'S YOU PEOPLE WHO WANT THE THRONE!

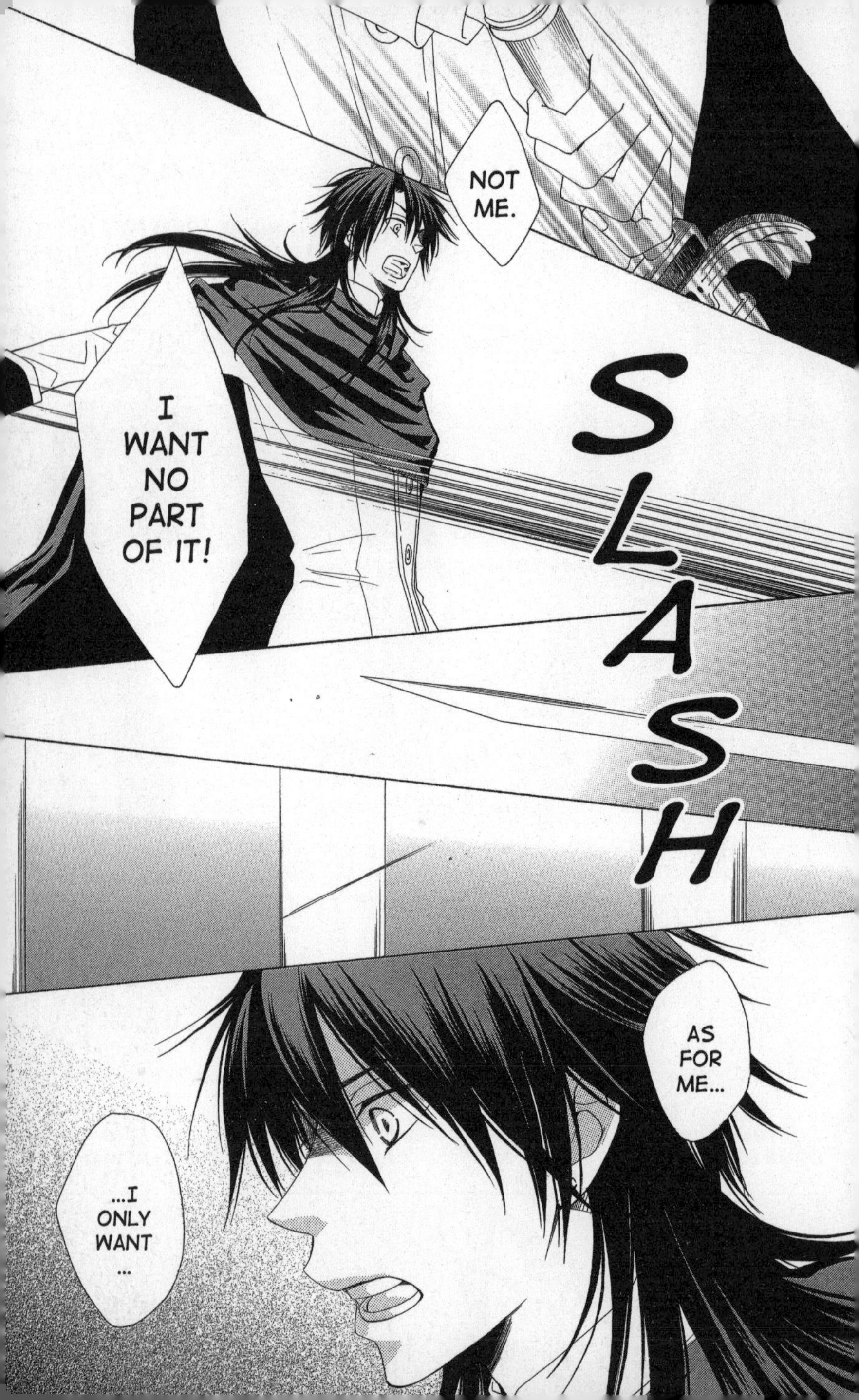
NOT ME.
I WANT NO PART OF IT!
SLASH
AS FOR ME...
...I ONLY WANT ...

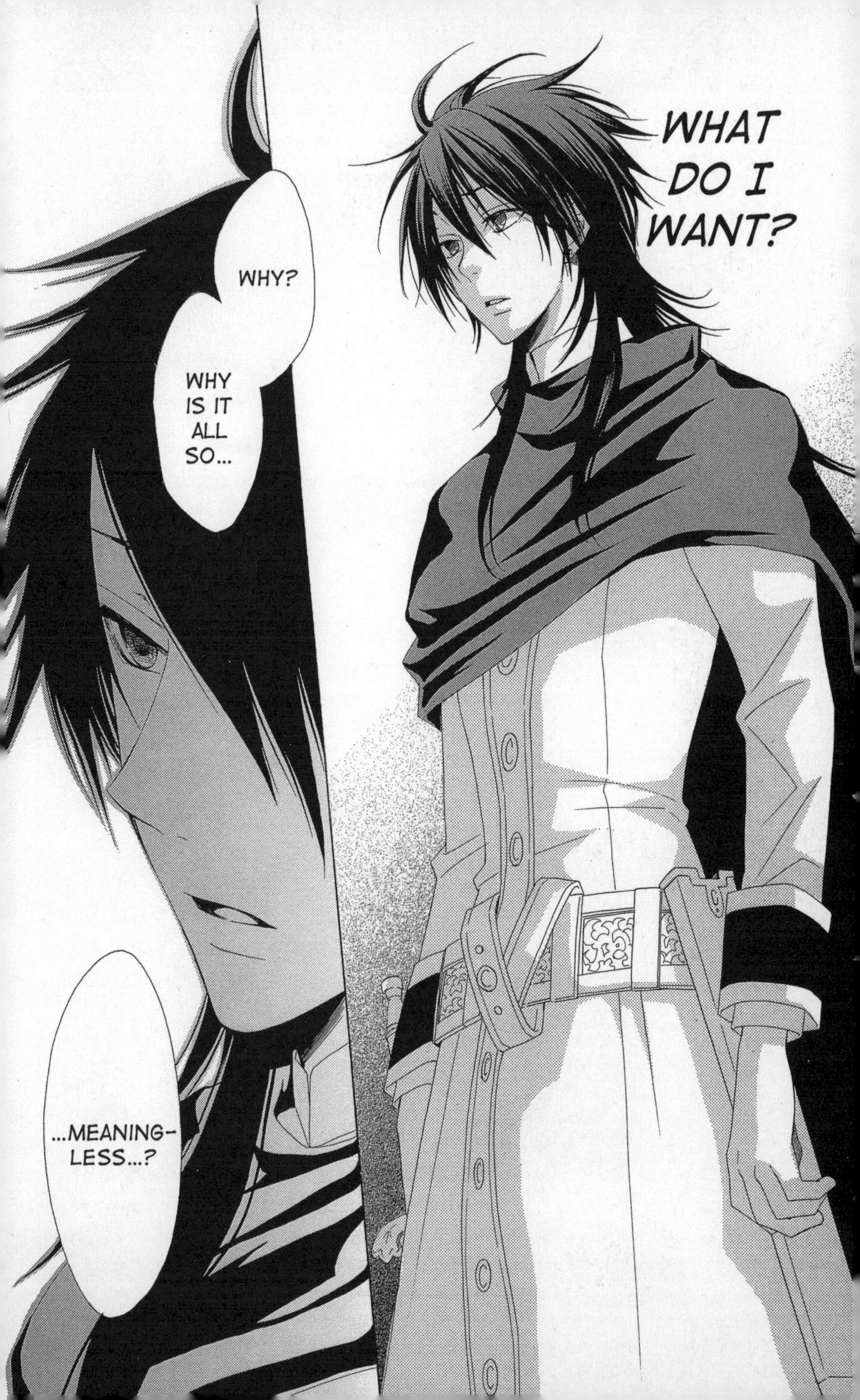
WHAT DO I WANT?
WHY?
WHY IS IT ALL SO...
...MEANING-LESS...?

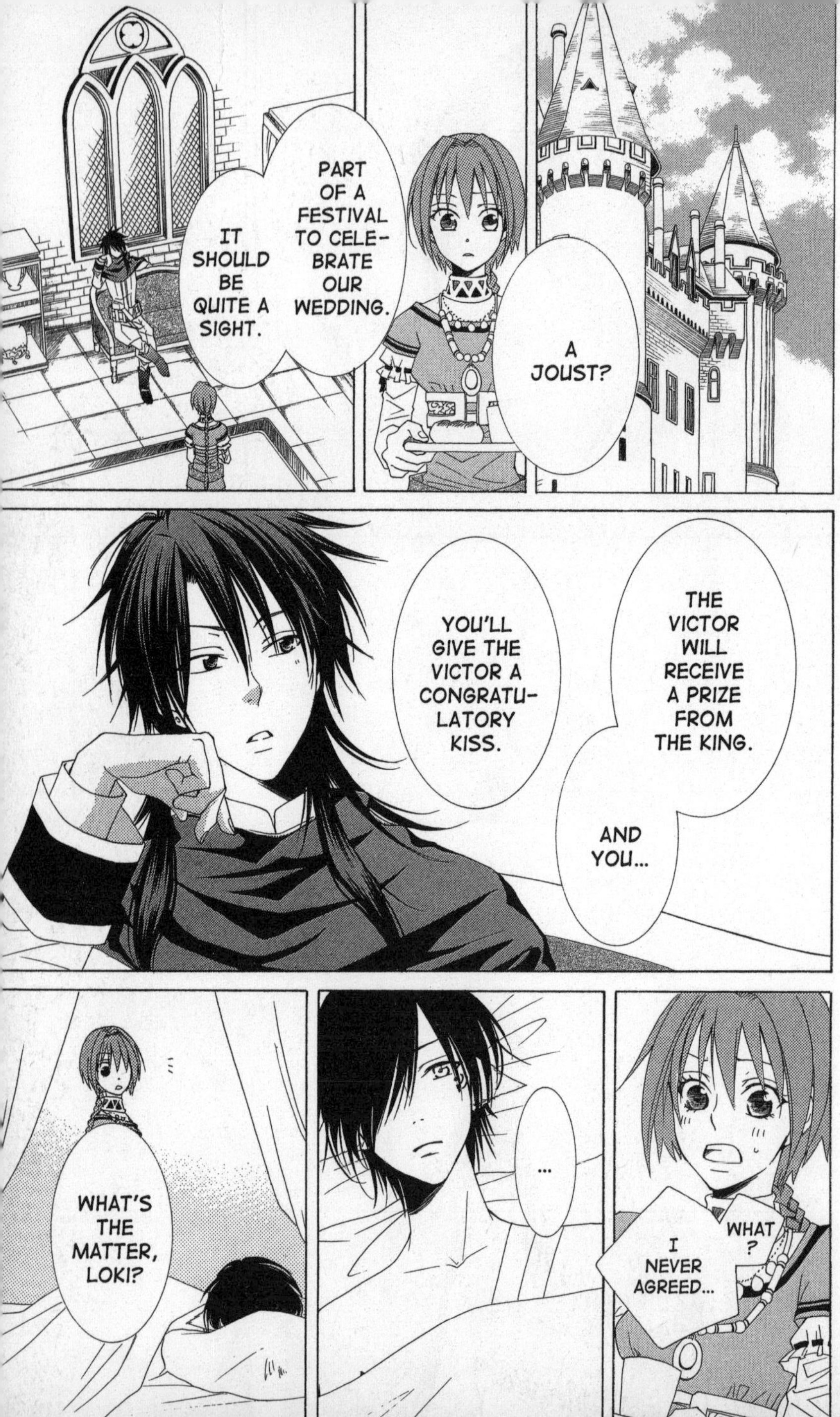
A JOUST?
PART OF A FESTIVAL TO CELEBRATE OUR WEDDING.
IT SHOULD BE QUITE A SIGHT.
THE VICTOR WILL RECEIVE A PRIZE FROM THE KING.
AND YOU...
YOU'LL GIVE THE VICTOR A CONGRATULATORY KISS.
WHAT?
I NEVER AGREED...
...
WHAT'S THE MATTER, LOKI?

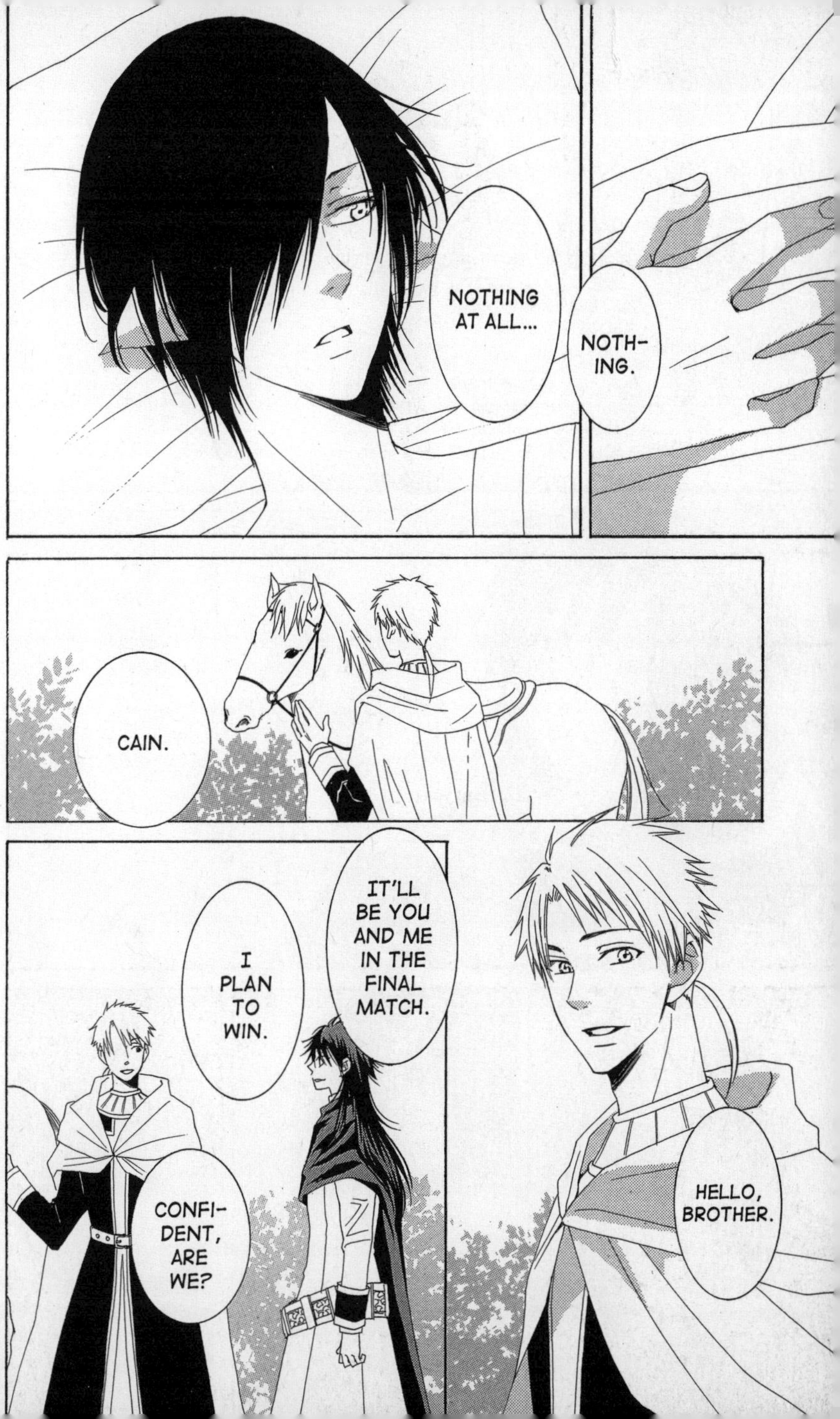
NOTH-ING.
NOTHING AT ALL...
CAIN.
HELLO, BROTHER.
IT'LL BE YOU AND ME IN THE FINAL MATCH.
I PLAN TO WIN.
CONFI-DENT, ARE WE?

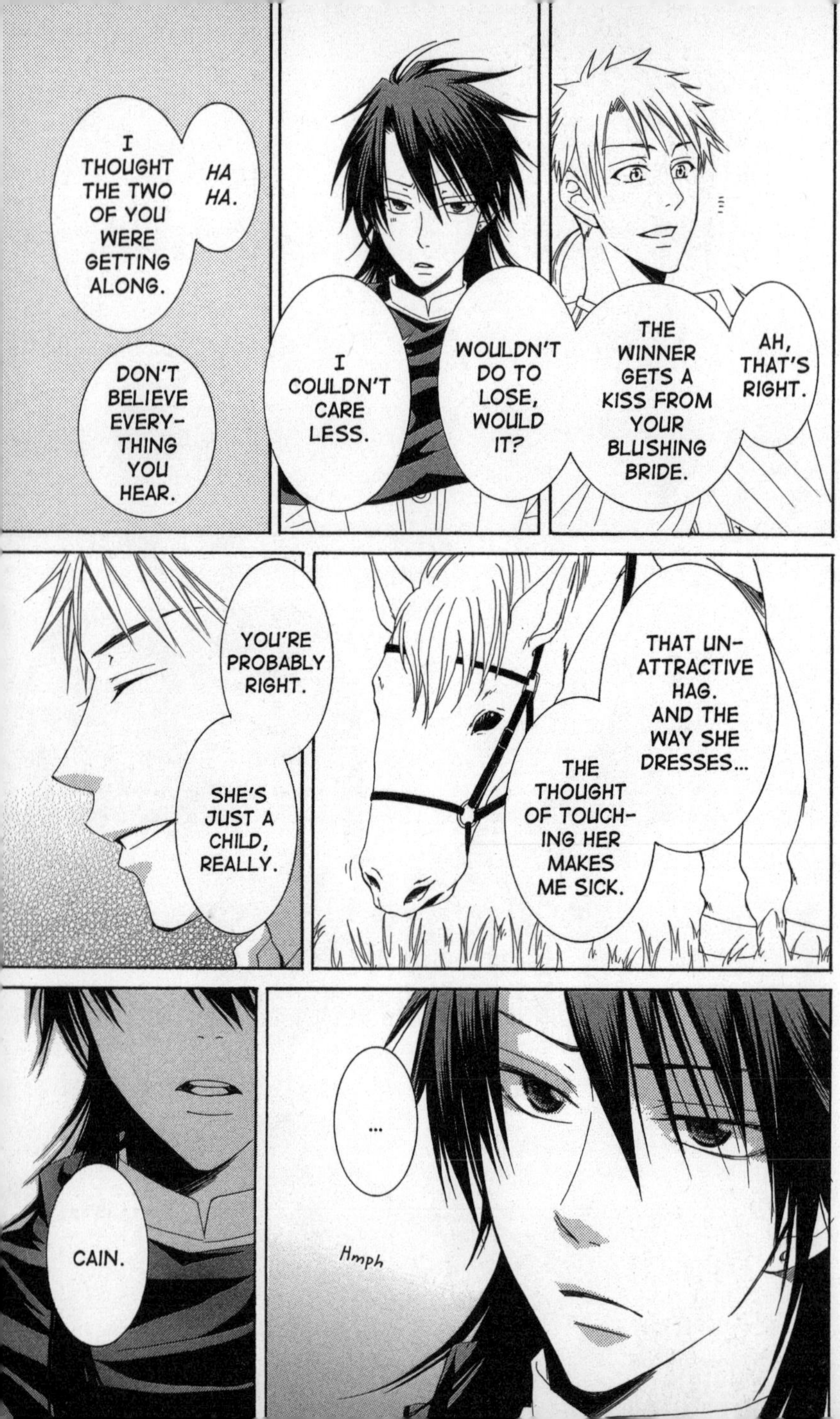
AH, THAT'S RIGHT.
THE WINNER GETS A KISS FROM YOUR BLUSHING BRIDE.
WOULDN'T DO TO LOSE, WOULD IT?
I COULDN'T CARE LESS.
I THOUGHT THE TWO OF YOU WERE GETTING ALONG.
HA HA.
DON'T BELIEVE EVERYTHING YOU HEAR.
THAT UN-ATTRACTIVE HAG. AND THE WAY SHE DRESSES...
THE THOUGHT OF TOUCHING HER MAKES ME SICK.
YOU'RE PROBABLY RIGHT.
SHE'S JUST A CHILD, REALLY.
...
Hmph
CAIN.

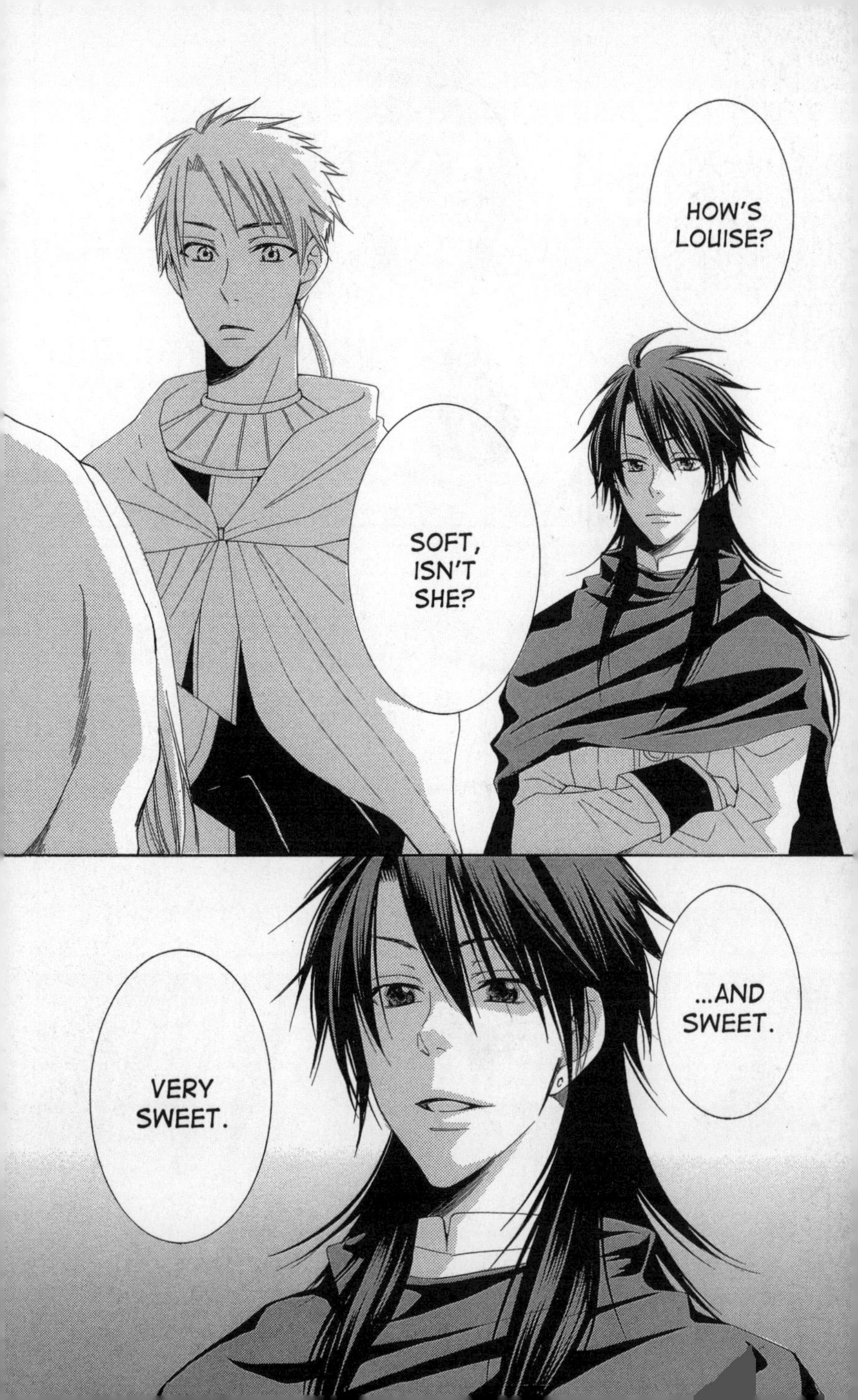
HOW'S LOUISE?
SOFT, ISN'T SHE?
...AND SWEET.
VERY SWEET.

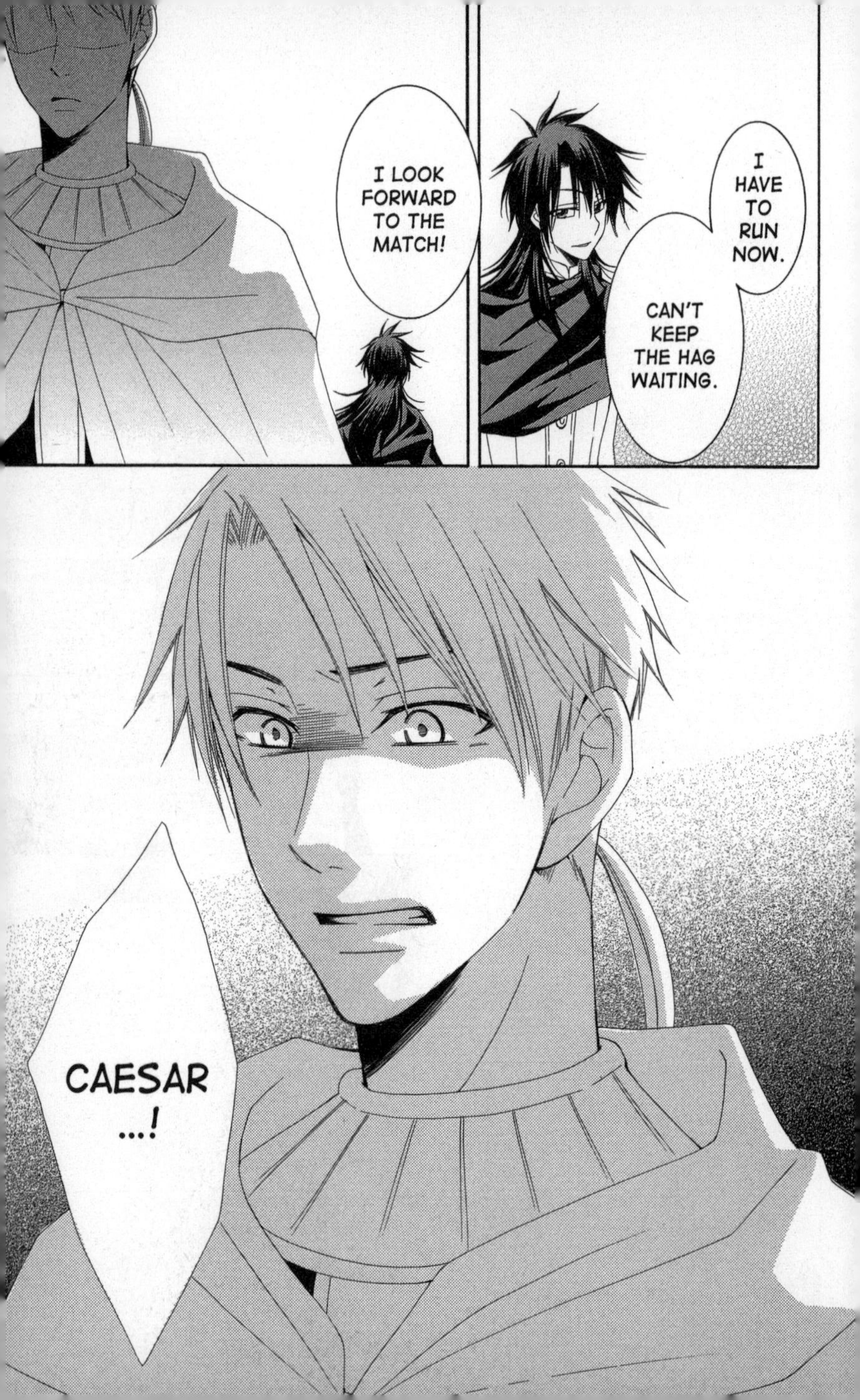
I HAVE TO RUN NOW.
CAN'T KEEP THE HAG WAITING.
I LOOK FORWARD TO THE MATCH!
CAESAR ...!

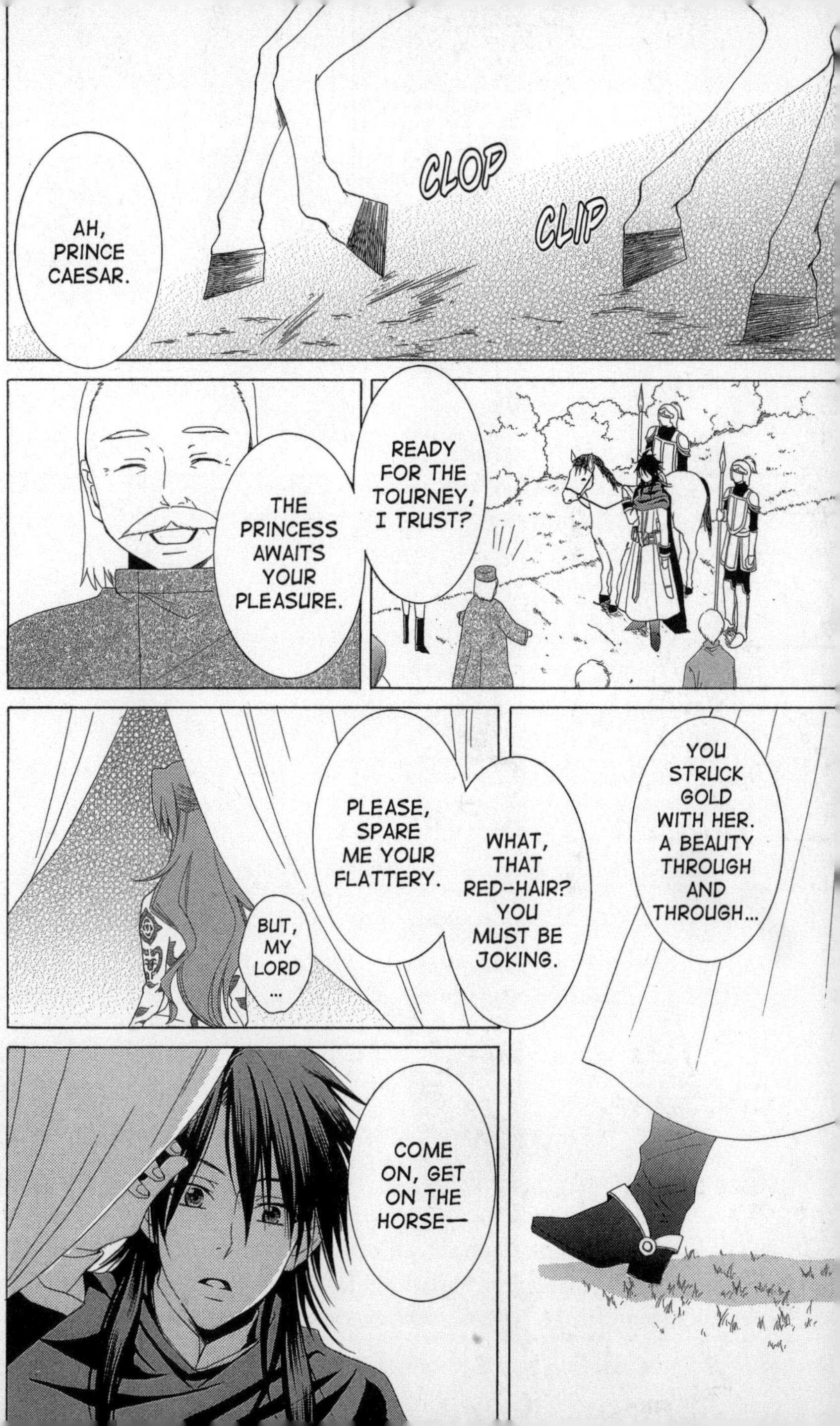
CLOP
CLIP
AH, PRINCE CAESAR.
READY FOR THE TOURNEY, I TRUST?
THE PRINCESS AWAITS YOUR PLEASURE.
YOU STRUCK GOLD WITH HER. A BEAUTY THROUGH AND THROUGH...
WHAT, THAT RED-HAIR? YOU MUST BE JOKING.
PLEASE, SPARE ME YOUR FLATTERY.
BUT, MY LORD ...
COME ON, GET ON THE HORSE—

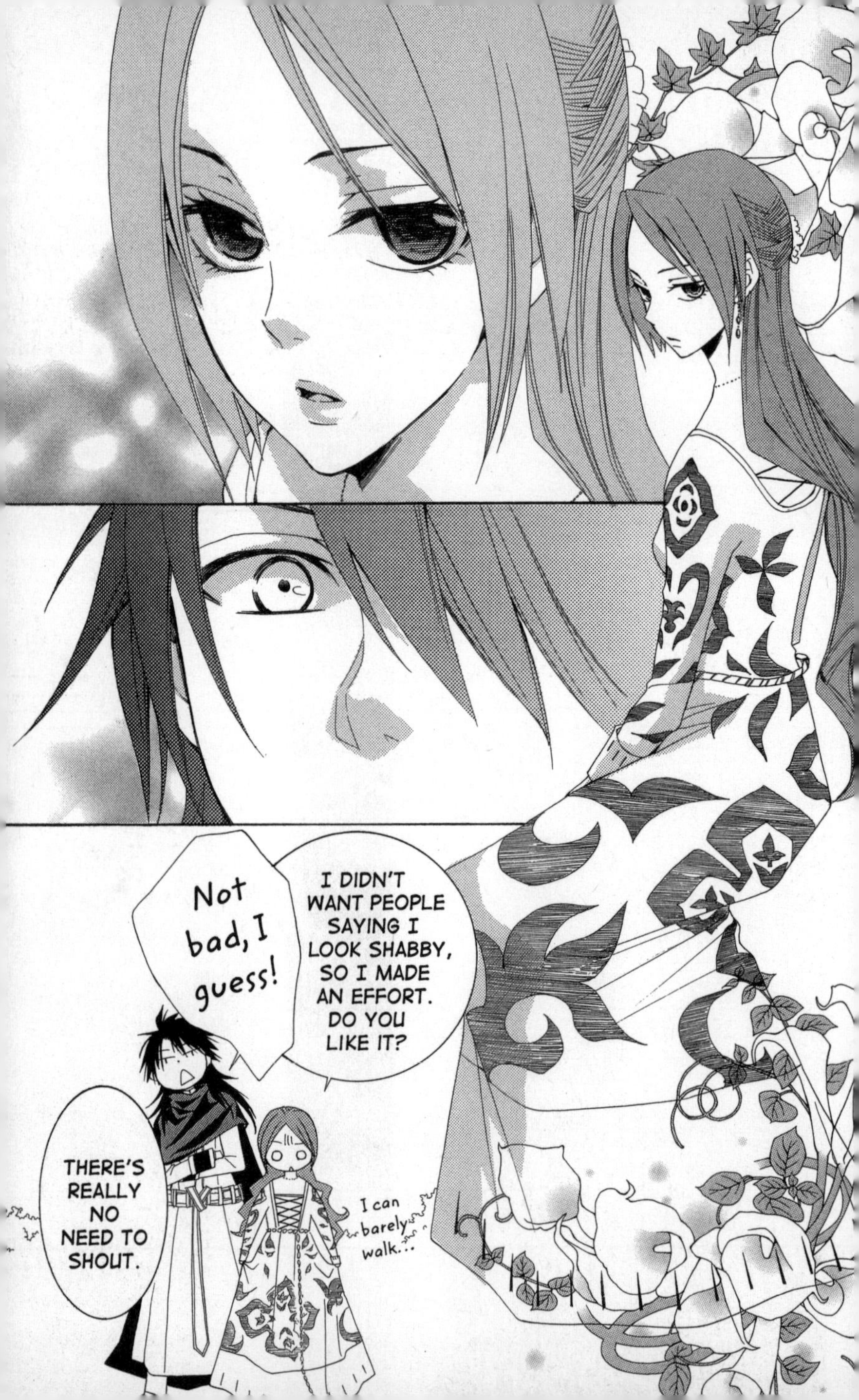
I DIDN'T WANT PEOPLE SAYING I LOOK SHABBY, SO I MADE AN EFFORT. DO YOU LIKE IT?
Not bad, I guess!
THERE'S REALLY NO NEED TO SHOUT.
I can barely walk...

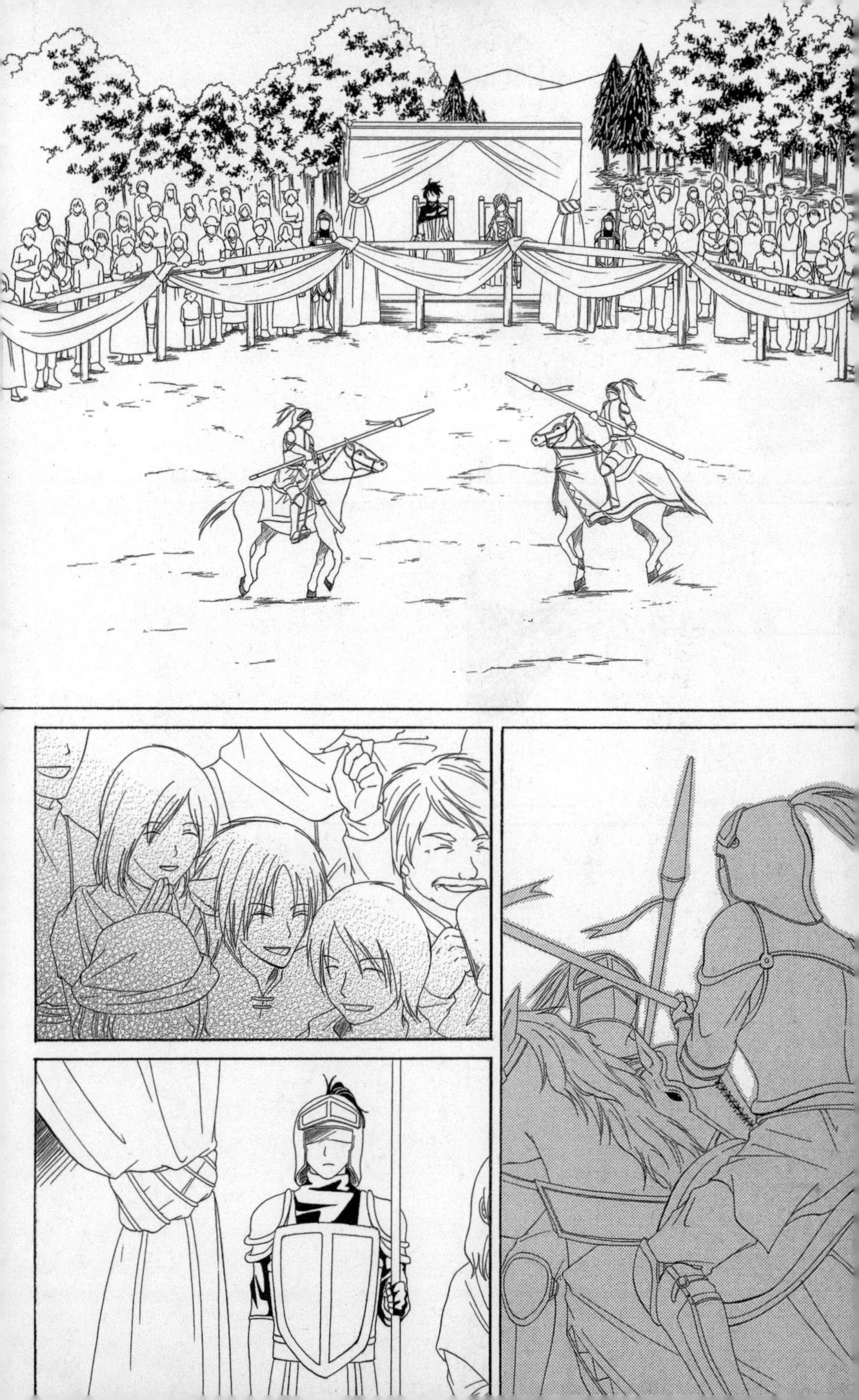

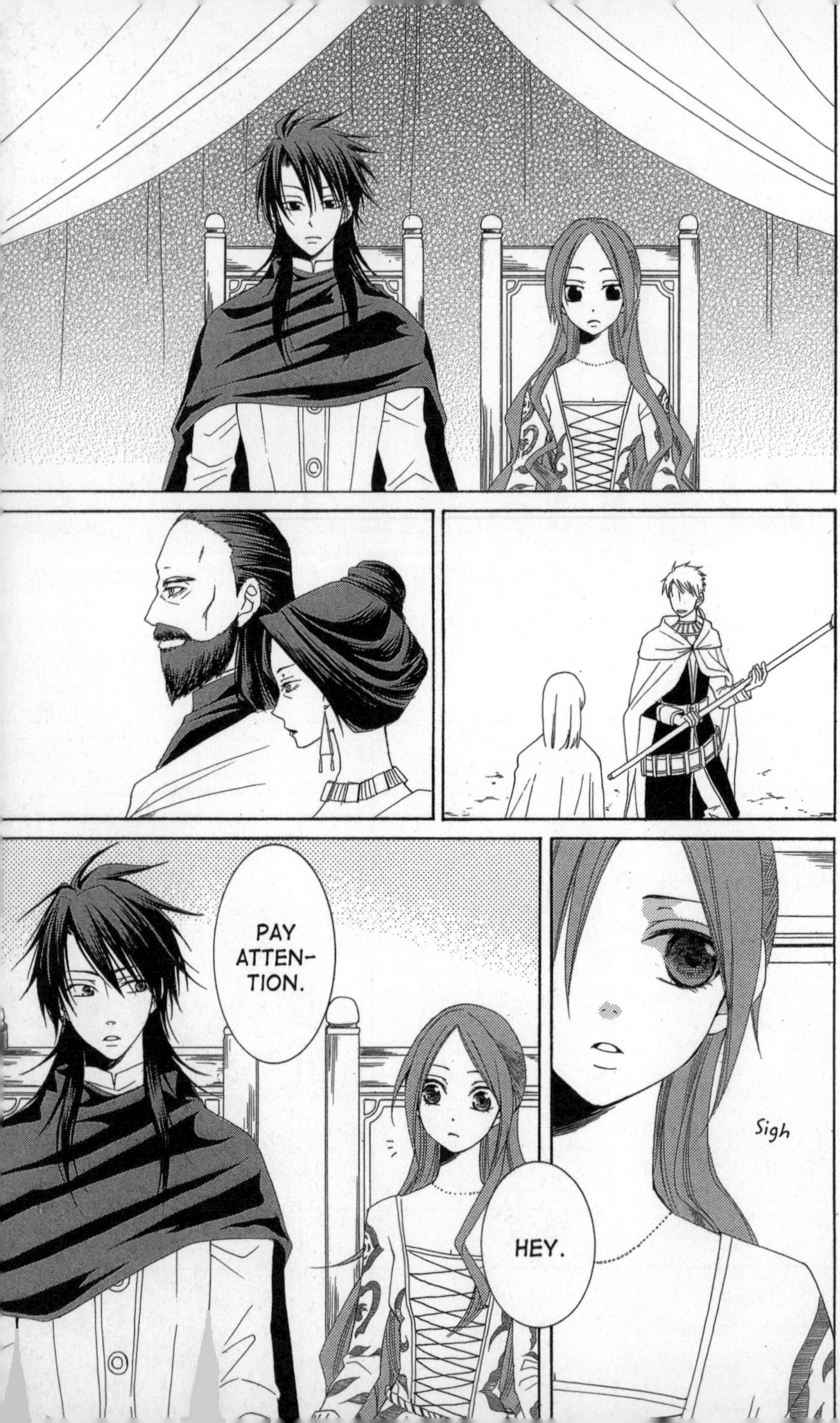
Sigh
HEY.
PAY ATTEN-TION.

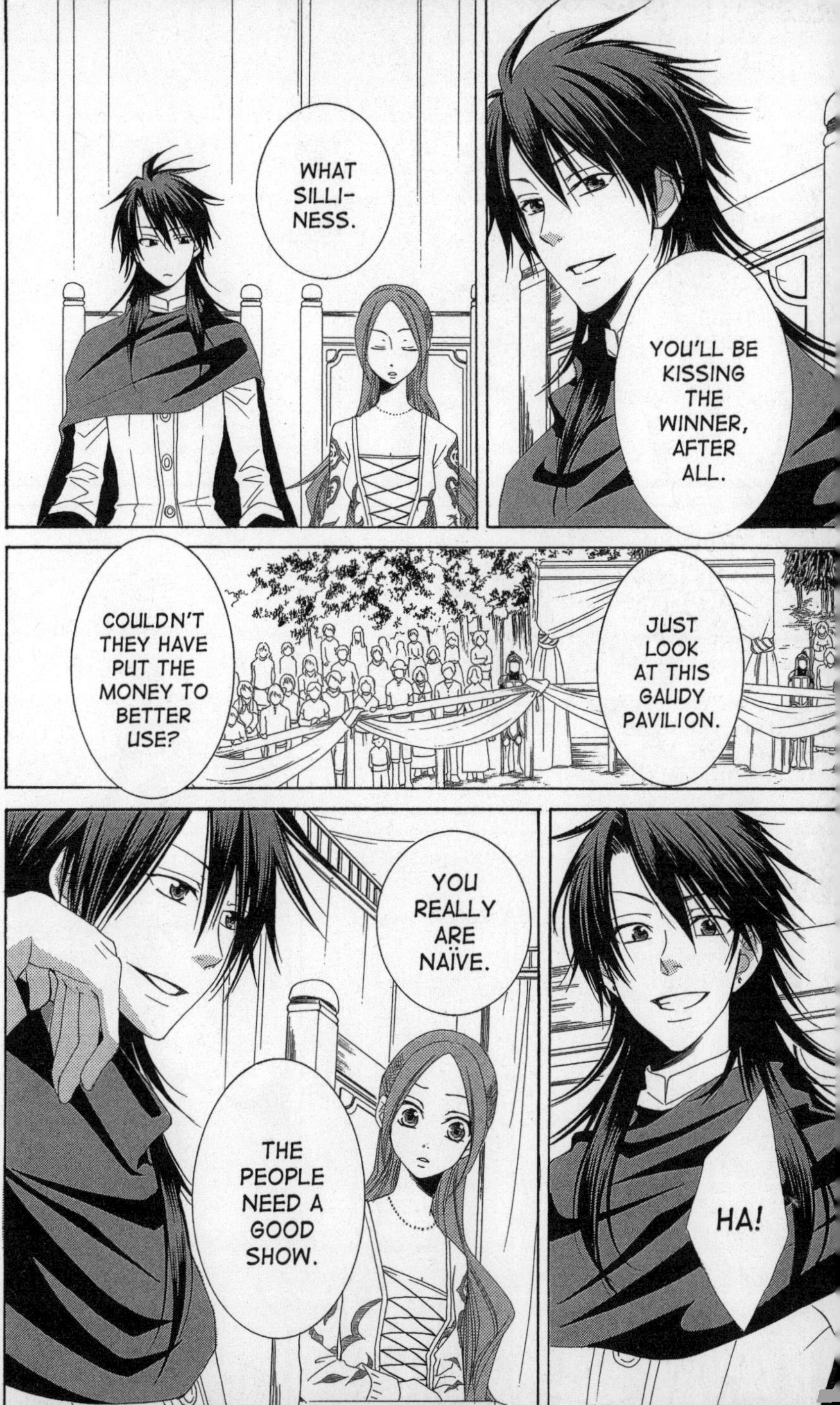
YOU'LL BE KISSING THE WINNER, AFTER ALL.
WHAT SILLI-NESS.
JUST LOOK AT THIS GAUDY PAVILION.
COULDN'T THEY HAVE PUT THE MONEY TO BETTER USE?
HA!
YOU REALLY ARE NAÏVE.
THE PEOPLE NEED A GOOD SHOW.

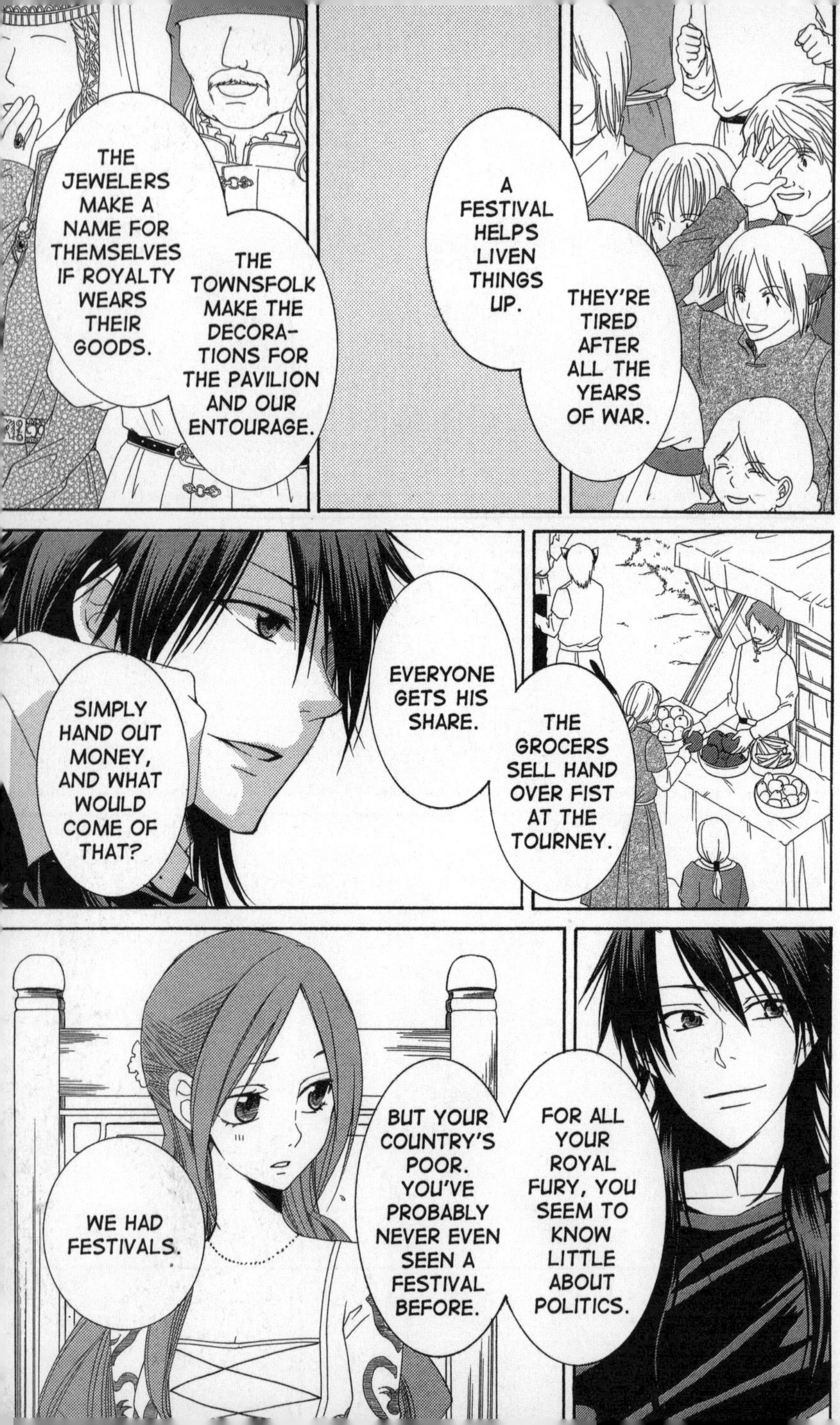
THEY'RE TIRED AFTER ALL THE YEARS OF WAR.
A FESTIVAL HELPS LIVEN THINGS UP.
THE TOWNSFOLK MAKE THE DECORA-TIONS FOR THE PAVILION AND OUR ENTOURAGE.
THE JEWELERS MAKE A NAME FOR THEMSELVES IF ROYALTY WEARS THEIR GOODS.
THE GROCERS SELL HAND OVER FIST AT THE TOURNEY.
EVERYONE GETS HIS SHARE.
SIMPLY HAND OUT MONEY, AND WHAT WOULD COME OF THAT?
FOR ALL YOUR ROYAL FURY, YOU SEEM TO KNOW LITTLE ABOUT POLITICS.
BUT YOUR COUNTRY'S POOR. YOU'VE PROBABLY NEVER EVEN SEEN A FESTIVAL BEFORE.
WE HAD FESTIVALS.

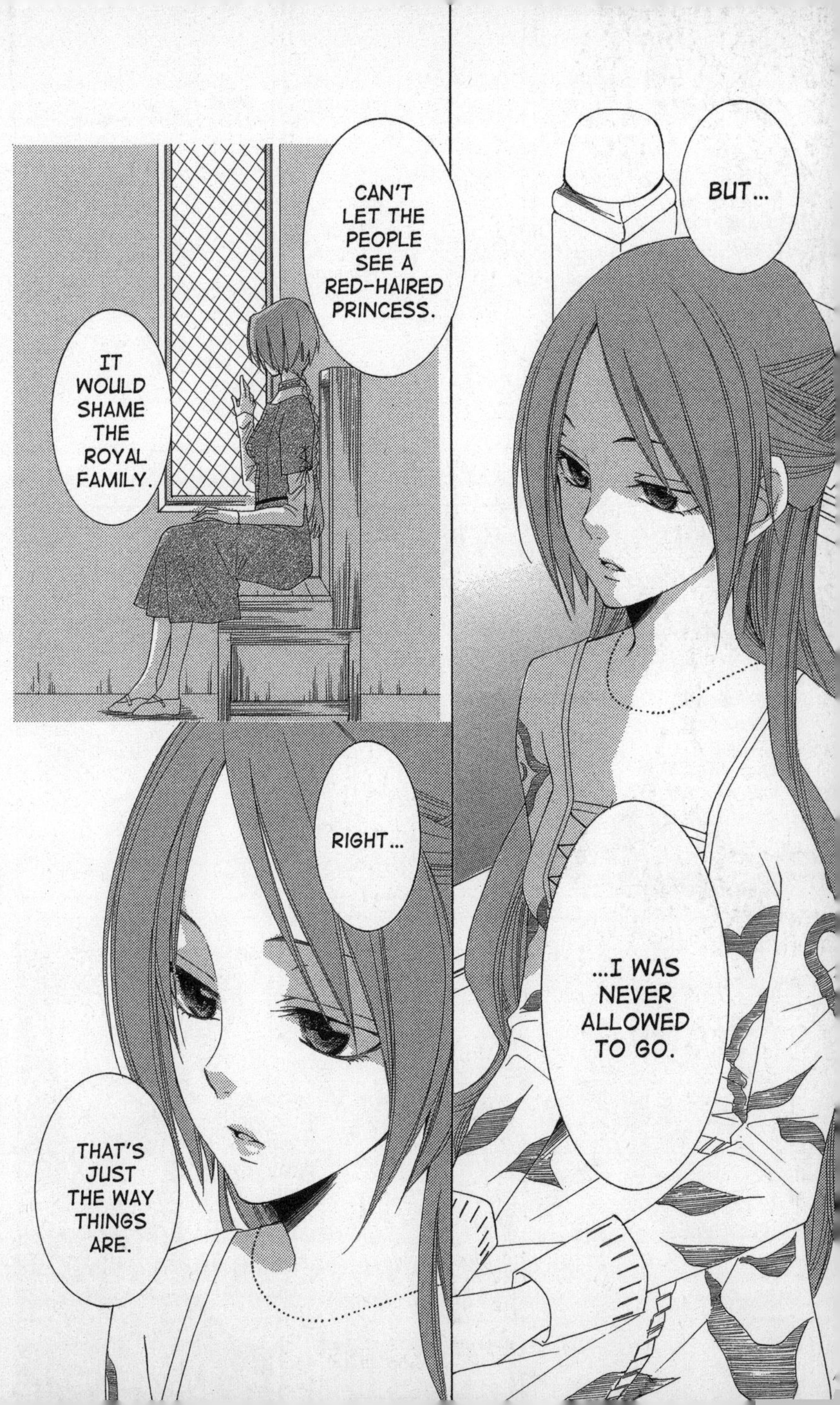
BUT...
...I WAS NEVER ALLOWED TO GO.
CAN'T LET THE PEOPLE SEE A RED-HAIRED PRINCESS.
IT WOULD SHAME THE ROYAL FAMILY.
RIGHT...
THAT'S JUST THE WAY THINGS ARE.

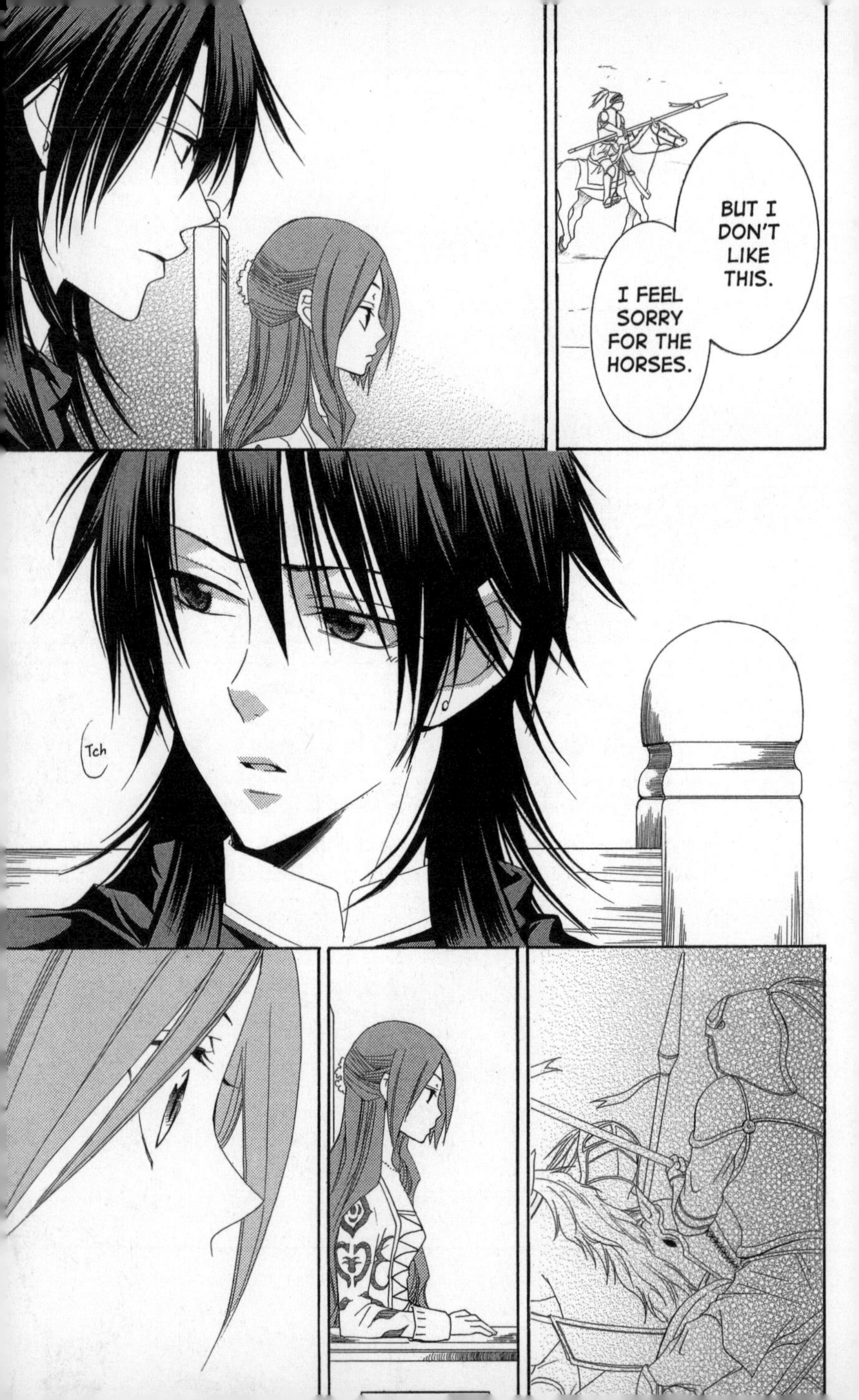
BUT I DON'T LIKE THIS.
I FEEL SORRY FOR THE HORSES.
Tch

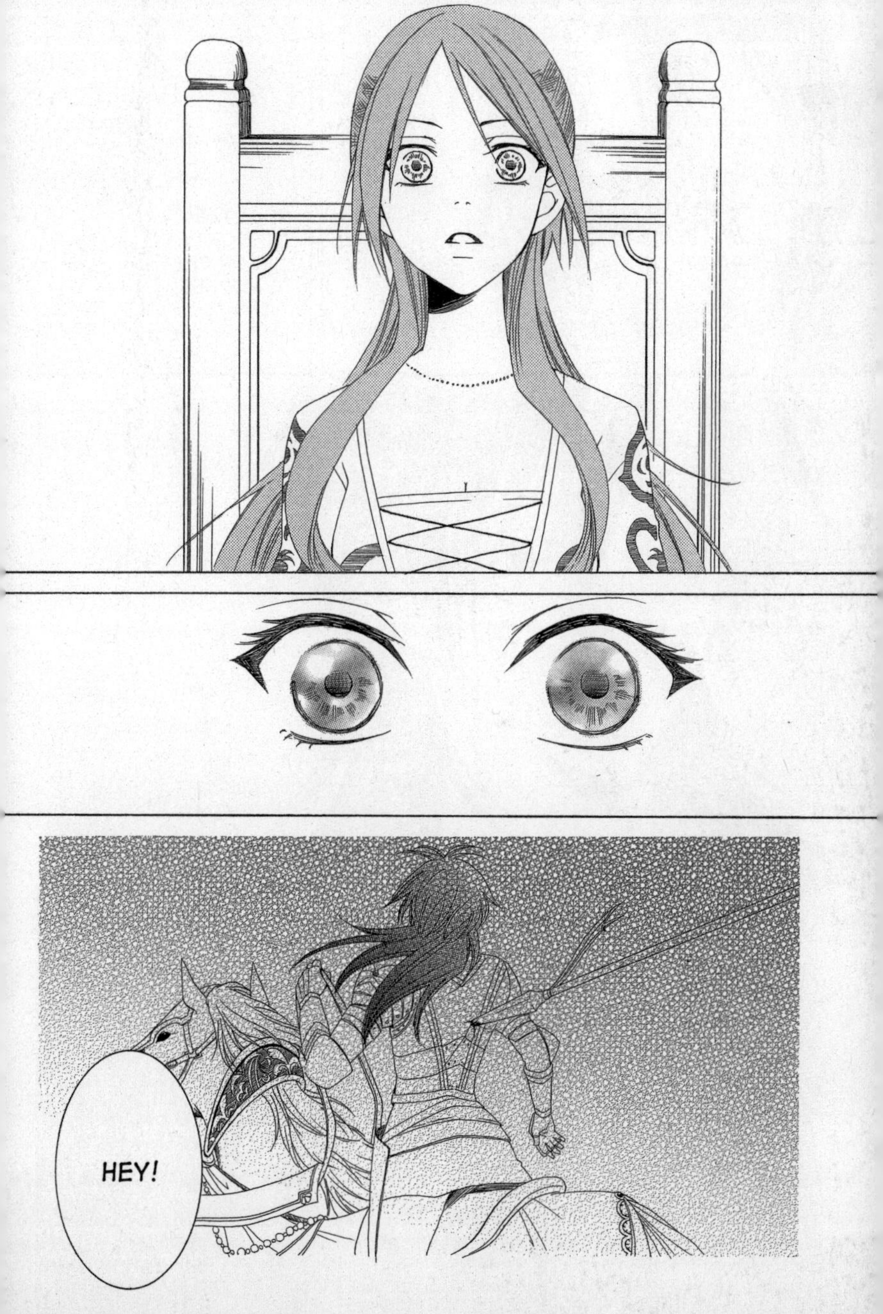
HEY!

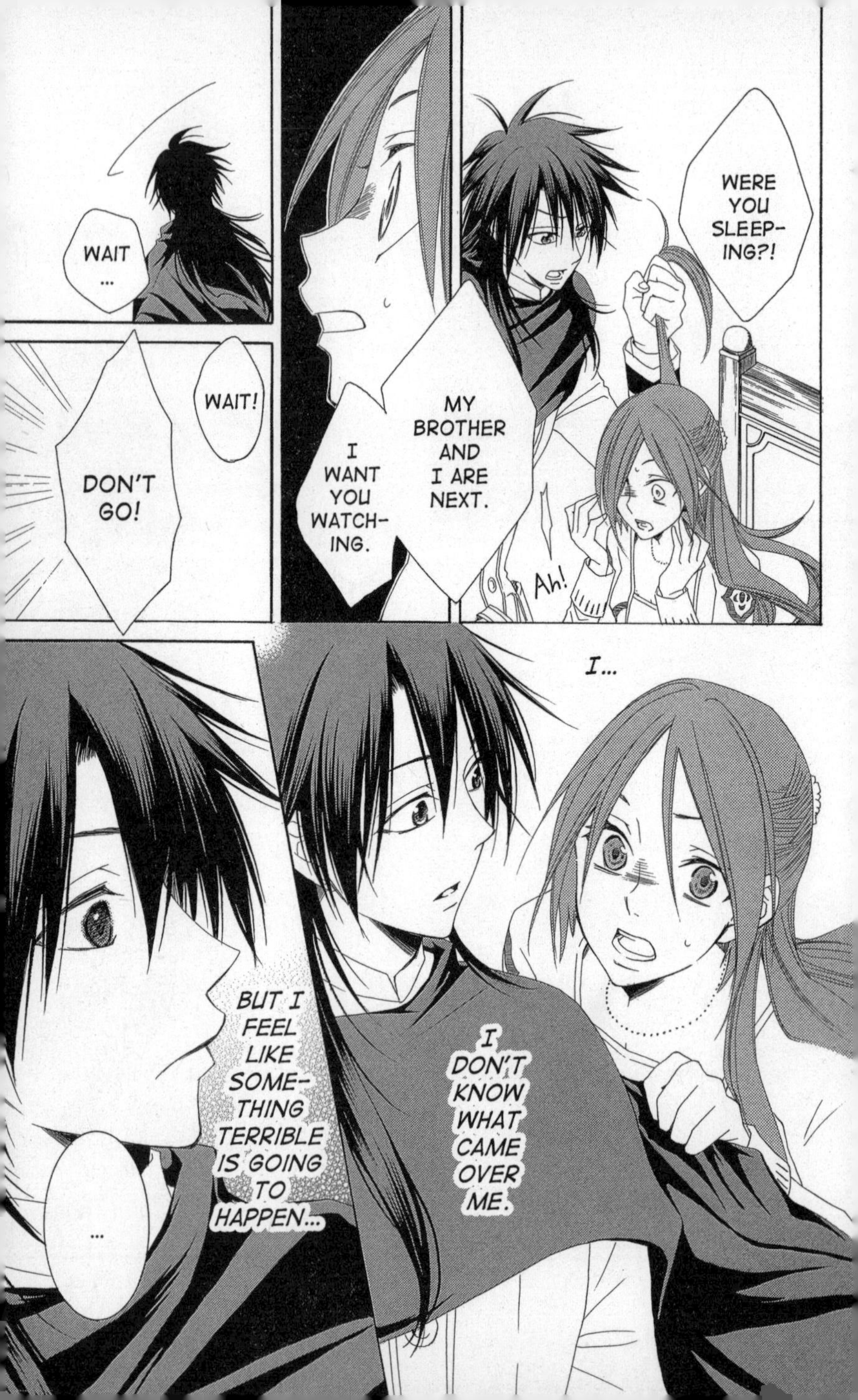
WERE YOU SLEEPING?!
Ah!
MY BROTHER AND I ARE NEXT.
I WANT YOU WATCHING.
WAIT ...
WAIT!
DON'T GO!
I...
I DON'T KNOW WHAT CAME OVER ME.
BUT I FEEL LIKE SOMETHING TERRIBLE IS GOING TO HAPPEN...
...

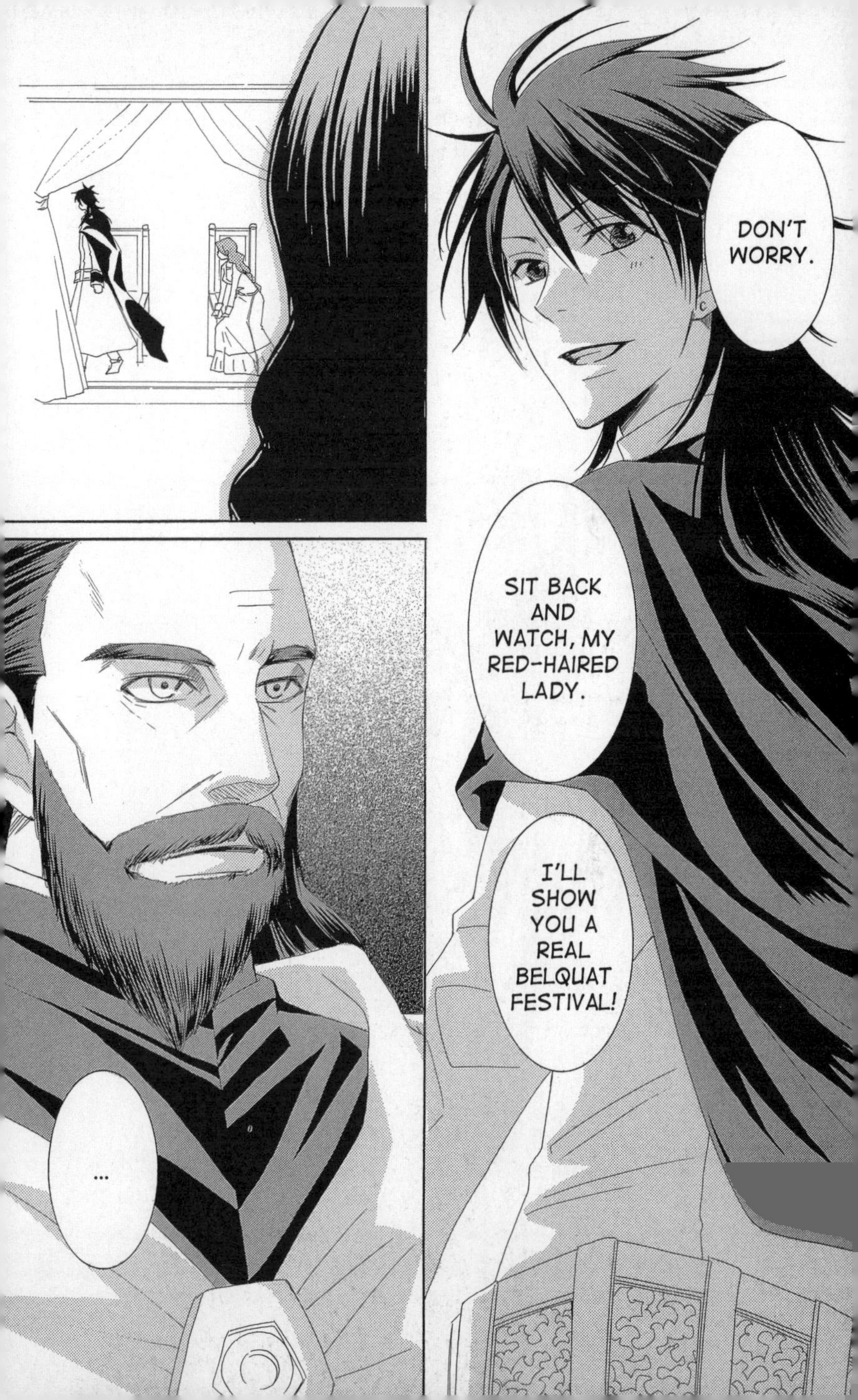
DON'T WORRY.
SIT BACK AND WATCH, MY RED-HAIRED LADY.
I'LL SHOW YOU A REAL BELQUAT FESTIVAL!
...

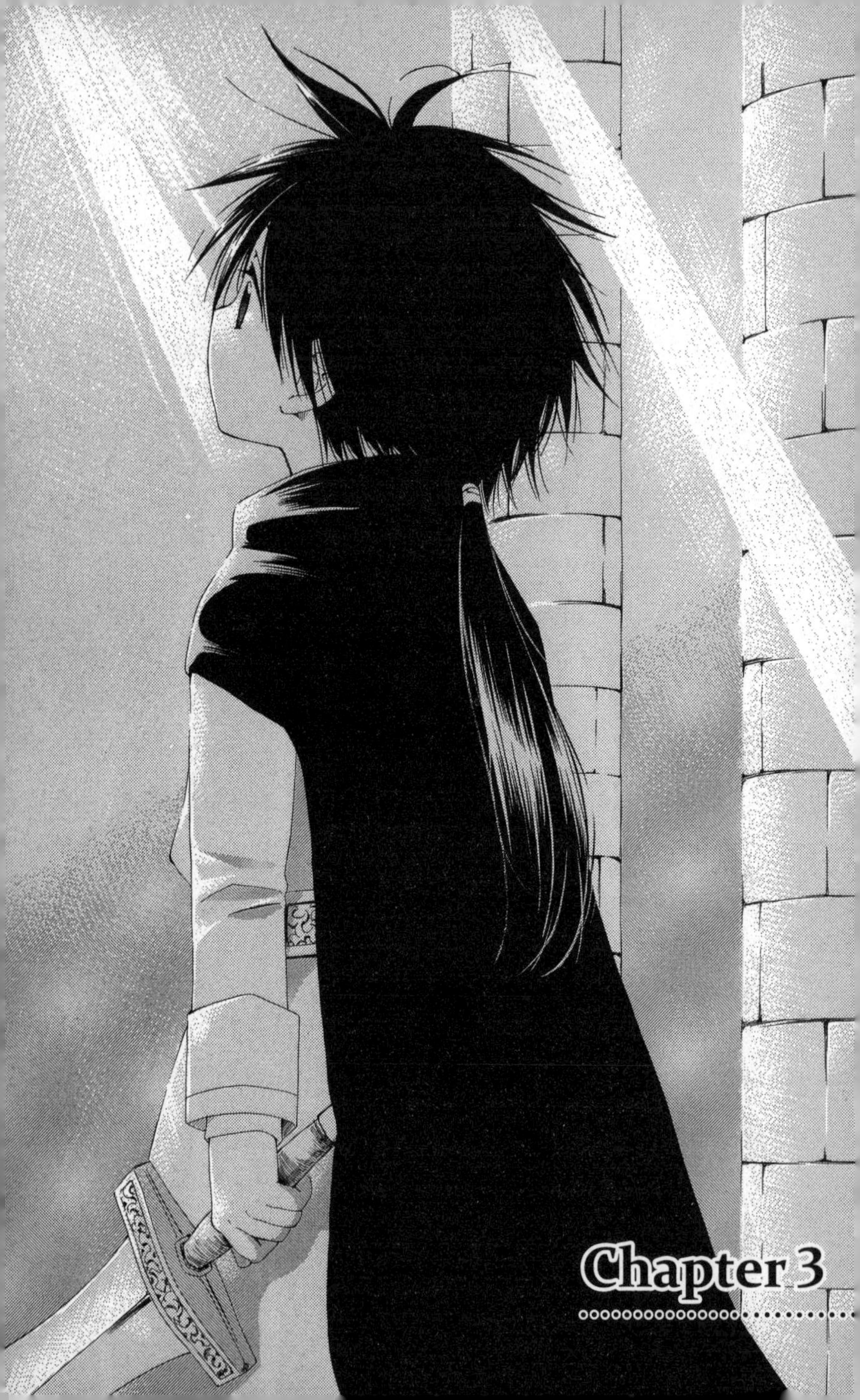
Chapter 3

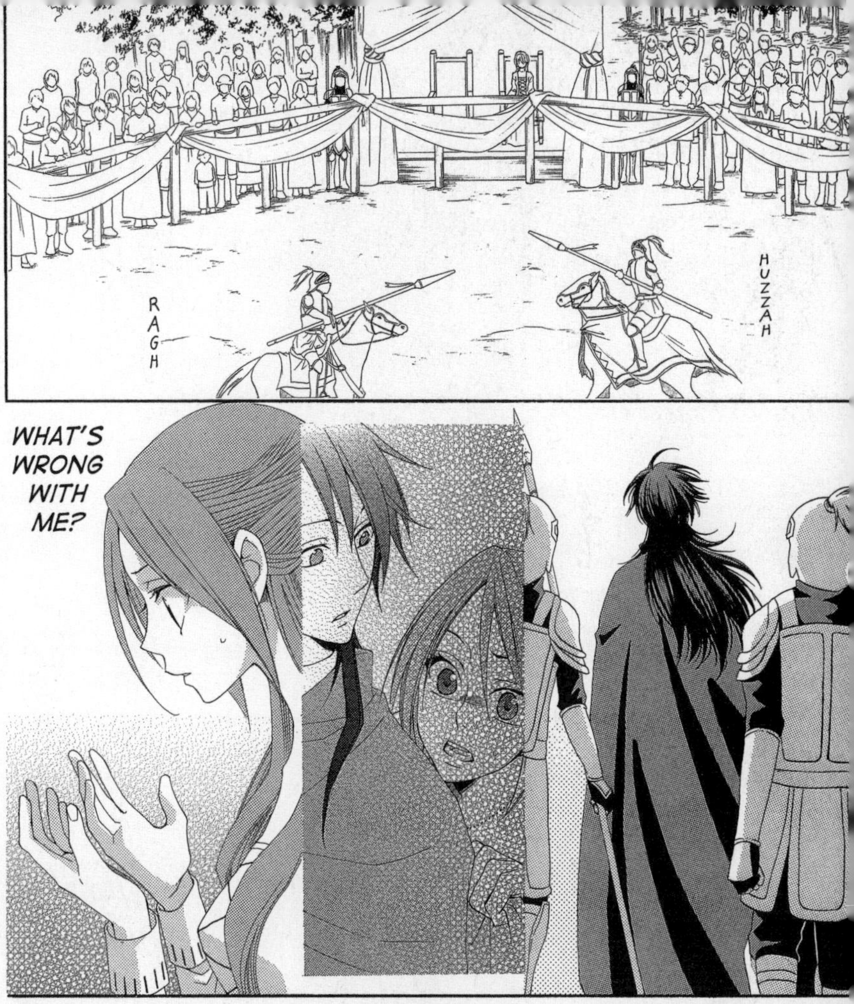
HUZZAH
RAGH
WHAT'S WRONG WITH ME?

Dawn of the Arcana

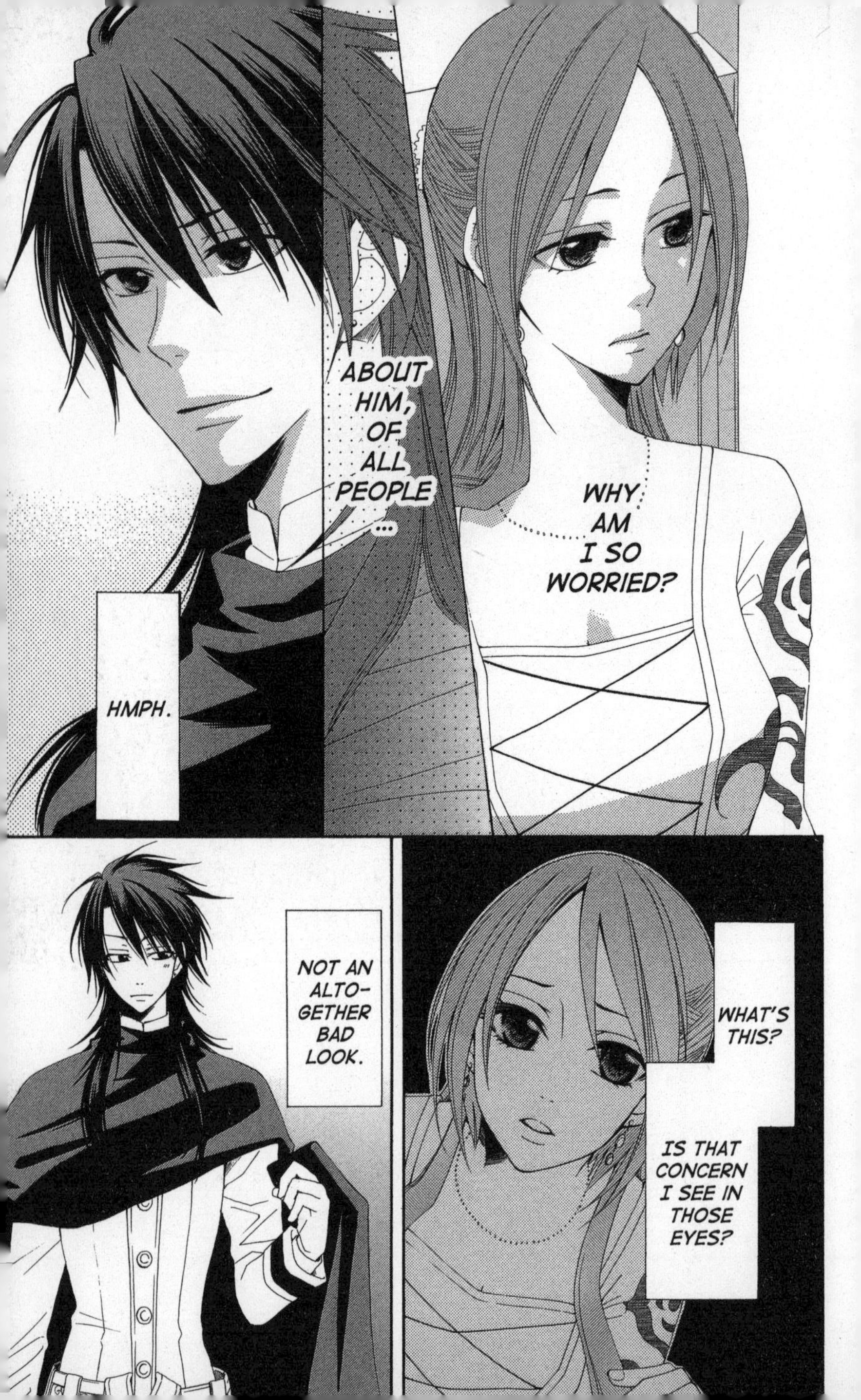
WHY AM I SO WORRIED?
ABOUT HIM, OF ALL PEOPLE...
HMPH.
WHAT'S THIS?
IS THAT CONCERN I SEE IN THOSE EYES?
NOT AN ALTO-GETHER BAD LOOK.

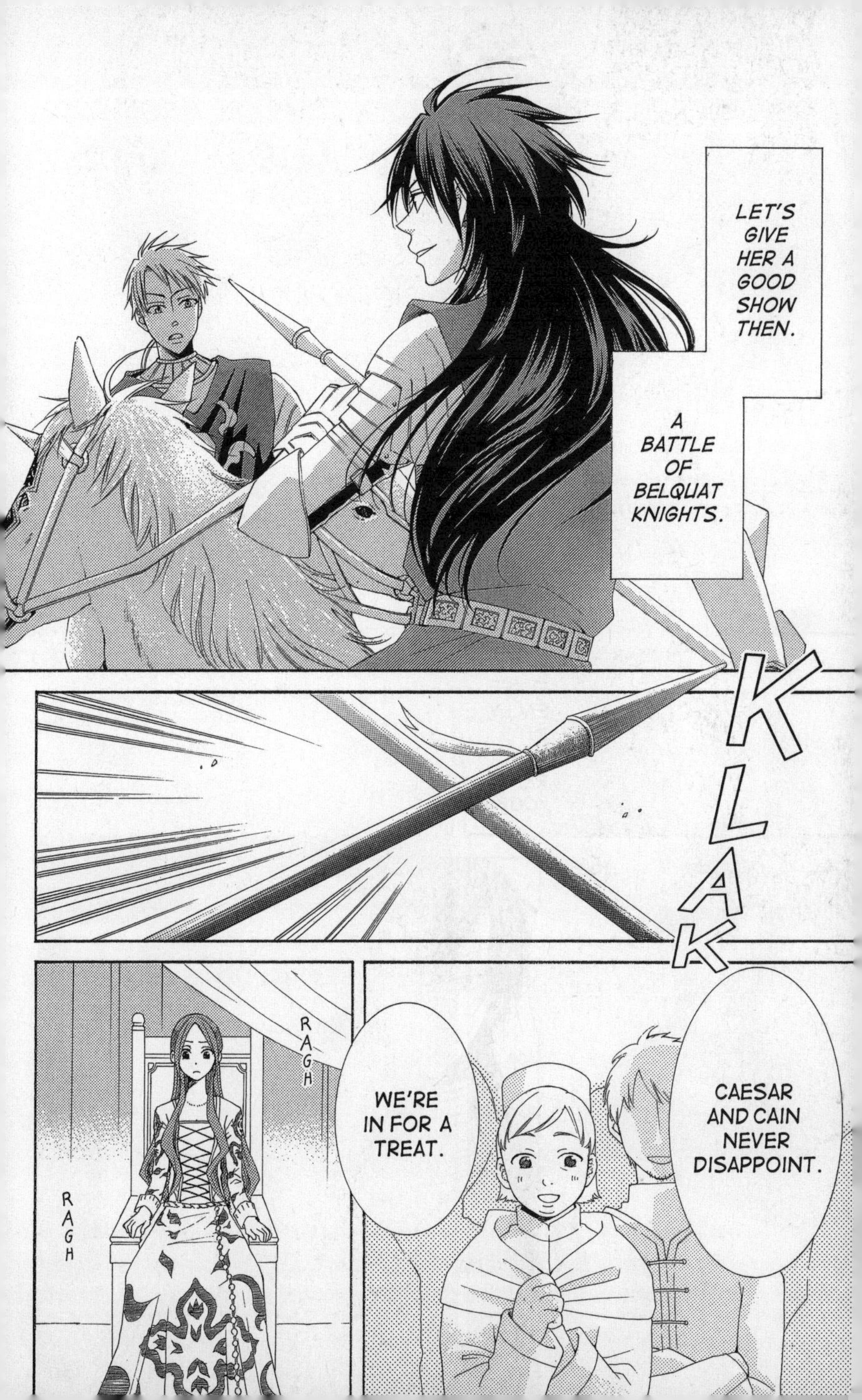
LET'S GIVE HER A GOOD SHOW THEN.
A BATTLE OF BELQUAT KNIGHTS.
KLAK
CAESAR AND CAIN NEVER DISAPPOINT.
WE'RE IN FOR A TREAT.
RAGH
RAGH

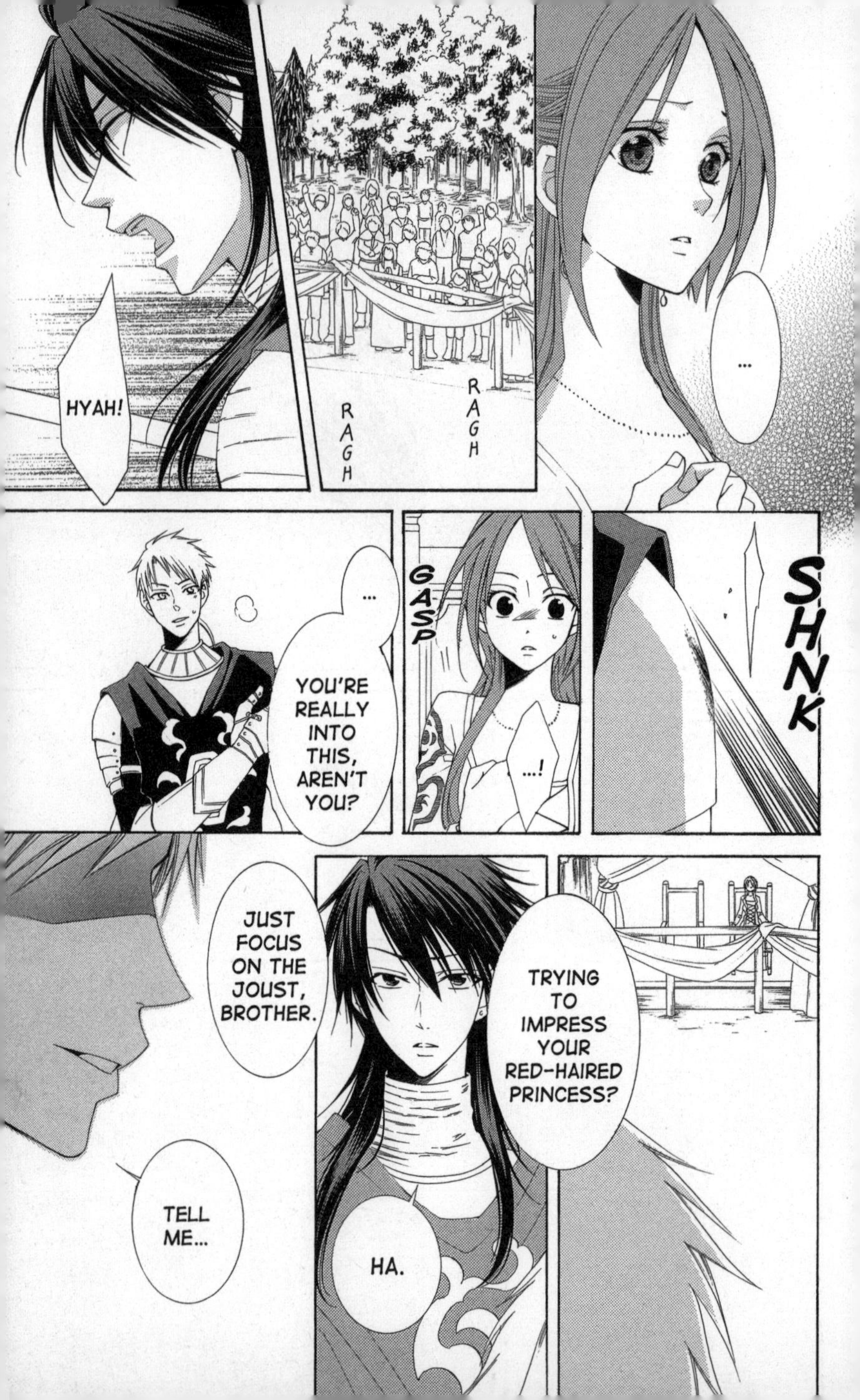
...
RAGH
RAGH
HYAH!
SHNK
GASP
...!
...
YOU'RE REALLY INTO THIS, AREN'T YOU?
TRYING TO IMPRESS YOUR RED-HAIRED PRINCESS?
JUST FOCUS ON THE JOUST, BROTHER.
HA.
TELL ME...

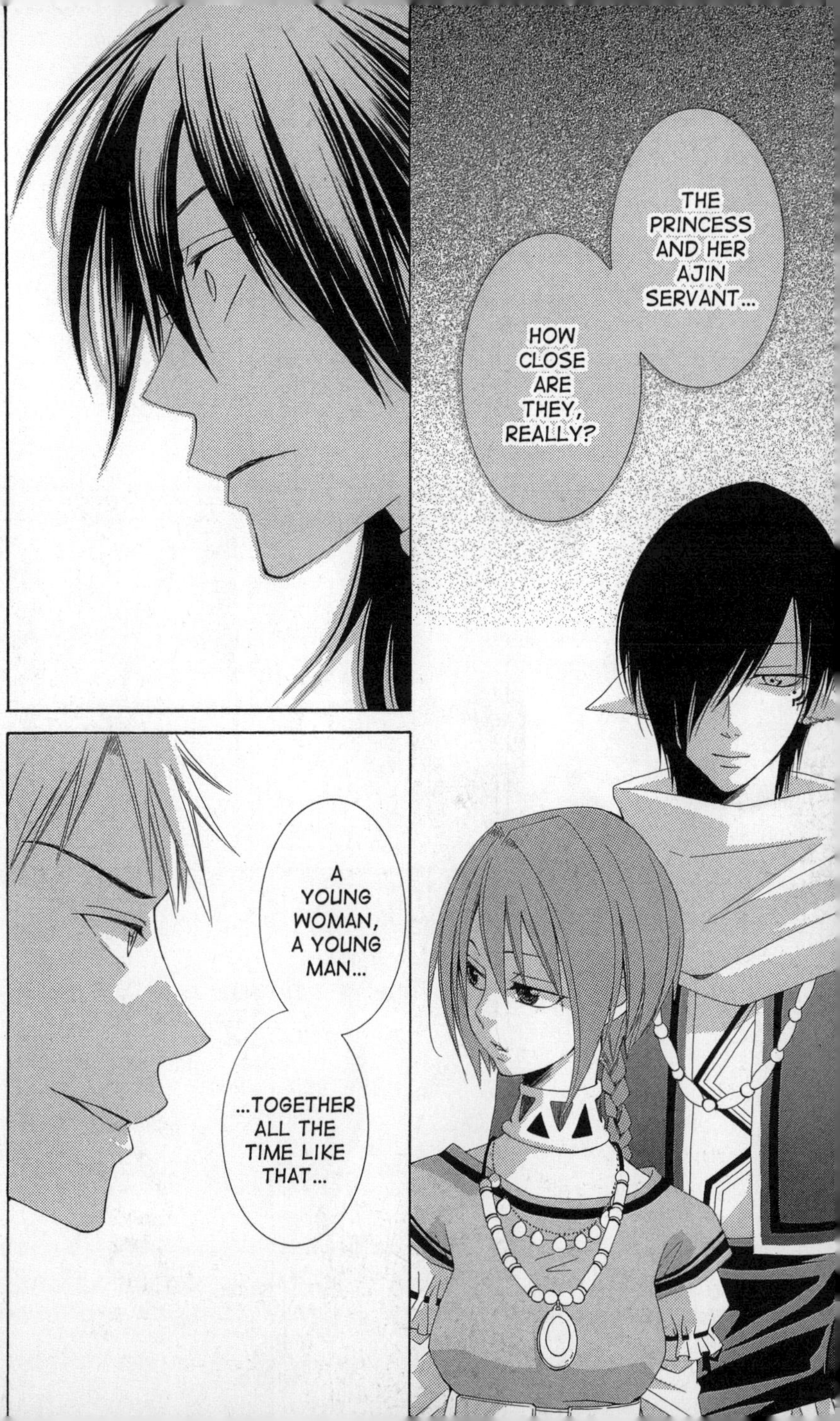
THE PRINCESS AND HER AJIN SERVANT...
HOW CLOSE ARE THEY, REALLY?
A YOUNG WOMAN, A YOUNG MAN...
...TOGETHER ALL THE TIME LIKE THAT...

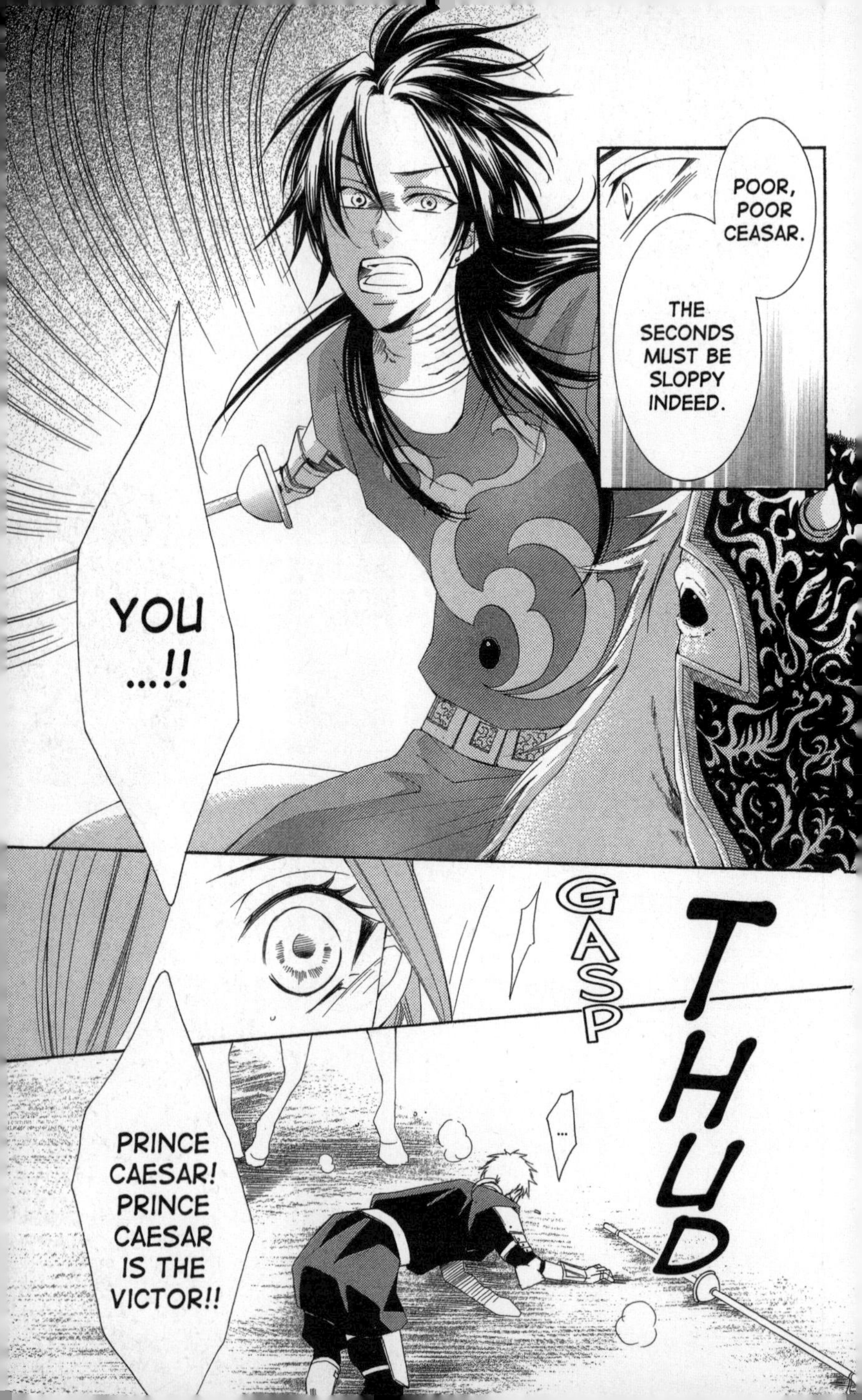
POOR, POOR CEASAR.
THE SECONDS MUST BE SLOPPY INDEED.
YOU ...!!
GASP
THUD
...
PRINCE CAESAR! PRINCE CAESAR IS THE VICTOR!!

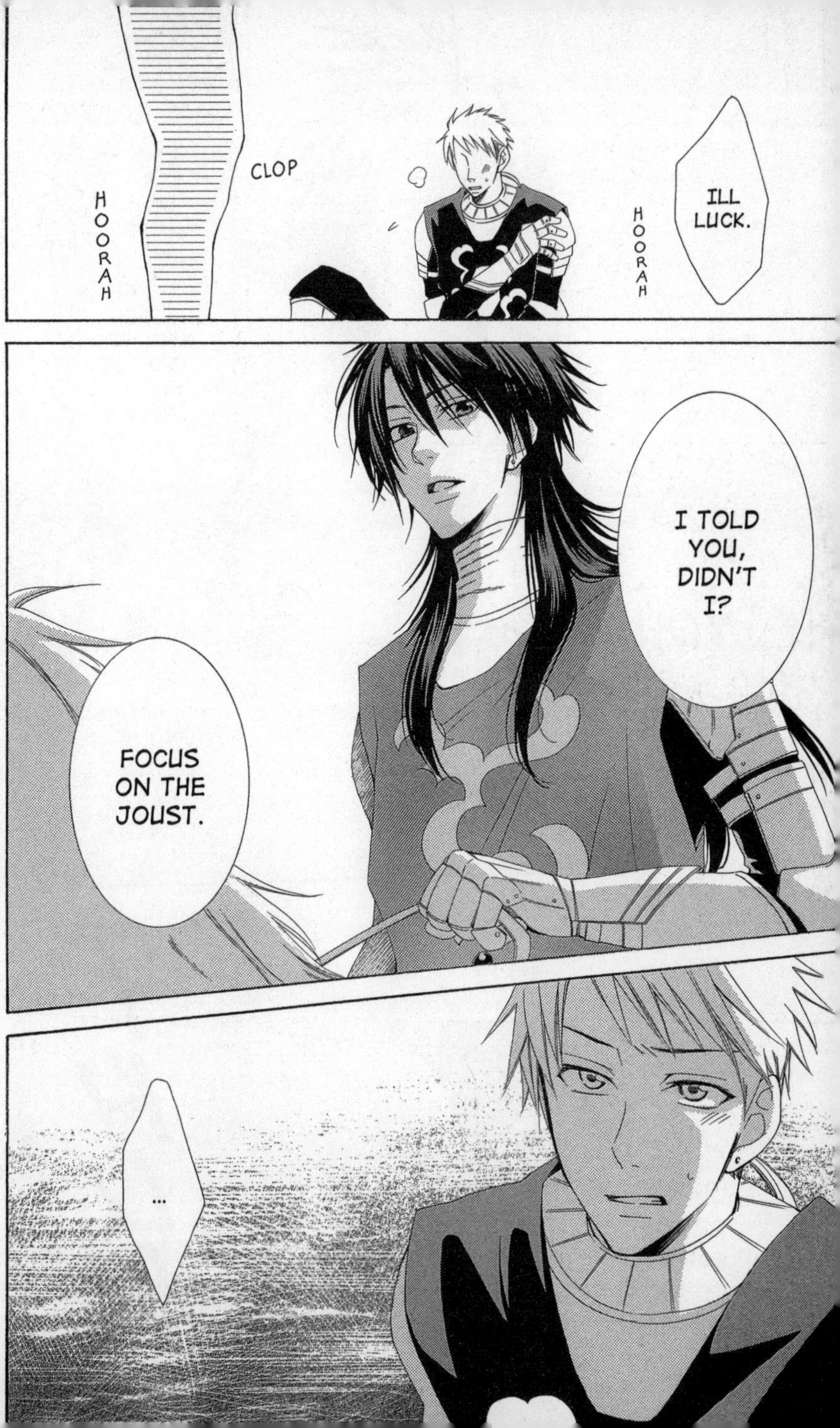
ILL LUCK.
HOORAH
CLOP
HOORAH
I TOLD YOU, DIDN'T I?
FOCUS ON THE JOUST.
...

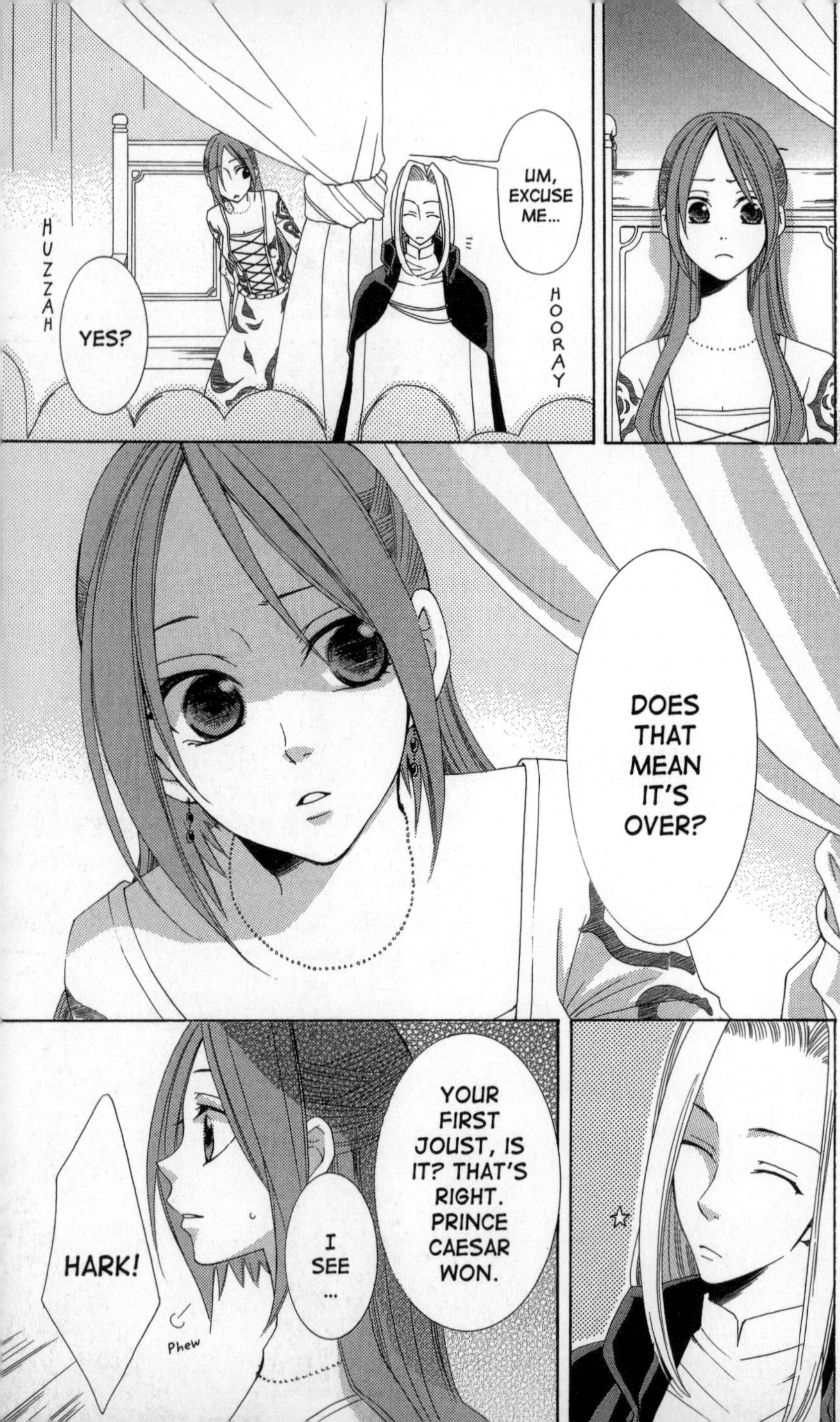
UM, EXCUSE ME...
HOORAY
HUZZAH
YES?
DOES THAT MEAN IT'S OVER?
YOUR FIRST JOUST, IS IT? THAT'S RIGHT. PRINCE CAESAR WON.
I SEE ...
HARK!
Phew

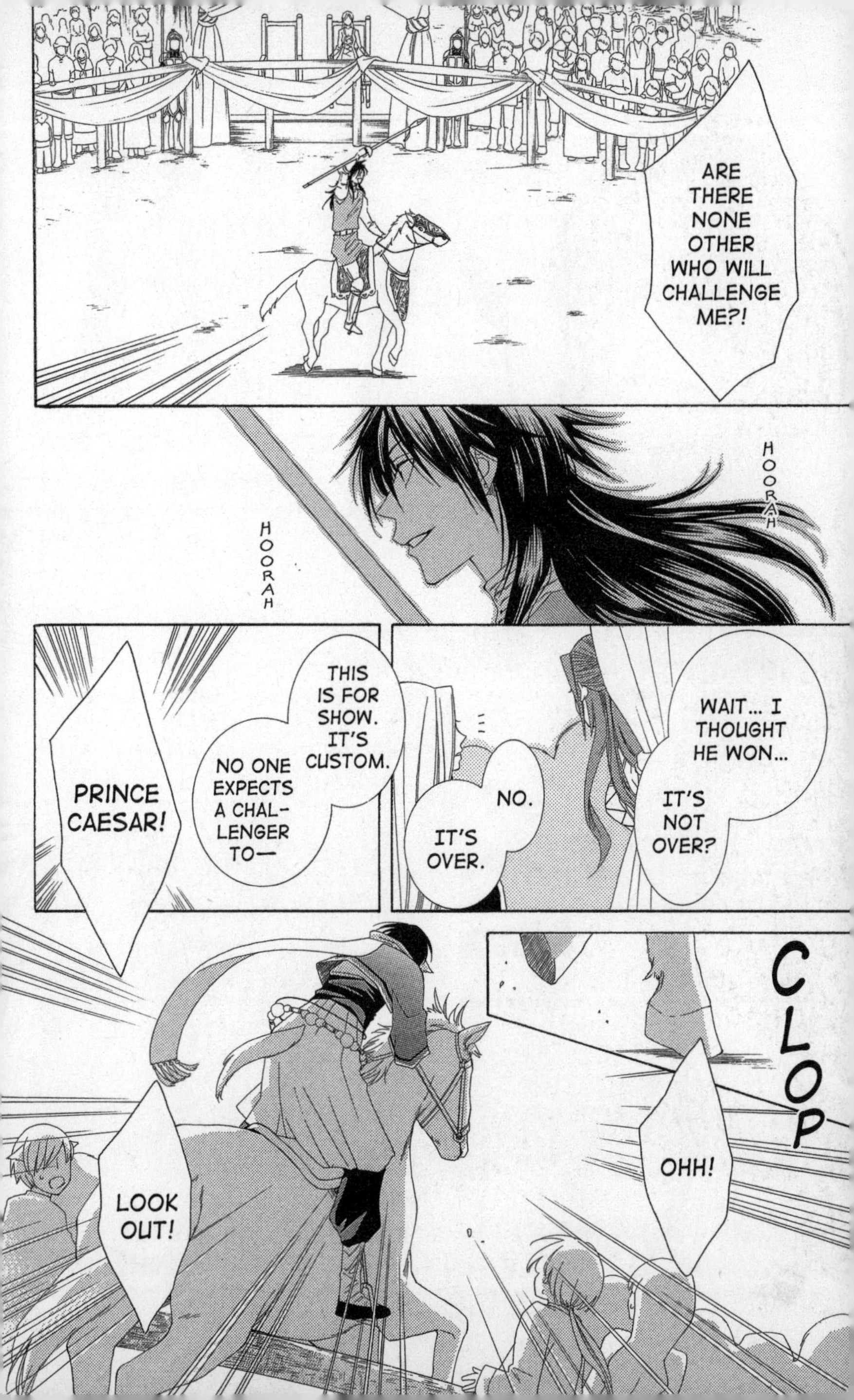
ARE THERE NONE OTHER WHO WILL CHALLENGE ME?!
HOORAH
HOORAH
WAIT... I THOUGHT HE WON...
IT'S NOT OVER?
NO.
IT'S OVER.
THIS IS FOR SHOW. IT'S CUSTOM.
NO ONE EXPECTS A CHALLENGER TO—
PRINCE CAESAR!
CLOP
OHH!
LOOK OUT!

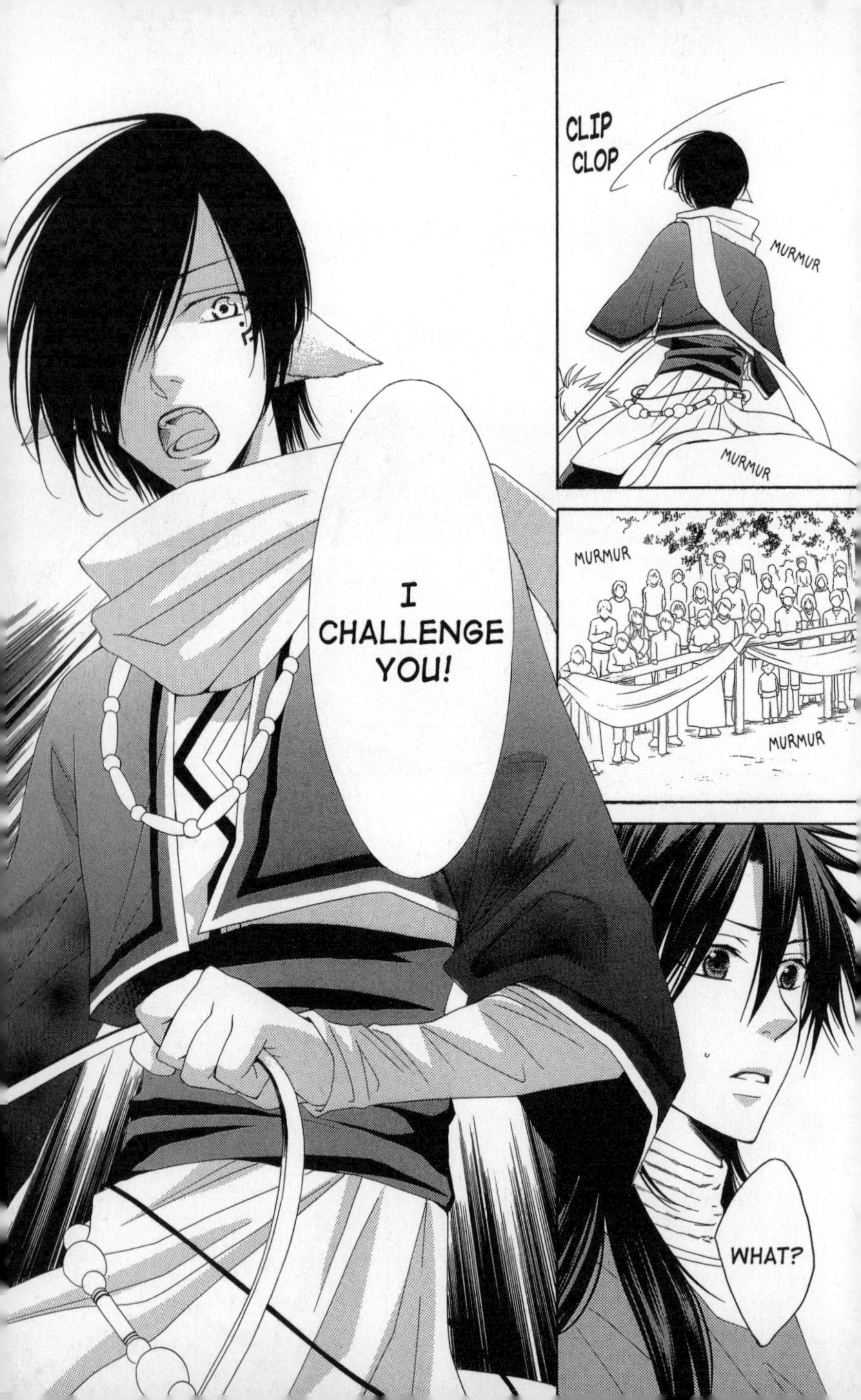
CLIP
CLOP
MURMUR
MURMUR
MURMUR
MURMUR
WHAT?
I CHALLENGE YOU!

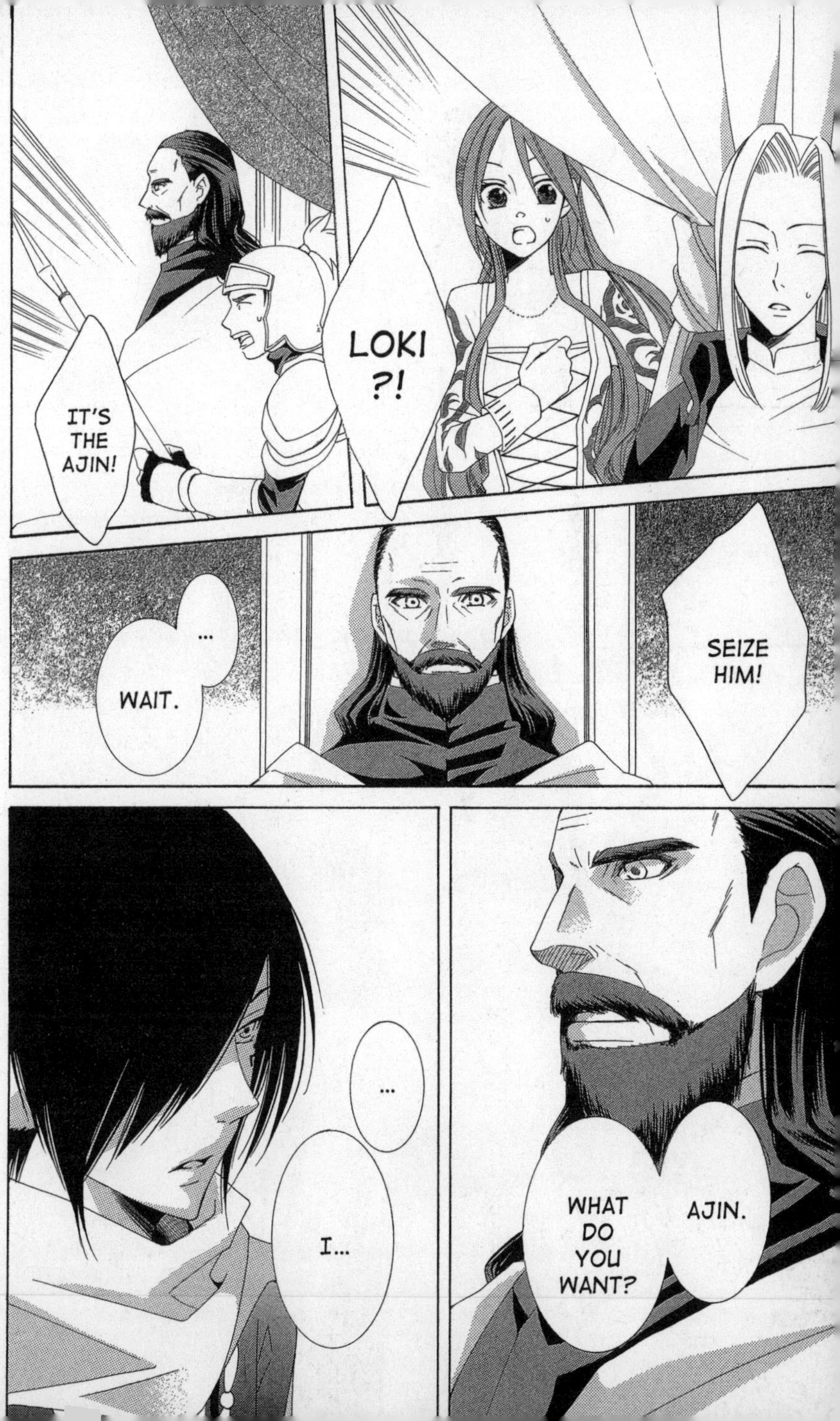
LOKI ?!
IT'S THE AJIN!
SEIZE HIM!
... WAIT.
AJIN.
WHAT DO YOU WANT?
...
I...

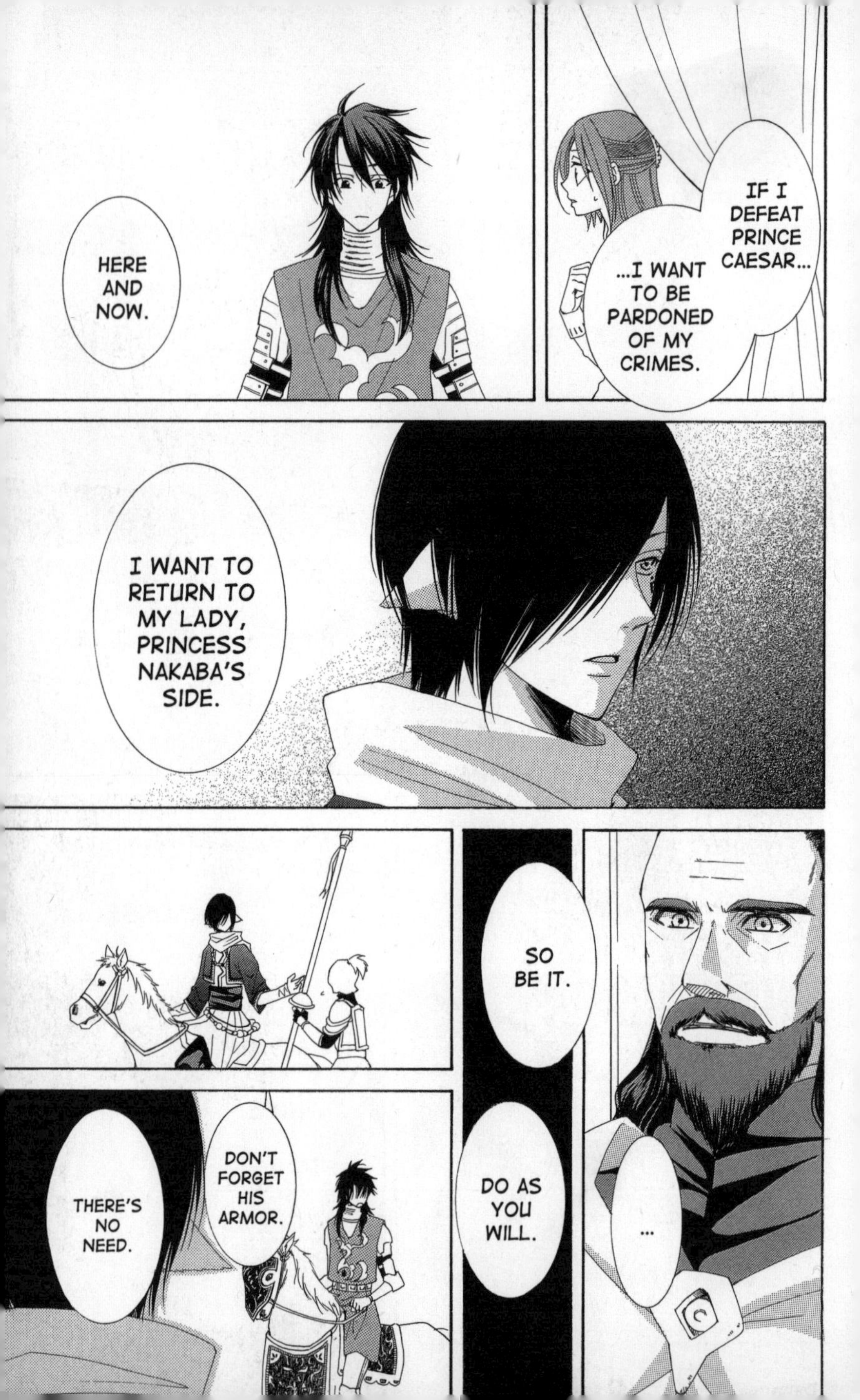

IF I DEFEAT PRINCE CAESAR...
...I WANT TO BE PARDONED OF MY CRIMES.
HERE AND NOW.
I WANT TO RETURN TO MY LADY, PRINCESS NAKABA'S SIDE.
...
SO BE IT.
DO AS YOU WILL.
DON'T FORGET HIS ARMOR.
THERE'S NO NEED.

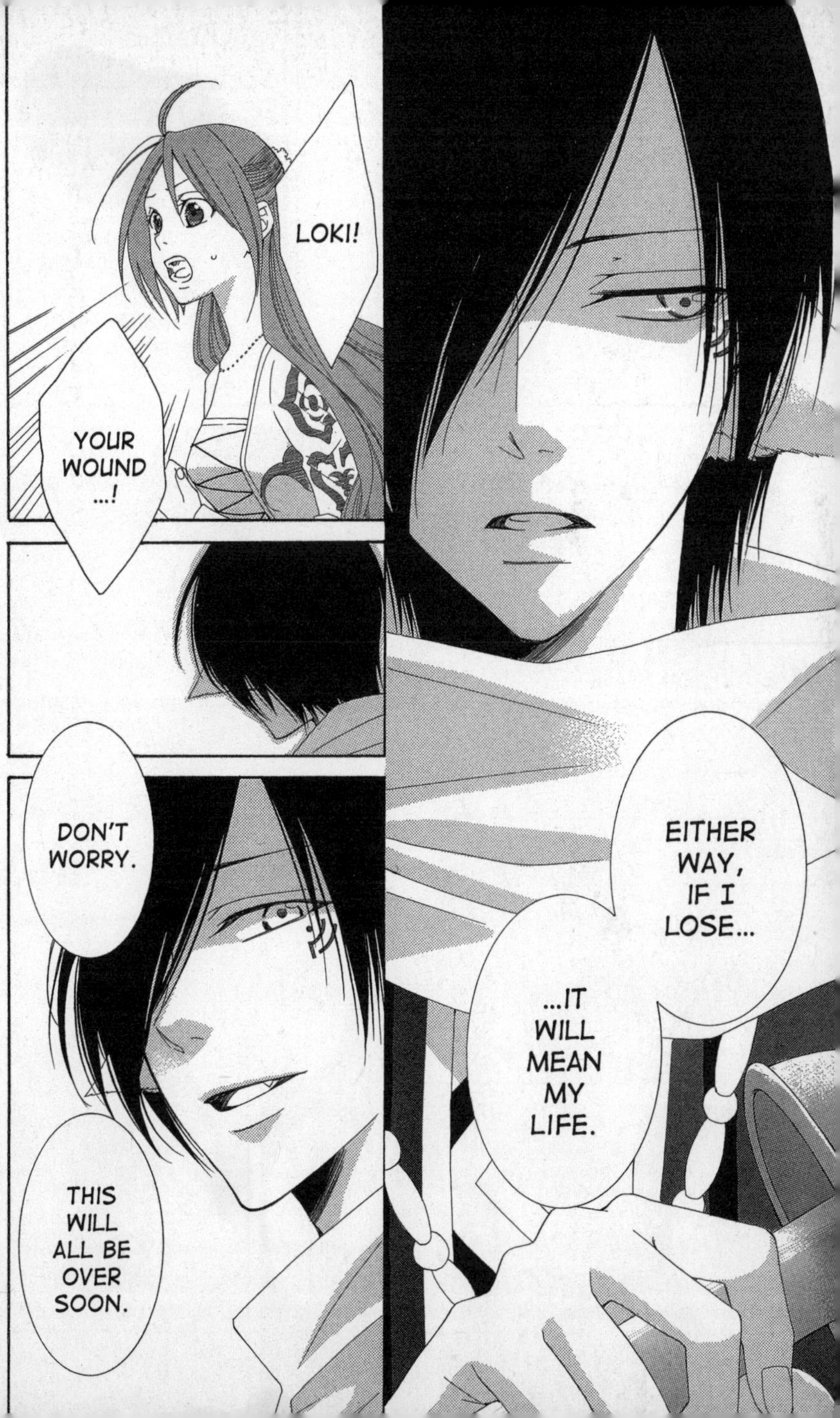
LOKI!
YOUR WOUND ...!
DON'T WORRY.
THIS WILL ALL BE OVER SOON.
EITHER WAY, IF I LOSE...
...IT WILL MEAN MY LIFE.

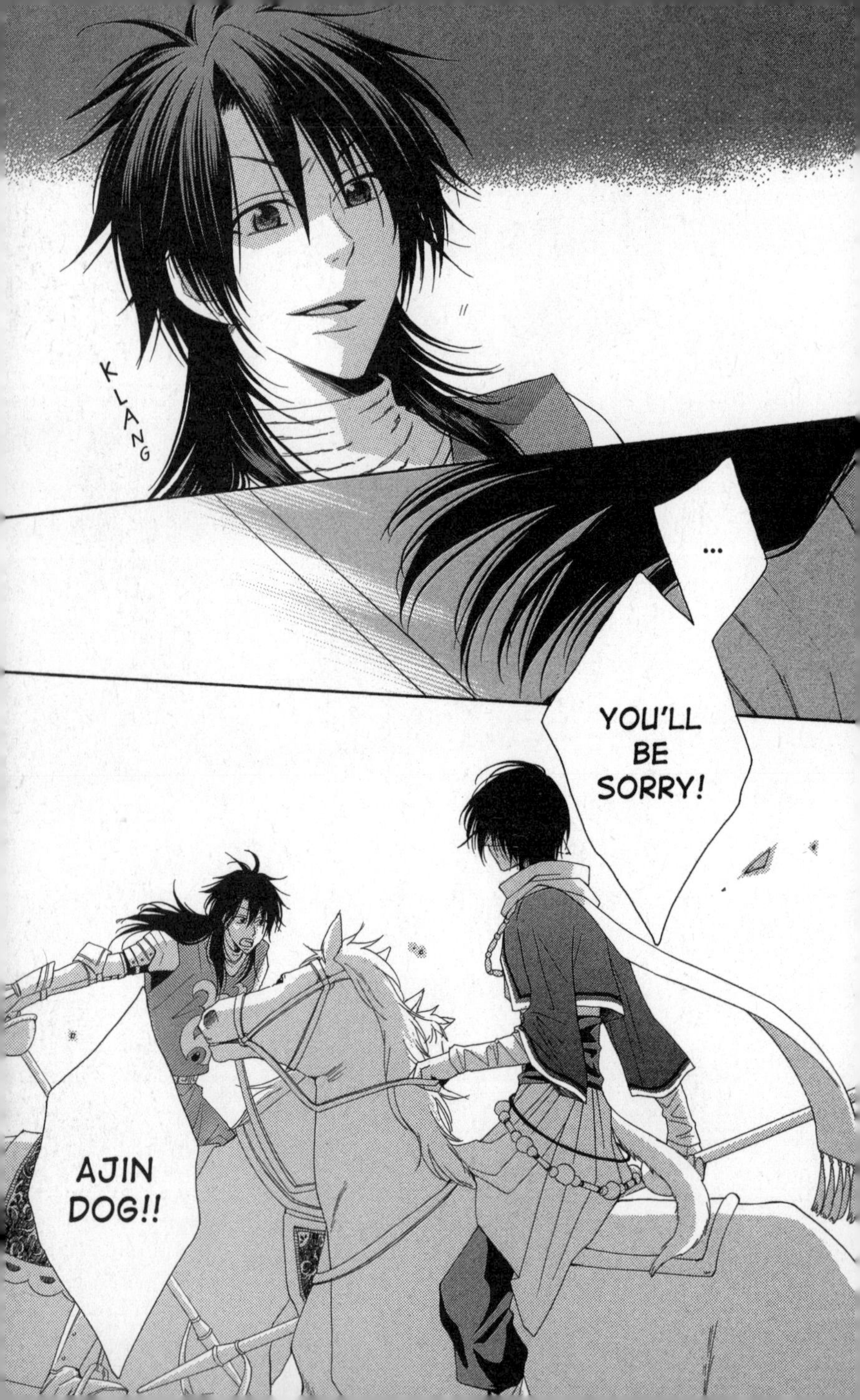
KLANG
...
YOU'LL BE SORRY!
AJIN DOG!!

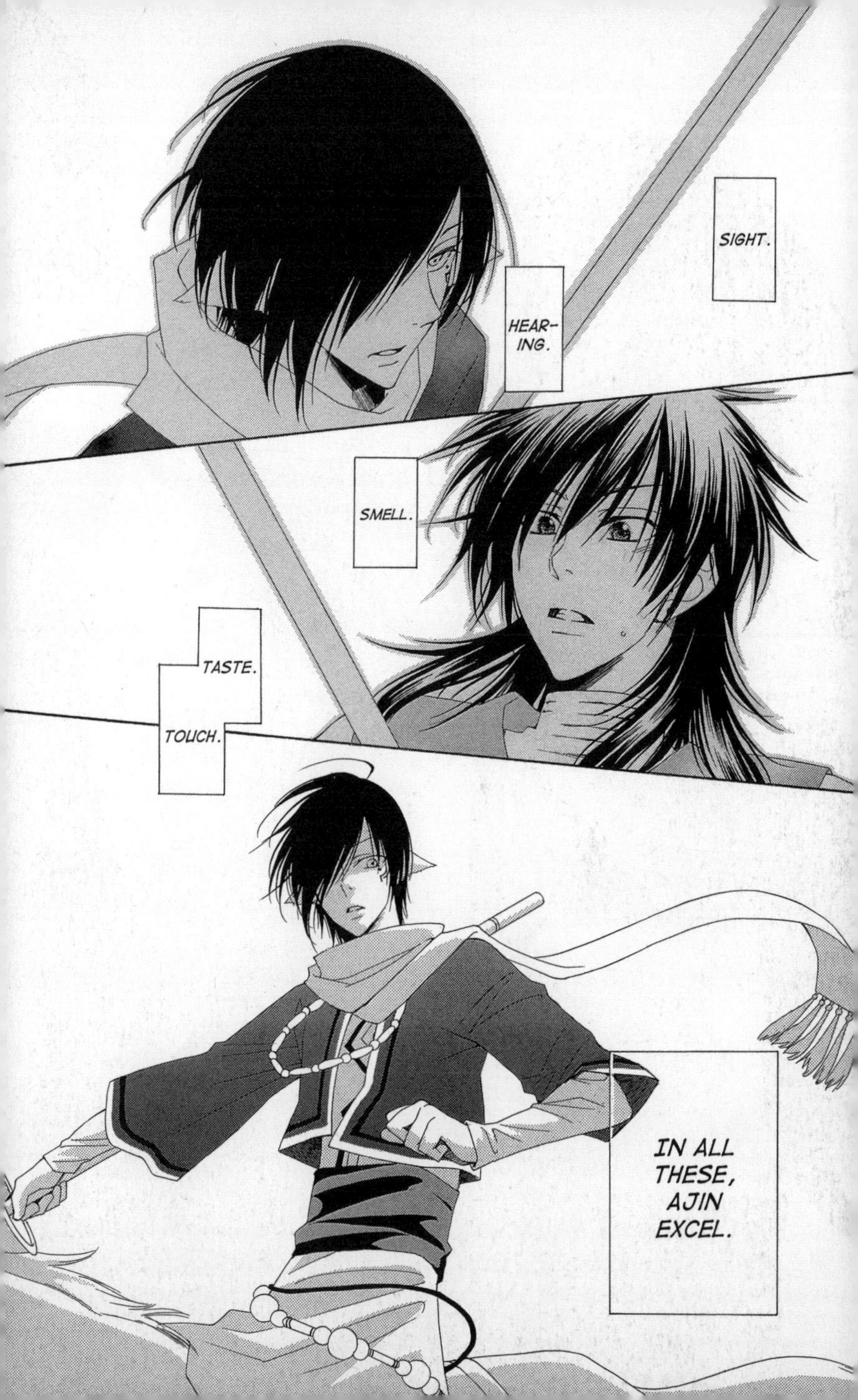
SIGHT.
HEAR-ING.
SMELL.
TASTE.
TOUCH.
IN ALL THESE, AJIN EXCEL.

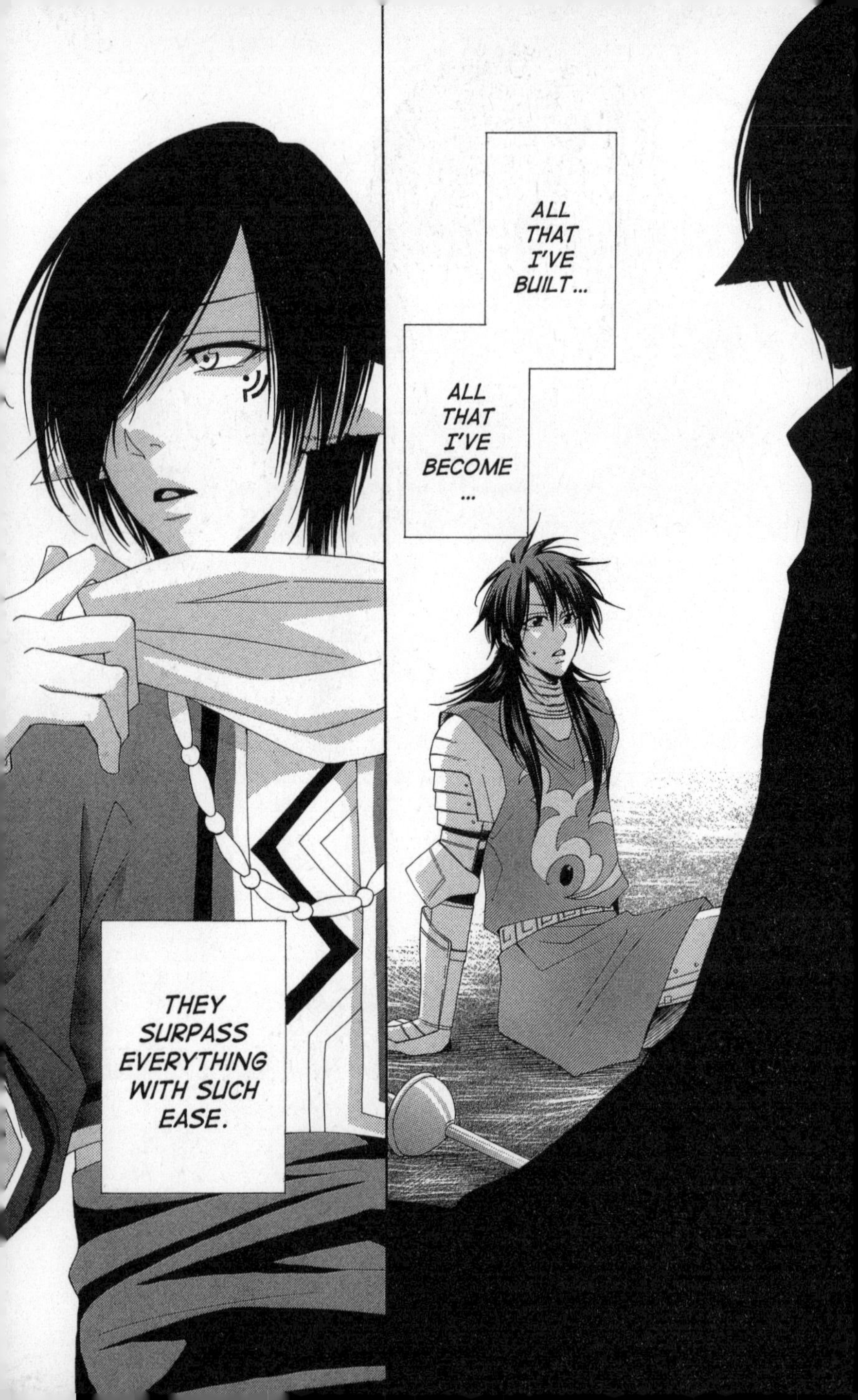
ALL THAT I'VE BUILT...
ALL THAT I'VE BECOME ...
THEY SURPASS EVERYTHING WITH SUCH EASE.

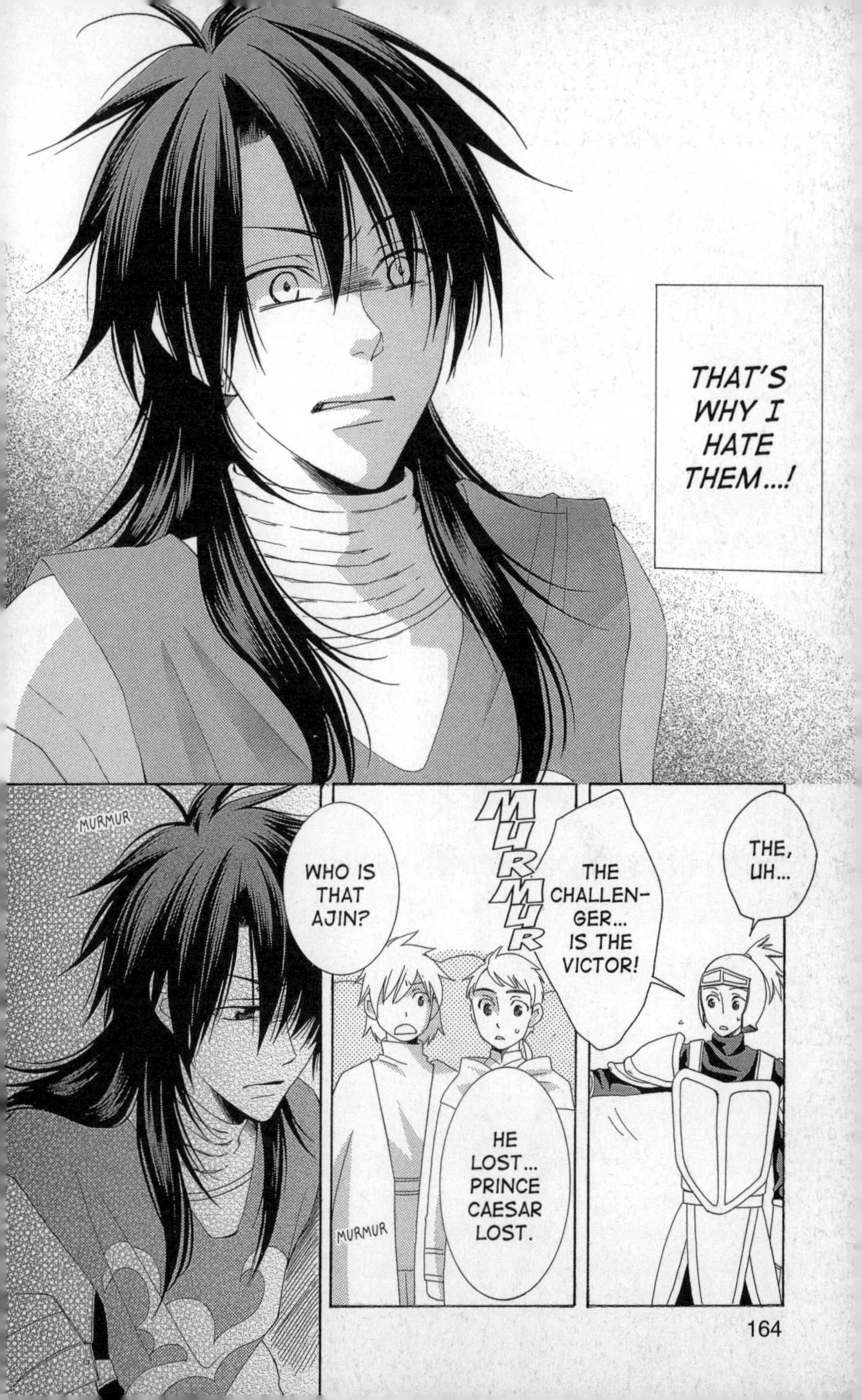
THAT'S WHY I HATE THEM...!
THE, UH...
THE CHALLENGER... IS THE VICTOR!
MURMUR
WHO IS THAT AJIN?
HE LOST... PRINCE CAESAR LOST.
MURMUR
MURMUR

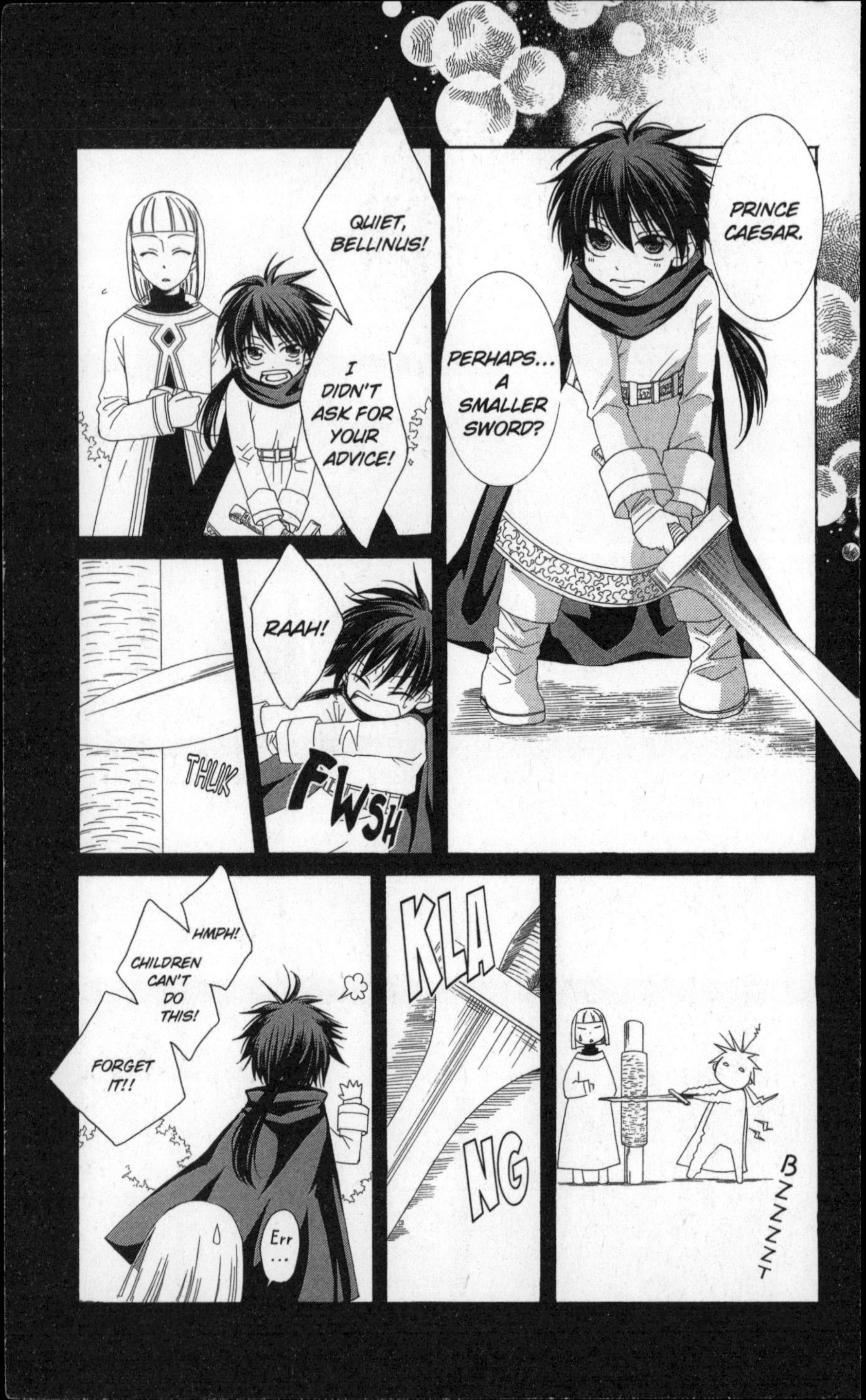
PRINCE CAESAR.
PERHAPS... A SMALLER SWORD?
QUIET, BELLINUS!
I DIDN'T ASK FOR YOUR ADVICE!
RAAH!
FWSH
THUK
BZZZZT
KLANG
HMPH!
CHILDREN CAN'T DO THIS!
FORGET IT!!
Err...

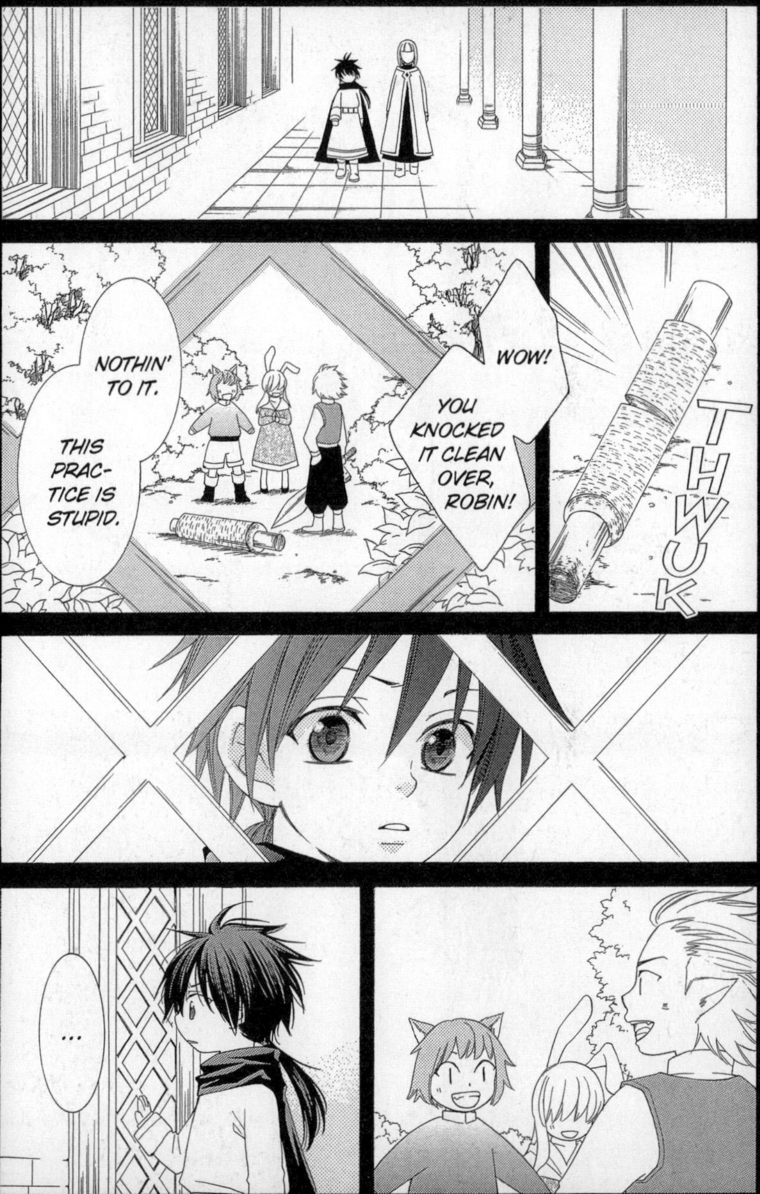
THWUK
WOW!
YOU KNOCKED IT CLEAN OVER, ROBIN!
NOTHIN' TO IT.
THIS PRAC-TICE IS STUPID.
...

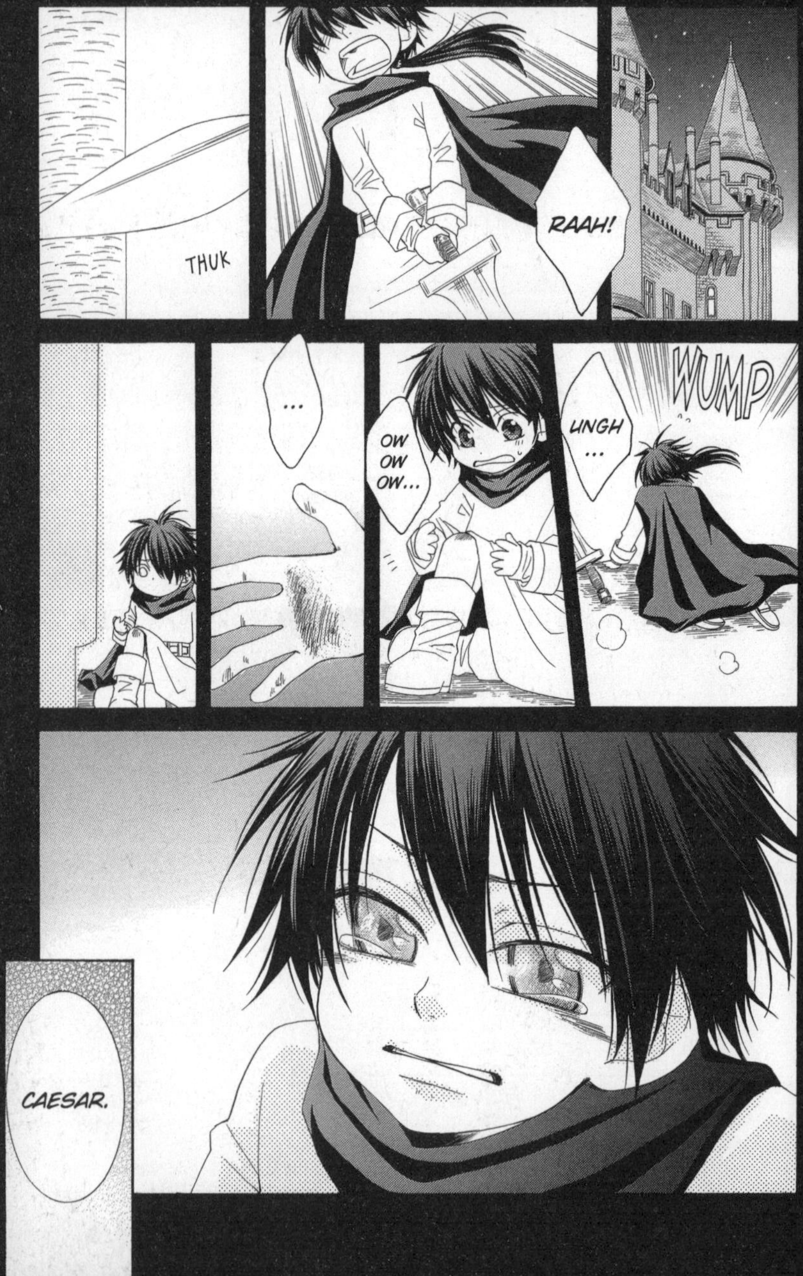
RAAH!
THUK
WUMP
UNGH...
OW OW OW...
...
CAESAR.

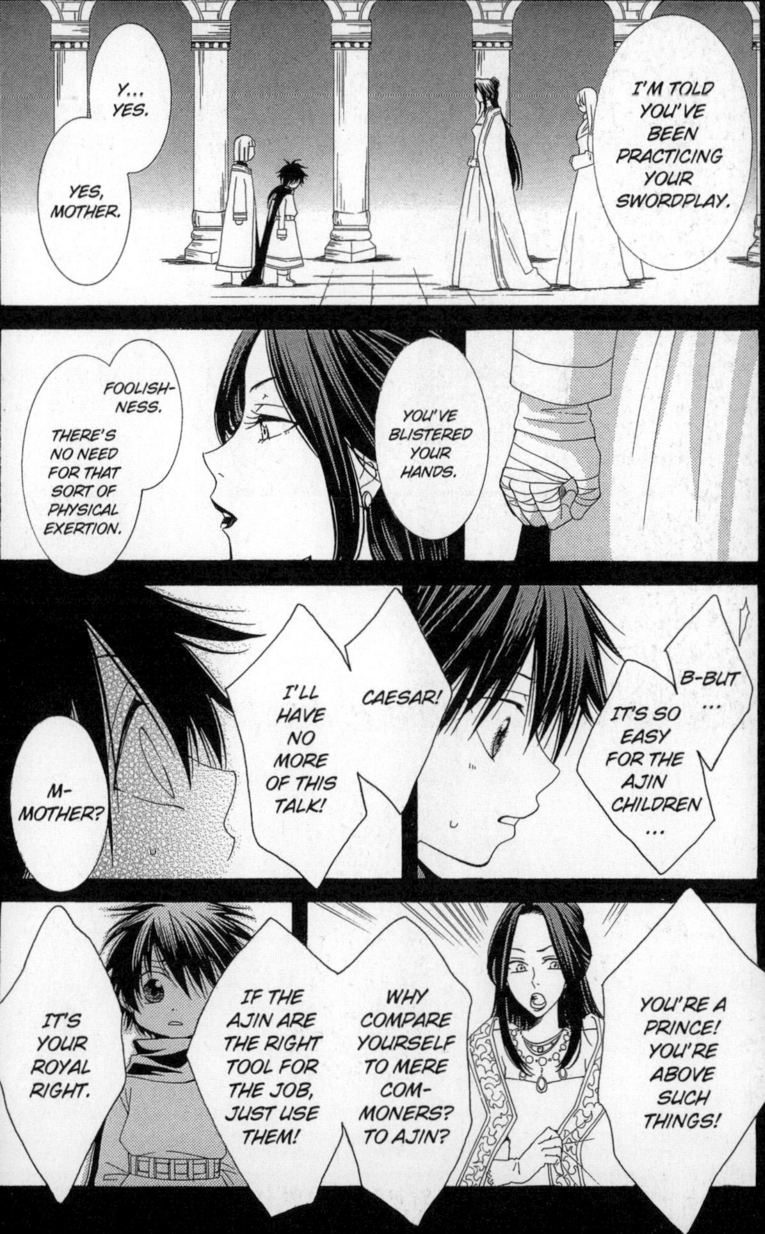
I'M TOLD YOU'VE BEEN PRACTICING YOUR SWORDPLAY.
Y... YES.
YES, MOTHER.
YOU'VE BLISTERED YOUR HANDS.
FOOLISH-NESS.
THERE'S NO NEED FOR THAT SORT OF PHYSICAL EXERTION.
B-BUT...
IT'S SO EASY FOR THE AJIN CHILDREN...
CAESAR!
I'LL HAVE NO MORE OF THIS TALK!
M-MOTHER?
YOU'RE A PRINCE! YOU'RE ABOVE SUCH THINGS!
WHY COMPARE YOURSELF TO MERE COM-MONERS? TO AJIN?
IF THE AJIN ARE THE RIGHT TOOL FOR THE JOB, JUST USE THEM!
IT'S YOUR ROYAL RIGHT.

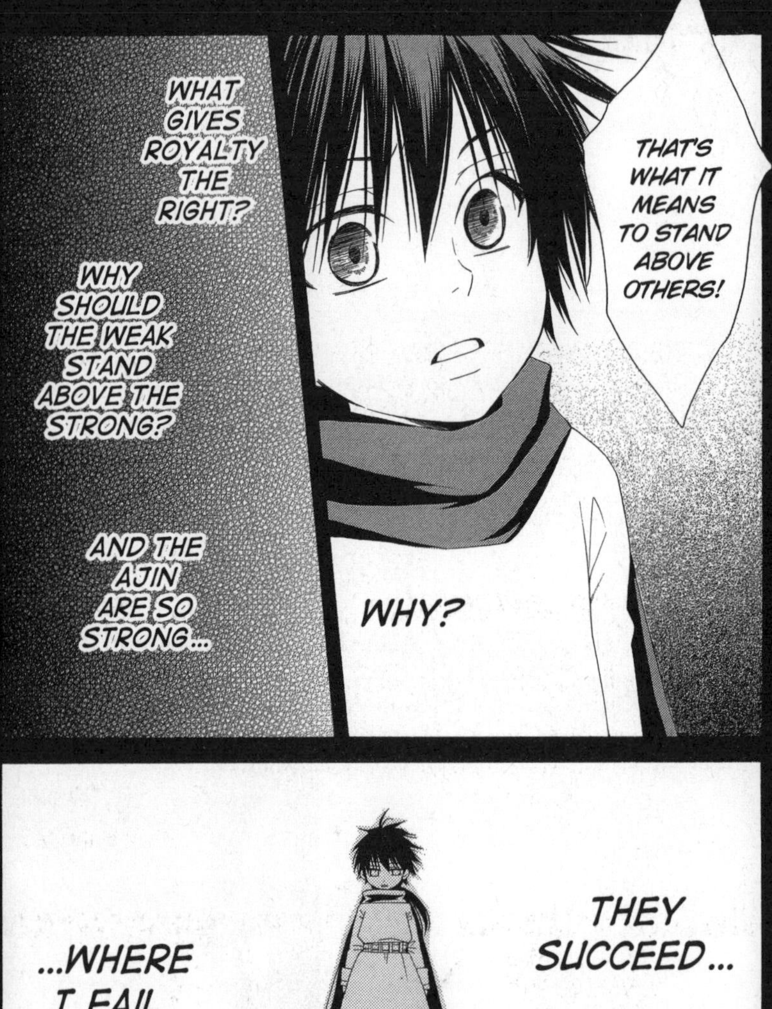
THAT'S WHAT IT MEANS TO STAND ABOVE OTHERS!
WHAT GIVES ROYALTY THE RIGHT?
WHY SHOULD THE WEAK STAND ABOVE THE STRONG?
AND THE AJIN ARE SO STRONG...
WHY?
THEY SUCCEED...
...WHERE I FAIL.

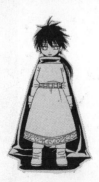

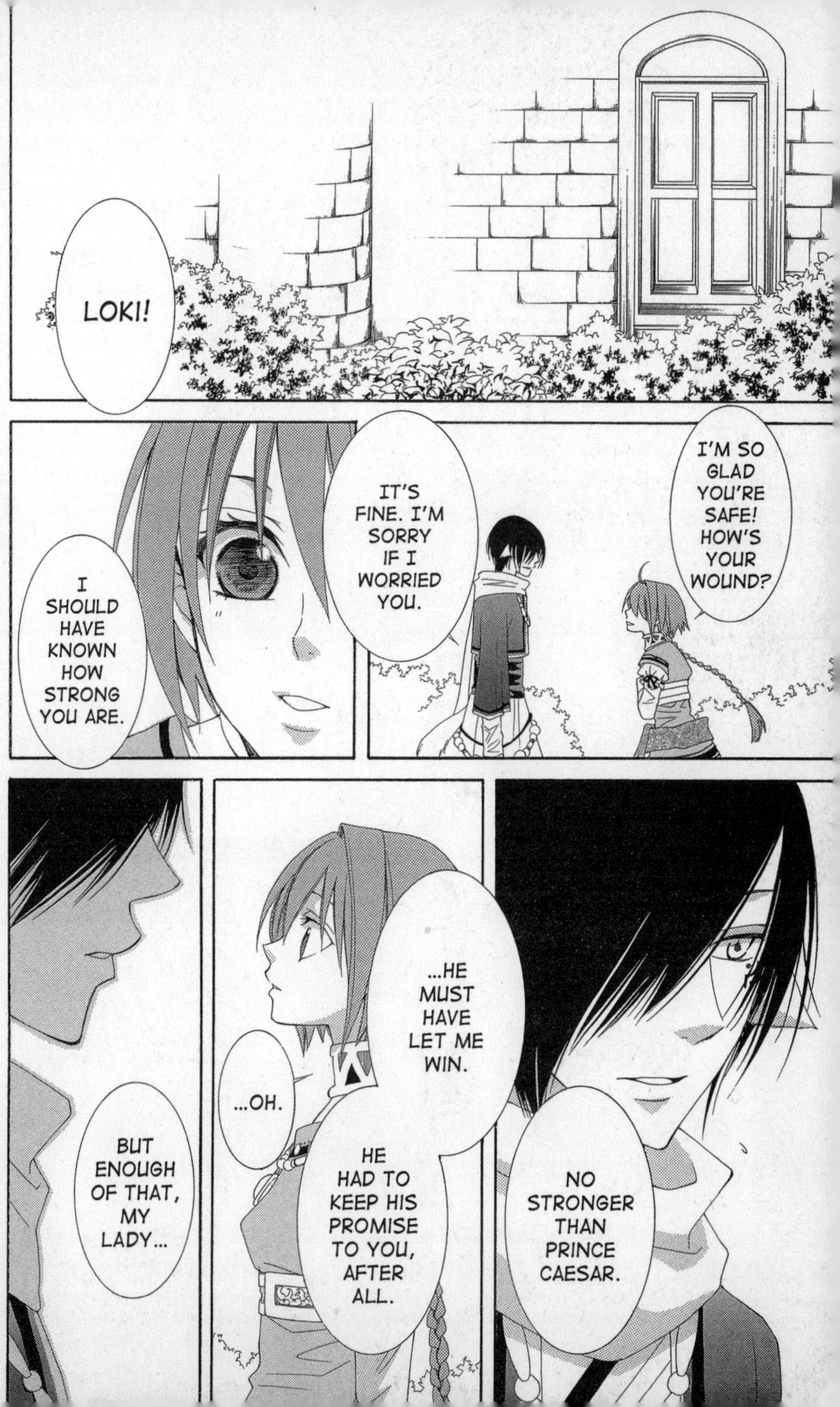
LOKI!
I'M SO GLAD YOU'RE SAFE! HOW'S YOUR WOUND?
IT'S FINE. I'M SORRY IF I WORRIED YOU.
I SHOULD HAVE KNOWN HOW STRONG YOU ARE.
NO STRONGER THAN PRINCE CAESAR.
...HE MUST HAVE LET ME WIN.
HE HAD TO KEEP HIS PROMISE TO YOU, AFTER ALL.
...OH.
BUT ENOUGH OF THAT, MY LADY...

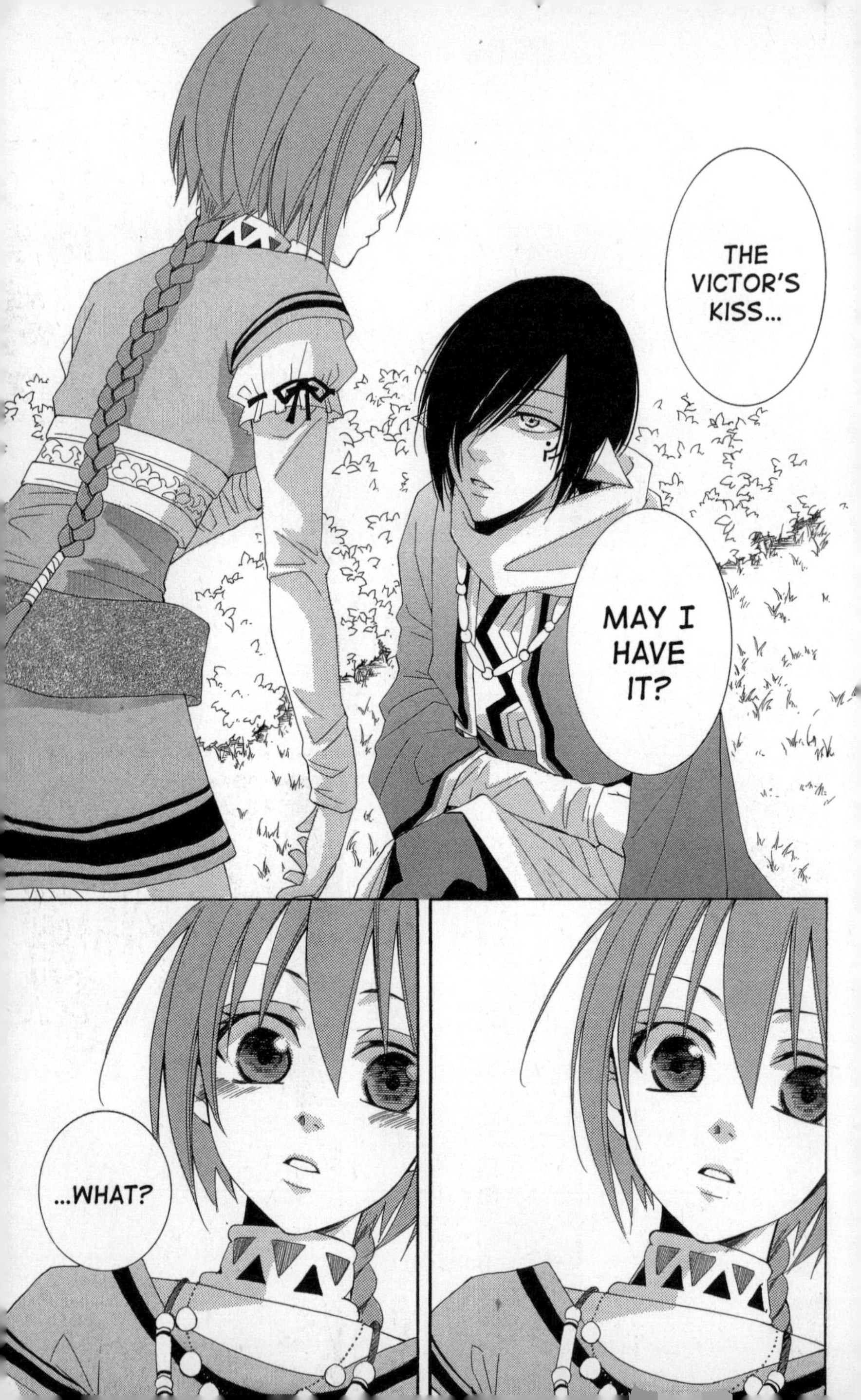
THE VICTOR'S KISS...
MAY I HAVE IT?
...WHAT?

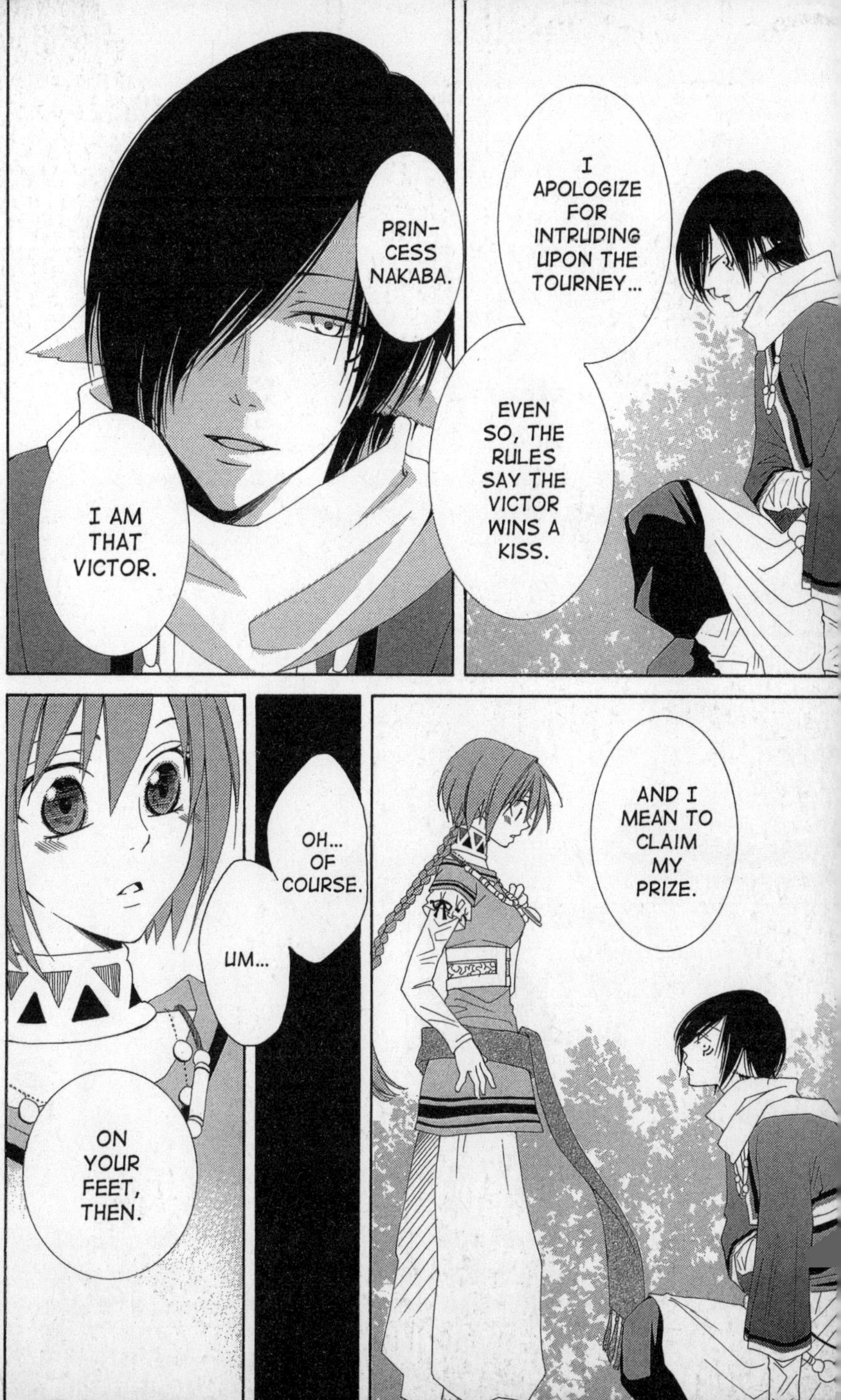
I APOLOGIZE FOR INTRUDING UPON THE TOURNEY...
EVEN SO, THE RULES SAY THE VICTOR WINS A KISS.
PRIN-CESS NAKABA.
I AM THAT VICTOR.
AND I MEAN TO CLAIM MY PRIZE.
OH... OF COURSE.
UM...
ON YOUR FEET, THEN.

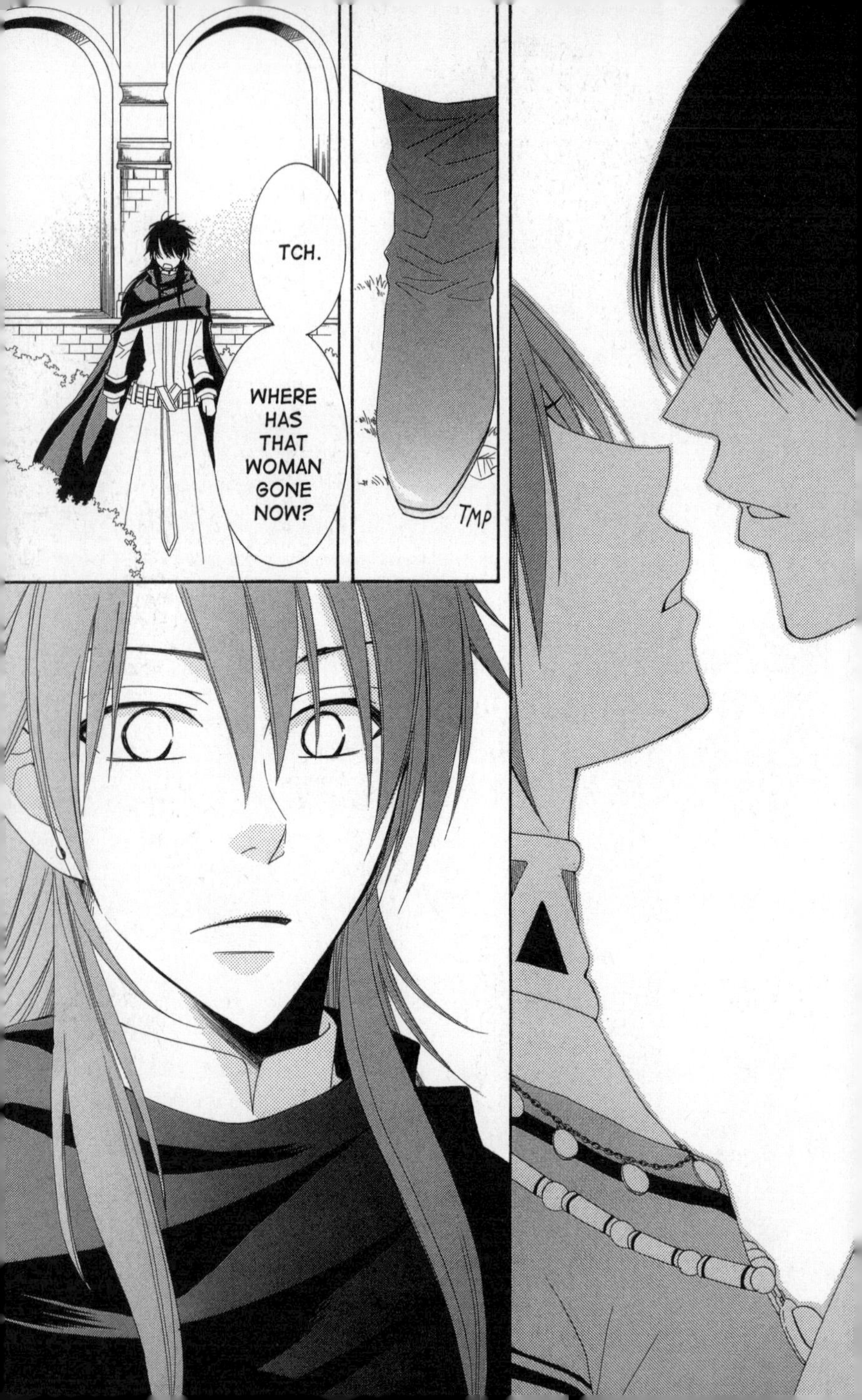
TMP
TCH.
WHERE HAS THAT WOMAN GONE NOW?

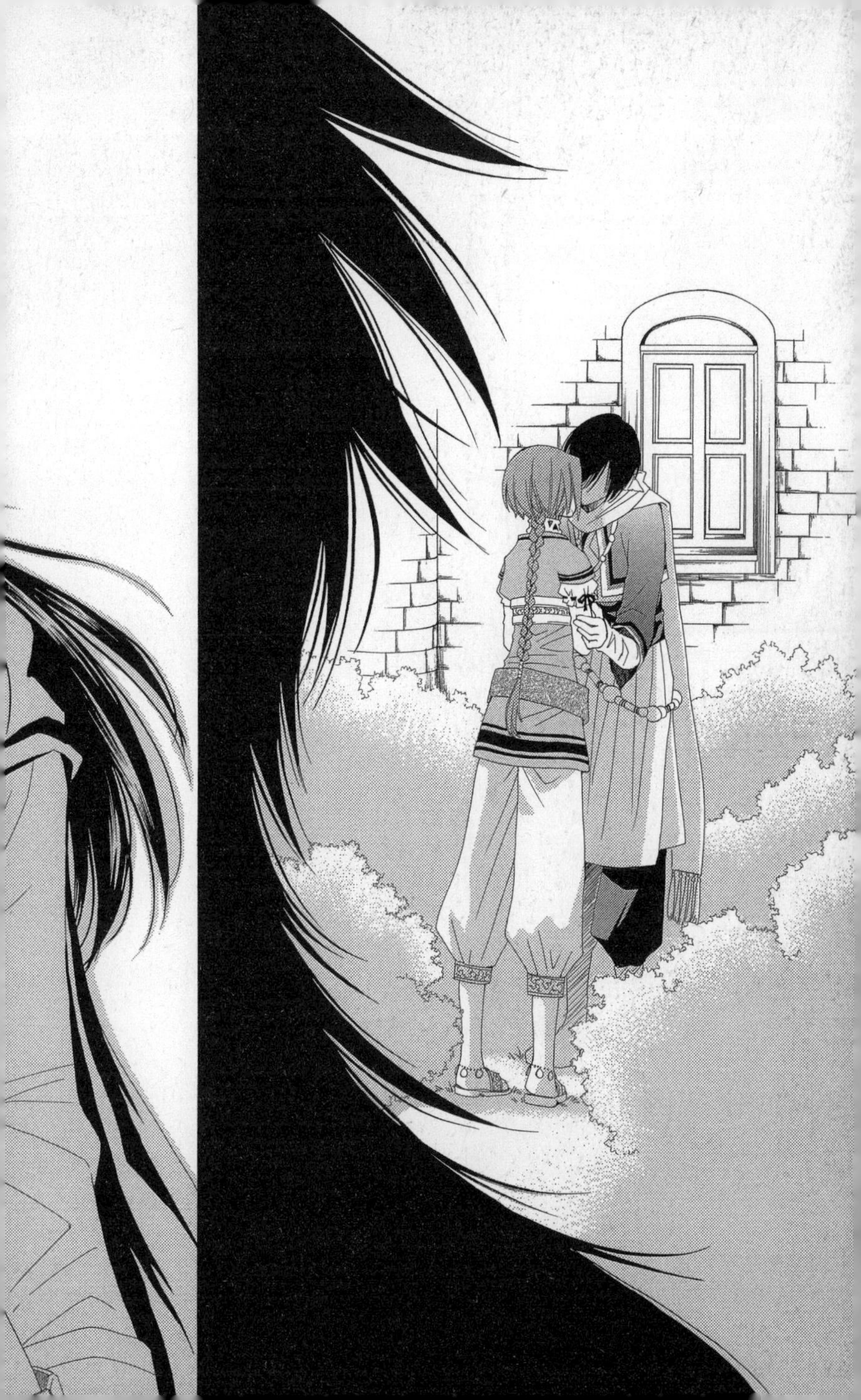

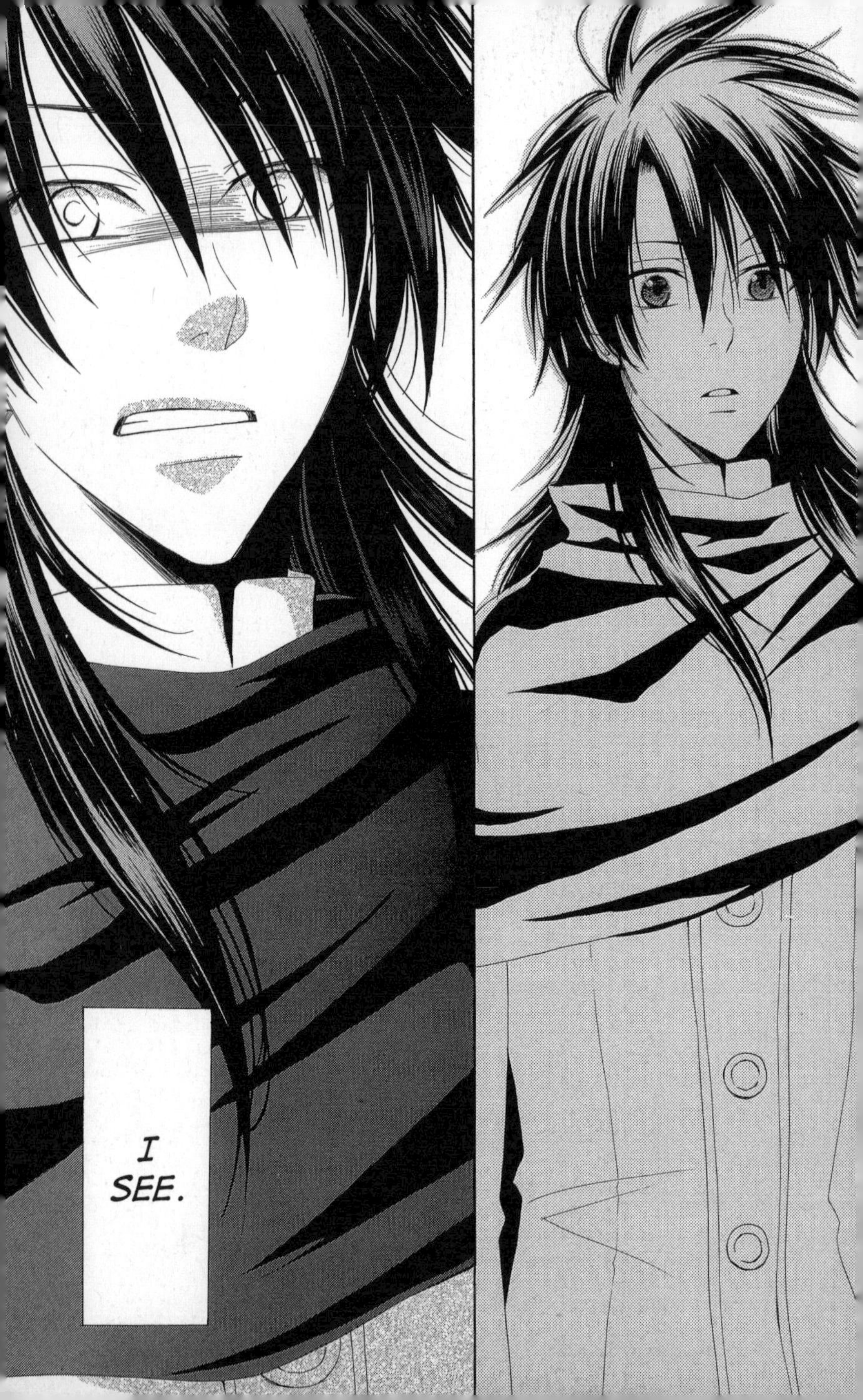
I SEE.

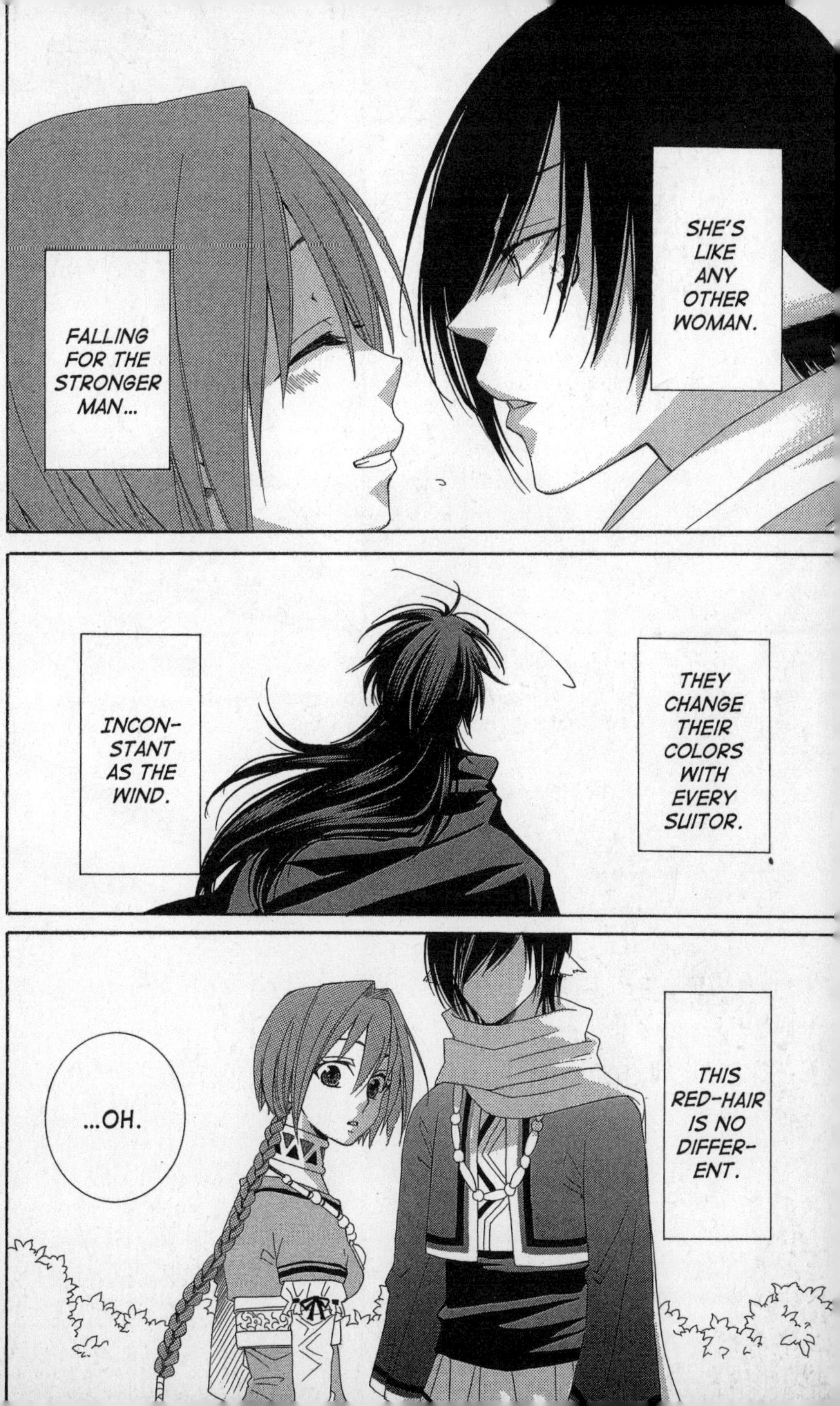
SHE'S LIKE ANY OTHER WOMAN.
FALLING FOR THE STRONGER MAN...
THEY CHANGE THEIR COLORS WITH EVERY SUITOR.
INCON-STANT AS THE WIND.
THIS RED-HAIR IS NO DIFFER-ENT.
...OH.

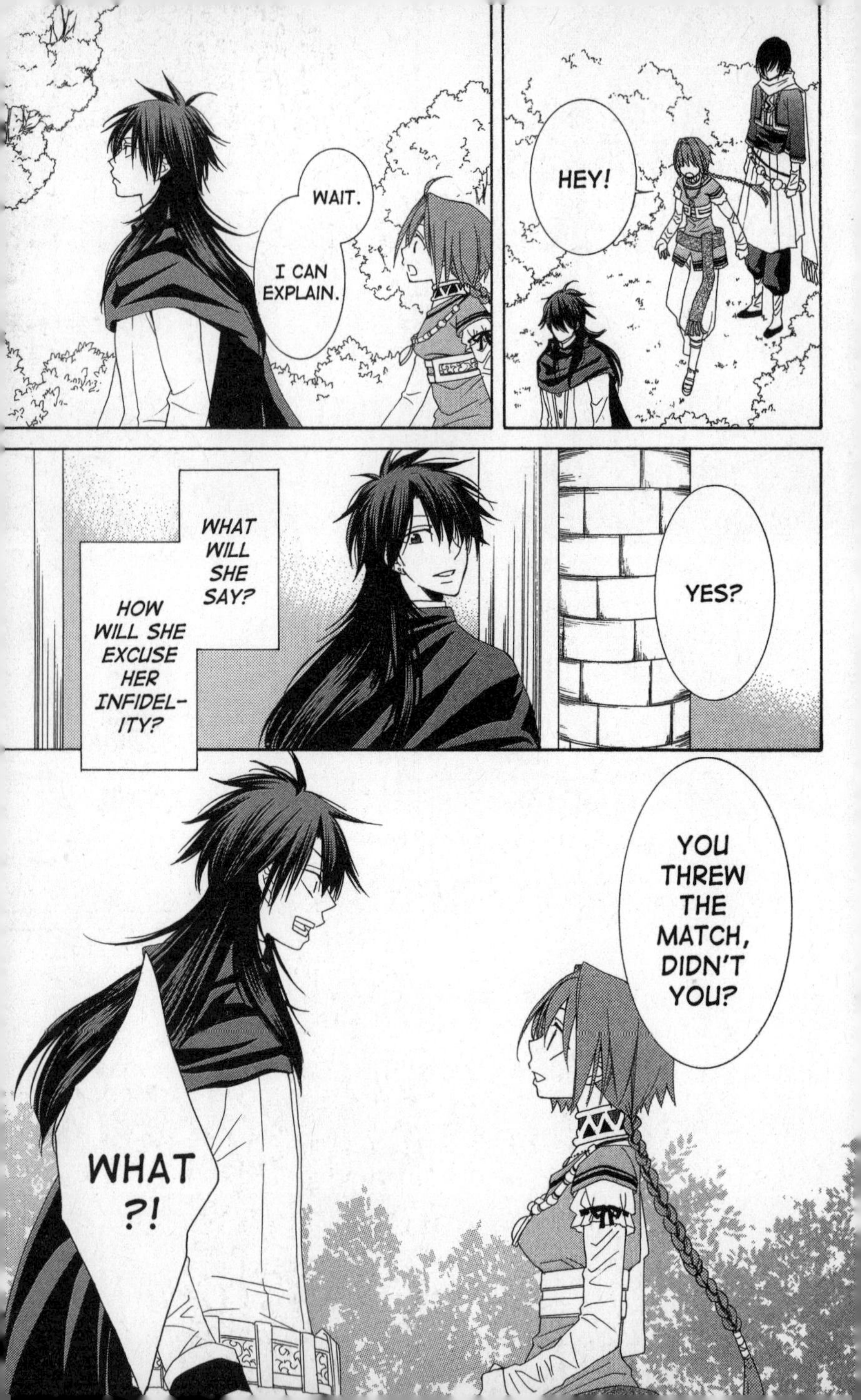
HEY!
WAIT.
I CAN EXPLAIN.
YES?
WHAT WILL SHE SAY?
HOW WILL SHE EXCUSE HER INFIDELITY?
YOU THREW THE MATCH, DIDN'T YOU?
WHAT?!

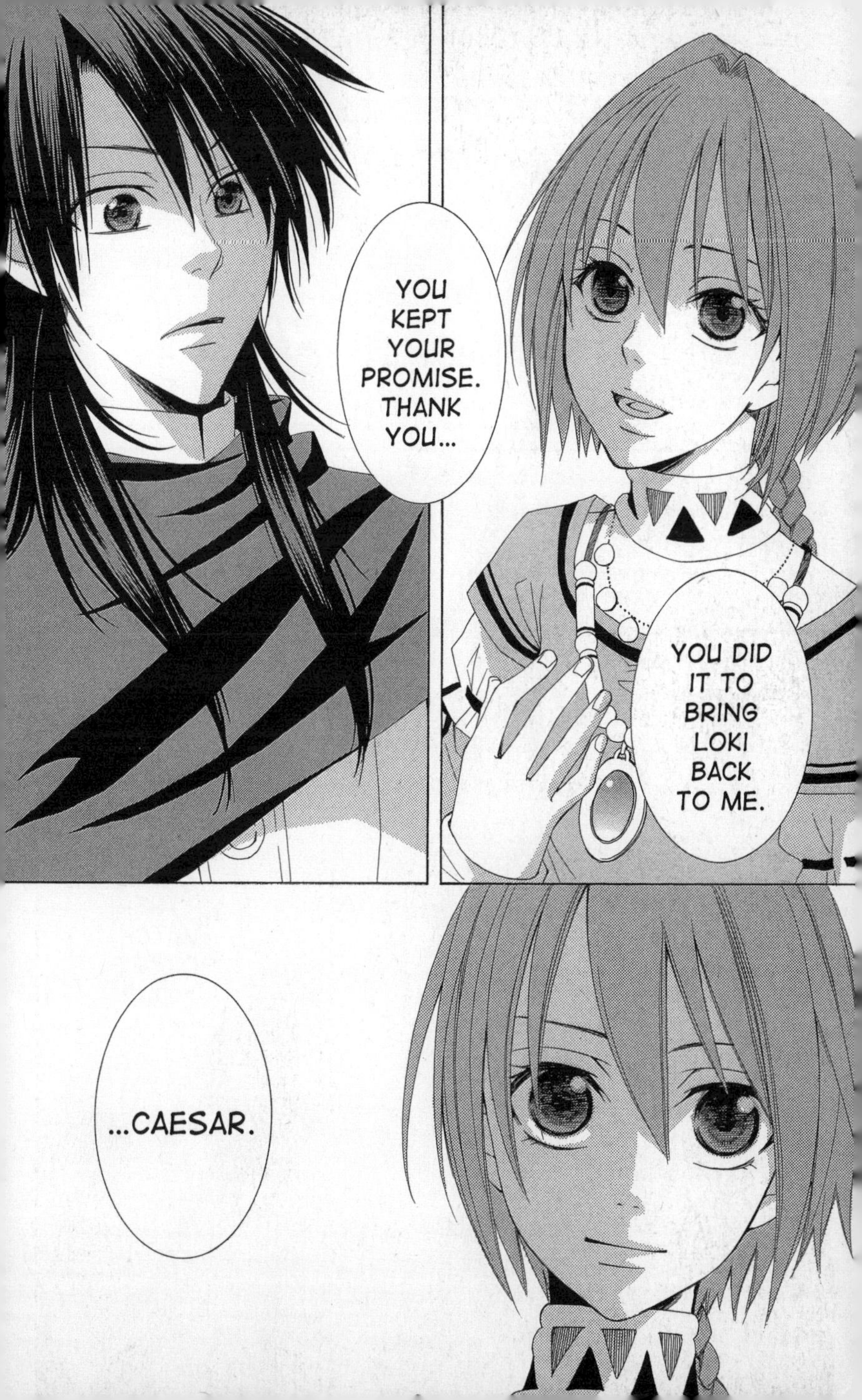
YOU KEPT YOUR PROMISE. THANK YOU...
YOU DID IT TO BRING LOKI BACK TO ME.
...CAESAR.

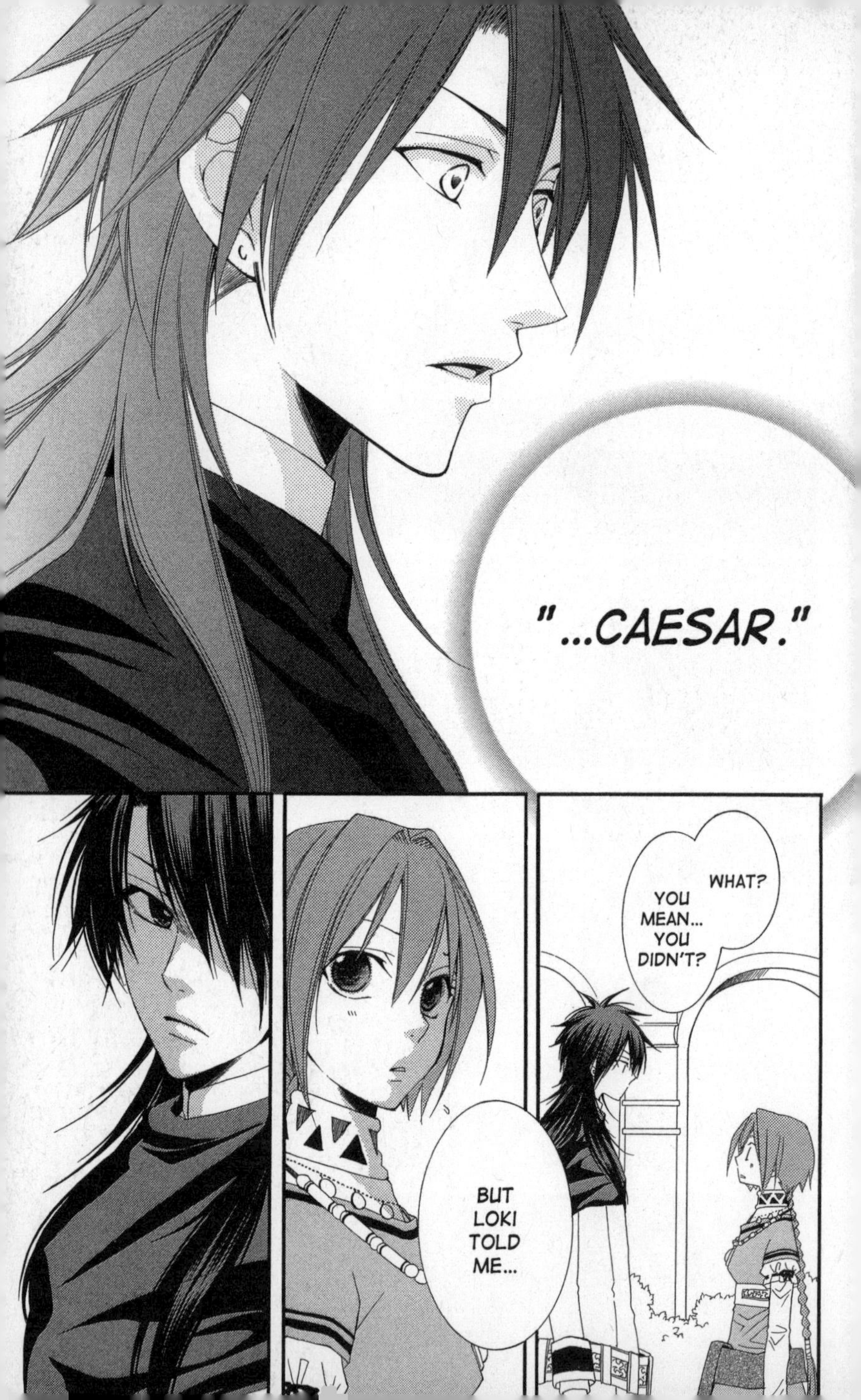
"...CAESAR."
WHAT? YOU MEAN... YOU DIDN'T?
BUT LOKI TOLD ME...

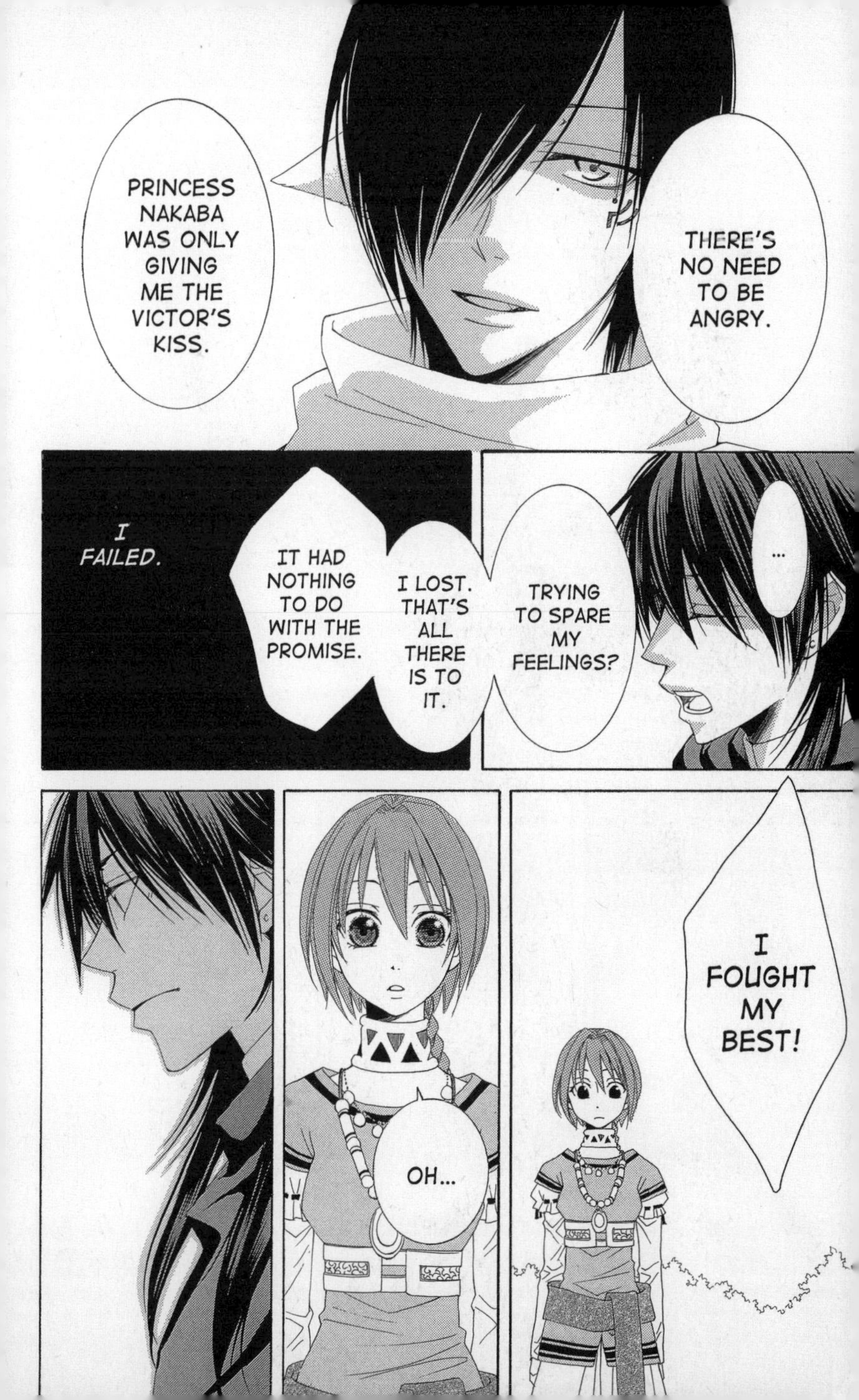
THERE'S NO NEED TO BE ANGRY.
PRINCESS NAKABA WAS ONLY GIVING ME THE VICTOR'S KISS.
...
TRYING TO SPARE MY FEELINGS?
I LOST. THAT'S ALL THERE IS TO IT.
IT HAD NOTHING TO DO WITH THE PROMISE.
I FAILED.
I FOUGHT MY BEST!
OH...

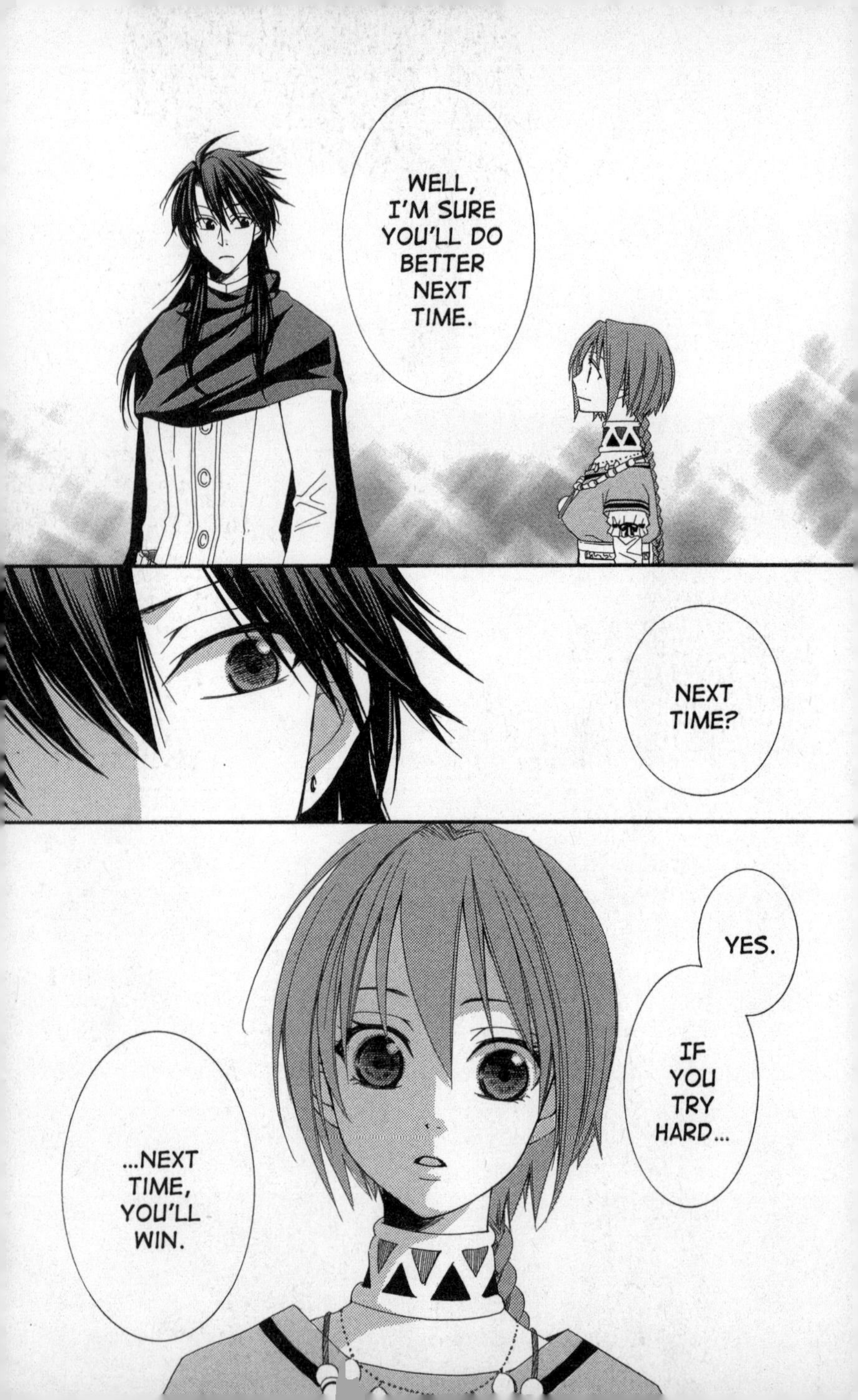
WELL, I'M SURE YOU'LL DO BETTER NEXT TIME.
NEXT TIME?
YES.
IF YOU TRY HARD...
...NEXT TIME, YOU'LL WIN.

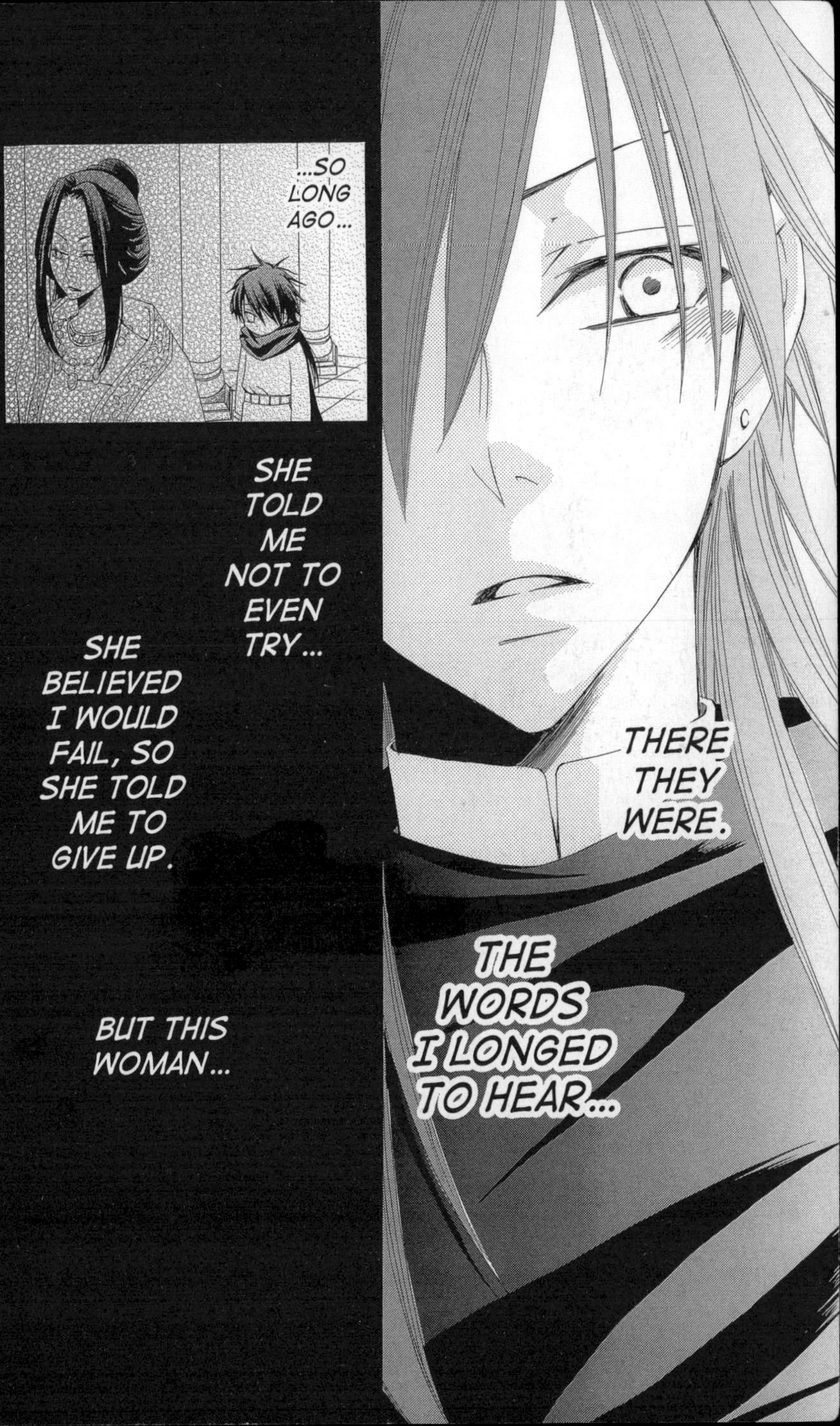
...SO LONG AGO...
SHE TOLD ME NOT TO EVEN TRY...
SHE BELIEVED I WOULD FAIL, SO SHE TOLD ME TO GIVE UP.
BUT THIS WOMAN...
THERE THEY WERE.
THE WORDS I LONGED TO HEAR...

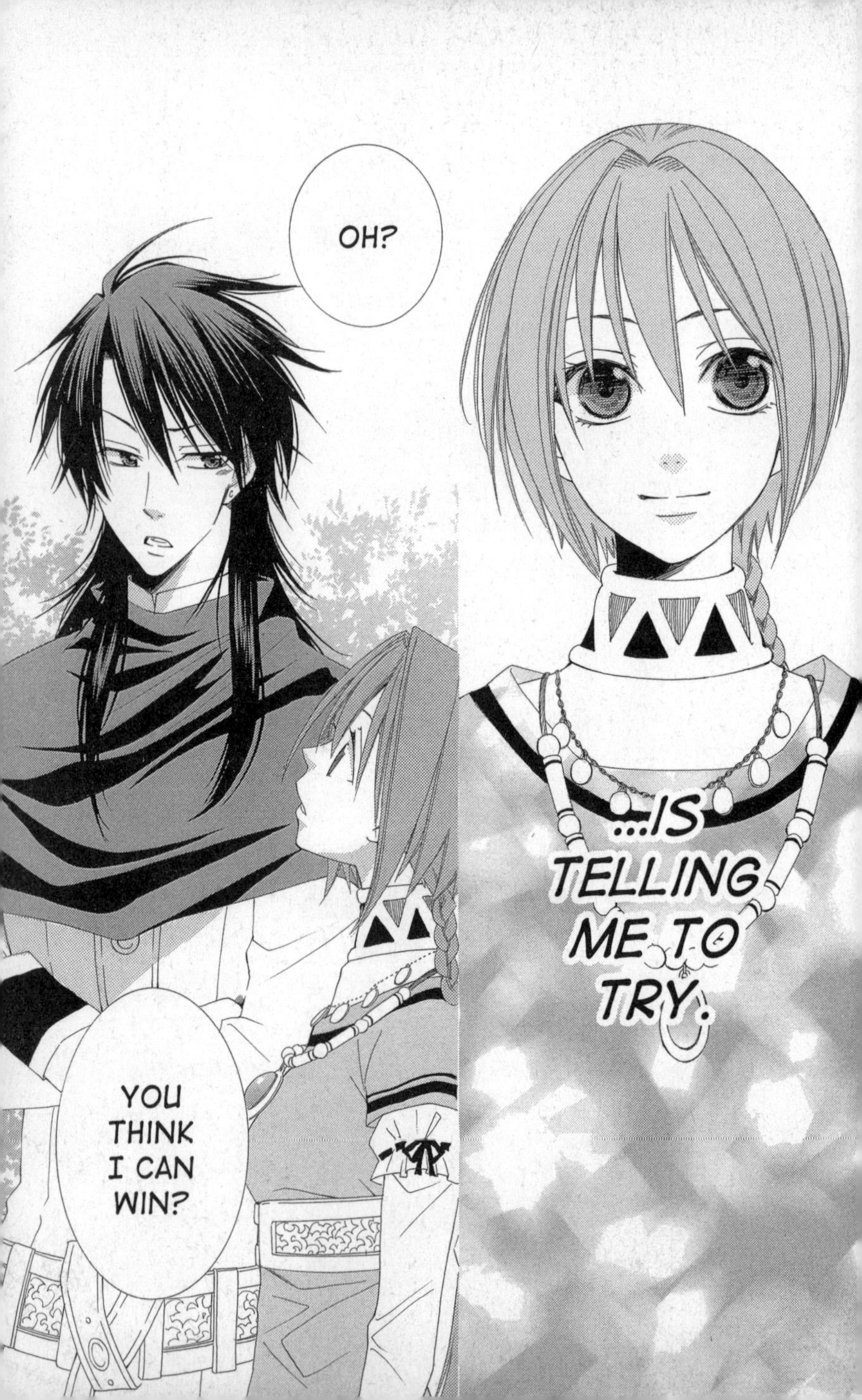
...IS TELLING ME TO TRY.
OH?
YOU THINK I CAN WIN?

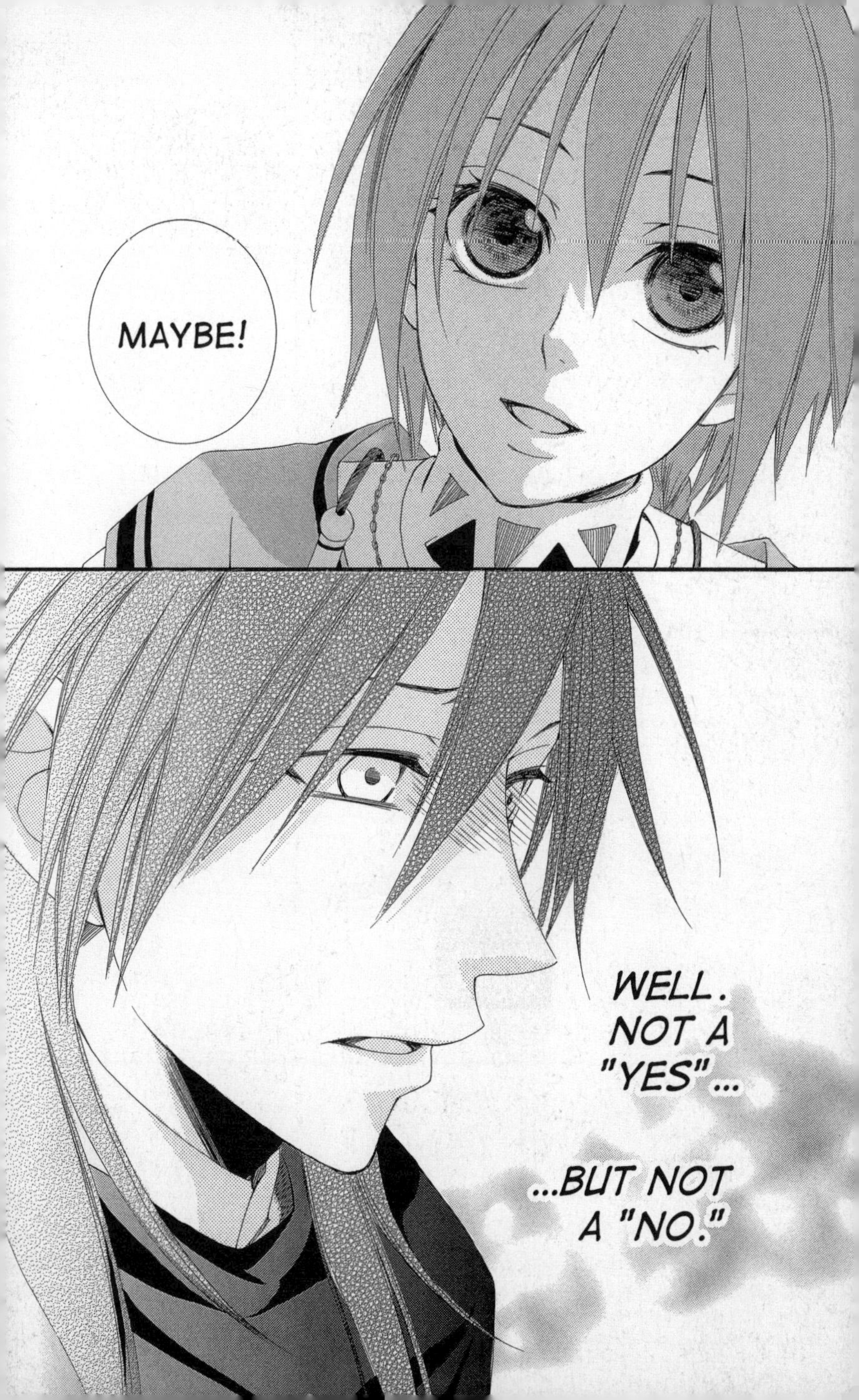
MAYBE!
WELL. NOT A "YES"...
...BUT NOT A "NO."

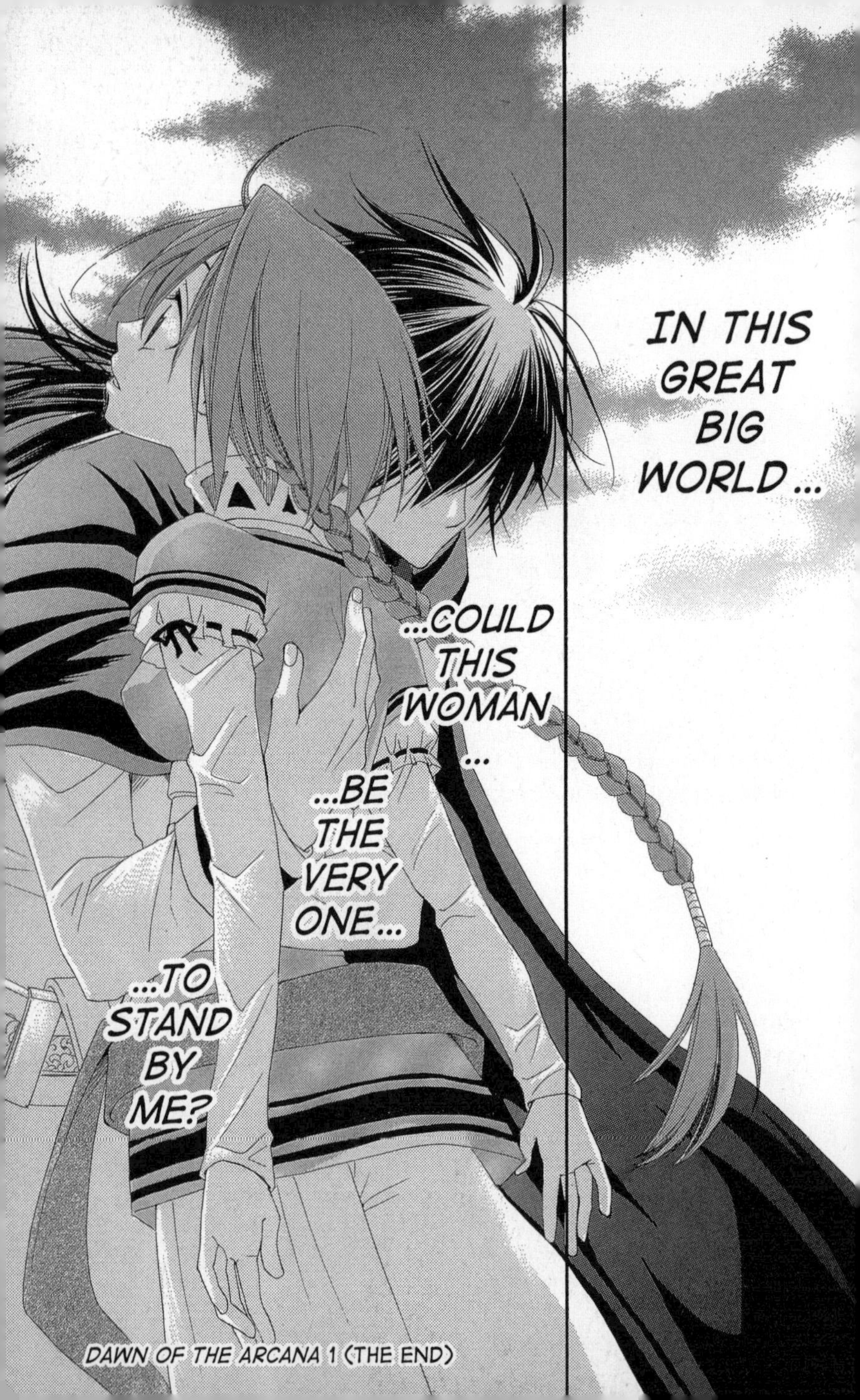
IN THIS GREAT BIG WORLD...
...COULD THIS WOMAN...
...BE THE VERY ONE...
...TO STAND BY ME?

DAWN OF THE ARCANA 1 (THE END)

This is my first fantasy manga, and I'm giving it my all. The clothes are different than in modern settings, and coloring them can be a real pain in the...I mean, fun! It's really fun! (*laugh*)

–Rei Toma

Rei Toma has been drawing since childhood, but she only began drawing manga because of her graduation project in design school. When she drew a short-story manga, *Help Me, Dentist,* for the first time, it attracted a publisher's attention and she made her debut right away. Her magnificent art style became popular, and after she debuted as a manga artist, she became known as an illustrator for novels and video game character designs. Her current manga series, *Dawn of the Arcana,* is her first long-running manga series, and it has been a hit in Japan, selling over a million copies.